Church Growth in Central and Southern Nigeria

Church Growth Series

CHURCH GROWTH IN MEXICO: Donald McGavran, John Huegel, Jack Taylor

WILDFIRE — CHURCH GROWTH IN KOREA: R. E. Shearer

NEW PATTERNS OF CHURCH GROWTH IN BRAZIL: W. R. Read

CHURCH GROWTH IN CENTRAL AND SOUTHERN NIGERIA: J. B. Grimley, G. E. Robinson

Church Growth in Central and Southern Nigeria

by

John B. Grimley
Gordon E. Robinson

William B. Eerdmans Publishing Company
Grand Rapids, Michigan

Library of Congress Catalog Card Number, 65-18084

Contents

List of Figures

List of Maps

List of Tables

Church Growth in Central Nigeria

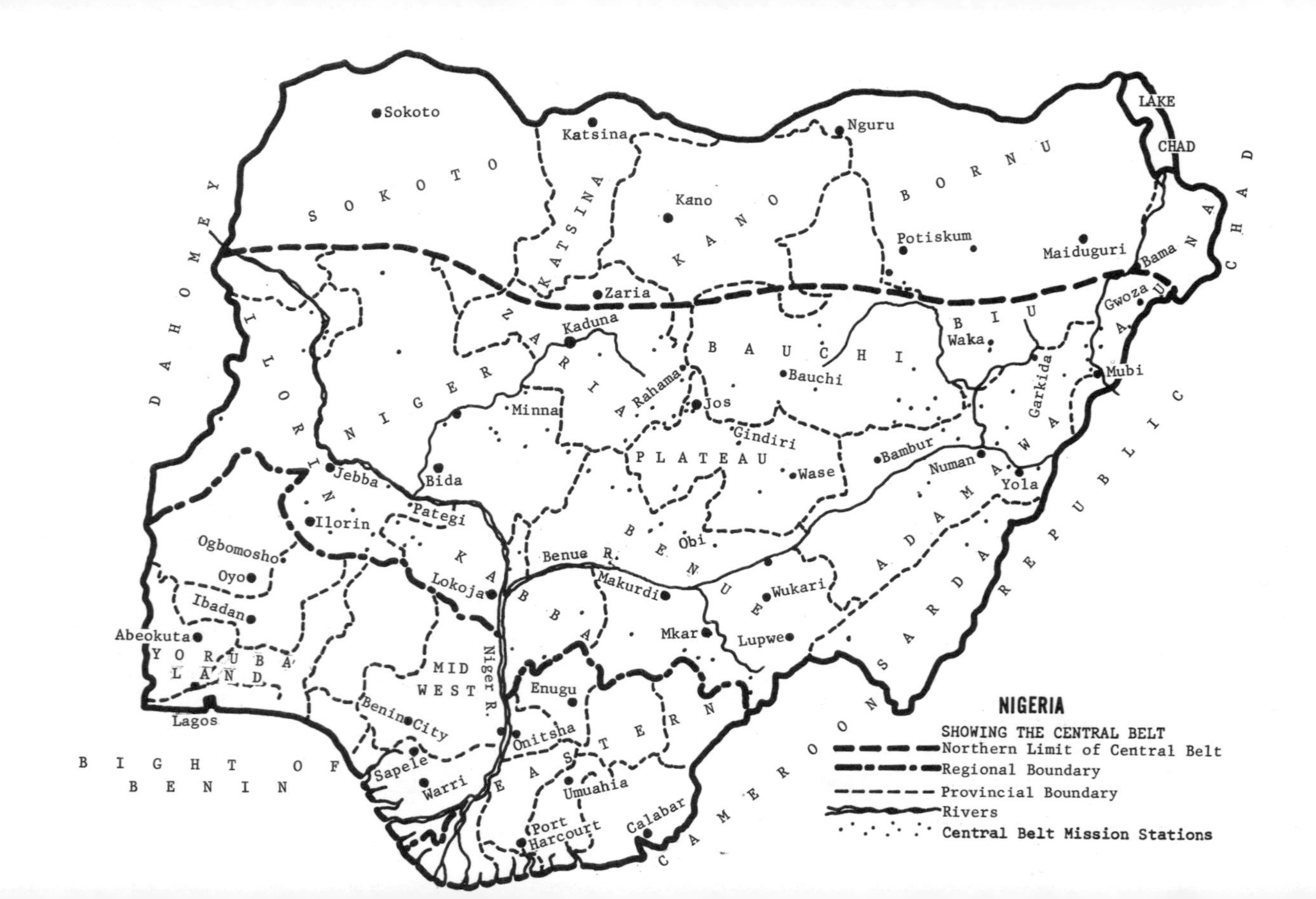
NIGERIA
SHOWING THE CENTRAL BELT
Northern Limit of Central Belt
Regional Boundary
Provincial Boundary
Rivers
Central Belt Mission Stations
SOKOTO
KATSINA
KANO
BORNU
LAKE CHAD
CHAD
DAHOMEY
ILORIN
NIGER
ZARIA
BAUCHI
BIU
PLATEAU
ADAMAWA
SARDAUNA
BENUE
KABBA
MID WEST
YORUBA LAND
EASTERN
CAMEROON REPUBLIC
BIGHT OF BENIN
Sokoto
Katsina
Nguru
Kano
Potiskum
Maiduguri
Bama
Gwoza
Mubi
Zaria
Kaduna
Waka
Garkida
Bauchi
Rahama
Jos
Gindiri
Minna
Wase
Bambur
Numan
Yola
Bida
Jebba
Pategi
Ilorin
Ogbomosho
Oyo
Ibadan
Abeokuta
Lagos
Lokoja
Benue R.
Obi
Makurdi
Wukari
Mkar
Lupwe
Niger R.
Enugu
Benin City
Onitsha
Sapele
Warri
Umuahia
Port Harcourt
Calabar

Foreword

The Central Belt of Nigeria is full of young missions and young Churches.* Most missions are from the United States and arrived in the twenties and thirties. Until after 1950 the Churches were clusters of small "mission station approach" congregations, experiencing relatively little growth. In recent years beginnings of people movements to Christ have become evident in many areas.

John B. Grimley's revealing volume *Church Growth in the Central Belt of Nigeria* vividly describes this kind of church planted by this kind of mission. His book corrects a view which considers that the only mission in the world is that to lands of large old "younger Churches." Missions in the Central Belt are different and much more like beginning missions everywhere.

Mr. Grimley knows his Central Belt. He has worked there for almost twenty years. He loves the country, people, and rising Churches. Belonging himself to the Church of the Brethren, he has cordial relations with the other Churches and missions. In gathering data for this study he traveled widely, visited most of them, and speaks from first-hand knowledge. He was a Research Fellow of the Institute of Church Growth in 1962-1963.

Mr. Grimley writes from within the missionary movement. He is a protagonist of Nigerian Churches and of Christian mission. He is optimistic and forward-looking. Both in Nigeria and at the Institute of Church Growth, he has studied church growth to good effect. His considered conclusions, after living with church growth victories and defeats, are backed up with a wealth of factual evidence, painstakingly displayed. His picture has the convincing

* In this book, Church (with a capital C) means either a proper name or denomination or the Church universal; but church (with small c) means congregation or is used as a adjective.

quality of a photograph. His charts and graphs of growth are illuminating. It will be difficult to challenge his data or his conclusions.

Serious students of mission in every land should read this book. Africasians and Euricans alike will profit. In it readers will see reflected many of the situations and problems they face. They will understand more of the relationships that exist between church planters (nationals and missionaries) and churches. Missiologists will find this a rich lode from which to mine facts concerning mission theories and how they have (and have not) worked out in practice. For a contrasting look, Gordon Robinson's *Church Growth in Southern Nigeria* – the second half of this book – should also be read.

Missionaries and nationals in Africa will find special delight in Mr. Grimley's perceptive study of church growth opportunity and achievement from their own part of the world. This would be a good book to send as a gift to any missionary – but specially to any missionary at work in Africa. English-speaking nationals will appreciate it too.

—DONALD MCGAVRAN
School of World Mission
and Institute of Church Growth
Fuller Theological Seminary
Pasadena, California

Introduction

Nigeria is one of the foremost countries of the new Africa. The progress of the Church here has meaning for the Church everywhere in Africa and, indeed, the world around.

This book deals neither with solidly Moslem Northern Nigeria nor with the substantially Christian South,[1] but with the largely pagan rural Central Belt.[2] The growth of the Church in the Moslem North is a special subject requiring another study. The large tribes of the South present homogeneous populations much in contrast to the splintered tribalism of the Central Belt. Christianity has been in the South longer, has made far more headway, and is more institutionalized. Also, African Churches unrelated to any mission are common in the South but practically unknown in the vast rural areas of the Central Belt – though at least ten such denominations are found in the larger cities of the Central Belt. To see the Central Belt Churches in the context of Christianity in the South and Islam in the North enables one to understand the vitality of the situation and underlines the magnitude of today's opportunity.

J. Spencer Trimingham suggests that in West Africa Christianity and Islam have reached a stalement and that "Christianity is still winning adherents (only) in . . . regions where Islam is not in competition as an alternative religion."[3] However, this cannot be said of the Central Belt. There Islam and Christianity are in competition, but there is no stalemate. The Christian Church has experienced great growth since World War II and since 1955 has entered a new age of expansion. The tribal populations are on

[1] Such problems are dealt with in greater detail by my colleague Rev. Gordon E. Robinson in the second half of this volume, *Church Growth in Southern Nigeria.*

[2] See Frontispiece.

[3] J. Spencer Trimingham, *The Christian Church and Islam in West Africa,* pp. 13-14.

the move. The question is whether the Church is ready and able to reap the harvest.

Church growth in the Central Belt affords a fascinating interplay of historical and physical environment, of past and present, of the moving of the Holy Spirit through the vicissitudes of life and the culmination of things in a "fullness of time." Before 1900 the Gospel of Jesus Christ was not effectively known north of the confluence of the Niger and Benue Rivers. In the short span of sixty-four years the Gospel has extended throughout the Central Belt, won more than 72,000 communicant members, and established a wider "Christian community" of over 277,000. It appears on the edge of a still more rapid extension.

I believe that the Church grows because the Holy Spirit is at work in the life of a nation and in the hearts of its people. In 1945 when my family and I first went to Northeast Nigeria to live at Lassa, a station of the Church of the Brethren Mission, we were welcomed by Rev. and Mrs. H. Stover Kulp, pioneers for Christ among the Margi and Bura tribes. On the wall of their dining room hung a picture of a window in the chapel of St. Colm's College, Edinburgh, depicting Jesus, shod and ready to travel. In His hand He held a long staff, topped with a cross. The motto was: "He Goeth Before."

Surely the Spirit of God has gone before us moving on the ocean of mankind, directing its currents, but being restrained by the rebellion and self-centeredness of man. Africa, so near the place where God in human form met man, has through the centuries been hindered from receiving the light of Christ. Christianity early lost its evangelistic zeal and stagnated in the highlands of Ethiopia. Though it won the Italian and Punic peoples in North Africa, it cut itself off from the common people – the Berbers – and when the Moslem advance wiped out the Italian and Punic population, Christianity disappeared. In West Africa the Portuguese missionaries of the sixteenth century made no lasting impression. They maintained a foothold at Benin for many years but planted no self-propagating churches. The trade of the Portuguese, French, and Dutch from the sixteenth to the eighteenth centuries, far from propagating the faith, degraded the West African and consisted largely in an exchange of gin for slaves.

The Spirit of God was brooding over West Africa in those days, but His will was frustrated temporarily by His servants. Christianity failed to penetrate that great land. Today, again, the Spirit of God, moving within the changing social milieu, has gone before, preparing the tribes of the Central Belt.

The student of church growth is sure *that* God makes churches grow; but he goes on to ask, How does the Church grow? What is its form? What does it look like in each local situation – the only place where growth occurs? Growth in a particular place cannot be explained by a phrase such as "The Lord has blessed here," true though it be, any more than lack of growth can be explained by the phrase "This is a very difficult place," true though that may be! Much in either case depends on what God's obedient servants do. Are they quick or slow to observe the "signs of the times"? Are they aware of or blind to the vivifying rain brought by the winds of change and the web of human relationships in today's strategic hour?

May the Holy Spirit lead His Church to recognize opportunity for the extension of Christ's Kingdom. May we enter into every open door for the "glory of God and our neighbor's good."

During 1962, on being appointed by my board to study at the Institute of Church Growth in Eugene, Oregon, I toured the central and eastern parts of the Central Belt, visiting churches and missions and consulting with missionaries and Nigerian Christians. I am most grateful for the hospitality shown me by missionaries of the Sudan Interior Mission and all branches of the Sudan United Mission. I regret I was unable to visit the United Missionary Society, the Assemblies of God Mission, and the Qua Iboe Churches.

The field secretaries of all the missions, whether by correspondence or in interviews, were exceedingly helpful in sharing their experiences, in making records available, and in setting up meetings with Nigerian church leaders. I thank all the Nigerian Christians who have been so patient with my questions.

Special thanks goes to Dr. Donald A. McGavran, Director of the Institute of Church Growth, for his invaluable insights in regard to church growth without which this study would not have been possible. I gratefully acknowledge the deep concern for the growth of the Church shown by Northwest Christian College in granting the research fellowship and by the Foreign Mission Commission of the Church of the Brethren in making my furlough year available for church growth research.

I am especially grateful to my wife, Mildred Hess Grimley, who typed and helped in editing the manuscript.

JOHN B. GRIMLEY
Uba, Nigeria

PART I: THE SETTING FOR CHURCH GROWTH

Chapter I. The Land, Its People, and the Winds of Change

A. THE CENTRAL BELT OF NIGERIA

THE CENTRAL BELT (SEE FRONTISPIECE), WHICH INCLUDES about four-sevenths of the Northern Region of Nigeria, lies between two extremes of topography, as well as between two extremes of religious thought. To the south are the luxuriant rain forests that merge into the mangrove swamps of the coastal area, and to the north are the dry, open savannahs and thorn thickets that fringe the encroaching sands of the Sahara. The Central Belt itself is a vast land of about 160,000 square miles; it stretches across Nigeria from the border of Dahomey on the west to that of the Cameroon Republic on the east. The Niger and Benue Rivers form a great Y with its junction in the south-central part of the Central Belt. Except for the grasslands under the arm of the Benue and on the central plateau, the Central Belt is characterized by low forests. Along the northern edge this low forest cover becomes open "bush country" with tall grass and an orchardlike scattering of trees.

Much of the Central Belt is less than 1,000 feet above sea level. However, higher elevations make several areas pleasant places in which to live. Jos, on the central plateau, at 4,000 feet, has been a haven from heat and insects for the missionary and government workers alike. The nearby hills rise over 5,600 feet. Other mountain ranges reach 3,000 and 4,000 feet, and in the southern part of Sardauna Province to over 6,000 feet.

In the Central Belt, in contrast to the monotony of the forests of the south and the low, sandy savannahs of the north, there is a fascinating variety of topography: rugged mountains and open grasslands, cool highlands and sweltering river valleys, dashing mountain streams and malarial swamps, wide rivers and parched volcanic cones. Erosion has cut deeply into many areas so that roads go up and down, with narrow bridges at the bottom of each downward sweep.

There are majestic rock formations sculptured by rain, blistering heat, and wind-blown sand. The Mandara Mountains and the Biu Plateau show evidence of ancient volcanic activity. Kamale, a pillar of volcanic rock 700 feet high and 150 feet in diameter, is an inspiring sight set on the high, windy ridge on the Nigerian border between Sardauna Province and the Cameroon Republic. Touched with mystery, the great pillar has led the people living in the village at its base to speak of it as: "The Only God There is."

On the Bauchi-Jos road the rolling plain is broken by bald projections of solid rock several miles long and hundreds of feet high. Like great "elephants" they lie upon the plain, exposing their black, hairless bodies to the erosion of the elements.

Then there is the massive, grey, pock-marked Wase Rock. It broods over the plains southeast of the central plateau. Rising like a sentinel of sheer rock, it has drawn pagan, Moslem, and Christian into its shade. For hundreds of years it has been a shrine for the neighboring tribes. The invading Moslems found it a natural site from which to exert their power, and the missionaries of the Sudan United Mission built their first station in 1904 just beyond the reach of its evening shadow.

Another historic rock is that of Jebba, which thrusts itself up from the waters of the Niger. It was here that the Church Missionary Society's first river boat, the *Dayspring*, met an untimely end.

Tilla Lake, one of the loveliest sights of the Central Belt, is seldom seen, for it is located on the Biu Plateau 300 miles east of Jos. This tiny lake, with its sacred crocodiles and fluttering egrets, is a jewel of sparkling beauty. Fringed with trees, the lake is set in a crater that was apparently formed when the side blew out of the now extinct volcano on whose slope it rests. Portions of volcanic "pipes" are visible along its shores. Many stories are told about this little lake: one of these stories states that it has no bottom, but soundings indicate that the lake is not more than seventeen feet deep.[1]

The mountains, plains, plateaus, and rocky ledges form a patchwork that compares to the pattern of tribes among which the church grows. The people themselves present a varied pattern. Some of the most "primitive" people are found within a few miles of the large city of Jos on the central plateau, as well as in the more remote areas of the eastern reaches of the Benue and the mountain ranges of Gwoza in Sardauna Province. "Duckbilled" women live just off the main road between Jos and Bauchi, and Fulani nomads are prominent throughout the area. Their herds of dark brown or white, long-horned, humped cattle are one of the country's most important assets. Hausa traders from the north, as well as artisans from the Ibo and Yoruba tribes of the southern regions are found in most of the cities.

Government and missions have established schools throughout many parts of the Central Belt. These have produced a "New Nigerian" found almost everywhere, and certainly often in the most unexpected places. School teachers, registered nurses, hospital workers and dispensers, pastors and evangelists, masons and carpenters, postal agents, agriculturalists, politicians, and members of the houses of representatives, veterinarians, forestry agents, school supervisors, midwives, and vegetable gardeners are all part of the new Nigeria so variously represented in the Central Belt.

Architecture is of a great variety. In towns the square, thick-walled, flat-roofed houses of the Hausa and town Fulani are prominent. Roof spires rise picturesquely from each corner of the house and long rain spouts protrude a foot or more from the walls. In the open "bush" one comes upon nomad Fulani encampments. Their beehive-shaped houses made of nothing more than cut grass thrown upon

[1] Helser, A. D., *Education of Primitive People*, p. 49.

a tree-branch framework, seem very fragile indeed in contrast to the three-foot-thick mud walls of the town houses. No type of building could more adequately fit the life of the nomad, however, for when the cattle move on to find new grazing lands the houses are simply left behind – with no loss but the short time it took to build them.

The most common architecture is that of the tribal villages located in river valleys, on mountain tops, in fertile lowlands, and on the precipitous sides of mountains. Everywhere the little round "hut" is the basic building unit. It may vary from five to fifteen feet in diameter. Its sun-dried mud wall is usually only a few inches thick. The door may have a wooden frame and hinged panel or be just a round hole cut in the wall. Windows have been nonexistent, but within recent years small ones of a foot or so square, with shutters, are found. The conical roofs are skillfully thatched and culminate in many different types of peaks. Indeed, one tribe can be recognized from another by the type of peak as readily as by language or tribal marks. These round houses constitute rooms of the home, and any one home may be composed of a dozen or more such "rooms" closely pressed together. The community found in such clusters of homes is comprised of units of close-knit clans and is especially fitted for a "discipling of the tribes" approach. Here, individuals are in strong family and village relationships, making it possible to win a whole community to Christ.

The first church building in the midst of such a round-house, conical-roofed society, will also be round with a conical roof. Structural difficulties will soon be met, however, as the number of disciples in the village increases and the church building must be enlarged. The maximum size of a conical roof with a framework of saplings and cornstalks is soon reached, and a larger rectangular building must be adapted. Split palm trees must soon replace saplings and cornstalks in the roof framework. The maximum size of a thatched building is finally reached and sheets of roofing metal become a practical necessity for the growing church.

Thus, in recent years a new style of house architecture has been introduced into many areas of the Central Belt.

It is the rectangular house with split-palm rafters, covered with either grass thatch or corrugated iron or aluminum roofing sheets. Such a house may be divided into three rooms, the central one being a living room for the family, with one of the adjoining rooms for the husband and sons, and the other for the wife and daughters. Corrugated roofing is a sign of economic achievement; and to be the first person to build a "pan-roofed" house in a village is to assure one's place in history!

B. THE ORIGINS AND COMPLEXITIES OF TRIBAL PATTERNS

To speak of the numerous tribes of Africa is commonplace. However, the extreme complexity of the situation is not usually recognized. Dr. E. W. Smith writes,

> . . . the details of their social organization present a bewildering diversity. Some are pastoral, some are agricultural, and others are both. The strong kingdoms of Ashanti and Buganda and Burotse form a striking contrast to the loose congeries of village communities found elsewhere. The language of the Hamites, Sudanese, and Bantu belong to distinct families of speech. At least 200 Sudanic tongues are known and 300 Bantu. . . .[2]

In so far as this shows the great diversity and complexity of the African situation it could well have been written of the Central Belt of Nigeria.

The cradle of humanity, once thought to have been in Asia, seems now, as a result of recent archeological discoveries, to have been in the eastern and southern parts of Africa.[3] From these areas of origin, humanity moved out across the world, with the probability that as the diffusion continued, migrations would become confused. There were movements in both directions – inward as well as outward. Thus the Bantoid people of South and Central Africa today are not direct descendants of those earliest inhabitants. Developing through the centuries as a branch of a sub-family of

[2] Smith, E. W., *The Christian Mission in Africa,* p. 6.

[3] Murdock, C. P., *Africa, Its People and Their Cultural History,* p. 9; Oliver Roland, *The Dawn of African History,* pp. 1, 2.

Nilotic stock, they began their movement south not more than 2,000 years ago[4] from the central plateau and eastern border area of what is now Nigeria – that is, from the very heart of the Central Belt. The people with which our present study of church growth is concerned were left behind to compete with other groups pressing in from the north and east.

Ethnologists distinguish between the central Nigerian Bantoid people and the Chadic people of the eastern Central Belt. The latter also had Nilotic origins and in many cases they refer to "the east" as their original home. Thus the present Central Belt population, whether Bantoid or Chadic, had very ancient eastern Sudanic origins.

One wave of migration followed on the heels of another. Those coming later sometimes obliterated those whose territory they invaded, or simply pushed them on. Those pushed on put pressures upon those into whose areas they were forced to move. The present Margi, Kilba, Bura, Higi, and Fali are the latest wave from the north and east. And now, with peace established between the tribes of the Sudan across all of West Africa, and with the formation of independent nations with fixed, politically defined boundaries, the geographical movements of tribes have come to an end.

By way of illustrating the complexity of local situations, let us note a small portion of the Chadic populace of southern Bornu and northern Adamawa Provinces. In the northeastern portion of this area the Margi-speaking people of Duhu and Gulak have become fused with immigrants from Gudur in the French Cameroons. To the west the Bura and Kilba have become fused with the central groups of Margi, Higi, and Fali. This fusion is especially noted in the area where Kilba and Margi meet: the South Margi of Wamdi, Uba, and Hildi. These could be called North Kilba just as readily as South Margi, for their villages "look more like Kilba than Margi towns."[5] The South Margi language is also a merging of the Margi and Kilba languages.

The Margi of Dille, Ngurthlavu, Musa and Wiyam look

[4] Murdock, C. P., *op. cit.*, p. 99; Oliver, R., *op. cit.*, pp. 4, 5.
[5] Meek, C. K., *Tribal Studies in Northern Nigeria,* pp. 216, 232.

to Bazza, with its Pabir (Biu Plateau) origins, for their chieftainship authority; but those of Wamdi and Uba look toward Hwong in the Kilba tribe for their authority. The "cult of Guti" at Uba, mentioned by Meek, made decisions not only for the local Margi people, but for the whole of Kilba as well. The Guti (or Buti) pool is located a mile or so from the Church of the Brethren Mission station at Uba, where I lived from 1955 to 1964. When I visited it, I found it an example of the decay that is seen in many pagan sacred sites. Reduced in size, covered over with encroaching swamp grass, cleared of crocodiles, with most of the trees of the grove cut for firewood, it was difficult to imagine that upon the successful crossing of this pool important decisions once depended. In 1961 the Uba Church baptized in the Guti pool.

The Margi groups of Bazza, and Dille, in the Yedseram River Valley west of the Mandara range, claim Pabir origin. Yet the Pabir, who have been the overlords of the Bura, claim Mandara origins. To further complicate the picture of origins, the Gadzama, one of the primary clans of the Margi, and the ruling clan in Wiyam, Chul, Lassa, and Madagali are immigrants from a place called Gadzama, located somewhere west of Mulgwi, an important North Margi center in Bornu. They claim they formerly originated from the Kanuri stock of the old Bornu capital of Ngsar-Gomo.

There are 248 distinct languages in Nigeria. If mutually unintelligible dialects were included, the count would be much higher. One estimate is that "There are 400 and more languages and dialects in daily use."[6] The list of the tribes of the Central Belt found in Chapter II, pp. 71, 72, could be expanded a great deal if all the smaller language groups were included. Even so, I have included eight "tribes" that are made up of several small tribes. Such are numbers 1, 12, 41, 44, 73, 85, 99, and 102. So, the actual count of the tribes varies greatly in any list, depending on whether certain small, related tribes are grouped together or counted separately. Having grouped these numerous smaller tribes into

[6] Niven, C. R., *Nigeria*, p. 9.

eight "tribes," we receive a total of 110 tribes in the Central Belt.

In these days of rapid social change it is amazing, and in many ways gratifying to all who seek unity in Nigeria, to note that intermarriage between tribes is on the increase. I suppose it has never been uncommon for Fulani men to take pagan tribal women as wives, and intermarriage between some pagan tribes was practiced. Today it is not unusual to find Margi and Higi and Bura intermarrying. In such cases the father might speak Margi; the mother, Higi; the children, Margi and Higi and Fulani (the language of the overlords), and Hausa (the trade language), and after a few years in primary school, English. Thus it is likely that both Margi and Higi are spoken less and less and Hausa is becoming predominant in the home. Yet tribal distinctions have remained surprisingly strong in spite of the acculturation that results from intermarriage.

In the area covered by the Fellowship of Churches of Christ in the Sudan, to be described in Part II, there are fifty-five of the 110 tribes. I have listed the seven Churches of the Fellowship of the Churches of Christ in the Sudan, giving the number of tribes represented in their spheres of influence and an estimate of the population in each group of tribes.

THE CHURCH	NUMBER OF TRIBES	POPULATION	
Plateau	13	382,000	
Mada Hills	6	250,000	
Tiv	1	800,000	(possibly 1,000,000)
Benue	8	150,000	
(This figure includes the "Tigon Complex" as one)			
Muri	5	265,000	
Lutheran	13	500,000	
Eastern	9	500,000	
	55	2,847,000	

To illustrate further the tribal complexity and at the same time to point up one problem it presents to the church, I refer to the Pastoral Training Class held at Bambur in the Muri Church area. In March of 1962 there were fifteen men from the Muri and Plateau Churches attending this class. Twelve different tribes were represented! It would have been impossible to have used any one of the twelve languages for the medium of instruction, for only one or two in the whole class would have understood. The language used was Hausa, the mother-tongue of 5.5 million Northern Nigerians, but no one of the fifteen students was a Hausa man. All could understand and speak it fluently, however, for Hausa is the trade language of the Northern Region of Nigeria.

The isolation of the Central Belt peoples played an important part in their comparatively late reception of the gospel. In many parts of the Central Belt a mountain culture with terraced farming had developed through the centuries. Tribal warfare and the pressures of immigating clans played an important part of this development. During the early years of the nineteenth century the Fulani *jihad* (holy war) heightened the tendency of the tribes to live in the most difficult-of-access parts of their habitation. The rocky plateaus of Jos, Bauchi, and Biu, and the ranges of the Mandara and Mambila Mountains, as well as every granite outcropping, became havens of refuge. The mountain retreats did not always protect them from fire and sword, but they very definitely increased their isolation and cut them off from outside cultural and trade influences. Some of the villages attacked by the Fulani were completely wiped out, or their inhabitants carried off into slavery. However, there are many who in these days of increasing freedom relate with a great deal of pride how their village suffered when under attack, and how they were finally able to beat off the invader. The numerous villages that were never subjugated are situated on mountain tops where water in caves was sufficient to hold them over the dry season and where paths were too steep and rocky for the Fulani horses.

The government is carrying out resettlement plans (the Resettlement Projects out of the Gwoza Hills of Sardauna Province, and near Langtang in Plateau Province, are good examples), but it is a slow process. Fear and uncertainty for the future, as well as a reluctance to leave their old homes and religious shrines and develop a new type of culture on the plains, hinders many from accepting the government help to find better and less crowded homes and farm lands. So even today many of the Central Belt tribes live in their mountain retreats. But the isolation will not long remain. Roads, commerce, and political parties are breaking through the isolation of the centuries.

The widespread agrarian culture of the Sudan characterized the tribes of the Central Belt long before the coming of the Fulani. Though geographically south of the actual path of the diffusion of both Sudanic agriculture and Neolithic animal husbandry, no traces of earlier forms of subsistence survive today.[7] Thus it is likely that the forms of agriculture and animal husbandry that are now practiced were brought in with the tribes during their original prehistoric migrations into the Central Belt. This Sudanic agriculture includes millet, sorghum, cow peas and earth peas, gourds, pumpkins, okra, roselle, sesame, yams, and cotton.

South of the Central Belt and merging into it are found the Malaysian plants, including yams, taro, and bananas, as well as American crops such as maize, manioc, peanuts, peppers, squash, sweet potatoes, and tomatoes.[8] The domestic animals are mainly goats, sheep, chickens, guinea fowl, cats, dogs, ducks, donkeys, a few horses, and a few cattle. Pigs are very common in some tribes. The very small breed of short-horned, humpless cattle are a marvel to see and counted of great value by the hill tribes who herd them.

The staple food is a thick mush made from sorghum (guinea corn) flour, and is usually eaten with a sauce made from a few vegetables and edible leaves, and cooked with meat, if it is available. Plenty of red peppers, which from time immemorial have been a part of the trade of West Africa, liven up the sauce.

[7] Murdock, C. P., *op. cit.*, p. 90.
[8] *Ibid*, p. 254.

C. THE WINDS OF CHANGE

The Harmattan of West Africa blows from the Sahara Desert in the dry season, making everything dry and hot, casting a pale haze across the countryside. But just preceding the coming of the rains the winds change. There is a period of a few weeks when they seem uncertain as to which way to blow; one day from the north and the next from the south, or from any point of the compass. The first storms are windstorms bringing dust and destruction and only a spattering of rain. But soon the winds have made up their minds, as it were, and the white clouds from the ocean, carrying life-giving moisture, pile high in the sky. Then the rain falls, beating the dust and ash of the burned fields into rich loam waiting for the seed.

This is a parable of Nigeria. In recent years dry winds have struggled with those laden with promise of planting and harvest. Now the winds of change are laden with great promise for the future. While there are still many cross-currents, the ultimate direction is well determined, and all feel much more than just a stir with the awakening breeze of full nationhood.

The Second World War brought an awakening to Nigeria that began with the youth. The army took young men to faraway places. They fought side-by-side with British soldiers and some received commissions. Many who had no education previous to their enlistment were trained in trades and services valuable to the army and potentially valuable in civilian life. They visited foreign countries and "came in contact with new people, new ideas and fresh influences."[9]

Torn from ancestral ways, the soldier observed the ways of other people — people he had never before even dreamed existed. He came home with hopes never before known and became an important factor in bringing change to Nigeria. Many of the returned soldiers were disillusioned when they came face-to-face with the primitive patterns of life in their home communities. Hopes for quick change on a broad base were shattered, but the returned soldier had money, and his dreams to a certain extent could come true on the level

[9] Epelle, Sam, *The Promise of Nigeria,* p. 30.

of immediate needs. Superior resources put him into a better position to get the wife he desired, to build a better house in his own village – with a sheet-metal roof and a cement floor – and his new knowledge led to establishing himself in some trade, if not in his own village, then in some large town to which he moved with his new wife. He became a part of the new spirit of progress that had come to Nigeria.

Many of the tribes of the Gongola-Yedseram-Benue Watershed and of the Plateau and its escarpment and lowland areas in the triangle of the Niger and Benue have felt increasingly out of step with the great political and technological changes that are coming upon Nigeria. Such changes are pressing in upon their isolation and they have begun to break out of their "parochial attitudes and loyalties, which, combined with linguistic diversities, have been obstacles to economic and political integration in Nigeria."[10] Their very fractured and splintered pattern of existence, which was once brought into being by, and maintained by, the struggle to exist, is now, with a broader base of existence – through travel and trade, education and medical facilities – being looked upon as confining and dissatisfying. This desire to break out of the confines of a tribe's shell has not been felt by the older adults to any great extent, but it is a primary, though often unconscious, drive in the lives of the youth and younger adults.

James Coleman writes,

> In this century and a half since the Fulani jihad, there have been two somewhat contradictory developments: the tendency of the leaders and more educated members of these tribal groups to become assimilated to the dominant Fulani-Hausa culture; and the British effort to stimulate their own group consciousness. Intermingled with these two influences has been the energetic evangelization of these people by Christian missionaries. Under the impact of many conflicting external influences, these Central Belt groups are being stirred to consciousness; the rate and direction of their cultural and political development are among the most important but unpredictable aspects of future Nigerian politics."[11]

[10] Coleman, J. S., *Nigeria, Background to Nationalism,* p. 13.
[11] *Ibid.,* p. 24.

And, may I add, of future church growth in the Central Belt.

Commercially, politically, and socially a new day is dawning. Up to and during the Second World War, Nigeria's total trade had never exceeded £50,000,000. Following the war, since 1949, it had risen steadily to over £175,000,000 in 1959.[12]

Nigeria's high potential as a market for the manufactured materials of the new day is shown by its rising imports. The export of its own products – mineral and agricultural – indicates the possibility of vast progress as technical skills and leadership develop.

The average annual income per person is between twenty and twenty-five pounds;[13] yet for many this has been increasing very rapidly. Four-fifths of the population are farmers, hunters, fishermen, cattlemen, or timbermen. Less than one-tenth of the population work as craftsmen or skilled industrial workers. Another tenth are traders. The biggest employers of labor are the regional and federal governments and trade and oil companies. The planting of cash crops, and groundnuts (peanuts) in particular, the development of cattle-improvement techniques, and increasing mechanization will continually raise the standard of living all over Nigeria. The nomadic Fulani and some very remote mountain villagers will be the last to leave the old ways, but even for them change will come.

The strongest wind blowing is that of politics and the spirit of nationalism. The nationalist movement was born in the life and dedication of Herbert H. S. Macauly, the great-grandson of Bishop Samuel Crowther. Macauly founded the Nigerian Democratic party in 1923 and was active for the next twenty-three years in the nation's half-century journey to independence. He died in 1946 at the age of eighty-two.

Political leaders, such as Dr. Nnamdi Azikwe, the first Nigerian Governor General of Nigeria, and now President of the Republic, had joined Macauly in pressing for Nigerian

[12] *Nigeria* Magazine, Independence Issue, p. 37.
[13] Epelle, S., *op. cit.*, p. 167.

participation in the government. As early as 1914 a Nigerian Council had been established that included six Nigerians. In 1922 a Legislative Council had been formed with ten Nigerian members, and in 1942 there was an Executive Council to which the first Nigerian was appointed. The Governor, Sir Arthur Richards, inaugurated a new constitution in 1946, thus encouraging the postwar awakening. He also arranged for an itinerate Legislative Council, which met in Lagos, Ibadan, Kaduna, and Enugu, in turn. He created the regional Houses of Assembly in addition to the central legislature. This made it possible for Nigerians to observe and participate in their own government to a larger degree than at any previous time and gave much impetus to political development. Five years later the Constitution was revised and Nigerians were given ministerial appointments. Then in 1954 the pre-independence Constitution was adopted, and in 1959 the Secretary of State for the Colonies let it be known that the British Government would look favorably upon Nigeria's request for independence. The next month (Jan. 16, 1960) the Nigerian Federal House made this formal request, and only eight and one-half months after this request Nigeria celebrated its independence on October 1, 1960.

The premier of the Northern Region, Alhaji Sir Ahmadu Bello, Sardauna of Sokoto, speaking on Self-Government Day for the Northern Region, said,

> In the name of God: the Compassionate and the Merciful. Let thanks be given to God, everywhere in the Northern Region of Nigeria, for the blessing of self-government which we have received this day through His help and for the blessing of progress which has long been a feature of our lives within this region. In our prayers let us beseech Almighty God for continued and peaceful progress. . . . I am beset with many emotions. The emotion of gratitude to Almighty God. . . . May God grant that His blessings shall always be with us in our endeavors.

The Sardauna's remarks show a consciousness of great change brought about by God's help. The motto of the Northern Region, emblazoned upon the coat of arms, "Work and Worship," clearly proclaims the interrelationship between God and man. This recognition of man's relationship to God and the stated policy of religious freedom[14] are most encouraging to Christians in the Northern Region of Nigeria today.

But the winds of change have included some cross-currents that have disturbed and detribalized, and yet all – both good and bad – have been important in "the rapidity of upward mobility in this revolutionary transformation (which) is possibly unparalleled in history."[15]

Mr. A. A. Nwafor Orizu describes the negative aspects of the change which has come to Nigeria:

> As time went on, English schools were established in Nigeria and young boys attended these with but one ambition: to learn enough to become clerks and interpreters, or employees of European traders. From these "pinnacles" they thenceforward surveyed their ancestral culture with high contempt, obeying no laws and observing no rules but the Englishman's. This contempt of culture and institutions of their own people then became the sign of "education." The educated class became a privileged class – "privileged" because they felt themselves above the Nigerian diet, above the Nigerian attire, above the Nigerian form of marriage, above the people's ceremonies, in fact, above Nigeria! Later this privilege expanded into study abroad, and now the young men who go to Oxford or Cambridge – when the return to Nigeria – become more English than the English themselves. . . . This educated class now exploits the masses. It has no use for the poor and underprivileged millions of the country. All that its members care about is to have a beautiful mansion and many servants, and to be very respectful to their wives. They apply for jobs from the British Government and they usually obtain them. They are the high-salaried class . . . they prefer it (clerical jobs at £300. per year) to returning to a creative aspect of Nigerian life – the reclamation and acceptance of things Nigerian, the construction of new institutions upon the best in the old ways added to the new ideas.[16]

[14] See the Sardauna's remarks on page 30.
[15] Coleman, J. S., *op. cit.*, p. 115.
[16] Orizu, A. A. Nwafor, *Without Bitterness*, p. 99.

The above was written in 1944. It well illustrates aspects of change that might have led to disturbances: rebellions against oppression and against the breakup of old culture patterns. However, political developments moved so rapidly toward independence through the new constitution of 1946 and other legislative changes that even the more radical decided upon independence through evolution rather than through revolution. It could not be said that none of the above elements of sophisticated westernization no longer exist! They can still be found among the "new elite" as well as among schoolboys in the most "primitive" areas, but the context is different. Now Nigeria belongs to the Nigerians, and a new appreciation for their own land, without reaction against things "Western," can be found on every hand. There is an encouraging interest in Nigerian history, institutions, customs, and the preserving of artifacts and other material evidences of the past.

Our observations concerning the changes that have come and are now coming to Nigeria are background for our study of the growth of the Church in the Central Belt. This climate of rapid change is more than just friendly to church growth; it has, in fact, been a cause of growth.

The situation is complex, for not only have changing conditions been the fertile ground from which the Church has grown, but the Church itself has been one of the main elements in bringing change. The message of Christianity played an important part in awakening Nigeria, and is vital to her development.

"Without the missionary enterprise," says James Coleman of the Department of Political Science at the University of California, "both the timing and nature of the awakening of racial and national consciousness would probably have been very different."[17] Through the centuries static, animistic tribalism had not been vitalized by any other contacts, but with the coming of the Christian message there were stirrings that preceded and permeated the winds of change. Coleman continues, "Through extensive evangelical activity and long monopoly in the field of education, Christian missions played

[17] Coleman, J. S., *op. cit.*, p. 91.

a critical part in the rise of nationalism in Nigeria."[18] The message of evangelists and village schoolteachers entered the most remote areas as well as into most of the large towns. Leadership began to appear in the most unexpected places, from among peoples who until very recently had been thought of as something less than human and merely the source of slaves.

A great many of the emerging leaders, especially in the South and in the Central Belt area, began their careers in the employ of missionaries or as teachers in mission schools. The Christian teaching of the worth of every man, and the impact of western education through the missions awakened unsuspected powers and directed them to constructive ends.

The enlightenment of education, the breakdown of tribal loyalties, a desire to make progress materially and to reach a higher level of living, and an increasing mobility of the youth – all produced an unrest and a realization that animistic fetishism is insufficient for today's "scientific" living. The Christian message comes to the fore as the philosophy of life that gives purpose and balance amidst the confusions of the times and unites man with a loving God in personal, national, material, and social advancement.

The opportunity for great response to the gospel in the Central Belt, where the winds of change buffet all the tribes, is reminiscent of conditions in Indonesia during the nineteenth century when the Church grew very rapidly – the Batak tribal area of Sumatra being the primary example. Rapid tribal moves to Christianity have also been experienced in the islands of the Pacific, some areas of India, Burma, Ethiopia, Uganda, Mexico, and elsewhere.

The present response to the gospel in the mountain areas of West New Guinea is large and dramatic. The potential response is enormous. The tribes there, very "primitive" and practically untouched by any aspects of modern life, are turning dramatically through fetish burnings and tribal decisions within the pattern of their ancient culture without schools, medicine, or other auxiliaries of modern missions. In the Central Belt the possibility of such response still

[18] *Ibid.*

exists in some of the more remote areas, but as a whole the winds of change have blown so strongly that most tribes desire education, medicine, political stature – in a word: "progress," all wrapped up with Christianity in one package.

As a result, missions, and to some extent national churches, have become involved and will remain involved in the material and visible aspects of Nigeria's new day. Educational, medical, agricultural, and village-improvement plans have taken and are taking much mission time and many resources. The importance of this in the eyes of the Nigerian can be seen from the following quotation from Mr. Orizu:

> When the proper light operates among the Africans and regenerates their society, to emancipate their mentality, to nationalize their activities, and to secure their existence, Christianity will have accomplished its mission in Africa. But if Christianity fails to solve these basic problems in Africa, it will have no basis for a preferred position over other organized religions in Africa. Then the African will have to make his own choice, not on the basis of the dogmatic claims of any religion, but on the visible utility of its principles in the matter of physical, mental, and spiritual growth of the whole people.[19]

The Church in the Central Belt of Nigeria is neither asking nor hoping for a "preferred position over other organized religions" on any grounds, though it certainly could already claim it upon those suggested by Mr. Orizu. As long as missions from overseas are present in Nigeria the "visible utility" of Christianity through various mission services will be clearly seen. How many of these services may be continued by the Churches themselves is impossible to predict, for while voluntary agencies are encouraged and some Churches, such as the Evangelical Church of West Africa, are taking over schools and dispensaries from the Sudan Interior Mission, the welfare state is likely to look upon all social services as primarily its own responsibility. Government grants have for many years been given to voluntary agencies "in aid of payments" for teachers' salaries and the building of new facilities.

[19] Orizu, A. A. N., *op. cit.*, p. 174.

Just how substantial these grants have been can be illustrated by the fact that in 1960 one mission alone received approximately $204,000 from the government as grants to its social services of education, general medical work, and leprosy treatment. Of the total, $191,250 went toward general education on the primary level and a teacher-training college that includes a new secondary school.

The Church, however, though not a social service agency, is an extending fellowship of awakened and transformed Nigerians moved by the Spirit of God in paths of constructive witness and service to all men. Its primary goal is that of bringing all men into fellowship with God in Christ Jesus. Its greatest service to Nigeria is to bring its citizens into this liberating, energizing life of Christ. Practically, this means that in the environment of change and "progress" new churches must be established everywhere and these churches must grow in numbers until the redeeming fellowship of Christ is at work in the lives of all. Then entirely new dimensions of health, education, integrity, and cooperation will become possible for all. No greater wind of change is blowing anywhere than that of the Spirit of Christ in the life of the individual, one strand stirred in the web of the whole, with vibrations moving out to the other strands, to family, clan, tribe, and nation, until substantial parts of whole communities move into the new life of the Spirit.

In the next chapter we shall outline the entrance of Christian missions into the Central Belt of Nigeria — an entrance, beginning before the winds of change had come, into a tribal, feudalistic, and self-destroying society in which both the Fulani invader and the Nigerian tribesman preyed upon each other.[20]

[20] *Nigeria* Magazine, Independence Issue, p. 61.

Chapter II. Missions in the Central Belt

A. THE BEGINNINGS

COMPARED TO OTHER PARTS OF WEST AFRICA THE GOSPEL MESSAGE came late to the Central Belt of Northern Nigeria. In 1841 an attempt was made to enter Nigeria by way of the Niger River.[1] Two English societies, the African Society and the Agricultural Association, raised £4,000 to begin a "model farm" on the Niger. A popular slogan, "The Bible and the Spade," was directed toward the regeneration of Africa. The two societies supplied the "spade" and the Missionary Society of the Anglican Church supplied the "Bible." The British government took a large part of the responsibility for the expedition, making an initial outlay of £38,000. Three boats, the *Soudan,* the *Albert* and the *Wilberforce,* equipped for agricultural experimentation and evangelization, headed up the Niger. One of them, the *Albert,* penetrated 350 miles up the Niger to Egan. The official purpose of the expedition was to make with the chiefs treaties under which slavery would be abolished and trade established. It was also hoped that the model farm would be an example of progressive and sound agriculture that would be copied by surrounding tribes and thus have its effect upon beginning a profitable and peaceful life that would in turn ultimately bring an end to slavery. Several treaties were made and the model farm started in the present area of Lokoja.[2] But scarcely had the work begun when tropical fever brought a terrible end to this expedition. During the first two months on the Niger 40 of the 145 Europeans in the party died, and 90 more suffered fever. Though the expedition failed, one of the members of the party, Samuel Adjai Crowther, was

[1] Stock, Eugene, *History of the Church Missionary Society,* Vol. I, pp. 454, 455.

[2] Warren, J. S., "A Story of Peaceful Progress . . . ," pp. 4, 5.

destined to play a leading part in the planting of the Church of Christ in the middle Niger area.

From 1837 to 1842 more than 500 freed slaves had been returned to Nigeria from Sierra Leone. Mr. Sam Epelle says,

> The slave trade had its favorable repercussions in Nigeria, for, with the establishment of British Colonies in the West Indies and Sierra Leone (Freetown), Negroes who had imbibed European culture at first hand returned as educational, commercial, and governmental pioneers to enlighten their brethren.[3]

Many of these were Anglican Christians. They entered Yoruba country and found it to be their homeland from which they had been taken as slaves. From Badagry and Abeokuta Christians began to call for pastoral help. In response to this call, in 1844, the Church Missionary Society sent Henry Townsend and Samuel Crowther from Sierra Leone to Badagry.[4] When they passed through Badagry to Abeokuta, they found that Thomas Birch Freeman, a Wesleyan Methodist missionary, had preceded them by just three months.[5] Both societies became active in establishing churches in Abeokuta and the surrounding countryside.

As the Church grew in Yorubaland, interest increased concerning the vast unexplored areas to the north of the Niger and the Benue Rivers. Dr. Barth's travels in the Sudan were soon to arouse the interest of the world at large, and of the Church in particular, to the importance of evangelizing Hausaland.[6]

In 1854 Dr. W. B. Baikie, a British naval officer appointed to direct activities along the Niger, with Rev. Samuel Crowther as an advisor, led an expedition nearly 400 miles up the Benue in the "Pleiad." Mr. Crowther wrote,

> The reception we met with from the kings and chiefs of the countries was beyond expectation. I believe the time has fully come when Christianity must be introduced on the banks

[3] Epelle, S., *op. cit.*, p. 19.
[4] Walker, F. D., *The Romance of the Black River*, p. 33.
[5] *Ibid.*, p. 35.
[6] Stock, E., *op. cit.*, Vol. II, p. 121.

> of the Niger. God has provided instruments to begin the work in the liberated Africans of Sierra Leone who are natives of the Niger territories.[7]

An agreement was made in early 1857 between the government and Mr. Macgregor Laird (who had fitted out the 1841 expedition) to penetrate as far north as possible by way of the Niger River. By July the *Dayspring*, with Mr. Crowther on board, and commissioned by the Church Missionary Society to begin the "Niger Mission," was steaming up this mysterious river.[8]

The *Dayspring*, a small ship of 77 tons and 76 feet long, was not destined to conquer the river that had been the doom of others. She came to an inglorious end on the Jebba rocks, 175 miles above Lokoja. The members of the party were rescued from the island by friendly natives and Crowther spent more than a year visiting the many villages along the river and studying the Nupe languages.[9] Thus, in spite of the sinking of the *Dayspring*, the message of Christ was given opportunity to reach the people all along that part of the Niger River by the mouth of a Nigerian.[10]

In 1879, in the river boat *Henry Venn*, Crowther, accompanied by J. H. Ashcroft, a layman of the Church Missionary Society, traveled 550 miles up the Benue. The Church Missionary Society chronicler, Eugene Stock, wrote in 1899, "That voyage opened up inviting mission fields, with large populations, but alas! those populations still remain, today, wholly unevangelized. No missionary has ascended more than one-fifth of the distance above mentioned."[11]

It is impossible to trace Christianity's advance into Northern Nigeria without being keenly aware of the part trade and government played and how these two aspects of western civilization became entwined with Christianity. All three seemed to be mutually forwarded by this relationship at the time.

[7] *Ibid.*, pp. 119, 120.
[8] *Ibid.*, p. 121; Warren, J. S., *op. cit.*, p. 10.
[9] Walker, J. S., *op. cit.*, p. 94.
[10] *Ibid.*, p. 101.
[11] Stock, E., *op. cit.*, Vol. II, pp. 384, 385.

In 1886 the Royal Niger Company received its charter giving it control of the Niger and its banks. This commercial development brought about added facility in the travel of missionaries. The extension of river-steamer trade and the preaching of the gospel went forward hand-in-hand.

But the Moslem Fulani rulers with a stronghold at Bida were not favorable to these new, disrupting influences. Traders and missionaries were deeply impressed by their complete disdain of foreign powers. Eugene Stock wrote,

> The great Mohammedan Potentates of the Central Soudan cared nothing for England. All they knew was that their own great Mahdi had killed a famous Englishman in Khartoum and put an end to his sway over their brethren in the Eastern Soudan.[12]

In 1890 John Alfred Robinson and Graham Wilmot Brooks led a new mission development: the "Soudan and Upper Niger Mission." Their goal was the vast Hausa population "north of the rivers." But Robinson and Brooks faced a new development. The Royal Niger Company announced that while they were willing to facilitate missionary travel among the pagan people they could not do so among the Moslems.

This did not discourage Brooks and Robinson. Rather it gave them opportunity to express their convictions concerning missionary identification with the people and their desire to separate the Christian advance from that of trade and government. In those early years civilizing influences were looked upon as being inseparably related to the message of Christ. Certainly it is not surprising that this should have been so, considering the devastating effects of the slave trade, human sacrifices, and cannibalism that surrounded the early messengers of Christ. But Brooks and Robinson decided to separate from their European relationships. They laid their plans to enter Hausaland without protection from the trade company or from government, stating "if they (the Moslems) imprison us, the British Government is not to interfere; if they kill us, no reparation

[12] *Ibid.*, Vol. III, p. 390.

is to be demanded." Theirs was perhaps the first strong statement to the effect that Christianity and western civilization were not synonymous, and "the Church Missionary Society committee cordially approved the desire of these two brethren to identify themselves with those they sought to save."[13]

It is lamentable that Brooks and Robinson, along with their mission party of four others, never took the opportunity to move forward and put their ideas into practice in Hausa country. Instead they became overwhelmed with church purity problems at Lokoja.[14] They believed it necessary to "root out" and "pull down" before they could "build" and "plant." So, Brooks and Robinson never reached Hausa country. They died of fever while engaged in the disciplinary problems of the Church.[15]

This was a dark period in the history of the expansion of the gospel into the North. The first Nigerian bishop, Samuel Adjai Crowther, suffered a stroke in July, 1891, and died in December of the same year. In his case, as in that of Robinson and Brooks, death was hastened by anxiety and disappointment as a result of the Lokoja troubles.[16] Bishop Crowther's 46 years of service had been essential in the establishment of the Church in the middle Niger as well as in the Delta, and argued eloquently for the fact that Nigerians could be both efficient and creative church leaders.

In December, 1893, a trio of Canadians – Walter Gowans, Tom Kent, and Rowland Bingham – arrived in Lagos, intent upon taking the Good News to the Sudan. They received discouraging words from the superintendent of the Methodist Mission in West Africa, who told them, "Young men, you will never see the Soudan; your children will never see the Soudan; your grandchildren may." Although they laid plans for going north by the way of Bida and Bingham, nevertheless weakened by fever, they stayed in Lagos to take care of supplies. Illness temporarily turned

[13] *Ibid.*
[14] *Ibid.*, pp. 393-397.
[15] *Ibid.*, p. 392.
[16] *Ibid.*, p. 396.

Kent back and Gowans alone reached Zaria. When he arrived there he was too ill to go further and on his return he died at Girku in November, 1894. A month later Kent also died at Bida. This double tragedy turned Bingham homeward. However it was not the end of the dream of reaching the Sudan. After several difficult years Bingham succeeded in organizing what was to become the Sudan Interior Mission.[17]

In the same year that Walter Gowans died in his attempt to reach Kano, the first [?] Christian with a missionary purpose, Charles H. Robinson, successfully reached that great earth-walled city of the Hausas. He had been sent by the Hausa Association of England to collect materials for the study of the Hausa language, for their task of translating the Scriptures into Hausa.[18]

Another "first" occurred in 1897 when Bishop Herbert Tugwell of the Church Missionary Society Niger diocese, after a tour that took him as far as Keffi, established the first organized work north of the rivers in the Basa (Base Komo) tribal area.[19]

In 1900 Bingham returned for a second try, but did not get beyond Lagos. Malarial fever and discouragement turned him and his two companions back again.[20]

The most important missionary incident of this period at the turn of the century was the journey of an expedition that finally reached Kano. In January of 1900 four Church Missionary Society missionaries, including Bishop Tugwell and Dr. Walter R. Miller, left Lagos with 240 carriers. They reached Zaria in April and were received with interest and kindness by the Moslem Emir. They pushed on to Kano and arrived there on April 19. Here their reception was very different. The Emir of Kano was openly hostile. After many appeals to be allowed to stay, if even for one month, they received the discouraging answer, "You are allowed three days to do your business. . . ." This was lengthened

17 Hunter, J. H., *A Flame of Fire,* pp. 51-59.
18 Walker, F. D., *op. cit.,* p. 177; Stock, E., Vol. III, p. 726.
19 *Ibid.,* p. 174.
20 Hunter, J. H., *op. cit.,* p. 78.

to seven days, and the party celebrated communion in the city before their departure.[21]

Upon returning to Zaria they found that the friendly attitude of that city had changed to one of hostility. The British West African forces had come up the Kaduna River and were encamped at the village of Girku near the present site of Kaduna, so the missionaries retreated to Girku.[22] Their short period of work was not without sorrow. They buried one of their party, Dudly-Ryder, beside the grave of Walter Gowans.

The Sultan of Sokoto and the Emir of Zaria were not satisfied with the mission remaining at Girku. Pressures were brought to bear and in January of 1901 they left Girku and returned to Lokoja.[23]

In 1901 the Sudan Interior Mission made its third, and this time successful, attempt to establish work in northern Nigeria. They entered the Nupe tribe and built their station at Patigi on the Niger.[24] Even so, one of the four missionaries, Mr. Taylor, died there, and two others were invalided home. The lone survivor, Rev. A. W. Banfield, showed exceptional ability with the Nupe language and made rapid progress in the translation of the Gospels. When he returned from his first furlough he brought with him copies of the Gospels in Nupe that had been printed by the Bible Society.[25] During furlough he visited conferences of his own Mennonite Brethren Church in Canada and the United States. His enthusiasm caught fire, and a Mennonite mission was organized. In 1905 Banfield and his wife returned to Nigeria and opened a station at Shonga about 70 miles upstream from the Sudan Interior Mission station at Patigi. "Before Banfield left Africa as a result of ill health, he had translated the whole Bible into Nupe, a remarkable feat that has seldom been duplicated."[26]

[21] Walker, F. D., *op. cit.*, p. 178; Stock, E., *op. cit.*, Vol. IV, pp. 71, 190.

[22] Stock, E., *op. cit.*, Vol. IV, p. 71.

[23] Walker, F. D., *op. cit.*, p. 193.

[24] Knight, C. W., "A History of the Expansion . . . ," p. 154; Hunter, J. H., *op. cit.*, p. 89.

[25] *Ibid.*, p. 91.

[26] *Ibid.*, p. 92.

At this time there was no reading public in Nupe country, and his translation of the Bible was practically unused for years.[27]

In 1905 Dr. Miller, of the original Church Missionary Society party to Zaria and Kano, received permission from both the High Commissioner and the Emir of Zaria to return to Zaria.[28] He opened a small dispensary within the walls of the city. (In 1925 this station was moved outside the city about two miles to Wusasa.) The mission buildings were patterned after the houses of the Hausa people, for it was Dr. Miller's intention to live as much like the people as possible.[29]

Thus far we have noted three attempts to enter the Sudan made at great loss of life: the Anglican Church Missionary Society; the interdenominational Sudan Interior Mission; and the Mennonite in Christ, whose mission was to be known as the United Missionary Society. Another large mission now comes upon the horizon of West Africa: the Sudan United Mission. This mission was born out of the tremendous unmet needs in the Sudan. Enough had been done to reveal to the Christians in England and America and Germany that the Sudan "was one of the largest untouched mission fields in the world." It also was evident that the larger denominations were not going to meet the challenge through their usual channels.[30] About 1900 a conference of the leaders of the Evangelical Mission Societies of England was called in Edinburgh to consider the problem.[31] The Annual Report of the Sudan United Mission of 1908 speaks of this meeting and gives the decision that resulted in the formation of the Sudan United Mission.

> In view of the present crisis in the West Central Sudan, where, unless the Gospel of Christ be brought within the next few years to Northern Nigeria, the million numbered pagan people of that new British Protectorate . . . will go

27 Traub, O. R., Correspondence, April, 1963.
28 Knight, C. W., *op. cit.*, p. 161; Coleman, J. S., *op. cit.*, p. 136.
29 Knight, C. W., *ibid.*
30 *Ibid.*, pp. 125, 127.
31 Tett, W., Correspondence, Feb. 19, 1963.

> over to Islam, and, in view of the fact that none of the missionary societies of Baptist, Congregational, Methodist, or Presbyterian Churches of Great Britain or Ireland feels itself at present able to do anything for the evangelization of the Soudan, we should rejoice if the Lord should enable the Free Churches of this country to join in a United Soudan Mission.[32]

A new and dynamic aspect of the Sudan situation had been added: they "will go over to Islam." This was to become the rallying point for Christian missions in the Sudan. The call went out to "stem the tide of Islam" and give the pagan populace a fair chance to choose between Islam and Christianity. The Edinburgh and Lucknow World Missionary Conferences stressed that the "whole strategy of Christian missions in Africa should be viewed in relation to Islam." The Lucknow Conference resolved:

> We are strongly of the opinion that concentrated action among missionary boards and organizations is necessary, in order to coordinate thoroughly the process now at work in Africa and to regulate their distribution in such a manner as to provide a strong chain of mission stations across Africa, the strongest links of which shall be at those points where Moslem advance is most active.[33]

Now we see the validity of such an appeal, for many of the pagan tribes *have* made their decision – for Islam! The fact that there are still vast populations – especially in the Central Belt of Nigeria – that have not as yet made their decision is a witness to the "staying power" of paganism, and, in part at least, is due to the establishment of a row of mission stations across the Sudan. While Islam is spreading, especially in the towns, its success among the pagan tribes would have been much more rapid if, in these years since World War II, the people of the distintegrating animistic tribes had not had the possibility of being Christians. For many the very presence of Christian missions and Nigerian Christians has given courage to resist the religious sway of

[32] Knight, C. W., *op. cit.*, p. 157.
[33] Coleman, J. S., *op. cit.*, p. 93.

Islam, even though as yet they may not have become Christian.

In 1902 the Soudan Pioneer Mission was founded in England as the result of the inspired work of a young German, Herman Karl Wilhelm Kumm, and his wife Lucy. Coming at the time when the churches had just made the statement, "We should rejoice if the Lord should enable the Free Churches of the country to join in a United Soudan Mission," it brought cooperation on an interdenominational level. Before their marriage Karl and Lucy had both seen mission service in Egypt, Libya, and the Eastern Sudan. Now their attention was turned toward Nigeria by Mr. C. L. Temple, the government official in charge of the Bauchi area "in which there lies a great plateau of comparatively healthy country with a large population of pagans."[34] He invited Mr. Kumm to consider this plateau country as the area for his proposed mission to the Sudan.

The name Sudan United Mission was chosen in 1904, and in July Dr. Kumm, Dr. A. H. Bateman, Mr. J. E. Burt, and Mr. J. Lowry Maxwell set sail on an expedition of investigation. While this mission party began its orientation with the aid of two Church Missionary Society missionaries at Lokoja, Dr. Kumm went on north to meet with the High Commissioner, Sir Frederick Lugard, to speak of his plans to enter Bauchi. He returned with word that Sir Frederick had suggested that they need not go so far and should consider beginning at Wase, about halfway between the Benue River and the Bauchi Plateau.[35] Thus it was that in 1904 the first station was built almost in the shadow of the great Wase Rock. (See Frontispiece.)

From Wase in 1905 the mission explored north into Birom land. But J. L. Maxwell reveals in his book *Half a Century of Grace* that exploration might have been taken more seriously in those beginning days. He says,

> I have sometimes thought that it was a pity that we did not, right at the first, settle it in our minds that we would not dig ourselves in anywhere until we had done a good deal

[34] Maxwell, J. L., *Half a Century of Grace,* p. 26.
[35] *Ibid.,* p. 38.

> more investigation. We were too easily brought to follow the suggestion of the High Commissioner, and stay at Wase. If we had looked around us more, we might have done better both for ourselves and for the work which was the reason for our coming to the country at all. We had not begun our work of getting a house built at Wase before the Resident of Bauchi passed through our camp on the way up to his district. It was he who had invited Dr. Kumm to open work among the tribes in the Bauchi hills. That area began only one day's journey beyond Wase. There at Kwunkyam and Kantana we were actually in it. We might then have settled down at once among the Birom, and straightway hurled ourselves into direct mission work, instead of spending life and time and money at Wase, which is a Moslem town. As a matter of history we did finally abandon Wase in 1909. Had we gone just that one day's journey further up in the Resident's Company we should have had this evident friendship and patronage to give us a good start, at the very place near which, 19 years later, we opened Tutung Station. We should have had delightful upland country to live in and numbers of pagan villages around us to provide us with opportunities for the work of an evangelist, and later, to furnish the converts who would constitute the membership of the young and growing Church. But there is also the other side of the question. It may well have been that Wase was God's place for us at the first, in order that we should not be tempted to keep too long to one tribe. He had it in His good pleasure that we should branch into three main directions, where He had prepared to bless us. Perhaps, if we had got too much preoccupied with an attractive work in the pleasant hill country at first, we might have hesitated to divide our forces as we actually did to the great forwarding of the work. God's grace does not always lead as man's wisdom would dictate.[36]

There was considerable friction with the Moslem chief of Wase,[37] and in 1907 a rather difficult period culminated in the burning of the Wase mission house. After the burning of Wase, Maxwell adds,

[36] *Ibid.*, p. 54.
[37] Kirk-Greene, A. H. M., *Adamawa Past and Present,* p. 121.

> Although that seemed disastrous enough at the time, it was perhaps really a help in the long run, for it tended to forward the task by spreading ourselves out to the pagan districts which were waiting for us.[38]

In 1906 a second station was built south of the river at Wukari and in 1908 the Lucy Memorial Freed Slaves Home was built at Rumasha. In 1918 this home was closed and moved to Wukari and finally in 1926 discontinued altogether. It was there in that same year that the Sudan United Mission performed its first baptism, that of Tom Aliyana.

In 1909 the Wase station was abandoned and moved to Langtang, twelve miles to the west, and then from the lowlands of Langtang the mission extended to the highland plateau among the Birom tribe.

The Sudan United Mission became a federation of missions, each raising its own staff and funds, but cooperating closely on the field. The originating group is known as the British Branch and is made up of missionaries from Baptist, Anglican, Methodist, Plymouth Brethren, Congregational, and in fact, practically every main Protestant denomination in England.[39]

In 1909, resulting from the visit of Dr. Kumm to South Africa, the South African Interdenominational Branch was formed.[40] Three South African missionaries – Rev. J. G. Botha, Mr. V. H. Hosking, and Mr. Carl Zimmerman – accompanied Dr. Kumm up the Benue River on the first part of his expedition across the Sudan. They chose a site at Mbula along the upper Benue for the beginning of their work, and Dr. Kumm went on across the Sudan.

However, the three missionaries soon found they were very far removed from other mission stations and also that the Mbula tribe was too small, numbering only 7,000.[41] Instead of branching out to the other tribes of the area they returned down the Benue in 1911 and established work at Salatu (Sai), about twenty-five miles from Wukari and

[38] Maxwell, J. L., *op. cit.*, p. 66.
[39] Tett, W., Correspondence, Feb. 19, 1963.
[40] Maxwell, J. L., *op. cit.*, pp. 96, 99.
[41] *Ibid.*, p. 96.

among the great Tiv tribe, numbering 800,000. In 1911 the Dutch Reformed Church Mission from South Africa arrived to take over this work among the Tiv.

In a 50th anniversary talk Rev. W. D. Gerryts of the Dutch Reformed Church Mission said,

> This was a time when the church in South Africa was not looking for new mission fields; there was enough inside and outside its borders to absorb all of its energies. Even though the church later decided to take responsibility for the Tiv field, it was not in full agreement. Considering these factors, it is evident that the establishment of the mission came along a detour that was unplanned by man but was an accomplishment of God.[42]

After its early associations with the Sudan United Mission the Dutch Reformed Church Mission became a completely separate denominational mission; and the South African Interdenominational Branch missionaries, not members of the Dutch Reformed Church, sought fields of service north of the Benue,[43] where Mr. Judd made an extensive tour of investigation and chose the Mada tribe. But since it was not possible to open a station within that tribe at that time, a temporary station was opened at Keana in 1917.[44] A second tour took him into Bornu and parts of Adamawa Provinces, where he visited many tribes that were later to hear God's Word through the Sudan United Mission.

At Sandwich, England, in 1912 a conference was held to consider the development of the church in the Sudan as a fellowship of believers "who would look to the mission for some guidance in the shaping of their church life and practice."[45] Dr. and Mrs. Bronnum of the Danish Lutheran Church were present and by the end of that year the Danish Society was formed.[46] The Bronnums arrived at Rumasha looking for an area of service for the Danish

[42] Christian Reformed Church publication, "The Coming of the Gospel into Tivland."

[43] Maxwell, J. L., *op. cit.*, p. 123.

[44] *Ibid.*

[45] *Ibid.*, p. 100.

[46] *Ibid.* p. 99.

Lutheran Church. There the beginning was made in sorrow with the death of Mrs. Bronnum. After this, however, Dr. Bronnum entered Adamawa Province to attempt work among the Bachuma tribe, beginning at Numan in 1913.

In 1915 Takum and Lissam became out-stations from Wukari and four years later Miss Johanna Veenstra, a member of the Christian Reformed Church, was sent by the Sudan United Mission to work at Lupwe among the Jukun and Kutab tribes. The enthusiasm of her letters and her speeches persuaded the Christian Reformed Church to support a mission to the Sudan. But it was not until 1940 that they were able to send Rev. Edgar H. Smith and wife, Jennie Stielstra, and Tena Huizenga to the Lupwe-Takum area to serve as part of the interdenominational Sudan United Mission. Mr. and Mrs. Smith have remained through the ensuing years, and he is now the Secretary of the Fellowship of the Churches of Christ in the Sudan.[47] When the Christian Reformed Church later took fuller responsibility, it insisted upon being a branch of the Sudan United Mission without its denominational name.[48]

Dr. Kumm's contacts with Rev. C. W. Guinter at Albright College in the United States brought about the formation of an Evangelical Brethren Mission. Mr. Guinter came to Nigeria with four others and arrived at Ibi. They moved south to Wukari, which had been opened in 1906 by Maxwell.

On a tour of investigation in 1916 Mr. Guinter made inquiry of the Resident of Yola concerning entry into the Mumuye tribe east of Donga and south of the river. Permission was not granted on the grounds that the time was not yet ripe for work among these people.[49] Instead it was suggested that work begin at Kona, 120 miles east of Donga, as a "key to Mumuye land."[50] Yet not until 1921 was any attempt made to begin work at Kona.[51]

[47] Knight, C. W., *op. cit.*, p. 217; Smith, E.H., Personal interview, August, 1963.

[48] Smith, E. H., Personal interview, August, 1963.

[49] Kirk-Greene, A. H. M., *op. cit.*, p. 121.

[50] *Ibid.*

[51] Maxwell, J. L., *op. cit.*, p. 131.

But the Evangelical Brethren were destined to find an area of their own north of the Benue and to the east among the Wurkum and Jukun, beginning at Bambur in 1923 and later reaching the Mumuye through its southern stations. Previous to this date the Evangelical Brethren were serving as part of the Interdenominational U.S.A. Branch of the Sudan United Mission. After this it became an Evangelical Brethren branch of the Sudan United Mission. Later the name was changed to Evangelical United Brethren.[52]

These branches of denominational and interdenominational missions had chosen to affiliate with each other in the great push into the pagan Central Belt under the single banner of the Sudan United Mission. The British and South African branches were unions of missionaries from many different denominations. This exceptional spirit of cooperation and oneness in Christ's service was to come to fruition in later years in the birth of the Fellowship of Churches of Christ in the Sudan.

One other group, independent of the Sudan United Mission, was to become associated with this Fellowship of Churches: the Church of the Brethren Mission. Dr. Kumm visited several Church of the Brethren colleges in America. Students were caught up with his enthusiasm and the challenge of the Sudan. The possibility of an African mission was presented to the mission board of the church.[53] A deputation into East Africa to make a preliminary investigation was cut short by the death in Mombasa of one of the party, J. H. B. Williams, who had contracted typhoid fever during the deputations visit of Brethren Missions in India.[54] The fact that the Brethren had so suddenly given a life in Africa to the witness of Christ deepened the interest of the church in such a mission. In 1922 the Board sent H. Stover Kulp and Albert D. Helser on a further tour of investigation to Nigeria. The government granted them permission to work among the Bura tribe in southern Bornu

[52] Smith, E. H., Personal interview, August, 1963.

[53] Mow, Annetta, "In African Villages," p. 1.

[54] Baldwin, E. R., "The Establishment of the Church of the Brethren Mission in Africa," p. 5.

Province and north of the area in which the Danish Lutheran had begun their work about ten years before.

Mr. Kulp wrote from Garkida, the first of the Church of the Brethren mission stations:

> Saturday morning, March 17, 1923, was a great day for us. . . . We had a ground breaking service for the first house to be built by the Church of the Brethren in Africa. Two scriptures were read: Eph. 2:4-22 and portions of the 5th and 6th chapters of II Corinthians. We knelt to pray, the sun had not yet risen; but after prayer, its glorious light was beaming full upon us.[55]

He continued:

> With native hoes we removed some earth where the building was to be placed, with a prayer in our hearts that the structure thereon erected would be a haven of peace for souls burdened with sin.[56]

By 1924 the Garkida mission group had increased to six, including the wives of Kulp and Helser and Dr. and Mrs. Homer Burke. But in the 1920s Africa was still claiming the lives of many who dared to enter into its secret places, and one of these pioneers, Mrs. Kulp, died in June, 1924, baptizing them, as it were, into the fellowship of sorrow that had played so large a part in the advance of the Christian gospel in West Africa.

B. MISSIONS AND GOVERNMENT

It is evident that the missionary played an important role in bringing the benefits of government and civilization to Northern Nigeria. Sir Frederick Lugard wrote in 1906,

> This friendly attitude (of the Emir of Zaria) and the most remarkable results achieved are probably and almost entirely due to Dr. Miller's exceptional tact and personal influence, together with his absolute mastery of the Hausa language. The Resident . . . cannot too warmly express his gratitude to Dr. Miller. . . . The Emir himself has apparently formed

[55] Mow, A., *op. cit.*, p. 3.

[56] Church of the Brethren Publication, "Our Churches in Other Lands," p. 38.

> a close friendship with Dr. Miller and invites a frank expression of his opinions on social abuses which come under his notice. I believe that a very great deal of good has resulted.[57]

H. H. Johnson, Commissioner of Uganda, wrote "In fact, the C. M. S. [Church Missionary Society, Anglican], for good or ill, has done more to create British Nigeria than the British Government."[58] As beneficial as the missionary was for the success of the British, it is this and similar coincidental relationships, which, throughout the world, has so embarrassingly associated Christianity with military conquest. The British government in Nigeria, however, in spite of the friendly relations created by missionaries, was not enthusiastic about mission work, especially among the Moslems. In 1859, in deference to the Fulani rulers, Dr. Baikie had closed Rebba to missionary visits.

In 1897 the Fulani slaving activities in Nupe territory brought action by the British. Sir George T. Goldie of the Royal Niger Company drove the Fulani out of Bida, but failure to maintain a strong follow-up resulted in the Fulani Emir's early return. Nevertheless, slavery had been struck a devastating blow.[59]

The British flag was raised at Lokoja on January 1, 1900. The charter of the Royal Niger Company was withdrawn and the Protectorates of Southern Nigeria and Northern Nigeria were established. The British had concluded an agreement with France and Germany that, "by the stroke of a pen," made the whole Fulani Empire a British Protectorate — without the Fulani knowing it! This extension of the Protectorate over Northern Nigeria coincided with the attempt to take the gospel into this same area.[60] As Bishop Tugwell and party were entering the Sudan a West African Frontier Force was making its way up the Kaduna River looking for a place for the new High Commissioner, Sir Frederick Lugard, to establish his headquarters. This coincidence was most un-

[57] Stock, E , *op. cit.,* Vol. IV, p. 74.
[58] *Ibid.*
[59] Walker, F. D., *op. cit.,* p. 160; Stock, E., *op. cit.,* Vol. III, p. 726.
[60] Walker, F. D., *op. cit.,* p. 181.

fortunate, for while the missionaries apparently knew nothing of the military action on the Kaduna River, it can hardly be thought that the Emir of Kano, with the Moslem traditional view of theocratic government, could have thought otherwise than that these two movements into his domain were part of one and the same plan to unseat him from his position. And certainly Lord Lugard thought of the mission enterprise as being aided by the government. He wrote in his Annual Reports of 1900-1911 that "without the support of the government, these missionaries would not be tolerated (by the Moslem Emirs). In effect, therefore, the mission obtains its footing on the support of British bayonets. . . ."[61]

The Christians in England and America also looked upon the British conquest as opening the doors to the gospel message. Speaking of Sir Goldie's victory at Bida in 1897, Eugene Stock wrote, "It has certainly opened Hausaland to the messengers of the Gospel, if only they will enter in."

In 1903, subsequent to the murder of an English officer, Lord Lugard marched against the city of Kano. The cannonballs scarcely damaged the great earth walls, but when a weak spot was found the city soon fell. A few weeks later Sokoto was also taken. A new day dawned in Hausaland.[62] Yet the next few years were not to be marked by any great extension of Christianity. In fact, while the British authorities showed personal kindness to the missionaries, they declined to permit their advance.[63] However, in this same year in which Kano and Sokoto fell, Bishop Tugwell established a mission station at Bida, which only six years before had been the very heart of slavery. The more marvelous is this accomplishment when it is realized that this station was built by the invitation of the Emir of Bida.[64]

Reluctance to allow missionaries to establish Christian work in Moslem areas became a definite policy.[65] When Sir Frederick Lugard, as High Commissioner of the Pro-

[61] Coleman, J. S., *op. cit.*, p. 136.
[62] Walker, F. D., *op. cit.*, p. 193; Stock, E., *op. cit.*, Vol. IV, p. 71.
[63] Stock, E., *ibid.*
[64] Coleman, J. S., *op. cit.*, p. 136.
[65] *Ibid.*, p. 133.

tectorate of Northern Nigeria, assumed responsibility on January 1, 1900, "he agreed to maintain, on behalf of Queen Victoria, all pledges and undertakings which had been assumed by the Royal Niger Company, including its policy of not supporting Christian missions in the Muslim North."[66]

This policy was applicable mainly to the predominant Moslem Emirates of Bauchi, Bornu, Kano, Katsina, Sokoto, and Zaria, which were peopled by the Moslem tribes of Hausa, Fulani, and Kanuri. On the other hand, missionaries were encouraged to work among the pagan tribes. In 1906 Sir Frederick Lugard stated, "I have . . . held out every encouragement to establish missions in pagan centers, which appear to me to need the influence of civilization and religion at least as much as the Mohammedans." Also the government allowed the missions to open stations where invited by Moslem Emirs. The invitations given to Bishop Tugwell in 1903 and to Dr. Miller in 1905 from the Emirs of Bida and Zaria respectively are evidence that such invitations were, in fact, at times given.[67]

It was a discouragement to many missionaries not to be able to take a more direct approach to the Hausa peoples of the North. Yet this government policy of missionary exclusion was providential. One writer observes, "Forbidden to advance into Moslem emirates, the missionaries turned their eyes elsewhere. To the south, between Zaria and the rivers, a great pagan belt stretches across the Sudan, and in this the government freely gave permission to work."[68]

With the exception of the Church Missionary Society breakthrough into the Moslem North at Zaria, the remaining missions directed new advances toward this pagan population of the Central Belt. While the Sudan Interior Mission has established many stations in recent years north of the Central Belt, at least thirty-three as of 1961, the number becoming Christian has been very small in comparison to that in the Central Belt area. The Sudan Interior Mission report of 1960 shows that out of a communicant membership of over

[66] *Ibid.*
[67] *Ibid.*, p. 136.
[68] Walker, F. D., *op. cit.*, p. 229.

14,000 in Nigeria only 403 are from the Sokoto-Kano-Katsina Districts. The Sudan United Mission likewise, working among the Moslem Kanuri of Bornu Province, was unable over a period of twenty-five years from 1937 to 1962 to plant any churches except for the one in Maiduguri town, made up almost entirely of Christians from pagan tribal areas in Sardauna Province to the south and from the neighboring nation of Chad. The United Missionary Society (Mennonite), working largely with the Moslemized Nupe, have had very slow response. The Sudan United Mission with all of its branches, and the Church of the Brethren Mission working almost entirely with the non-Moslem tribal populations, have had notable response.

The attitude of government toward missions remained friendly, although not without some local difficulties at times. The British government, since World War II, has greatly encouraged schools under the proprietorship of voluntary agencies (primarily missions), and government grants for education have been continued since independence as well.

The policy of "indirect rule" in Northern Nigeria, whereby Britain ruled through the local chiefs and their councils, with advice and assistance of British administrators, was a system of government beneficial to the progress of missions and the resultant churches. Government officers were few and literally far between. They confined themselves to matters of government administration. Most missionaries found that the local pagan chiefs were friendly and interested in the new ideas they brought. To the tribesmen the missionaries were often a symbol of the British government, which had saved them from the raids of the Fulani. In this respect the identification of missionary and government in the minds of tribal people was definitely an aid to the furtherance of mission activity.

On the regional government level independence has brought a continuation of friendly and cooperative attitudes between government and missions. The Nigerian Constitution upholds freedom of religion, and Moslem leaders make hearty expressions of toleration and good will.

Speaking during independence celebrations in Kaduna,

the premier of the Northern Region, Alhaji the Honorable Sir Ahmade Bello, said:

> The Northern Region, as it is today, is the product of three main factors: geography, history, and the character of its people. These three factors have produced a feeling of real unity among the people who inhabit our region. We have divergencies in customs, religion, and language. But we have emerged and progressed out of the stage in the life of a people where such differences constitute a barrier to unity. We have sought for unity; not conformity. Our unity, which we have now gained and which we celebrate today, is therefore all the more genuine and strong. All right-thinking people in the region know full well that toleration and goodwill must and shall prevail. We shall never adopt measures which will discriminate against any section of our communities because of their religious beliefs or because of their customs; provided only that those beliefs and customs do not militate against the requirements of law and order. To this I pledge myself and my colleagues in the government of the Northern Region.

C. THE PRESENT EXTENSION OF THE MISSIONS THROUGHOUT THE CENTRAL BELT OF NIGERIA

The map, Fig. I, shows the location of the various missions, and the map, Fig. II, shows the numerous mission stations. In this description of the present mission extension, we will begin with the north-central and western part of the Central Belt, swing south to the Niger and Benue Rivers, and then eastward.

The Sudan Interior Mission is the largest single mission in Northern Nigeria with about 550 missionaries and 101 major mission stations as of 1958. (Both the Sudan Interior and the Sudan United Mission have extensive work outside of Nigeria in other parts of the Sudan.) Of the 101 stations seven are south of the Central Belt and 37 north of it, leaving 57 stations within the Central Belt. From the first station at Patigi,[69] on the Niger River, the mission expanded north and south. The northern arm of the Yoruba tribe and the

[69] See Map, Fig. II.

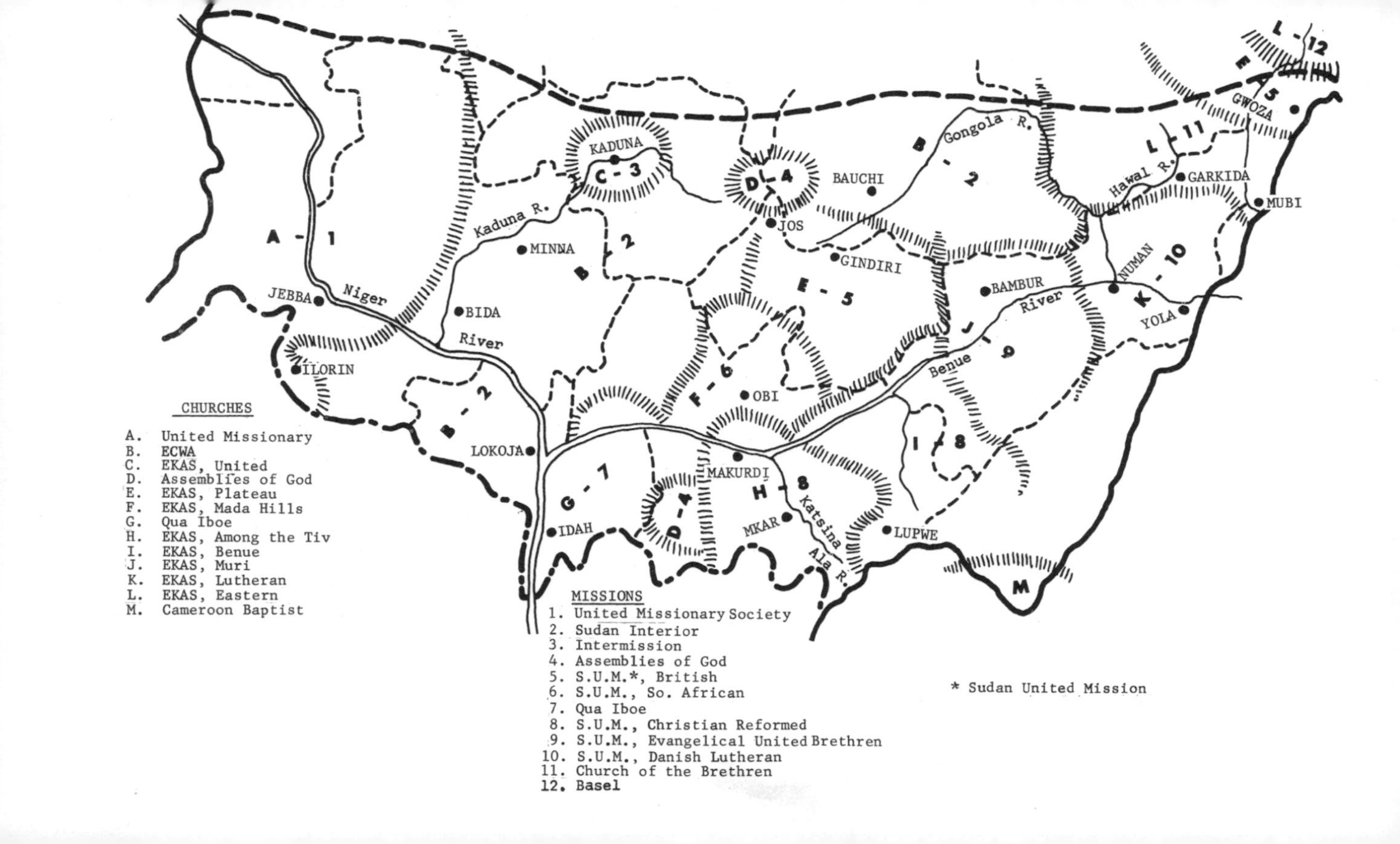

A - 1
JEBBA
Niger
River
ILORIN
KADUNA
C - 3
Kaduna R.
MINNA
B - 2
BIDA
LOKOJA
D - 4
JOS
BAUCHI
Gongola R.
GINDIRI
E - 5
F - 6
OBI
G - 7
IDAH
MAKURDI
H - 8
MKAR
Katsina
Ala R.
I - 8
LUPWE
Benue
J - 9
BAMBUR
NUMAN
K - 10
YOLA
Hawal R.
GARKIDA
L - 11
MUBI
GWOZA
E - 5
L - 12
M

CHURCHES
A. United Missionary
B. ECWA
C. EKAS, United
D. Assemblies of God
E. EKAS, Plateau
F. EKAS, Mada Hills
G. Qua Iboe
H. EKAS, Among the Tiv
I. EKAS, Benue
J. EKAS, Muri
K. EKAS, Lutheran
L. EKAS, Eastern
M. Cameroon Baptist

MISSIONS
1. United Missionary Society
2. Sudan Interior
3. Intermission
4. Assemblies of God
5. S.U.M.*, British
6. S.U.M., So. African
7. Qua Iboe
8. S.U.M., Christian Reformed
9. S.U.M., Evangelical United Brethren
10. S.U.M., Danish Lutheran
11. Church of the Brethren
12. Basel

* Sudan United Mission

southern portion of the Nupe tribe are south of the Niger River in Ilorin and Kabba Provinces. There are twelve mission stations, including Patigi, in this area.

In the Y formed by the meeting of the Benue River with the Niger there are two stations in the Igbira tribe, staffed with Nigerian evangelists. Along the road east of Bida are three stations in the northern tip of Benue Province. These are in the country of the Gabari, Koro, and Lungu people.

Among the northern Nupe and Basa is a cluster of ten stations about and including Minna, and the Niger Leprosarium. Farther north are the Kaduna station (in the capital of the Northern Region) and a second station only a few miles outside this city to the east. These stations are in Zaria Province and in the Gbari tribe, although the Kaduna station is in a multitribal population characteristic of all large towns.

The largest cluster of stations, fifteen, includes Jos and reaches down the escarpment to Kafanchan and Kwoi. This area is an excellent example of the complex tribal mosaic, for there are many different tribes here including the Afus, Birom, Irigwi, Aten, Chawai, Katab and Gwandara.

Moving east from Jos there is a leprosarium at Bauchi and two other stations south of that town. Between Bauchi and Potiskum there are four others, of which the two northernmost are outside the Central Belt, as designated on the map, but still within the multitribal conditions. The tribes there include Jara, Saya, Jul, Kerikeri, Ngam, and several other partially Moslemized ones.

The stations farthest east are the six clustered in the southeastern corner of Bauchi Province, among the Tanggali, Tera, Kushi, Buruk, Bangganji, Alwak, Tula, and Waja tribes. Kaltungo and Biliri are the main stations here.

Thus the Sudan Interior Mission has extended into six Central Belt Provinces: Ilorin, Kabba, the southern part of Niger, Zaria, the northern edge of Plateau, Bauchi, and the east-central edge of Bornu, and into at least twenty-seven tribes.

The United Missionary Society in Ilorin, Niger, and Sokoto Provinces, extended from Shonga in 1905 to Jebba in 1909, and then to Ilorin. A glance at the map will show a cluster of six stations in the Jebba-Ilorin area. Share opened in 1915 and Igbetti in 1921. Ilorin and Jebba are in Yoruba country. Mokwa was received from the Church Missionary Society in 1915 or 1916. Shonga and Mokwa and Bida are in the Nupe tribe.

There is another cluster of four stations about and including Yelwa. Yelwa was opened in 1938, and both it and Shabanda station are among the Gungawa Island people. Agara, Iwa, and Salka (1922) are among the Kamberri. There are two more stations, Zuru, far to the north in the Dakakari and Dukawa tribes, and Gurai, on the western border of Nigeria among the Bariba.

The stations of the British Branch of the Sudan United Mission are found in three areas: the Langtang lowlands, the central plateau, and the eastern extension in Bornu and Sardauna Provinces. In the Langtang lowlands, the Langtang and Kwalla and Lalin stations are prominent among the Yergum, Kwalla, and Garkawa tribes. By 1909 Ibi, on the Benue, had become a station, and Forum was opened in 1910 among the Birom. By the 1920s Ibi was the Mission Headquarters. Dampar, farther up the Benue, on the route to Wase, also became a station, but later missionary residence was discontinued at both of these stations.

There is a cluster of ten stations on the plateau, of which Panyam and Kabwir were originally opened by the Cambridge University Mission Party in 1907 and 1910 respectively under the direction of the Church Missionary Society, but transferred to the British Branch of the Sudan United Mission in 1930. Panyam is located in the Sura tribe and Kabwir in the Angas. The Gindiri station began in 1953, became a Bible-teaching center, and has since developed into a large educational institution. It is surrounded by at least eight different tribes: Birom, Fyam, Jarawa, Sura, Angas, Kanka, Sigidi, and Saya. The leprosarium at Mongu, only a few miles from Gindiri, was opened in 1949. Other extensions of the British Branch have been into the eastern part of Bornu at Molai Leprosarium (1937) near Maiduguri, and in Sardauna Province at Bama and at Gwoza (1956). In 1963 a new station was opened at Limankara, eight miles south of Gwoza. A recent extension is into the tribes of the shore and the islands of Lake Chad, where there is a population of more than 200,000.[70]

The Assemblies of God Mission entered the Central Belt from their Southern Nigerian Delta work, which had begun spontaneously in 1930 when Ibo Christians read a copy of the Assemblies of God paper, "Pentecostal Evangel." They wrote to the Assemblies of God in the U.S.A., inviting them to come to help them. In 1939 Assemblies of God missionaries settled at Port Harcourt. But before this, as early as 1934, Southerners, employed by the railway, conducted Assemblies of God prayer services in their homes in the larger cities of the North.[71] In the early 1950s Assemblies of God missionaries were living in Kaduna. In 1954 the Faith Mission to the Sudanese assigned a missionary to the Assemblies of God, and a second station was opened at Rahama, north of Jos among the Kurama tribe. A third station was located on the Plateau in 1958, and in 1961 a fourth was opened in the Oturkpo area of the Egede tribe of southern Benue Province.[72]

From the beginning the South African Branch of the Sudan United Mission desired to enter the Mada tribe, which numbered 100,000. Since moving from Keana, the first station, to Randa in 1920, eight other stations have been opened in the southwestern tip of Plateau Province and north-central Benue Province: Wana (1924); Alushi, as a leprosarium (1948); Lafiya (1932) later moved to Muriya; and Ancho (1937). Obi was opened as a Bible school in 1960. The tribes, in addition to the Mada, are Egon, Ninzam, Mawma, Rindire, Migili, Arago, and an increasing number of Tiv north of the Benue.

The Qua Iboe Mission, an Irish mission, receiving its name from the Qua Iboe River of the Eastern Region where it began its work in 1887, extended in 1932 into the Igala tribe in the eastern part of Kabba Province. This advance was the result of the Qua Iboe Church seeking a home mission field. Their evangelists established churches east of the

[70] Carling, David, Correspondence, August 20, 1963.
[71] Pennington, Harry, Correspondence, April 20, 1963.
[72] Publication of the Assemblies of God: "Nigeria," pp. 9, 10.

Niger in Kabba Province at the towns of Idah, Ankpa, Adoro, Gwolarwo, Ochandamu, Asaba, and also north of the Benue at Kainyehu.

The extension of missions south of the Benue and east of the Qua Iboe work involves the Dutch Reformed Church Mission of South Africa and the Christian Reformed Church (U.S.A.) Branch of the Sudan United Mission.

The extension of the Dutch Reformed Church Mission west of the Katsina Ala River is shown on the map by a cluster of six stations south of and including Mkar, the Mission Headquarters. Makurdi station is one of four in the northern part of Tiv, with Apir located just south of it. Isherev, opened in 1960, is the one station north of the Benue River, and is in the northern extension of the Tiv tribe.

By 1940 the Christian Reformed Church Mission had committed itself to work among the Jukun and Kuteb tribes east of the Katsina Ala River. However the Tiv extend east and meet Jukun in Wukari district. Around the Lupwe station, opened in 1919, and Takum town and eastward there are many other tribes: Chamba, Ichan, Kamino, Tigon, Jibuwa, Ndoro, and Ipango. All of these became the Christian Reformed Church Mission's responsibility, and Lupwe station and Takum Church became the center of their activities. Wukari, Sai, and Donga all came under their direction. Baissa was opened in 1951, Harga in 1955, the Takum Hospital in 1958, and Serti in 1962. Zaki Biam and Sevav, between Wukari and the Katsina Ala River, were turned over to the Christian Reformed Church Mission in 1950. The following year conversations were begun concerning the total transfer of the remainder of the Dutch Reformed Church Mission area. The transfer was completed in October, 1961.

After delays and unfulfilled plans to enter the Mumuye tribe, the Evangelical United Brethren Branch of the Sudan United Mission expanded on both sides of the Benue River, including the Mumuye tribal area. The map shows a cluster of five stations on the north side of the river: Bambur (1923), Kirim (1924), Filiya (1929), Bambuka (1936), and Jen.[73]

[73] McBride, I. E., Personal interview, March, 1962.

Kirim, northeast of Bambur, was the largest town in Wurkum land, but when fear of the Fulani raids no longer kept the people in the mountains they began to spread out and away. Many went to Bambur.[74] These migrations from the area brought about the closing of Kirim station. Likewise Bambuka station was closed after it had received a severe blow due to a smallpox epidemic. Though 1956 was the last year of missionary residence, a small, faithful Christian group continues to worship there.[75]

South of the river are the stations of Gandola (1926), Zinna (1932), Lankaviri (1941), and Kassa (1955) – all in the Mumuye tribe. Gandola had been opened by Mr. Fleming, a New Zealander, working under the British Branch.[76] The response was so poor – not a single convert – that it was closed, and Mr. Fleming moved to Gurum in the Chamba tribe. Later the Danish Lutheran Mission took over Gurum from the British Branch.

The Danish Lutheran Branch of the Sudan United Mission has extended into three areas: along the Benue River; south of the river in Chamba country; and north of the river under the Y of the Gongola-Hawal confluence. The Numan station is in the midst of Bachama (to the west) and Mbula (to the east) tribal populaces, but being in a large town finds all the thirteen tribes of the lower Gongola and Belwa Rivers meeting on its doorstep. The river area stations, in addition to Numan, are Lamurde (1921) in the Bachama tribe; Dille (1929) in the Mbula tribe (where the South African Branch attempted unsuccessfully to begin work in 1909); Jemeta, the river port of Yola; and Nzoboliyo – these last two in the Batta-Vere tribal area. Almost 100 miles to the south in the Chamba tribe are the Dashen and Gurum stations.

Under the Gongola-Hawal Y are four stations: Gwuyok (1930), in the Languda tribe, which we shall consider later; Shellem (1918) in the Kanakuru tribe; Dungma in the Yangur tribe; and Gaanda in a tribe of that name. Farther

[74] *Ibid.*
[75] *Ibid.*
[76] *Ibid.*

to the east is the station of Pella (1922) in the Kilba and Paka tribes.

Before World War II the Church of the Brethren Mission opened five stations: Garkida (1923), including Virgwi (a leprosarium), was on the eastern edge of the Bura tribe near the Whona tribe. Lassa (1927) brought entrance into the Margi tribe. Marama (1931) took the message back on to the Biu Plateau among the Bura. Chibuk (1938) in the Chibuk tribe was begun by an African evangelist, and visited by missionaries from Lassa until resident missionaries arrived in 1941.[77]

After the war Gulak (1948) was opened in the eastern extension of the Margi tribe. It is near to Waga and other mountain tribes. Wandali (1946), Shafa (1950), and Waka Teacher Training College (1951) were all opened in the Bura tribe.

Thus by 1951 there was a cluster of six stations in the Bura tribe, with one other station to the north among the Chibuk and two stations among the Margi. The fast development of the United Nations Trust Territory of the Northern Cameroons, as well as the insistent call of the Higi Christians in this area for more definite help from the mission, caused attention to be directed east where a station was opened in 1954 in the government and trade center of Mubi on the edge of the Fali and Gude tribes. Uba (1955) was opened in the South Margi area, and the Higi tribe was entered at Mbororo in 1957. The Mbororo extension was made possible by the cooperation of a sister denomination (the Brethren Church, with headquarters in Ashland, Ohio), which supplied both staff and funds for the station. The last station to be opened is a Rural Life Center between Uba and Mubi. The cluster of six stations to the west covering the Bura-Babir-Whona tribal area is balanced by the cluster of six stations in the east covering a more widely diversified tribal area, including Margi, Higi, Waga, Fali, and North Kilba. The station of Chibuk to the north stands out alone on the edge of a vast West Margi area, which has

[77] Church of the Brethren Publication, "Our Church in Other Lands," p. 4.

been acculturated toward the very large Moslem, Kanuri tribe of Bornu Province.

Two missions have extended their witness into the Central Belt from the Cameroon Republic. The first is the Cameroon Baptist Church Mission from Bamenda in the Cameroon Republic. At the time of extension Bamenda was in the United Nations Trust Territory of the Southern Cameroons, under the administration of the British in Nigeria. A plebescite has now separated the Southern Cameroons from Nigeria and it has become a part of the Cameroon Republic. Its one Central Belt Nigerian station is at Wuwar on the Mambila Plateau in the Mambila tribe.

The second is the Basel Mission, which has reached out from its extensive work in the Cameroon Republic to the northern part of Sardauna Province. It has built its first station at Gavva (1959), just across the mountains from the British Sudan United Mission station at Gwoza.

The Church Missionary Society, which played such an important part in the beginning of Christian witness in the Central Belt, has done very little in this part of Nigeria. Following the War thousands of Yoruba and Ibo Christians from Southern Nigeria flooded into the large cities of the North in search of government, trade, and clerical jobs. The struggling work of the Church Missionary Society among the Moslems was thus given a more satisfying direction as it served its immigrant members in the cities of Kano, Wusasa, Kaduna, and Bida.[78]

The earlier work that was begun at Panyam and Kabwir on the edge of the Central Plateau and among pagan tribes had been turned over, as previously noted, to the Sudan United Mission in 1929. Thus except for Bida, where there is an extensive work but few Christians in the surrounding Nupe areas, the Church Missionary Society turned from the pagan belt to exert its energies in the larger cities of the North.

As of 1963 the Northern Diocese of the Anglican Church had a communicant membership of 5,398, and 4,281 others who were not yet confirmed, and an average Sunday-morn-

[78] Walker, F. D., *op. cit.*, p. 230; Knight, C. W., *op. cit.*, p. 212.

ing-church attendance of about 6,800. There were 39 clergymen, only five of which were English, 103 Nigerian lay readers, thirty-two vicarages, and sixty-eight church buildings.

The Methodists,[79] as well as the Assemblies of God and Qua Iboe, followed their members north, and many strong city churches have resulted. In addition to the city churches of Kaduna, Jos, Zaria, and Iloria, there are churches in Offa, Oju, Igumale, Oturkpo, and Igo Okpaya, all in the southern part of Benue Province, east of the Christian Reformed Church Mission Tiv area. There is also one church in northern Ilorin Province south of Iwa.

Another important extension following immigrants from the South is that of the Southern Baptist Mission (U.S.A.), which has established stations in the cities of Kaduna, Jos, Zaria, Minna, Keffi, Kontagora, and Kafanchan. Churches have also been established in Saminaka, just north of Rahama, and in Eke, Kabba, Mubi, and Okuta, the latter being along the western border south of the United Missionary Society's station of Gurai. A new station is to be opened in Gombe. The Nigerian Baptist Convention has now stated its purpose to evangelize the cities and the surrounding countryside. Considering the numerous cities in the North, in which there are Baptist churches made up of immigrants from the South and the generally receptive state of the tribes, the Baptists should experience rapid church growth.

There is much room for church (as distinct from mission) extension in the Central Belt. In the next section we shall see that there are many unevangelized tribes, and in Chapter III we shall note that an interchurch plan has emerged that gives opportunity for cooperative planning in advance. Difficulties can now be dealt with creatively as a part of the common dynamics of church growth.

In the fifty-eight years (1904-1962) of mission extension into the Central Belt the geographical and tribal coverage has been phenomenal. A glance at Fig. II shows how well distributed the mission stations are. The following table indicates how well the tribes have been reached. However,

[79] Johnston, T. A., Correspondence, Sept. 16, 1963.

FIG. II

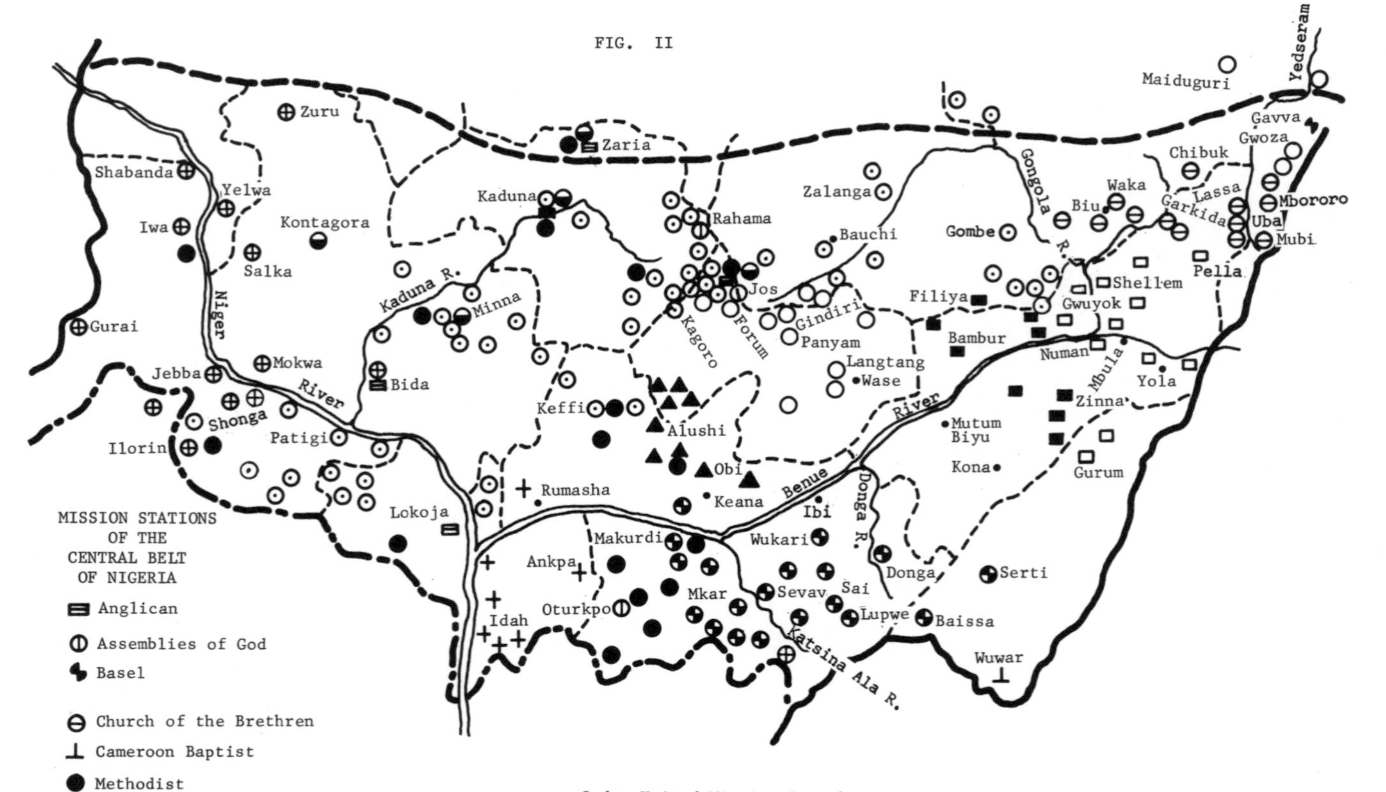
Yedseram R.
Maiduguri
Gavva
Gwoza
Chibuk
Lassa
Mbororo
Garkida
Uba
Mubi
Waka
Biu
Pella
Shellem
Gwuyok
Gongola R.
Gombe
Filiya
Bambur
Numan
Mbula
Yola
Zinna
Mutum Biyu
Kona
Gurum
Zalanga
Bauchi
Rahama
Jos
Kagoro
Forum
Gindiri
Panyam
Langtang
Wase
Zaria
Kaduna
Zuru
Shabanda
Yelwa
Iwa
Kontagora
Salka
Gurai
Niger
Kaduna R.
Minna
Mokwa
Jebba
Bida
River
Shonga
Patigi
Ilorin
Keffi
Alushi
Obi
Keana
Rumasha
Lokoja
Benue
River
Ibi
Donga R.
Wukari
Makurdi
Ankpa
Oturkpo
Idah
Mkar
Sevav
Sai
Lupwe
Donga
Serti
Baissa
Wuwar
Katsina Ala R.
MISSION STATIONS
OF THE
CENTRAL BELT
OF NIGERIA
Anglican
Assemblies of God
Basel
Church of the Brethren
Cameroon Baptist
Methodist
Nigerian Baptist
Qua Iboe
Sudan United Mission Branches:
British

undue optimism is not in order, for while numerous tribes have been entered and many churches born, the great turning to Christ that this area should see has only just begun in a few places. In most station areas it is still only a hope.

Missions of the Central Belt	Year of Beginning	Number of Stations[80]	Number of Tribes Reached
1 Church Missionary Society	1857 (*Dayspring*)	3	1
2. Sudan Interior Mission	1894	57	21
3. British Branch, S.U.M.[81]	1904	17	13
4. United Missionary Society	1905	12	7
5. South African Branch, S.U.M.	1909	9	6
6. Danish Lutheran Branch, S.U.M.	1913	12	13
7. Evangelical United Brethren Branch, S.U.M.	1921	7	5
8. Church of the Brethren Mission	1922	13	9
9. Methodist Church Mission	1925	10	4
10. Qua Iboe Church Mission	1932	4	2
11. Assemblies of God Mission	1938	4	2
12. Christian Reformed Church Branch, S.U.M.	1940	20	9
(Dutch Reformed Church Mission .... 1911)			
13. Nigerian Baptist Mission	1940's	7	1
14. Cameroon Baptist Mission		1	1
15. Basel Mission	1959	1	1
		177	95

14 tribes are reached by two or more missions 14

Tribes reached 81
Tribes unreached 29

Total tribes in Central Belt 110

Fifteen different mission societies are active in the Central Belt, one having entered the country as early as 1857 and

[80] In Central Belt.
[81] Sudan United Mission.

one as recently as 1959. These missions maintain at least 177 mission stations, which reach eighty-one of the 110 Central Belt tribes. Eleven tribes are each reached by two missions, and in three cases (Birom, Nupe, and Yoruba) by three missions. Thus there are twenty-nine tribes unreached by any Protestant mission.

The missions that have extended into the greatest number of tribes are the Sudan Interior Mission, with one-third the total number of stations and twenty-one tribes, and the British and Lutheran Branches of the Sudan United Mission, with a total of twenty-nine stations and twenty-six tribes between them. However, the population and its density may be of more significance, as some tribes may be comparatively small, while others very large. An estimate of the population of the tribes reached, as shown on page 24, indicates that the Plateau Church (British Branch, Sudan United Mission), and the Lutheran Church (Lutheran Branch, Sudan United Mission), together have in their twenty-six tribes about the same population that the Christian Reformed Church Mission has in one tribe, the Tiv: over 800,000 population. Furthermore, "reaching" the tribes is not sufficient. We are commanded not to "reach" them, but to "disciple" them. We rejoice that the missions have gotten into a position from which discipling can now proceed.

D. THE UNREACHED

There are two closely related aspects of this subject. The first relates to unreached tribes and the second to unreached areas.

Unreached Tribes

In Figure III each circled number represents an unreached tribe. It should be noted that eight of the numbers include more than just one tribe. For instance, on this map number 41 is a complex of thirteen hill tribes. Other tribal complexes in this listing are as follows:

1, The Kamuku Complex: Kamuku, Uru, Banshi, Pongu
12, The Mawma Complex: Mawma, Rindiri, Migili
44, The Afawa Complex: Afawa, Ajawa, Warjawa, Diryawa

77, The Tigon Complex: Tigon, Amburu, Magu, Ambo, Ashuku
85, The Kaltango Complex: Kushi, Buruk, Bangganji, Alwak, Kamo, Tula, Waja
99, The Gwoza Hill Tribes
102, The Mandara Hill Tribes: Sukur, Tur, Wula

Of these eight complexes, four (1, 41, 44, and 102) are listed among the twenty-nine unreached tribes.

UNREACHED TRIBES

Tribe	Number on map	Tribe	Number on map
Kamuku Complex	1	Butawa	43
Laka	2	Afawa Complex	44
Fulani	4	Kabbawa	45
Lungu	8	Shangawa	47
Ayu	9	Boko	52
Kanka	21	Dibo	57
Ngam	25	Ibaji	60
Jerawa	28	Gade	61
Jaba	35	Base Komo	62
Kamantan	36	Afu	64
Ikulu	37	Uria	65
Chawai	38	Daka	77
Kadara	39	Matakam	101
Jajaru	40	Mandara Hill Tribes	102
13 Hill Tribes	41		

These twenty-nine unreached tribes are found in four main areas. Far to the northwest, north of the United Missionary Society Mission's Shabanda station are the Kabbawa (45), Shangawa (47), and farther south the Boko (52). The nomadic, cattle-herding Fulani (4) are also found here and in many other parts of the Central Belt. There has been no satisfactory contact made with the Fulani nomads by any mission, and very few have made any profession of Christianity.

The second concentration of circled numbers is found on the western edge of the Central Plateau, between Jos and Kaduna, in areas very close to stations of the Sudan Interior Mission, British Branch Sudan United Mission, and Assemblies of God Mission. Much of this country is cut through

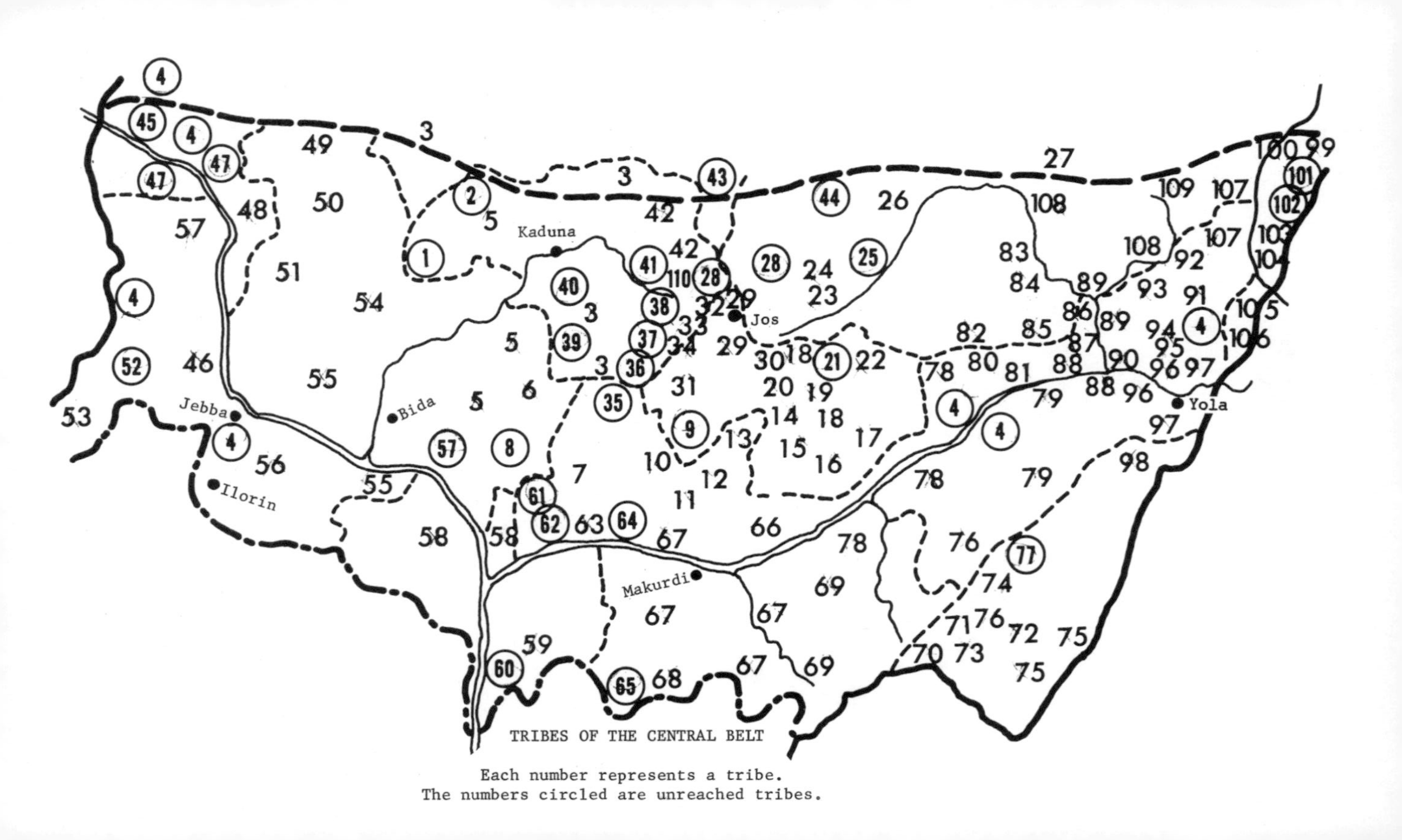

TRIBES OF THE CENTRAL BELT

Each number represents a tribe.
The numbers circled are unreached tribes.

with a rugged network of mountains and broken ridges, and the tribes living there (35 to 41 inclusive), make up one of the most interesting tribal complexes in the Central Belt. The type of country in which they live makes continuous contact by missionaries and Nigerian evangelists very difficult. Numbers 44, 43, and 28 are continuations of similar conditions.

In the following listing of the tribes, letters represent the missions that are working in the various tribes:

SIM	Sudan Interior Mission
Br	British Branch, Sudan United Mission
SA	South African Branch, Sudan United Mission
R	Dutch Reformed and Christian Reformed Branches of S.U.M.
EUB	Evangelical United Brethren Branch, S.U.M.
L	Danish Lutheran Branch, S.U.M.
CBM	Church of the Brethren Mission
QI	Qua Iboe Mission
AG	Assemblies of God Mission
B	Basel Mission
CB	Cameroon Baptist Mission
NB	Nigerian Baptist Mission
M	Methodist Mission
A	Anglican Church Missionary Society

1. Kamuku Complex		56. Yoruba	UMS, SIM, M
2. Laka		57. Dibo	
3. Hausa	SIM	58. Igbira	SIM
4. Fulani		59. Igala	QI
5. Gbari	SIM	60. Ibaji	
6. Koro	SIM	61. Gade	
7. Gwandara	SIM	62. Base Komo	
8. Lungu		63. Idoma	QI, M
9. Ayu		64. Afu	
10. Mada	SA	65. Uria	
11. Egon	SA	66. Arago	SA
12. Mawma Complex	SA	67. Tiv	R, SA
13. Rinzam	SA	68. Egede	AG
14. Sura	Br	69. Kuteb	R
15. Kwalla	Br	70. Kamino	R
16. Garkawa	Br	71. Ichan	R
17. Yergum	Br	72. Ndoro	R
18. Angas	Br	73. Tigon Complex	R

No.	Tribe	Missions
19.	Sigidi	Br
20.	Kwamba	Br
21.	Kwanka	
22.	Saya	Br, SIM
23.	Jarawa	Br, SIM
24.	Zul	SIM
25.	Ngam	
26.	Kerikeri	SIM
27.	Kanuri	Br
28.	Jerawa	
29.	Afusara	SIM
30.	Fyem	Br
31.	Birom	Br, SIM, AG
32.	Irigwi	SIM
33.	Aten	SIM
34.	Katab	SIM
35.	Jaba	
36.	Kamantan	
37.	Ikulu	
38.	Chawai	
39.	Kadara	
40.	Jajaru	
41.	13 Hill Tribes	
42.	Kurama	AG
43.	Butawa	
44.	Afawa Complex	
45.	Kabbawa	
46.	Busawa	M
47.	Shangawa	
48.	Gungawa	UMS
49.	Dakakari	UMS
50.	Dukawa	UMS
51.	Kambari	UMS, NB
52.	Boko	
53.	Bariba	UMS
54.	Basa	SIM
55.	Nupe	UMS, SIM, A
74.	Jibuwa	R
75.	Mambila	CB
76.	Kam	EUB
77.	Daka	
78.	Jukun	EUB
79.	Mumuye	EUB
80.	Wurkum	EUB
81.	Jen	EUB
82.	Pero-Pia	EUB
83.	Tera	SIM
84.	Tanggali	SIM
85.	Kaltango Complex	SIM
86.	Languda	L
87.	Piri	L
88.	Bachama	L
89.	Kanakuru	L
90.	Mbula	L
91.	Kilba	L, CBM
92.	Whona	CBM
93.	Gaanda	L
94.	Lala	L
95.	Yangur	L
96.	Bata	L
97.	Bere	L
98.	Chamba	L, R
99.	Gwoza Hill Tribes	Br, B
100.	Waga	CBM
101.	Matakam	
102.	Mandara Hill Tribes	
103.	Higi	CBM
104.	Fali	CBM, NB
105.	Gude	CBM, NB
106.	Paka	L
107.	Margi	CBM
108.	Bura	CBM
109.	Chibuk	CBM
110.	Kaji	SIM, M

About the confluence of the Niger and Benue Rivers, 57, 8, 61, 62, and 64 are unreached, but are in country that should soon be reached by churches bordering them to the east and west. 60, 65, 28, and 77 are small groups also bordering areas where there are strong Christian churches.

The Mandara Hill Tribes (102) in the Northeast are on the edge of Church of the Brethren Mission territory. Matakam (101) is included as part of the Central Belt because, though the great majority of the tribe is located in the Cameroon Republic, they spill over into Sardauna Province and are completely unreached in this border area.

Most of these people live in the mountains and are difficult to reach, but nevertheless they demand attention. The population of the Tur, Wula, Sukur Complex is about 10,445.[82] Sukur is a very important cultural center for the whole Margi (107) tribe, and casts its spiritual influence upon many of the mountain groups of the Mandara range.

The Unreached Areas

We look at the map, Fig. III, and notice that the western "upright" of the Niger River has few mission stations. The United Missionary Society reports that in 1952 this vast area contained only sixty places of worship.[83] From this it is evident that great opportunities exist for further extension.

The tribes east of the river (Dakabari, Dukawa, and Kambari) number over 143,000 together, and on the west side of the river are the Busawa, Boko, and Shangawa. The 1960 map of Nigeria distributed by Shell shows 182 villages and towns of various sizes in this area. These are the homes of a large number of people who still maintain their animistic traditions.

A second area is that between the Christian Reformed and the Evangelical United Brethren Branches of the Sudan United Mission south of the Benue. After the Australian-New Zealand Branch of the Sudan United Mission was driven from the Sudan, East Africa, it considered relocating in this area. However, it decided that the evident scarcity of population did not warrant the entrance of a new mission.[84] In 1962 I drove over the new road from Donga to Lankaveri and observed that the population along the road

82 Kirk-Greene, A. H. M., *op. cit.*, p. 2.
83 *World Christian Handbook*, 1952.
84 Gilliland, D., Personal interview, March, 1962.
Smith, E. H., Correspondence, April, 1963.

is sparse indeed. However, it may be that the view from the road is deceiving, for it was built primarily, I would suppose, to get through this "bush area" and connect Yola with Makurdi, and not as a route to reach remote villages. There may be numerous farming hamlets in this area of 6,000 square miles. The largest town is Mutum Biyu, which is Moslem. Beli, at the fork of the road that turns south to Serti, contains some Tiv who have moved into the area. Tribes from the surrounding countryside meeting in the area are Mumuye from the northeast, Jukun from the west, Tiv from the south, and Daka, Kam, and Chamba from the east.

The Shell map locates twenty-eight villages and towns south of the Benue, west of Lankaveri, and including no part of Benue or Sardauna Provinces. It is difficult to judge from this what the population might really be, for it is quite evident that only the most important and largest villages are indicated on this map. In the entire Church of the Brethren Mission area this map pinpoints only twenty villages, but from personal visitation I know that there are hundreds. In the Margi tribal area of 100,000 population there are only four villages designated on this same map!

Thus it is possible that there is a much larger population in this unoccupied area than is supposed. One thing is certain. There is much "bush country" here, drained by the Wurkam, Kam, and Taraba Rivers, which must have great agricultural, and therefore Christian community, potential. At present, though there is no mission station in the area, the Muri Church has sent in several evangelists. One is at Beli and another at Mutum Biyu, and a third between these two in the Kam (76) tribe.

In Sardauna Province, bordering the above area, the Mambila Plateau appears to be another largely untouched area. The Lutheran Branch extends south a short distance beyond Gurum, and the Christian Reformed Branch is at Baissa. Serti, opened in 1962 at the foot of the Mambila Plateau, is still in its exploratory stage. The other mission in this southernmost part of Sardauna is the Cameroon Baptist Mission with its northern extension at Wurwar in the

Mambila tribe. A.H.M. Kirk-Green gives a striking description of the Mambila Plateau:

> The grassy highlands of the Mambila Plateau rise to over 7,000 feet and carry the best cattle ranges in Nigeria and some of its most majestic scenery. But this mountainous country (is) wild and hard of access. . . . (No one) who has trekked among these hills (can) forget the superb panoramic view over the plains towards Serti, or the storm clouds rolling up over the undulating grasslands. The term "plateau" is perhaps misleading, for once you have struggled up the escarpment the land is anything but flat; it is, rather, a saucer-shaped offshoot of the Cameroon highlands, where a trek from one village to the next may involve a whole day's laborious descent to the valley and the weary ascent of the opposite slope, though only a mile or so separates them as the crow flies. . . . The greatest concentration of cattle is on the Mambila Plateau, where over 150,000 head make overgrazing a very real danger. This plateau now carries one adult bovine per 6.3 acres per year.[85]

The major tribe is the Mambila tribe numbering over 18,000 in Sardauna Province.[86] North of the Mambila is the Dakka tribe of about 8,000[87] and beyond is the southern extension of the Chamba tribe of 58,000.[88]

Certainly this high grassland, cattle country, broken as it is by plains and valleys, though at present very remote and difficult to enter, will be an increasingly important part of Nigeria, and, because it is still largely pagan, gives promise of becoming strongly Christian.

In addition to these unreached areas, every tribe "reached" by mission stations still has untold numbers of persons who have not accepted Christ, and hundreds of villages and hamlets that have no churches. Furthermore, as a result of movement from traditional village sites, new villages are springing up everywhere. Like most newly located villages, these are much more receptive to the gospel than the ancestral villages were. Yet among these also we find very few churches.

85 Kirk-Greene, A. H. M., *op. cit.*, pp. 11, 12, 112.
86 *Ibid.*, p. 2.
87 *Ibid.*
88 *Ibid.*

The opportunity for multiplication of churches is overwhelming, and though, in independent Nigeria, this coming great expansion of Christianity will be made primarily by the churches now established throughout the Central Belt – not by the missions – what a tremendous responsibility nevertheless rests upon missions and missionaries to make resources and experiences available at the strategic moments that come and so quickly pass by!

What then is the Church in the Central Belt like? What is its structure? What have been its successes? What of its dedication and how vital is its inner life? Does it feel the urgency of the present opportunity to such a degree that it will very quickly possess all the land for Christ? To seek an answer to these questions we now turn our attention to the indigenous churches.

PART II: INDIGENOUS CHURCH GROWTH

Chapter III. The Establishment of the Indigenous Church

A. THE SETTING

WE HAVE SEEN HOW THE CHURCH FIRST ARRIVED IN THE Central Belt through the witness of the various missions. All of these had in mind only one purpose: the establishment of an indigenous Church. One important element in the setting for the emergence of the indigenous Church was the harmonious inter-mission relationships that existed from the very beginning. The Sudan Interior Mission, the Church Missionary Society, and the Sudan United Mission were in close accord in the attainment of their common goal. Between 1905 and 1907 the Sudan Interior Mission and the Sudan United Mission coalesced as a result of the meeting of Dr. Kumm of the Sudan United Mission and Rev. Rowland Bingham of the Sudan Interior Mission.[1] The November, 1906 issue of *Lightbearer*, the Sudan United Mission publication, lists the missionaries of both societies, and for a period of time Bingham was secretary both for Canada and the United States.[2]

A series of inter-mission conferences (1910 and 1913 at Lokoja, and 1926 at Miango) expressed this spiritual accord as well as gave opportunity to deal with practical aspects of bringing the gospel to the Central Belt. In 1910 the first inter-Mission Conference discussed, among other things, church organization, training of Nigerian helpers, polygamy, wives for converts, the dowry, the posture one should take in prayer,

[1] Maxwell, J. L., *op. cit.*, pp. 62-65.
[2] *Ibid.*

a common outline for worship, scripture translation, language study, grants-in-aid for schools, and the liquor traffic. The conference at Miango was an historic one in that the Sudan United Mission presented a draft of a church constitution hoping for a United Church of Africa. At the next conference in 1929, with fifteen delegates representing five mission societies, it was decided that it would not be possible to go forward in a United Church, but that efforts should be directed toward bringing about a "Federation of the missions in the Northern Provinces which are officially represented at this conference," and that "this Federation shall earnestly endeavor to secure such unity of fellowship and action as shall be approved by the Council of Missions for the Northern Provinces in consultation with their home boards."[3]

The missions met annually to discuss common problems, to plan for a Church of Christ in the Sudan, and together to work out difficulties created by the Moslem bias of the British government. These meetings were formally organized as the Council of Missions, and included at least ten mission societies, which later became the Northern Missions Council. It was made up of missionaries and did not include Nigerians, except that from time to time the Church Missionary Society's representative was a Nigerian. The Sudan Interior Mission withdrew from the Council, but continued harmonious relationships with the individual missions of the Council and at times sent an observer to the Council.

Indigenous churches, as formed, were encouraged to consider the possibility of a Council of Churches. In 1960, after such a Council of Churches had finally been formed, the Northern Missions Council ceased to exist. The Council of Evangelical Churches of Northern Nigeria (C.E.C.N.N.) has a constitution, but no statement of faith. The word "Evangelical" in its name is the only governing factor in this respect.

Nine of the member churches have grouped themselves in the two fellowships to be discussed in this chapter: the Fellow-

[3] *Ibid.,* pp. 160-162.

ship of Churches of Christ in the Sudan, and the Evangelical Churches of West Africa. Four other churches that belong to this Council are: the United Missionary Church, the Qua Iboe Church (Northern Region), the Anglican Church (Northern Region), and the Nigerian Baptist Convention (Northern Region). The Council meets at least once a year, discusses common problems, and is the liaison between government and its member bodies. Its chairman is usually an African minister, and in 1963 was the Rev. Gin Mai Gari, leader of the Evangelical Churches of West Africa.[4]

Decisions of the Council of Churches are not binding upon its member bodies, but their significance for united action and mutual aid in social, moral, religious, and other matters relating to the welfare and growth of the churches can hardly be overestimated.

In the midst of these mission proceedings, which culminated in the formulation of the Council of Churches, the Church itself throughout the Central Belt was "bearing fruit and growing" (Col. 1:6). While the early beginnings seemed weak and uncertain in the face of the immensity of the task, these beginnings, both missionary and Nigerian, were made by consecrated men and women whose witness went forth in the power of the Holy Spirit. At first, though mission stations and missionaries were multiplied, the church grew very slowly. The remoteness, lack of roads, tropical illness, language difficulties, and poor lines of communication plagued and frustrated the labors of the early missionaries. The First World War caused a slowdown, yet it was amazing how well the missions were able to carry on in spite of staff shortages, and gain some expansion. But the dozen years following the war, though characterized by the expansion of mission activities, institutions, and preaching to a primitive and largely unresponsive population, saw little multiplication of churches. Mr. Maxwell, writing in 1935, says that conditions in those early days were not conducive to fast growth.[5] After speaking of an attack

[4] Smith, E. H. An unpublished paper on the organization of the Fellowship of the Churches of Christ in the Sudan, p. 9.

[5] Maxwell, J. L., *op. cit.*, p. 74.

that had been made upon the British Resident when he arrested a slave trader, he says, "Under such circumstances quick progress was scarcely to be looked for. A new tribe, a new language, a new setting, all had to be dealt with. . . . The ground must first be prepared, and then the sowing can be done."

Today we look back and contemplate the possibility of our having missed opportunities for more rapid response. Certainly the government and mission pressures against the slave trade gave the missionaries a great advantage in the eyes of the oppressed tribal populace. Yet even in areas such as New Guinea, where today there is a tremendous tribal responsiveness to the gospel, it is quite clear that the early years demanded great patience, as well as enthusiasm, on the part of the first missionaries. Ten-year periods of sowing the seed, with little response, was the usual pattern.[6]

In the Central Belt of Nigeria the graph of church attendance shows that there were long periods of preparing the ground and planting the seed, and very little sprouting before 1930. However, the winds of change have brought about a different situation from those early years. As the gospel enters new tribal areas quick sprouting of the seed is becoming increasingly common. Despite this, some Christian leaders still seem to expect slow church growth. An attitude of great expectancy must, in these days, replace that of stubborn patience.

In 1930 attendance at Christian worship began to increase significantly. Between 1935 and 1940 attendance at Sunday morning services more than doubled in the Sudan United Mission areas. This increase is partly due to two factors: (1) increased responsibility being taken by Nigerian evangelists in preaching, and (2) the resultant forming of many small worshiping groups far from mission stations. In 1935, in the Sudan United Mission area, 55% of the Sunday attendance was at mission stations and 45% at preaching points carried on by Nigerians away from the stations. But in 1940,

[6] Vicedom, G. F., *Church and People in New Guinea,* p. 10.

only 33% of the attendance was at the stations, and 67% was at outside preaching points.[7]

In the Plateau Church the average Sunday morning attendance in 1925, after twenty-one years of preaching, was only about 1,000, and in 1930 it had risen to over 2,000, but by 1942 it had passed the 10,000 mark.

The Eastern Church's line of Sunday morning attendance likewise began to rise in the middle of the 1930's. The place the increased number of preaching points plays in the growing attendance can be shown by the following chart of the Eastern Church:

Preaching	1955	1956	1957	1958	1959	1960	1961	1962	1963
points:	109	123	226	235	253	290	245	277	295
Sunday attendance:	7882	9274	14353	17000	15387	18089	19055	18420	21742

Note that both the preaching points and church attendance more than doubled in seven years.

For the Fellowship of Churches of Christ in the Sudan, of which the Plateau and Eastern Churches are a part, there were in 1962 2,778 places of worship and an attendance of 201,938. The places of worship had more than doubled in five years, and the Sunday attendance had increased 157% in the same period.

After World War II all of the churches experienced an amazing increase in Sunday morning church attendance, so that by 1962 the average attendance was over 270,000.

These 270,000 people meet to worship God in a great variety of places. There are only a few fine church buildings, such as those at Gindiri and Waka and Numan. Many churches, with a membership of from three to eight hundred, are improving their church buildings with cement floors, shining aluminum roofs, and cement-plastered walls. But the great majority meet in small, thatched, adobe buildings with floors of pounded earth and backless earth benches. Some of these may measure not more than ten-by-twenty feet, and many are the circular entrance houses of the leading Christian or evangelist in a community.

[7] Maxwell, J. L., *op. cit.*, p. 236.

In all the Central Belt we find a distinction made between an "organized church" and a "place of worship" or "preaching point." Places of worship are centers where Christians, and many non-Christians, meet regularly on Sundays and perhaps once during the week for worship and the study of God's Word. The attendance is made up of a cross section of the community with a predominance of youth. Few school children or ex-school children are present, as most such places of worship are far from any mission or government school. In such services there are always many non-Christians who are preparing for church membership. Usually the service is led by an evangelist or a local lay preacher. Most places of worship begin with a simple gathering of interested folk under the shade of a tamarind or wild plum tree in the doorway of the village chief during the dry season, and far from any mission station. As interest increases and the rainy season draws near, there will be talk about a building for worship. The first rainy season may be passed in the entrance house of the chief. But by the next, most groups of believers will have completed plans for a small building. From small centers such as this the church grows.

An organized church results when such a village group grows to eighteen or more baptized Christians with a minimum of one or two strong local leaders around whom a "church committee" for the planning and execution of church activities can be formed. In many cases there is no ordained pastor available for such a church, but the local committee members perform the pastoral and teaching duties. Such a group has elected officers and regular "council meetings" and arranges for the communion when an ordained pastor is available.

The extension of missions described in Chapter II, when seen in the light of the conditions outlined in Chapter I, "The Winds of Change," and the marked increase of interest on the part of the people of the Central Belt, made it clear that by the middle 1950s the time had come to organize a Nigerian Church. The matter was urgent. The Church had to be indigenous, not only in the eyes of Nigerians in general, but of the Government in particular. As long as missionaries are on the scene the Christian church, unfortunately, looks rather "foreign." Sunburnt white is so conspicuous in a populace of varying shades of brown! The missionary residence with its neat, tree-planted grounds sets the missionary off from his surroundings. Even though there are only a few missionaries to thousands of Christians, "Yours is a European religion" is nevertheless a charge thrown in the face of Central Belt Christians. It is impossible to free the Church of this charge as long as its true character is unknown by its critics. But a "self-governing, self-supporting, and self-propagating" Church goes a long way toward establishing it as a fellowship of Africans growing from the very soil of Nigeria.

The rapid and peaceful movement toward independence, the commercial and social development of the country, the widening base of education, and the emerging of mature leaders, and perhaps, most of all, the rapidly increasing membership – all made it necessary for the Church to become an independent, responsible organization. The fact that two Fellowships of Churches were organized at about the same time (1954), each originating from different "parent" missions, and that eight Protestant missions (including five denominational and three interdenominational missions) were involved, was evidence that the fullness of time for indigenous organization had come.

B. THE FORMATION OF THE ASSOCIATION OF EVANGELICAL CHURCHES OF WEST AFRICA (ECWA)

The Association of Evangelical Churches of West Africa is the indigenous Church which has resulted from the witness of the Sudan Interior Mission. Meeting each year from 1950 to 1954 it prepared a constitution. At a meeting in Kagora in 1954 the constitution was accepted by the leaders of the Church, and at Egbe on May 18, 1954 the Church of ECWA was founded.

There are three councils in the ECWA Association of Churches: (1) the Local Church Council, (2) the District Church Council, and (3) the General Church Council. The

Local Church Council is made up of delegates from one or more churches in a particular area. There are eight District Councils to which every Local Church Council sends one pastor and one elder. (In ECWA an elder is an experienced churchman, but not usually ordained. Elders are chosen by each congregation and they serve as a local board dealing with matters of church growth and discipline.) Each District Council is autonomous within the bounds of the constitution and thus local business may be dealt with differently from district to district. The General Council meets once a year primarily for fellowship. Delegates from all the District Councils meet in this assembly, and "even though it has no great power it is still very important because it helps to keep ECWA united."[8] The constitution may be changed through action of the General Church Council except for the doctrinal statement, which may not be changed.[9]

The Sudan Interior Mission is gradually turning mission property over to the Church. By the end of 1962 ECWA had received nine mission stations and nine more were in the process of being turned over.[10] Nigerians now live in some of the homes once occupied by missionaries. In other cases missionaries required in the area continue to live in the church-owned property.

A very important part of the Church is its evangelistic thrust through its "African Missionary Society," which has sent out 140 of its own missionaries.[11] (There were about 85 actually in missionary service as of July, 1963.) It has received an excellent response from its own churches. At Kaltango six couples were working under this society and more than twenty others from the Kaltango-Biliri area had answered calls to serve as evangelists in other parts of Nigeria.

In ECWA there are about 700 (1962) organized churches,[12]

[8] Sudan Interior Mission, "Lessons on What ECWA Stands For," p. 5.

[9] *Ibid.*

[10] Sudan Interior Mission Publication, "Sudan Witness," p. 3.

[11] *Ibid.*

[12] Olatayo, D. I., Personal interview, July 25, 1963.

an increase of 140 since 1960.[13] All but about sixty of these are among the pagan tribes. There are 391 evangelists and 159 pastors. The Church has opened four Bible schools and hoped to open three more in 1964.[14]

The Sudan Interior Mission has developed an extensive educational program. Its Church also became very much interested in continuing this emphasis under its own control and has become deeply involved in the educational activities. Education is increasingly important to the development of Nigeria, and missions have been expected by the government to participate as voluntary agencies in the expansion of educational facilities, especially on the primary level. The Christian Church feels this educational service is necessary, not only to make the development of Nigeria possible, but also to make the Christian community strong and enlightened.

In 1958, less than four years after its founding, the Church became a registered voluntary agency in the field of education. Thus ECWA, as reported by Pastor David I. Olatayo, (ECWA's General Secretary), was by 1961 proprietor of fifty-seven junior primary schools in Ilorin, Kabba, and Zaria Provinces, with over 7,900 pupils enrolled; and eighteen senior primary schools with 2,214 enrolled; and with Nigerian teachers, one Nigerian supervisor, and two Nigerian visiting teachers. Where Nigerian supervision is not as yet adequate, the Sudan Interior Mission is continuing to help. The Church plans to expand its educational work into the secondary (high school) level, to establish special training institutions, such as schools of agriculture and commerce, and also to expand into literacy and bookshop developments. It hoped to open two secondary schools in 1964.

The Church is also becoming involved in the healing arts. It has taken over five government-approved dispensaries, and has opened two new ones.[15] Pastor Olatayo concludes his review of the social services of the Evangelical Church of West Africa by saying, "We really want to play our part in the development of our great and beloved country,

[13] Hunter, J. H., *op. cit.*, p. 246.
[14] Olatayo, D. I., Personal interview, July 25, 1963.
[15] *Ibid.*

Nigeria, both spiritually and materially. To God be the glory; great things He has done."[16]

All missions have been greatly involved in educational programs. As can be seen from the above, the Churches will also become involved. In the thought of the missions, education is an entranceway into the Christian Church. Now that Churches are becoming agencies for the management of schools, their limited resources may prevent the opening of schools in unreached areas, and thus tend to change the emphasis from schools as a doorway to the Church to that of educating the youth of the existing Church for the development of the new Nigeria. Considering the great task of discipling the tribes that still lies before us, we may well ask the question: *will this degree of involvement in education divert the Church from its primary task to that of developing a Christian elite?*

C. THE FORMATION OF THE FELLOWSHIP OF THE CHURCHES OF CHRIST IN THE SUDAN (TEKAS)

The Tarayyar Ekklesiyoyyin Kristi A Sudan (TEKAS) becomes in English the Fellowship of the Churches of Christ in the Sudan. It is made up of people from fifty-seven or more non-Hausa tribes. However, Hausa is the *lingua franca* of Northern Nigeria and all educated Central Belt Nigerians speak it fluently. All of the business of the Church is conducted in Hausa, and all of the reports of proceedings are produced in it as well. The Hausa name lends a certain Nigerian flavor characteristic of the Church itself and of value in these days of independence.

Each TEKAS Church is assisted by a mission, as follows:

Church[17]	Mission
1. Plateau	British Branch, Sudan United Mission
2. Mada Hills	South African Branch, S.U.M.
3. Benue	Christian Reformed Branch, S.U.M.
4. Lutheran	Danish Lutheran Branch, S.U.M.
5. Muri	Evangelical United Brethren Branch, S.U.M.

[16] Hunter, J. H., *op. cit.*, pp. 246, 247.

[17] The Churches and their geographical locations are shown on Map, Fig. I.

6. Eastern	Church of the Brethren
7. Tiv	Christian Reformed Branch, S.U.M.
8. United	Christians from many areas now in Kaduna.

Rev. E. H. Smith, secretary of TEKAS, writes concerning the origins of TEKAS,

> . . . the harmony and unity of purpose which the Branches of the Sudan United Mission enjoyed was fruitful also among those who believed on Christ Jesus through their ministry. Moreover, the unison or togetherness was not introduced to Nigerian Christians after they had reached maturity, but was something with which they grew up from infancy.[18]

In keeping with the spirit of post-war Nigeria, Christians in the habit of gathering in biennial spiritual-growth meetings within the framework of the Sudan United Mission began to desire something more definite and permanent.[19] In 1954, at Langtang, as a culmination of long discussions between missionaries and Nigerian church leaders, a decision was reached to advise each cluster of congregations established by a Branch of the Sudan United Mission to organize as a Church and (together with the Church of the Brethren Mission area church) form a Fellowship of Churches of Christ in the Sudan.

In 1955 at Randa the Fellowship of Churches of Christ in the Sudan was formally established. In 1959 the Church among the Tiv, formed by the Dutch Reformed Church Mission, made application for membership in TEKAS and was warmly received as the seventh member body.

The establishment of the eighth Church in TEKAS, the United Church of Christ in Nigeria, located in Kaduna, is so significant for the future of TEKAS and the Christian community of Northern Nigeria that I quote the statement of its origin given by Rev. E. H. Smith, who was in close contact with the situation from its beginning.

> The eighth church of TEKAS is unique. . . . The capital city of Northern Nigeria is Kaduna, a city which had no existence prior to the British occupation; it has no native

[18] Smith, E. H., An unpublished paper on the Fellowship of the Churches of Christ in the Sudan, p. 3.

[19] *Ibid.*, p. 4.

> sons and daughters. During World War II it was a military centre where Nigerians from all parts of the North were trained. Those who were Protestant Christians worshipped together. This set a precedent and in time of peace which followed they continued in their common worship. Moreover, the progress of the country to independence meant a tremendous increase in indigenous Government servants which have been attracted by the thousands from all over the country. This naturally meant that the gathering of Christians was multiplied in size five or ten times. Disputations, especially over the matter of baptism, forced the group to carefully consider what it would do. Finally, those who derived their faith from many tribal and many denominational backgrounds as indicated in the seven Churches of TEKAS, decided, together with some others, to form the United Church of Christ in Nigeria. This Church enjoys a Constitution very similar to that of the TEKAS Churches but provides for a diversity of practices. It is well to remember that this organization was born out of a period of harsh adversity and so to know that its charter members are aware of the difficulties and are resolved that tolerance is to be practiced towards each other in the cause of Christian unity to be openly displayed in the Region's capital where Islam is the predominant religion. This United Church of Christ in Nigeria applied for and was granted membership in TEKAS.
>
> The TEKAS Fellowship is not a superficial organization. Its roots are deep and its members warmly intimate with each other. It is reasonable to say that in essence it has existed since the first believers were born again thirty or forty years ago. In the narrow confines of the word Church as defined by denominations, TEKAS is only a Fellowship, yet its warmhearted togetherness is probably a better demonstration of the true Church of Jesus Christ.[20]

The separate Churches all have similar constitutions; even the statements of faith are very much alike. The first part of the name of each is the same, viz, "Ekklesiyar Kristi a Sudan." The difference of each name appears after the first part of the name, for example, "EKAS,[21] Eastern," and

[20] *Ibid.*, pp. 5, 6.

[21] In the name TEKAS, the letter T represents the word for "Fellowship" and thus is dropped when reference is being made to one particular Church.

distinguishes the particular Church according to denomination or geographical area.

The constitution of the Fellowship of Churches of Christ in the Sudan provides for an Advisory Council. This council, composed of the official representatives of all the member bodies, meets each year in a different EKAS area. Its business is composed of matters of general interest to the Churches and any particular items of business that may be referred to it by its member bodies. Its decisions as they affect the Churches are advisory, but one of its strongest aspects is that it seeks to present a united front.

TEKAS is registered with the Government of Nigeria with trustees composed of one member appointed by each member Church. Also, each member Church is registered with the government separately or is in the process of becoming so. The Constitution of TEKAS may be revised only with the approval of the Advisory Council and ratified by the Councils of all the member Churches.[22]

Papers read and discussed at the Advisory Council (1962) at Waka in the Eastern Church points up the type of constructive study participated in at such a meeting. These papers on the responsibility of Christians in the new Nigeria included the following topics: Repentance; Bribery and Corruption; Christian Marriage and the Home; Students for the Ministry; Young Men and Farm Work; Faith and Good Behavior; Unity in Christ; Indigenous Worship Forms; and Literature. Reports were given by all of the Churches, and special reports were heard by TEKAS committees on Evangelism, the Christian Newspaper, and the Theological College of Northern Nigeria, which is a cooperative project being supported both by the Churches of TEKAS and their missions.

Each year TEKAS invites and receives fraternal delegates from ECWA, and sends fraternal delegates to the ECWA General Assembly. Figures V to XII give the membership increase of the Churches of Christ in the Sudan.

[22] Extracts from Sudan United Mission Field Committee minutes, February, 1954, Appendix iii, pp. 2-4.

Chapter IV. Church Growth on the Plateau and West

A. THE EVANGELICAL CHURCH OF WEST AFRICA (ECWA)

THE GRAPH OF CHURCH GROWTH FOR THE ECWA CHURCHES (Fig. IV) shows accelerating growth from 1911 to 1960. Communicant membership rises from less than twenty in 1911[1] to 2,000 in 1925[2] and to 2,337 in 1932; 4,199 in 1940; and then jumps to 14,258 in 1960.[3] The Mission began its work in 1901, and took thirty years to attain 2,000 members. But the second thirty-year period added 12,000. Incomplete reports indicate a still more rapid rise to almost 20,000 by 1963![4]

A closer view of the growth of this Church year by year reveals some losses as well as sudden gains. Yet church attendance steadily increased from 12,926 in 1936, to 17,439 in 1940, and to 42,260 in 1960.

Great differences exist in the responsiveness of the various districts of the ECWA Church.[5] About forty-two of the 101 mission stations lie outside the Central Belt. The eleven stations in Yoruba country, about half of them south of the Central Belt, show a substantial membership of 4,000, which is more than one-fourth of the total membership of ECWA. The thirty-seven stations north of the Belt in solid Moslem areas (Sokoto, Kano-Katsina, and Bauchi-Bornu) have only six percent of the total Church membership. The District of Sokoto reports only forty-eight communicant members and a Sunday attendance of only 120. Kano-Katsina reports 355 members and 1,200 Sunday attendance. Many of these

1 *World Atlas of Christian Missions* (1911), p. 93.
2 *World Missionary Atlas* (1925), p. 109.
3 ECWA Church Report, 1960.
4 Olatayo, D. I., Personal interview, July 25, 1963.
5 ECWA Church Report, 1960.

Christians are immigrants from the South or came from other Churches of the Central Belt. The Kano station is highly institutionalized with schools, hospitals, and leprosarium, all of which draw heavily from outside the Moslem North for leaders and workers in church and mission. However, the leprosarium church in Kano contains 110 converts from Islam and has produced more than thirty full-time Christian workers.[6]

In the Nupe District, Islam is very influential,[7] and this is part of the reason for the small membership of 185 in spite of twenty mission stations, twelve pastors in the District, and sixty years of labor. The average Sunday morning attendance is 1,240.

The largest membership is found in the Zaria-Plateau District (5,000), and a Sunday attendance of 12,600. The Yoruba District ranks next in size with 4,000 members and 12,000 attending Sunday morning services. The Tanggali-Waja District of southeast Bauchi Province, neighbor to the fast-growing Lutheran Church of the Numan area, has the third largest district membership of 2,700 with a Sunday morning attendance of 8,000.

There were about 550 missionaries and 101 mission stations in 1961. The following chart gives an overall picture:

Statistics of ECWA as of April, 1961[8]

Districts	Mission Stations	Evange-lists	Pastors	Places of Worship	Members	Av. Sun. Attend.
1. Sokoto	10	11	1	3	48	120
2. Nupe	20	1	12	11	185	1,240
3. Kano-Katsina	20	37	7	20	355	1,200
4. Bauchi-Bornu	13	21	7	30	399	1,100
5. Gwari	5	54	7	136	1,571	6,000

[6] Hunter, J. H., *op. cit.*, p. 210.

[7] In the Nupe tribe the 1931 *Census* gave 235,990 Moslems out of a total of 324,375 for all religions. But in many communities pagan rituals exist side by side with some Moslem observances, the latter being increasingly adopted for reasons of prestige (Ford, Brown, and Armstrong, *Peoples of the Niger Benue Confluence*, p. 45).

[8] Statistics from ECWA General Secretary Office, Jos, Nigeria.

6. Tanggali-Waja	6	115	25	135	2,700	8,000
7. Yoruba	11	10	70	150	4,000	12,000
8. Zaria-Plateau	16	142	30	255	5,000	12,600
Totals	101	391	159	740	14,258	42,260

The first column of figures compared with the membership shows that sixty-two percent of the stations are in areas not responsive to the gospel. Also some, such as the Bornu stations of Zalanga and Kukar Gadu, surrounded by large pagan populations, are finding strong Moslem pressures a hindrance to rapid church growth. Kukar Gadu, established in 1935, had 150 communicant members in 1962.

The Zalanga station in the midst of a large pagan populace was opened in 1941 and in 1962 had twenty-five local Christians. Perhaps another twenty-five had become Christians during the twenty years but had died or moved away. The Christian community was much enlarged by the presence of the students of the Zalanga Bible School who were from outside the area. The local response to education was so small as a result of Moslem pressures that only by the attendance of the children of the Bible school families was it possible to have a primary school at all. It is hoped that by maintaining a school with these children time may be gained in which to break through to the general tribal populace.

Though missionaries are concentrated in resistant areas, eighty-two percent of the Nigerian evangelists and eighty-three percent of the pastors are in the responsive areas. Strong Nigerian leadership is especially noticed in the Tanggali-Waja, Yoruba, and Zaria Plateau Districts (Columns 2 and 3). The large number of regular places of worship and the 38,600 Sunday attendance, with less than half of these attenders being members, indicates a great potential harvest in Districts 5, 6, 7, and 8. With the large number of Nigerian workers much progress can be made, if additional resources are available in these responsive areas. The question might well be asked whether a shifting of more missionary staff into these fields, white unto harvest, might not be a strategic move. Or, would increasing the missionary staff tend to take the initiative from the Nigerian leaders? Perhaps it would be more pertinent to ask if a lessening of the mis-

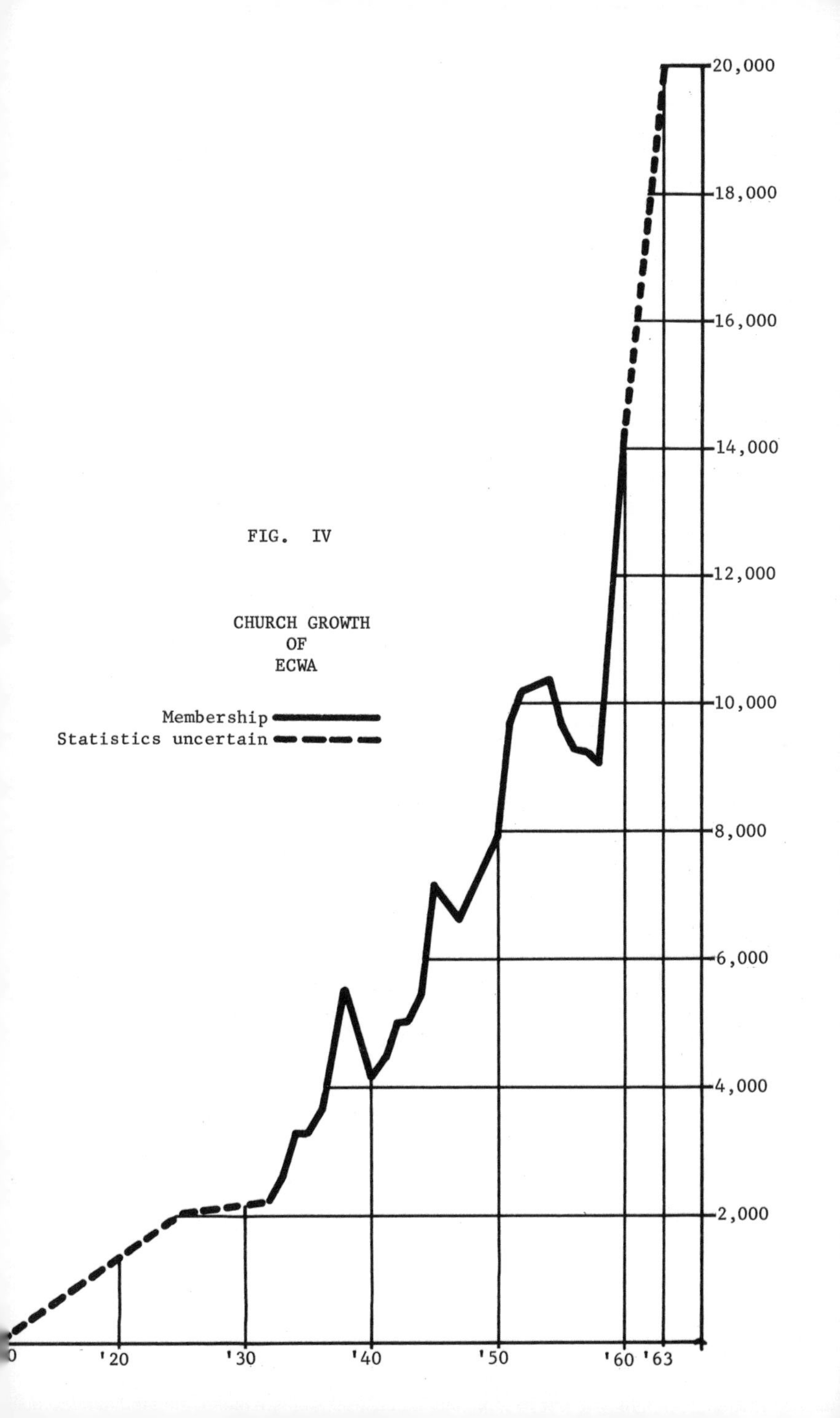
FIG. IV
CHURCH GROWTH
OF
ECWA
Membership
Statistics uncertain
20,000
18,000
16,000
14,000
12,000
10,000
8,000
6,000
4,000
2,000
'20
'30
'40
'50
'60
'63

sionary staff in the Moslem North would weaken the Christian position in the Northern Region as a whole? Is a strong Christian force in the North necessary to keep the Central Belt open for church planting? It is difficult to see large groups of people being left in spiritual darkness because attempts to win the "unwinnable" are being made in other places.

B. THE ASSEMBLIES OF GOD

The beginning of the Assemblies of God in the Central Belt stems from the spontaneous fellowship of Christians from the South who had come to the cities of the North in search of work. These small groups soon became desirous of pastoral care and were organized as churches. These churches then began to take the message of Christ to the surrounding countryside, and other churches were established.

In 1954 the Northern Church of the Assemblies of God was formed. This was the same year in which the fellowships of ECWA and TEKAS were formed. The Northern Church has an executive committee composed of an area supervisor and area leaders. Annual Meetings are held in which these leaders are elected. Since 1961 a Nigerian has led the Assemblies of God. The Mission acts in an advisory capacity. All offices of the Northern Church may be held by any ordained minister, whether Nigerian or missionary, as elected by the Annual Meeting.

The Assemblies have ninety-three churches in the Central Belt. The figures of membership do not distinguish between the whole Church in Nigeria and its northern, mainly Central Belt, branch. However, since the churches in the North are approximately one-fifth of the total number of churches in Nigeria, I here report one-fifth of the figures given to represent the Central Belt, which considering the strength of the Church in the South is likely somewhat higher than the actuality.

THE ASSEMBLIES OF GOD CHURCH IN THE CENTRAL BELT

	1958	1959	1960	1961	1962
Sunday attendance	5,075	5,507	6,668	7,506	7,777
Baptized in the year	291	443	327	300	416
Communicant members	1,192	1,481	1,746	1,687	1,936

Since there are ninety-three churches in the Central Belt and 1,936 members or less, the average Assemblies of God church would have about twenty members. While there is some extension into tribal, unchurched areas about the towns, the main work has been in the towns in the multi-tribal population. This kind of population creates difficulties relating to membership. Christians from many different denominations come together in the towns seeking church fellowship. In many instances their own church is not there and they desire to become a part of any Christian group that welcomes them. Rev. Harry Pennington, Field Secretary of the Assemblies of God, writes concerning this situation:

> I am inclined to be sympathetic to the idea of several different missions working together in an area and cooperating in commonly accepted evangelical principles. But one discouraging factor is the constant changing of adherents from one mission to another. We are becoming far more strict on acceptance of anyone from another mission without a letter of good recommendation from the originating mission.[9]

Sunday attendance has increased from 5,075 in 1958 to 7,777 in 1962 and membership has increased by 744 members in the same four-year period. Greater church growth may be anticipated as the center of emphasis shifts from the towns to the surrounding tribal villages and will be much greater if the Assemblies encourage the group approach.

C. THE UNITED MISSIONARY CHURCH

The United Missionary Society, which began its work in the Central Belt in 1905 organized an indigenous Church, the United Missionary Church of Africa, in 1950. While registered with the government as one Church, it includes within it three separately organized regions – the Yoruba, the Nupe, and the Hausa. The Yoruba and Nupe regions are composed largely of one tribe each, but the Hausa is a multi-tribal region that uses Hausa, as do the TEKAS churches, for communication across language barriers. The

[9] Pennington, H., Correspondence, April 20, 1963.

tribes in this region are the Dakakari, Dukawa, Kambari, Gungawa, and Bariba. (see Figure III, numbers 48, 49, 50, 51, 53) Each region has its own executive officers, and one trustee as required for government registration of the combined regions of one Church. Each region has its own yearly conference to which the mission sends two delegates as advisors. Also, each region sends two delegates to the annual mission conference as advisors. The three regions and the mission each send five delegates to a joint council once a year.[10]

The Sunday attendance as of 1962 was between 2,500 and 3,000. There were 130 baptisms in this year.

With the three regions of the Church largely autonomous, the reports for membership and Sunday attendance are not available in any complete form. A uniform system of reporting is now being introduced to the churches.

The 1952 and 1962 *World Christian Handbooks* give the following statistics, which indicate a rather static church when compared to others in the Central Belt. This is largely due to the highly Moslemized character of the Nupe and the fact that the winds of change have so lightly blown upon the other pagan tribes along the "upright" of the Niger River.

Communicants		Community – Sunday attendance
1949:	310	1,700
1952:	500	5,000
1957:	550	5,000
1962:	615	5,000
1963:	700+	5,000

D. THE CHURCH OF CHRIST IN THE SUDAN, PLATEAU

The Plateau Church extends over the Central Plateau and down its escarpment to the southeastern lowlands. In 1922 there were five organized churches with a total of 100 communicant members and in 1963 there were thirty-seven churches, but 734 places of worship, and 7,020 communicants served by nineteen ordained pastors and 584 evangelists.

[10] Traub, O. R., Correspondence, 1963.

The British Branch "parent" mission has entered into a period of partnership with the Plateau Church. Its Field Committee, made up of Nigerians and missionaries, is composed of twenty-one members representing the various areas of work: evangelism, education, medical, literature, faith, and farm. In 1963 there were eight Nigerians and thirteen missionaries, but the proportion fluctuates as there are some positions on the committee, such as school supervisor, which may be held by either a Nigerian or a missionary. This committee directs the placement of missionaries, as well as the various aspects of the work listed above.

Most missionaries are full members of the Nigerian Church. The previous ordination of missionaries has been accepted by the Church, but now the Church is calling lay missionaries and ordaining them into the ministry of EKAS, Plateau.[11] This is true of other TEKAS Churches as well.

The internal organization of the Plateau Church begins with the local church congregation. This is usually a village church which has a center where communion is celebrated and is under the care of a Nigerian pastor. The reference to a "center" is significant, for most churches have many places of worship, one of which is chosen as the primary one, or the center. The local churches send delegates to a district council, and each district council sends five delegates to the regional church council, one of whom should be a woman, and one of whom is a missionary. The regional council is the executive committee of the church, and works in close liaison with the field committee of the mission. It sets policy and gives direction to district councils. Missionaries are elected members of these councils. The mission field superintendent is an ex-officio member of the regional council.

There are two regions: Plateau-Bauchi with four District Councils, and Bornu-Sardauna with two.

The Forum District on the Plateau is typical. Forum, the "mother church" of the District, began about 1910. By 1945 Forum had a membership of 548. The awakening following the war is shown in that by 1950 there were three organized churches with a communicant membership of 945, in 1955

[11] Tett, W., Correspondence, February 19, 1963.

there were four with 1,180 members, and in 1960 six with a membership of 2,006 (310 had been baptized in that year). Attendance at the Forum District Sunday morning worship services rose from 3,806 in 1950 to 10,000 in 1960.[12]

The eight organized churches of the Forum District have numerous classes of religious instruction and 117 places of worship. One of the eight, Jarawa, whose members belong to the Jarawa tribe, is an example of how churches grow in the Plateau District. At the very beginning a leper by the name of Nyam, who had relatives in seven different villages, led some of his own tribe to Christ. Two Nigerian evangelists moved into the area and much later, when Moslem pressures had been circumvented, a missionary also settled among them. At the end of the first sixteen years there were only ninety adherents, but in 1962 there were about 200 communicants and about 1,000 adherents. Regulations concerning pre-baptismal examinations vary a great deal depending upon the strictness of the local elders, but high standards are characteristic.[13] At one church those disfellowshiped for beer drinking and adultery desired to build a church of their own and threatened the life of a Nigerian pastor. The Nigerian elders and pastors there met and tightened up the regulations, objecting not only to beer and adultery, but also to smoking.

In another church of the Forum District there were fifteen cases of reversion through beer drinking and adultery during its early years. Since then more severe requirements have been maintained and greater care taken in preparing people for baptism. It is not uncommon that young men want to become Christian in order to get a faithful wife from among the girls of the Christian community, and it is not surprising that the elders of the church take a dim view of such proceedings!

There are two mission stations in the Forum District with three to six missionaries serving as advisors to the church and mission auxiliaries, except the schools, which are now directed by a Nigerian Schools Manager. (Each

[12] Churchman, R. K., Personal interview, March 27, 1962.
[13] *Ibid.*

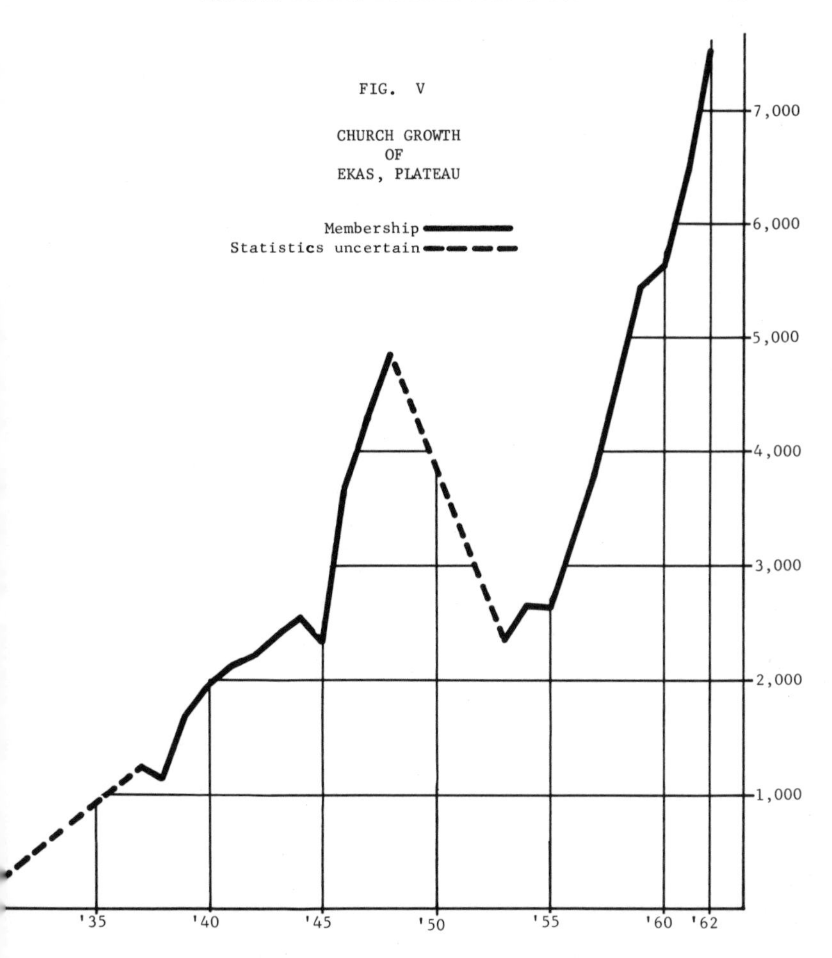

Church District has its own Nigerian Schools Manager. The overall school program at the primary level is coordinated by the school supervisor, Nigerian or missionary.) Since 1945 it has been usual that only ordained missionaries be assigned to work directly with the church organization.

The graph of the growth of the Plateau Church (Figure V) shows that during the first twenty years there was little growth. In 1911 it is recorded that there were eighteen converts "up country," which refers to the area north of the Benue River. By 1926 there were 146 members. Between 1926 and 1938 membership rose from 146 to 1,120. The first dramatic increase took place during World War II. Note how the line of increase rises. Communicant members increased from 1,100 to 2,519 in seven years. After a slight drop between 1944 and 1945 there is a 57% jump from 2,326 to 3,674 in one year! There is a further 30% increase of 1,126 in the next two years, but with the apex of 4,800 reached in 1948 the great surge comes to an end. The records of membership figures also come to an end, until in 1953, after a gap of five years, the membership is given as only 2,382. Here a shift from recording all the Sudan United Mission to that of recording only the Plateau Church took place. The graph of the Plateau Church then rises from 2,382 to 7,449 in 1962 – a 212% increase in nine years. In 1962, 990 new members were received by adult baptism, and in 1963, 1,172.

The potential for even larger church growth is clearly illustrated by the graph of Sunday church attendance (Figure XVI). The attendance soars from 18,549 in 1953 to 40,891 in 1962, a 115% increase in nine years, as compared with a 212% increase in church membership during the same period of time. Increase in Sunday attendance indicates the growth potential. Since the mission and Church are continuing to reach out into new areas such as Gwoza and Limankara, both in the northern Mandara Mountain Range, the attendance should continue to increase and the increased numbers hearing the gospel will increase church membership.

E. THE CHURCH OF CHRIST IN THE SUDAN, MADA HILLS

The growth of this church was very slow in the post-World War I years, and not until after World War II, as late as 1955, did Sunday attendance exceed 6,000 and membership top 700. From 1955 to 1957, as shown by Figure XVI, there was an awakening of interest resulting in an increase in Sunday attendance from 6,500 to 10,035, and a growth in

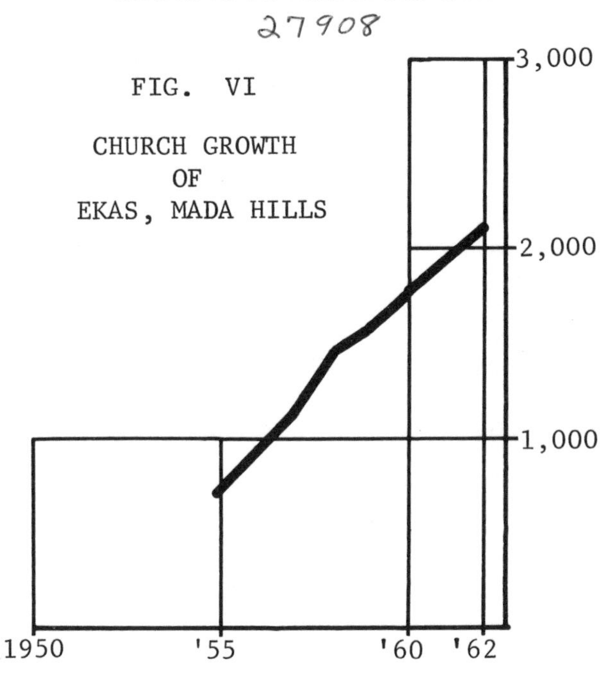

membership from 734 to 1,121. While membership growth (Figure VI) continued slowly during the next year, from 1,121 to 1,467, the church attendance took a discouraging drop to 8,476 and then back up to 9,610 where it leveled off for two years. From 1961 to 1962 the attendance jumped to 11,360 and membership that had been slowly increasing just missed topping 2,100.

In 1962 there were fifteen organized churches and five district councils in the Mada Hills Church. There were only four ordained pastors and nine catechists, but 220 evangelists and 215 places of worship. This large number of evangelists should open the door to more rapid growth in the future.

Preparation for membership is in two stages. The first is that of the catechumen class, in which the applicant prepares to "testify" in a church meeting. When he feels that he is ready to do this, he asks permission of the elders. If they pass him, he then stands before the church and makes a statement of repentance and faith in his own words, and thus enters the second stage, in which there is no special class to attend nor any date set for baptism. But the elders and others of the church simply observe him so that when he later requests baptism they will from their observations of his way of life be able to judge whether he is ready for baptism and church membership. All youth must be literate by the time of baptism. There is a week of special classes preceding baptism as a review of basic Christian faith.[14] All of this results in a long, slow, and uncertain preparation for church membership, which process, from the beginning, has been a primary reason for such slow growth.

[14] Judd, H. W., Personal interview, March, 1962; also correspondence from Adam, A. W., 1962 and 1963.

Chapter V. Church Growth in the Central Benue Area

A. THE CHURCH OF CHRIST IN THE SUDAN, AMONG THE TIV

THE CHURCH AMONG THE TIV HAS THE SINGULAR BLESSING OF being in the center of one great tribe that numbers close to 1,000,000. Its parent mission, the Dutch Reformed Church Mission of South Africa, has withdrawn as of 1961 and turned over all its stations to the Christian Reformed Church Branch of the Sudan United Mission.

Though mission work began among the Tiv at Salatu (Sai) in 1911, it was not until 1957 that the church was organized with 1,500 members. It is difficult to get a clear picture of the growth of the Tiv Church from its beginning for records are not complete. The total communicant membership for 1962 was 4,162; and then, amazingly, membership jumped to 7,352 in 1963![1] This sudden jump is certainly due to catching up on past records, for the new member increase of 1,501 for the same year does not substantiate the rise.

The Church covers a very large area with 1,296 places of worship. Record keeping and reporting by evangelists and pastors on such a large scale is very difficult. There are only twenty organized churches,[2] seventeen Nigerian pastors (ten of whom were ordained in early 1963), fourteen missionary pastors, and twenty-six evangelists. Considering the area and population this is a small pastoral staff. It can be seen that the unpaid but enthusiastic laymen of the church play a very important part in the day-by-day life of the numerous preaching and worshiping places. There

[1] Rubingh, E. R., Correspondence, September 2, 1963, and 1963 TEKAS report.
[2] *Ibid.*

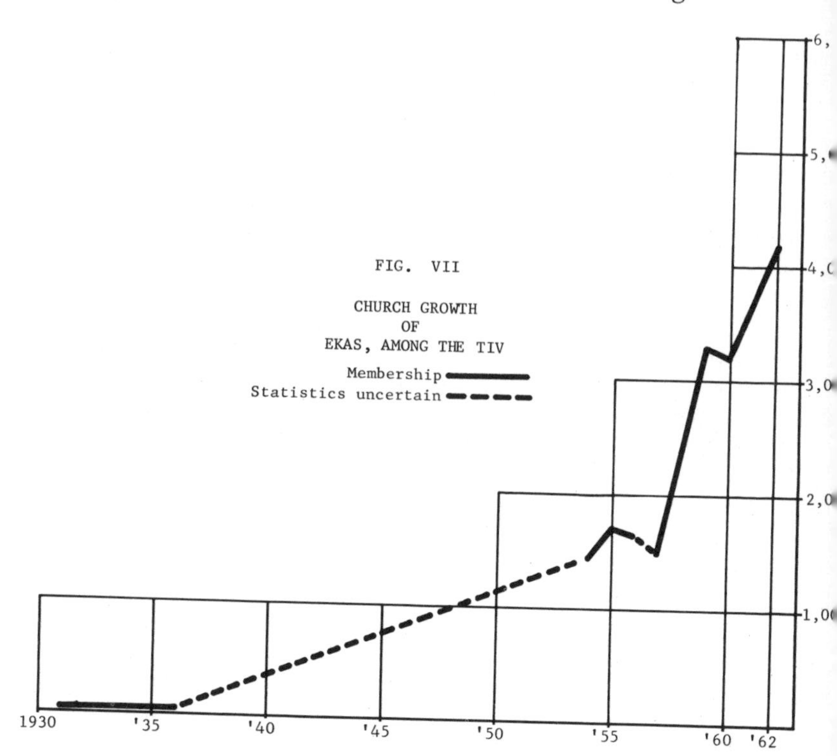

are 665 village classes of religious instruction, which are directed primarily by laymen. In 1958 there were 450 such lay workers teaching in the villages.

On the graph of Sunday attendance (Figure XVI) we note that in 1955 there was a Sunday morning attendance of just under 10,000. Two years later, in 1957, this had increased 140% to over 24,000, and from 1957 to 1962 an additional period of five years, it increased 200% from 24,000 to 73,140 (the conservative 1962 figure of the Tiv Report. The 1963 TEKAS report gives the Tiv Church as having an average Sunday attendance of 105,242!). Yet the increase in membership is not commensurate with the increase in attendance at worship (see Figure VII).

In 1942 there were twenty-five communicant members,[3] and in 1955 there were 1,688.[4] After a slight drop to 1,500 in 1957,[5] (the rounding off of a conservative figure),[6] the rise in membership goes up sharply with a 60% increase in one year to 2,409 in 1958, and in the next four years a 72% increase to 4,162 in 1962, and possibly up to 7,352 in 1963.

The true potential for church growth is shown in the 7,564 inquirers receiving preliminary instruction in 1962 and in the 3,632 catechumens preparing for church membership. Also there are 16,479 enrolled in classes of religious instruction. Most of these are included in the Sunday school enrollment of 30,718, but even so, this practically doubles the number receiving regular and intensive instruction.

With 73,000 attending worship on Sunday, and 30,000 of these in Sunday school in addition to hearing the Word in the preaching service, and over 16,000 of those in Sunday school receiving special instruction through the classes of religious instruction several days of the week, it is not unreasonable to ask the question, Why are there only 4,162 communicant church members?

Rev. Ralph Baker, Christian Reformed Church missionary at Zaki Biam, raises this question in a different context: "Why is there such a low church membership considering the large number of people contacted through the mission auxiliaries?" He gives the following figures.[7]

The Auxiliary Service	The number reached with the gospel and therefore "potential church members"
Medicine (General)	210,000
Medicine (Leprosy)	10,000
Education (Primary Schools)	9,000
Education (Village Bible Classes)	18,000
Direct Evangelism	200,000
	437,000

3 Christian Reformed Church publication, "The Coming of the Gospel to Tivland."

4 Records at Mkar, Christian Reformed Headquarters of EKAS, Tiv.

5 *Ibid.*

6 Rubingh, E. R., Correspondence, September 2, 1963.

7 Baker, R., "The Evangelization of the Tiv Tribe," p. 5.

Mr. Baker writes, "After subtracting 100,000 for overlapping, there still must be some 300,000 adults now living who in varying degree have had some contact with the gospel through the hospital, dispensaries, schools and village preaching."[8]

The Tiv situation warrants a study of the following chart:

The Tiv Church 1962

Organized Churches	Members	Sunday Attend.	Inquirers	Catechumens	Adult[9] Bapt.	Infant Bapt.
1. Mkar	846	7,715	724	504	229	26
2. Sevav	420	6,500	620	320	114	83
3. Adikpo	408	12,104	731	340	84	80
4. Zaki Biam	350	7,020	417	344	100	47
5. Kunav	316	6,877	417	259	63	39
6. Harga	247	3,500	431	350	58	52
7. Turan	200	4,000	300	250	60	30
8. Apir-Makurdi	198	3,120	1,348	264	80	15
9. B.L.S.	153	1,416	270	205	34	16
10. Ikaave	151	4,757	221	89	25	17
11. Aku	194	3,255	356	166	46	22
12. Abwa	164	4,384	785	157	38	33
13. Sai	156	1,023	387	153		18
14. N'aa	138	3,107	308	130	18	13
15. Shangev	123	2,200	129	97	32	3
16. Wannune	98	2,162	120	104	25	10
17. Gboko						
Totals	4,162[10]	73,140	7,564	3,632	1,006	304

The Mkar Church, with 846 members, is the largest of the seventeen organized churches of Tiv. It has 724 inquirers and 504 catechumens. This church is centered at the mission station which includes schools, hospital, orphanage, and mission-headquarters offices. However, it is distributed over

[8] *Ibid.*

[9] "Adult" is defined as "those who have arrived at the age of discretion" and in Tivland this would mean those who can read and write and have attended catechism classes for a long time. "Adult" baptisms may begin as early as fourteen years, but the average age is about 23. Unfortunately, very few over the age of 30 are being baptized. Rubingh, E. R., Correspondence, Aug. 24, 1963.

[10] 7,352 as of the 1963 TEKAS report.

an area that includes seventy-six places of worship with a total Sunday morning attendance of 7,715. The Adikpo church with 408 members has a Sunday attendance of 12,104, distributed among 140 places of worship.

It is significant that the highest number of inquirers (1,348) is in Apir-Makurdi, which is more urban than any of the other churches, and has only 3,120 Sunday attendance. The second highest number of inquirers (785) is found in the Abwa Church with 4,384 Sunday attendance. The third highest number of inquirers (731) is found in the Adikpo Church, which has the highest Sunday attendance of 12,104.

Thus there seems to be no correlation between Sunday attendance and number of inquirers. Apparently there are other factors in addition to the greater number of people in church services in one area than in another. The availability of schools to the youth may be an important factor, for in the Tiv area children of the schools are more likely able to meet the high membership requirements of the church. The buildup of large numbers of inquirers, as well as of catechumens, is abetted, or hindered also, by the methods employed by the church congregations in bringing these "believers" into full membership in the Church. The general policy of the Tiv Church has been one of long preparation for baptism, including one or two years of study as an inquirer and at least two years of study as a catechumen, followed by two weeks of special instruction preceding baptism. Not until 1962 was some progress made toward reducing the length of this preparatory period. Such long periods of required instruction discourage the increase of catechumens. "The long travail in catechism is one important reason why more of the attenders-at-church are not members."[11]

From its formal organization in 1957 the Tiv Church has administered its own affairs. If the Church chooses, missionary ministers may be voting members and hold office. In 1960 the mission invited representatives of the churches to sit as voting members on the mission councils, which deal with evangelism, education, and medical aspects of the

[11] Rubingh, E. R., Correspondence, September 2, 1963.

mission's work; the primary governing body is the church-mission Nigerian General Conference.

It is planned that the schools now under the proprietorship of the mission will be slowly turned over to the proprietorship of the Church. The orphanage at Mkar is scheduled to be completely in the hands of the Church by 1965. It is anticipated also that the hospitals will be run by their own advisory boards with executive powers delegated to them as soon as Nigerian Christians become qualified for responsibilities that demand technical knowledge.[12]

B. THE CHURCH OF CHRIST IN THE SUDAN, BENUE

The Benue Church has a close relationship to the Tiv Church, not only because they are neighbors, but also because the Dutch Reformed Church Mission, which has been the parent mission of the Tiv Church, has now turned its work over to the Christian Reformed Church Mission, the parent mission of the Benue Church. Thus one mission is now advisor to two very different Churches. While the Katsina Ala River (see Figure I) might seem a natural division between these two Churches, such is not the case, for the Tiv tribe reaches across and beyond Sai, which was the first mission station of the Dutch Reformed Church Mission among the Tiv. Sai, Zaki Biam, Sevav, and Harga, all east of the river, are part of the Tiv Church. However, the Benue Church, being virile and active, and with a much shorter period of preparation for church membership, is beginning to win some of the Tiv people. Since the Kuteb and the Jukun and many smaller tribes are represented in the Benue Church, it is in direct contrast to the one-tribe Church of the Tiv. There is strong outreach in every direction and a willingness to accept the Tiv as just one more tribal group. In 1962 a certain Tiv village on the east side of the Katsina Ala near Lupwe was turning out en masse for Christian worship and desired to be part of the Benue Church. It may be natural for the Tiv Church to feel that

[12] *Ibid.*

Tiv people should be members of the Tiv Church, but Tiv and Benue Church leaders are not always able to agree upon a mutually satisfying solution to this interchurch and inter-tribe situation.

Because there are so many tribes represented in the Benue Church, the Hausa language is used to a very large extent. Jukun is the most influential language, but Kuteb is also widespread. Farther south and east there is a great complex of languages.

There are three districts in the Benue Church: Takum (Lupwe), Wukari, and Baissa. Together these districts have 164 centers of worship, 12,683 attending services every Sunday, and 7,109 communicant members, according to the 1963 TEKAS report. In the Benue area the difference between Sunday attendance and membership is not nearly as great as in the Tiv Church. The Tiv proportion for 1963 is 7,000 members to 105,000 Sunday worshipers. The Benue proportion is 7,000 members to 12,000 Sunday worshipers. This difference in proportion may in part be due to the difference in the method of bringing "believers" into full membership. The Benue Church no longer has a two-stage preparation for church membership. There is no inquirers' class and no preparatory public "witnessing" in a church service. When an interested person desires to become a Christian he immediately enters the catechism class. There is no minimum length of time set for preparation before baptism, but it would hardly ever be less than six months. The catechism class is taught by an ordained pastor. A week before baptism the applicant is examined; if he passes, he enters a full week of special review, which culminates in baptism.

Baissa (see Figure II) is of special interest, for it is a multi-tribal district with a comparatively small population of about 20,000. The graph of membership and Sunday attendance of the Baissa District (Figure IX) shows a very noticeable in-gathering during the years 1957 to 1962, a 431% increase in membership.

The gospel did not reach Baissa until about 1940 when an early start was made by asking the chiefs to send young men to the Bible school at Lupwe. There they became some of the first converts in the Baissa area. At first a missionary,

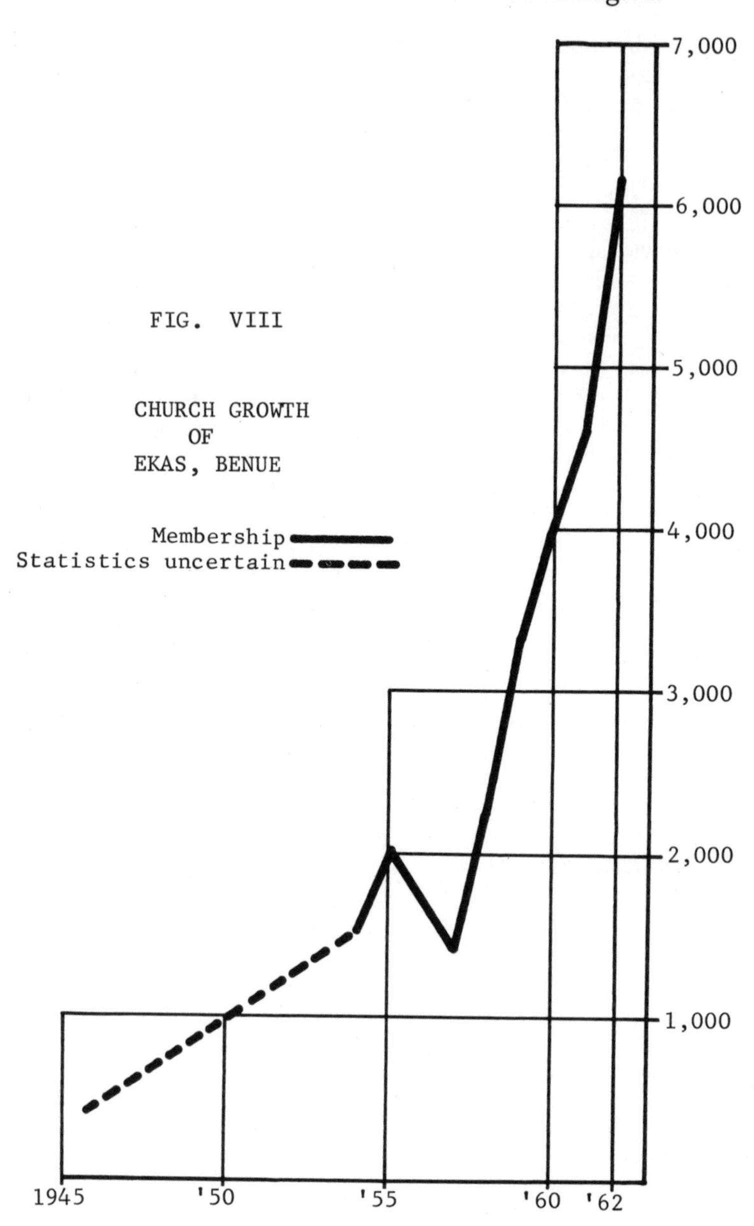

FIG. VIII
CHURCH GROWTH
OF
EKAS, BENUE
Membership
Statistics uncertain
7,000
6,000
5,000
4,000
3,000
2,000
1,000
1945
'50
'55
'60
'62

in company with a Nigerian pastor, made preaching tours. The Takum Church followed up the move to get young men from Baissa by sending in three evangelists between 1943 and 1945. They traveled throughout the area preaching the gospel intensively. About 1949 the Baissa mission station was opened by the first resident missionary. A year later medical work was begun by a Nigerian dispenser. In 1952 the Bible school was opened and from this point the graph of membership turns upward.

Rev. Bob Recker, missionary at Baissa since 1950, writes, "Most of the energetic young people of the district turned to Christianity, and many of them turned to it in a desire for literacy and progress." Primary schools were opened and attended by 100 pupils by 1954, and 556 by 1962. However, many of the older youth learned to read without any formal classroom instruction, simply by association with the evangelists and other youth who had learned to read – each one teaching another as the opportunity presented itself. Mr. Recker continues:

> The spread of the Gospel among the young people has been contagious, but the fact that we have not reached the older people is one of our sad burdens. Perhaps, in the past, we should have held up on accepting the young people; until after we had had a longer conversation with the adults – hoping that after their conversion, the young people would follow. Even now it would be well to arrange meetings with the older people, with no youth present – giving some dignity to the meeting and gaining opportunity to more fully explain the Gospel to the older generation.[13]

When this was written in March, 1962, a significant move into the Church was taking place. The Church grew by the addition of about 500 members in 1962, which, considering the comparative smallness of the Baissa District, is very notable. The increase seems due to saturating all communities with the gospel message. There are seventy-two places of worship in the Baissa District as compared to thirty-seven in the Takum District and forty-six in the Wukari

[13] Recker, R., Personal interview, March, 1962.

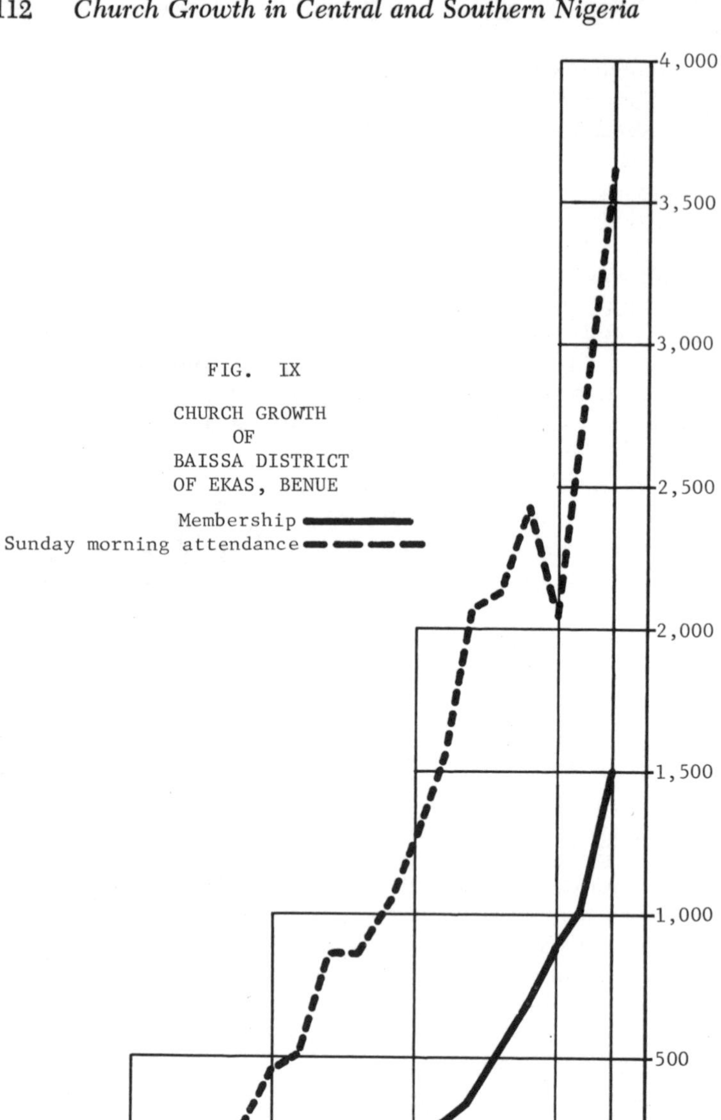
FIG. IX
CHURCH GROWTH
OF
BAISSA DISTRICT
OF EKAS, BENUE
Membership
Sunday morning attendance
4,000
3,500
3,000
2,500
2,000
1,500
1,000
500
1945
'50
'55
'60
'62

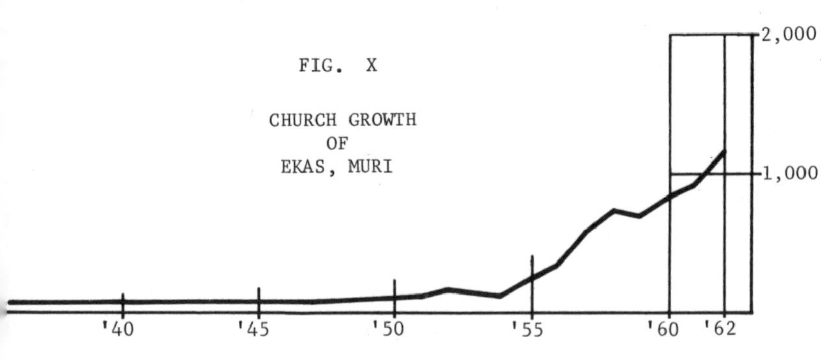

District. In 1962, 523 new members were added to the Takum District and 234 in the Wukari District.

C. THE CHURCH OF CHRIST IN THE SUDAN, MURI

The Muri Church (see Figure I) lies on both sides of the Benue River, northeast of the Benue Church and west of the Lutheran Church.

The graph (Figure X) reveals very little growth before 1950, a slow but steady growth from 1954, and a great fluctuation in attendance at Sunday worship services (Figure XVI). This fluctuation between 1952 and 1956, the great rise preceding 1960, and the drop of 1,700 in attendance during 1960 are all related to the revival of the Bori, devil-possession cult, the uphill pull in competition with Islam, and the political ferment of the area. The drop in attendance came during the months preceding Nigerian independence when there was great political activity. Many of the evangelists became lecturers for the political parties, received more salary than the Church had been paying them, and lost interest in church work. The revival of the Bori cult, including self-torture and complete license, was encouraged by the political situation, and youths feeling despair in not getting ahead in the new age, found it an outlet for their frustrations.

Between 1957 and 1958, when interest in the Church was sharply on the increase, the classes of religious instruction grew in numbers from forty-seven to sixty-one, and those attending increased from 651 to 802. But the drop in interest and church attendance was preceded by a drop in attendance at the junior primary schools from almost 950 in 1959, which was the record enrollment, to just over 700 in 1960, and under 700 in 1961. But 1961 and 1962 show an encouraging increase in church attendance, in enrollment in classes of religious instruction, in church membership, and enrollment in the junior primary schools – almost 900 in 1962. The number of evangelists in 1959 was eighty-nine, but this number dropped to less than seventy in 1960. By 1962 the evangelist force had begun a comeback and had increased to eighty-three, and then to ninety-three in 1963.

The Muri Church is governed by its regional church council, as of 1950. It is composed of representatives from each organized church, the representatives being the pastor and two elected members, and missionaries in an advisory position with voting privileges. There are four standing committees elected by this body, which, along with local church councils, refer business to the regional council.[14]

The mission council is separate and deals only with mission matters, all church matters being referred to the regional church council. Five standing committees (evangelism, education, medical, literature, and community development) make up both the church and mission councils. These committees of Church and mission have the option to meet jointly.[15]

As of 1962 there is a joint council, which handles business from the above-mentioned committees. The mission council and the regional church council review all business of the joint council, and action by both is required before items of concern to each are finalized. A proposal rejected by either body must be reconsidered by the opposite body together with suggestions for its alteration. When mutual agreement is reached the proposal is referred to the proper agency.[16]

[14] Gilliland, D. S., Correspondence, February 18, 1963.
[15] *Ibid.*
[16] Evangelical United Brethren publication, "A Paper on Church-Mission Relationships in the Sudan Mission," May, 1961.

There is a cumbersomeness about this organization of two equal councils with co-chairmen and a third joint council whose decisions need to be reviewed by each of the other two. Missionaries and Nigerian church leaders may too often find themselves hindered by the "machinery." The term "opposite body" in the organizational statement could be prophetic of each council being handicapped, rather than inspired, by the other. However, this is another of the several differing approaches being made in the Central Belt to preserve the values of missionary experience and resources and at the same time bring the indigenous church leadership to the fore.

Chapter VI. Church Growth in the East

A. THE CHURCH OF CHRIST IN THE SUDAN, LUTHERAN

THE LUTHERAN CHURCH COVERS AN EXTENSIVE AREA IN EAST-central Adamawa Province and central Sardauna Province. This area (see Figure I) is bisected by the Benue River into which the Gongola River flows from the north.

The graph of Sunday attendance, from 1953 to 1962 (Figure XVI) shows a steady rise from 10,000 to 37,000, with only two slight setbacks. In 1957 there was a Sunday attendance of 19,000. The following five years saw a 95% increase that brought the attendance figure to 37,452 in 1962.[1] Likewise there has been a rapid increase in church membership (Figure XI). In 1954 there was a communicant membership of 4,082, and the seven years following saw a 142% rise to 9,782 as of 1961. Then in the period of one year, 1961 to 1962, the communicant membership rose 55.8% to 15,251, an increase of 5,469. The following year, 1963, a further increase of 6,248 was indicated![2] The field secretary of the Lutheran Mission reports that those baptized in infancy are not confirmed until they reach the age of 25 years, and only those confirmed are counted as members.[3] A very significant movement to Christ is occurring in the Lutheran area. The 41,819 Sunday attendance points to the fact that the tribes of the Lutheran area are exhibiting a responsiveness equal to that of the Plateau and exceeded substantially only by the Tiv.

In 1961 the Church was composed of the Numan and

[1] 41,819 as of 1963 TEKAS report.

[2] The 1963 TEKAS report gives an increase of 10,000 in this one year, but the increase in "new members" of only 3,000 does not substantiate this tremendous rise.

[3] Hojvig, E., Correspondence, Nov., 1963.

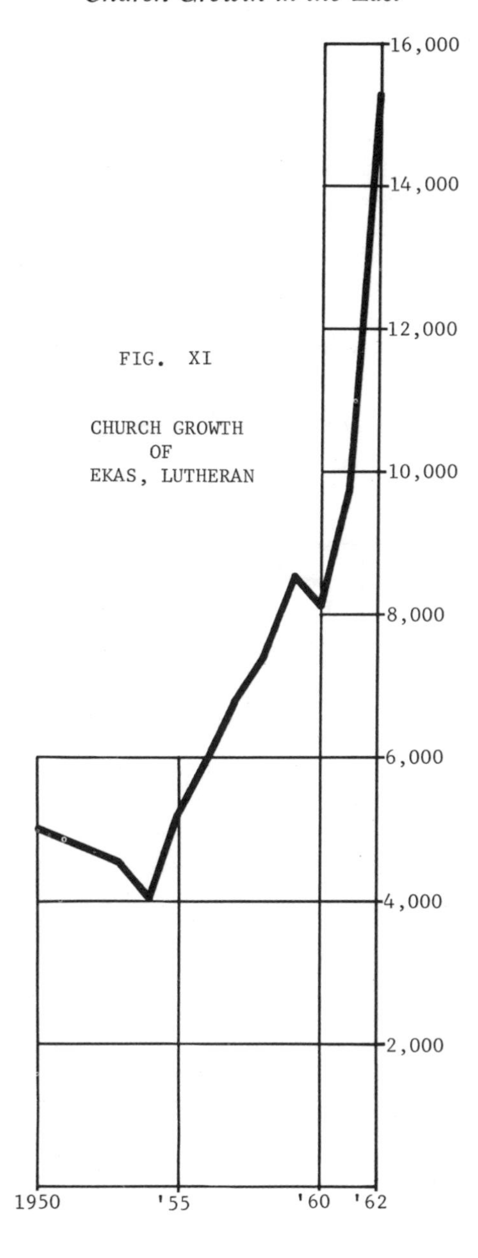

FIG. XI

CHURCH GROWTH
OF
EKAS, LUTHERAN

Pella divisions and three more divisions are now contemplated. Each division contains several districts. A local church is planted by a village evangelist. When there are eighteen or more baptized adult members a church may be organized by choosing elders from among charter members. They then send delegates to the quarterly meetings of the District Councils.

With more than 20,000 members as of 1963, the Lutheran Church had only 20 organized churches, but 528 places of worship. Thus it seems that the 528 evangelists scattered among the people and the 36 ordained pastors (an increase of 26 in five years preceding 1962) should do more toward the development of local leaders so that more organized churches can be formed. It may be that many of the worshiping groups are made up of schoolboys or ex-schoolboys and do not have the maturity for church leadership, but schoolteachers serving in their home communities should be urged to take a greater part in church leadership.

In Chapter VII our attention will be further directed to the Lutheran Church of the Languda area, fifty miles north of Numan.

B. THE CHURCH OF CHRIST IN THE SUDAN, EASTERN

The Eastern Church of the Hawal-Yedseram River area (see Figure I) is multi-tribal and multi-lingual, and until very recently all missionaries were assigned to learn either Bura or Margi as their first, and usually only, language. Bura was used in the District Council. However, within the last five years, while Bura, Margi, and Higi are spoken in the various churches, Hausa is used in District Meeting, and translated into English because many of the missionaries do not understand Hausa. In a few cases Nigerians speak in English, which is then translated into Hausa.

It is mission policy that all missionaries be members of the Nigerian Church and make their contribution to evangelism, not as professional missionaries but as church members. Nigerians have not come into a mission church, but rather, missionaries have come into the Nigerian Church. The

Church may call a layman (Nigerian or missionary) to the ministry and ordain him in any of its local churches. Every position in the Church held by a missionary is held because of church status, not missionary status, except the position of Assistant Chairman, which has been held by a missionary. In March of 1964 the position of Secretary was permanently taken by a Nigerian.

There are three areas (Western, Central, and Eastern) of EKAS, Eastern, but there is only one District, which is made up of delegates elected by each organized church congregation, plus all ordained ministers and the Directors of Youth and Women's organizations.

Becoming a Christian

Every Church should make clear the steps to be taken to become a Christian. The Eastern Church has an easily understood two-stage preparation for membership. During the first years of the mission at Garkida a medical missionary, Dr. Homer Burke, introduced the following covenant and baptism procedure, which is still in use.

1. Individuals are attracted to Christ through the witness of evangelists or some Christian in the community.
2. They enter a class taught by the village evangelist or by anyone the church may ask to do the teaching.
3. This class meets once or more times a week and studies the "covenant," which reads as follows:

> I believe that Jesus is the Son of God and that he showed us the true way to seek God.
> I follow him, and make him Lord of all.
> I am a sinner. I repent before God and the people. What I have spoiled I will make right.
> I believe that Jesus died for my sins.
> I believe that he alone is able to save me from sin, and give me strength that I may live a good life.
> I leave all fetish worship, and worship the one God alone. I desire to make my life consistent with the teaching of the New Testament.
> I desire to work with all my strength so that the things of God may prosper.

> I will always attend the place of learning so that I may increase my knowledge about being a follower of Jesus, so that I may receive baptism and thus enter the Church.[4]

While this covenant must be learned by heart, exceptions are made for the old or mentally retarded.

4. After several months of instruction, those who feel prepared are interviewed by the church committee. They must be able to recite the covenant and answer a few simple questions about the Christian life. Their engagement or marital condition is inquired into and if unsatisfactory will prevent them from receiving the covenant.

5. Those who pass the interview stand before the church congregation in a service of confession of faith and are asked questions similar to the following:

> Is it your desire to live in pleasantness with your neighbor?
> Do you leave those things which degrade a person such as immorality, beer drinking, and smoking?
> Do you understand and accept that the Christian way is one man and one wife?

After an affirmative answer to these questions, the group recites the covenant and kneels for a consecration prayer. These, then, are "people of the covenant," or catechumens.

6. The people of the covenant prepare for baptism under a person appointed to teach a catechism class, which meets once or twice a week for the next six months. Until a few years ago a person had to be a covenanter for at least two years before being baptized. The district council has changed this to a minimum of six months.

This baptismal class studies a shorter catechism. It is not required that this be learned by heart, but the learner must be able to give answers in his own words.

7. When the covenanters are ready for baptism, the church committee asks them questions concerning the Christian

[4] Translation into English from page 141 of "Kakadur Na aga Sur Gunggur Sili anu Iju," a song and worship book of EKAS, Eastern, in the Margi Language, Church of the Brethren Mission, Lassa, Nigeria, 1956.

way and their moral and marital situation. Those who pass are baptized.

On the edge of the water they are asked three questions:

> Do you believe that Jesus Christ is the Saviour of the world and your Saviour?
> Do you leave Satan and all his evil ways?
> Do you covenant with God to follow Jesus until death?

Baptism by trine immersion follows with the laying on of hands and prayer for the infilling of the Holy Spirit.

THE GROWTH OF THE CHURCH[5]

The graph of the Eastern Church membership (Figure XII) shows slow growth during the first thirty years. In 1927 there were twenty-four Christians at Garkida. The membership did not exceed 100 until 1932. By 1937 it had risen to 544, but by that time the shortage of missionary staff during the war years was beginning to take effect and a plateau under 600 was maintained until 1945. The post-war awakening is noted in the dramatic turning-up of the lines of growth for both membership and Sunday attendance (Figure XVI). Until 1945 there were four substantial church groups (Garkida, Virgwi Leprosarium, Marama, and Lassa) with a total membership of 623. Three of these were strategically located – Marama being on the Biu Plateau in the midst of the Bura tribe, Garkida on the eastern edge of the Bura with Whona and Kilba tribes very close to the south, and Lassa in the heart of the Margi tribe and facing Higiland across the valley. Virgwi with almost 1,400 leprosy patients quickly grew into the largest church until in the 1950s when its membership was scattered as the result of changed methods of leprosy treatment. Throughout the history of the Leprosarium Church its witness was continually enhanced by those patients who, after several years under treatment, returned as Christians to their home villages.

During the years of the awakening, 1945-1955, six new churches were organized, including Chibuk and Kaurwatakari,

[5] Records at Garkida, Church of the Brethren Headquarters of EKAS, Eastern.

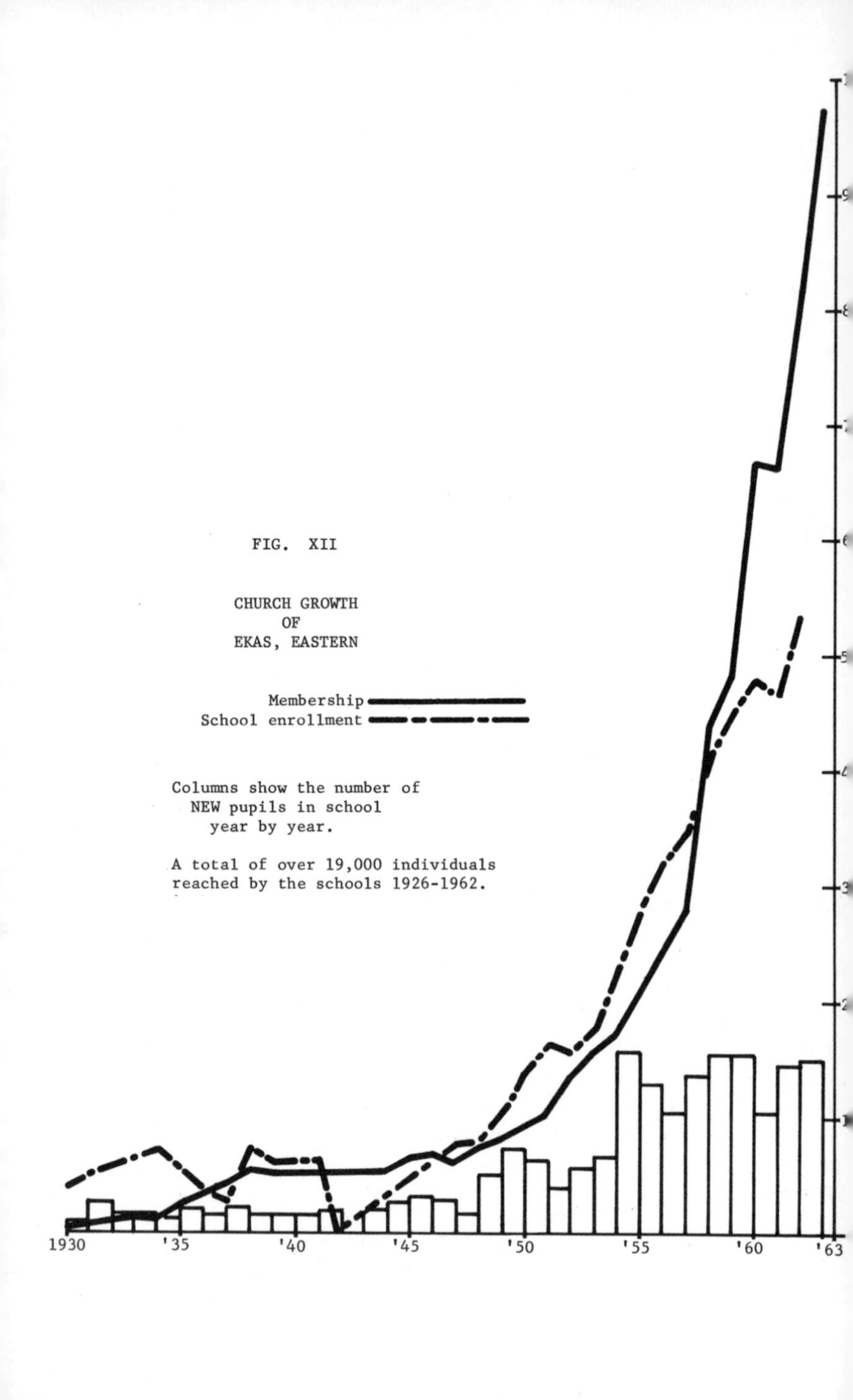
FIG. XII
CHURCH GROWTH
OF
EKAS, EASTERN
Membership
School enrollment
Columns show the number of
NEW pupils in school
year by year.
A total of over 19,000 individuals
reached by the schools 1926-1962.
1930
'35
'40
'45
'50
'55
'60
'63

both on the edge of the great Kanuri tribe, and Gashala, a church of Kilba people on the southern edge of the Margi tribe.

The years 1956 to 1963 were characterized by church multiplication. In this period twenty churches were organized. The awakening was dramatized between 1950 and 1960 by a 440% increase in Sunday attendance and a 635% increase in church membership. In 1958 four new churches were organized. This was the highest number for any one year. Two of these were in the Higi tribe, one in the South Margi tribe, and one in the multi-tribal town of Mubi. In this year the adult baptisms were 1,043, and an additional 1,246 became Covenant Christians. In 1963 there were 2,034 baptisms, bringing the communicant membership to 9,730. The following chart shows the increase from 1950 to 1963:

	1950	'51	'52	'53	'54	'55	'56	'57	'58	'59	'60	'61	'62	'63
New Covenants:			442	564		649		664	1246	1422	2396	1575	2251	2374
Baptisms:	103	187	314	319	349	347	443	518	1043	1305	1712	1231	1569	2034
Membership:	909	1009	1349	1564	1715	2059	2440	2810	4371	4818	6684	6649	8144	9730

Note the relationship between the "new covenant" figures for one year and the figures for those baptized the next. While each person receiving the covenant is usually required to be a Covenant Christian for at least six months, in actual practice few receive baptism under a year. The covenanters in any one year should be ready for baptism by the next. In 1961 there were 1,575 covenants, and in 1962, 1,569 baptisms. In 1958, 1959, and 1960 there were more baptisms than covenants the previous years, and this is due to a goodly number of the covenant people of each of those years receiving baptism before the year was out, as well as the baptism of some who received the covenant in the early 1950s. The discrepancy between numbers baptized and increase in membership between 1950 and 1963 is due to (1) the exceedingly mobile nature of the youth who go off to larger towns, (2) the disciplinary action of the Church, and (3) the difficulty of keeping church records complete in a society where individuals often change their names and white ants eat up membership card files! From 1950 to 1963 the figures indicate that 11,439 persons were baptized; this should have brought the membership to 12,243 in 1963. With 1963 membership being only 9,730, it is evident that somewhere along the way 2,513 members have been lost in about thirteen years. 396 out of 1,200 had been lost in the twenty-seven years previous to 1950.

The two-stage preparation for church membership has proven an inspiring and satisfying procedure because there are definite goals along the way that can be attained in a reasonable length of time and require a learning schedule not too difficult for beginners. Literacy, though encouraged, is not a requirement, and adults find that the emphasis upon dedication to Christ and the primary doctrines of the Church are not beyond their reach. In comparison, the Tiv Church preparation for membership seems long and demanding while the indefiniteness of the Benue Church plan with no time requirements and no public time of decision other than at baptism (after the catechism class) seems to take away something of the satisfaction of progression that is experienced in the Eastern Church. Outward form is very important in symbolizing the truths of the spirit and few people appreciate this more than those of West Africa. Nigerian church leaders must consider seriously the form of this very important step out of pagan life, for admittedly the plans now used are adaptations of European forms worked out by missionaries on the field, and they may not be a sufficient bridge from the old to the new. Not enough progress is being made in winning whole families and clans. Nigerian insight and leadership are essential to this broader approach.

PART III: THE DYNAMICS OF CHURCH GROWTH

Chapter VII. Dynamic Movements to Christ

THE DYNAMICS OF CHURCH GROWTH HAVE TO DO WITH THE forces that produce and assist church growth. We ask, "Why do churches multiply in the Central Belt? What factors and forces encourage increase? Lack of what influences retard it?"

The supreme dynamic is the power of God to salvation. It is "Christ in you the hope of glory." It is the "power with us . . . able to do far more abundantly than all we ask or think." The power of prayer cannot be emphasized too greatly and the infilling of the Holy Spirit enables a higher degree of Christian living than is possible to natural man. All this is so well known and so greatly emphasized that it is unnecessary here to do more than call attention to the primacy of the spiritual forces.

The consecration, labor, and sacrifice of African and missionary members of the Church are also important parts of the dynamics of church growth. The histories of both missions and Churches reveal the significant part these have played. They are well recognized.

Some significant forces that make for church growth, however, have not been recognized. These are the cultural and social forces that determine how societies change, how innovations occur, how churches grow, and how peoples become Christian. We shall present these in this chapter.

In the Central Belt up till the present time the chief mode of church growth has been that individual converts here and there (mostly boys and young men in Christian schools) have accepted Jesus Christ as Lord and Saviour and been instructed, tested, and baptized. Frequently they have acted with the approval of their elders, but more often they have broken with their compound, clan, or tribe to become Christian. As long as the growth of the Church occurs by one-by-one accessions that entail opposition to the majority of the adults in the community, church growth is certain to be slow and hesitant. The churches may well start in this fashion but they should soon break out of the one-by-one pattern into something more like the normal way in which societies change and churches multiply. If they do not there is grave danger that the Church will become an elite, educated society separated from the mass of backward, illiterate villagers.

Somewhere along the way *movements to Christ* should take place that bring to the Christian faith multitudes of men and women. The New Testament pattern is clear. The early chapters of Acts repeatedly tell about multitudes becoming Christian. Whole households, like that of Cornelius, frequently were added to the Lord. Whole villages like Lydda and Sharon full of illiterates became Christian on a single day.

A. INTIMATIONS OF MOVEMENTS TO CHRIST

As I have studied the growth of the churches in the Central Belt I have been agreeably surprised by numerous intimations of such movements. Though the need for such has not commonly been recognized by church leaders, and though the pattern of such movements is very different from that by which most missionaries in their homelands and most early Christians in the Central Belt have come to Christ, nevertheless movements to Christ have been occurring in this vast land. The tribesmen of the Central Belt want to become Christian in group fashion, of this there is much evidence. Small beginnings of people movements to Christ have often taken place. Not being welcomed nor skillfully conserved, and running into some difficult problems, most of them have failed to become powerful revivals sweeping whole communities into genuine Christian faith.

1. In the Plateau Church

For example, Pastor Dusu of the Plateau Church told me the following story.

> I first became interested in Christ by hearing Dan Sofo read the Bible to himself. It was amazing to me to hear him read about John the Baptist – a man far off in another country – as though he knew him. At Jal the first Christians were the evangelist and his family and another family and several young men. The people of the village wanted to force these Christians to do fetish worship. When four of the young men refused, they were punished. There were many difficulties in those days, persecution and sleeping sickness also. However, two years later the Christian faith grew stronger. Even the chief sent his son to become a Christian. In the evening when we returned from the fields, the chief would call us together for prayer. One Sunday he came to church with all his thirty-five wives, the elders of the village, and most of the people. Thus they came for three Sundays. But the evangelist was preaching things which did not harmonize with their usual way of life. This discouraged them and they stopped coming. The chief's wives, however, wanted to return to Christian worship. They were so anxious to receive a blessing from Christianity that the chief had to beat them to keep them from attending.
>
> A Native Authority policeman in the village had four wives. One wanted to leave him and marry a Christian so that she could become a Christian. As a result her husband beat her so severely that she bled from her ears. The Vom Mission doctor sent her to the government officer who gave her freedom to marry whomever she desired. This displeased the elders of the village. Nevertheless, the Christian faith grew stronger and thirty-eight people repented. Shortly after this, twenty-five more repented. In fact, the church leaders had to exercise great care for there were too many.
>
> In these days preaching continued all night. The number repenting moved the chief to repent as well. He wanted to return to the church with all of his wives. The church leaders and missionaries had a big meeting. I, myself, was present. In 1947 this group of believers at Jal was organized into an indigenous church. There was some backsliding then, partially due to organizing. Even so, great numbers continued to repent until it seemed that everyone was a Christian. In

> 1947 there were thirty-two baptized members: sixteen men and sixteen women. Then, only a married man was permitted to be baptized. Now, in 1962, there is a baptized membership of 198. But the total population of this Jal village area is about 1,000 tax-paying men or approximately 4,000 people of all ages.

Several things are evident in this report by Pastor Dusu. Most striking of all is his concern that "too many" were repenting. On the other hand, while it "seemed that everyone was a Christian" only one-twentieth of the population had become members of the Church by 1962, fifteen years after the original moving of the Spirit! Had something gone wrong? Perhaps the church leadership had not been expectant enough, or was not prepared to handle anything but one-by-one decisions. The group response seemed to surprise them. Perhaps little attempt was made to replace the fetishism of the year's cycle – planting, first fruits, and harvest festivals – with Christian rites. Church membership requirements were linked to much memory work and literacy. In the early years only married men were permitted baptism. All told, it seems as though a great opportunity was lost here. Whole villages and clans might have turned to Christ if greater encouragement and opportunity had been given. Had sound group conversions, such as are described by G. F. Vicedom in *Church and People in New Guinea* (Lutterworth Press, London), been customary in the Central Belt, a very large part of the 4,000 might well have become Christian.

Church leaders from Jal, describing how compounds, clan segments, and social wholes had repented of their sins, changed living patterns, built churches, and become Christian without social dislocation, would then have become available to spread the good news of a more Nigerian way of becoming Christian. Dr. A. R. Tippett of the Institute of Church Growth says that in the South Pacific new islands evangelized by missionaries took about 15 years to decide for Christ, but when evangelized by men from a recently converted island, the average time span between first hearing the message and baptism was usually only four years. The missionary preached the same gospel as the island men, but he preached it in an English setting. The island men, telling how "our tribe led by our elders became genuinely Christian, with improvement to our crops and benefits to our society," were far more persuasive than the missionary.

The Kwalla tribe of 18,000 heard the gospel in 1946 when a mission station was built in their midst. The first six baptisms were in 1953. In 1955 there were twenty-four baptized church members. In 1960 there were 123 baptized and 1,000 "believers."[1] Considering the large number of "believers," there is a good possibility for church growth in the Kwalla tribe. This area from the beginning of this century has been a Roman Catholic stronghold. However, the opposition from the Catholics has not been a deterrent to growth. In fact, much of the strength of the Kwalla Church has been attributed to Catholic opposition. But the strength of such a group must not be portrayed as that of a fortress simply holding its own within its walls. Its strength must be demonstrated in its successful outreach into the surrounding villages.

2. In the Church Among the Tiv

Several missionaries and Nigerian pastors at the Christian Reformed Church Mission station of Sevav reported the following: the Tiv have a great fear of Mbatsav, the being which "kills and brings to life – only to hide the person in the forest where finally all is eaten – even the bones and the skin – nothing is left." This fear has caused a great desire for life. As a result, through the years there have been movements in search of life. The latest has been "Inyam Ibuyom." One of the pastors said, "Just to think of seeing mother again! This is a great attraction to Christianity." These movements searching for eternal life have set the stage for movements toward Christ.

In 1932 and 1933, as a result of the many village Christian schools, there was a great response to Christianity in the bush country, away from the mission stations. Quite a few of the older Tiv pastors came to Christ in this movement of the Spirit.

[1] Crow, A. W., Personal interview, March, 1962.

The prominence and burden of witchcraft have prepared the Tiv for breaking out in search of true life. This reminds us of how the burden of the taboo system in Polynesia had become so heavy that whole tribes were throwing off these burdensome regulations just previous to the arrival of the Christian missionary. With 105,000 attending Sunday services, the Tiv search is gaining momentum. The Church, however, through its extremely stiff membership requirements, far from assisting the break out, is arresting it. Unless the ripe grain is reaped soon, it may be lost.

3. In the Benue Church

One man in the Pastor's class at Baissa reported, "The whole village of Nyita turned to Christ. I saw my pagan father become a Christian. So I followed him into the Christian way." Also Kwambai, a village of the Takum Church area, turned to Christ – first the chief, followed by the elders, then the youth as well. After this, some said they would make a new place for pagan rites, but only two village people showed up to help the old men with the work of building this shrine. When completed, the mat surrounding it was blown down by the wind and "even the women saw it," so the whole attempt to revive the old way collapsed.

There have been many such intimations of group movements to Christ in the Central Belt of Nigeria. However, too often any significant move is sealed off from neighboring villages – losing, at the same time, its own original fire.

4. In the Muri Church

At Gwomo in the 1940s it was thought that the whole village would become Christian. However, the first Christians became disappointed that their status was not greatly enhanced by the new way, and returned to the pagan way. This misconception of Christianity has been a hindrance to the progress of the gospel through the years.[2]

At Jen the church showed good progress until 1956. At times there was so much interest that groups talked about church problems and evangelisic work all night and only

[2] McBride, I. E., Personal interview, March, 1962.

dispersed when the rising sun called them to their fields. But since 1956 clan rivalry and political frictions have killed the spontaneity of the Jen church. There were fifteen evangelists who at first were receiving five shillings per month from the mission; later they received ten shillings per month. But of these fifteen only one is now continuing the work of the church. The others became "lecturers" for political parties. When political tasks grew less they were dropped from the political party payrolls, but did not return to the work of the church, for evangelists had less status in the eyes of the general populace than did the political lecturer.[3]

At Yandam before 1948 no one had heard of the gospel; in 1950 there were only a very few Christians. In that year the old men told the Christians that they would kill them through witchcraft. However, the Christians replied that since Christianity was the true way, they were not afraid of witches. While the Christians were praying in the open, a juju pot and stick were set up nearby. But the Christians were not in the least deterred by this show of pagan power. At the close of the prayer session the Christians divided into twos and threes and went to preach the gospel. When news spread over Yandam country that the Christians "had challenged the pagan ways and were unharmed" there was much interest and almost every village soon had a few Christians. Growth was steady between 1950 and 1960, though it never broke out into full bloom as had been expected.

These few intimations of movements to Christ illustrate how widespread group response has been. Numerous instances were related to me, and there must be many more of which I did not hear. Also, Mr. Robinson found many in Southern Nigeria. Great care and much prayer are needed in bringing such movements to Christ to their full fruition as ongoing, reproductive Christian Churches. True, tribal animosities, politics, pagan influences, and wrongly used mission aid have often nipped such movements in the bud. But suppose missionaries and church leaders learn how to shepherd these numerous and often spontaneous

[3] *Ibid.*

tribal movements, how to purify them and step up their power, lead them to genuine experience of Jesus Christ, and mould them into strong churches! Then, truly, would the "multitudes in the valley of decision" (Joel 3:14) come into the Kingdom of God!

I am convinced that God has much to teach us as to how tribes become Christian.[4] We must start, of course, in the Central Belt, with these Churches, missions, tribes, and these first tender beginnings of people movements. If we would look for them we would find more of them. If we knew how to conserve them, we would bring more sheaves to the Master's threshing floor.

B. TWO STUDIES IN CHURCH GROWTH

1. The Languda Response[5]

The Shellem station of the Danish Lutheran Mission was opened in 1918 in the midst of the Kanakuru tribe (No. 89, Figure III) on the east bank of the Gongola River. The valley is broad and flat. To the west lie the forbidding mountains of the Languda tribe, which numbers about 14,000. Though the gospel was preached first to the Kanakuru, the Languda showed signs of response fully twenty years before there was any substantial response among the Kanakuru. In 1961 church attendance among the Languda was seven times greater than among the Kanakuru.

Dawuda had heard the gospel at Wukari and was baptized there. Later he turned up at Numan and was employed by the mission as an evangelist to the Languda tribe. He settled in the village of Banjeram on the west side of the Gongola, south of Shellem, but his witness for Christ reached far beyond that village. While preaching the gospel he urged his people to go to the Shellem dispensary to receive treatment

[4] Pickett, Warnshuis, Singh, and McGavran, *Church Growth and Group Conversion*, available from the Institute of Church Growth, Eugene, Oregon, and *Bridges of God* by McGavran are essential reading for all who would understand how tribes become Christian.

[5] Jorgensen, A. and Jameta, Taddawus, Personal interviews, March, 1962.

for their ulcers. Many of the youth who responded entered the Shellem school and became Christians.

Later a Languda lad became ill with a throat infection. When he went to the mission hospital at Numan he became a Christian and entered school there. When he returned to his people he called them together for prayer and preaching. He urged four youth, including Taddawus (the present dispenser at Shellem), to go to the Shellem school. At Shellem they found many other Languda boys, some of whom had received stimulus toward Christ from Dawuda.

The Languda received their first and only mission station, built at Gwuyok about 1930. By that time there were fourteen Languda Christians, who, having gone to the dispensary at Shellem, stayed to enter the boarding school. While there they visited their own tribes at irregular intervals to preach the gospel.

The coming of World War II brought staffing difficulties to the missions, and Shellem station was unoccupied in 1936 and 1937. Young men attending school there scattered back into the hills of their Languda tribe spreading the gospel everywhere. Since 1937 the Shellem station has been occupied only about half of the time, but because of the good response of the Languda, the Gwuyok Station staff was continued. The following chart shows the relative responsivensss of the two areas:

Number of Persons Baptized Each Year

	1936	'37	'38	'39	'40	'41	'42	'43	'44	'45	'46	'47
Shellem (Kanakuru)	14	7	10	26	16	9	2	0	4	0	4	2
Gwuyok (Languda)	81	41	69	30	91	46	30	24	37	38	26	78

Total baptized at Shellem: 94

Total baptized at Gwuyok: 591

Many of the young men of the Languda tribe broke their fetish pots upon the rocks or threw them into the streams. Later many young women also responded to the gospel message, and a few of them went to the boarding school at Numan. The adults of the tribe were not pleased at these developments. It was common for them to threaten the youth by saying that they would not give food to them if they followed the new Way. But in time many of these adults also became Christians.

Two factors militated against this Languda movement to Christ. First, the Languda were a very isolated group. There are only a few motor traces into their mountain area. Secondly, the Languda have been a very primitive people with a savage way of life. Headhunting and cannibalism, also practiced by many other tribes of the eastern part of the Central Belt area, indicated strong beliefs relating to "mana," soul stuff, and ancestor worship. Such a pattern of life could not be broken into easily. Yet neither the isolation nor the pagan culture pattern kept the youth from responding. The graph of church growth (Figure XIII) will repay study. The first movement to Christ began in 1933, about six years after the arrival of the missionaries, and continued on to 1941. Eighty-one persons (see the columns) were baptized in 1936 and 91 in 1940. About 60 persons were baptized during each of the six years from 1936 to 1941 inclusive. Then between the years 1942 and 1946 baptisms show a slump. Only about thirty were baptized in each of these years. In 1947 the second movement into the church began and has continued on to 1961 with an average yearly baptism of 115 persons for this fifteen-year period. From 1947 to 1961 1,748 were baptized. The low year for this period (1947-1961) was 1948 with the baptism of seventy-two and the high year was 1961 with the baptism of 303. Sunday attendance ranged from 459 in 1940 through 743 in 1944; 1,370 in 1947; 1,400 in 1948; and 8,108 in 1961.

The total accumulated number of persons baptized between the beginning, 1930, and 1961 is the substantial figure of 2,319. During this same period only 743 had been baptized in the Kanakuru Church.

The church membership line shows a different picture. It goes steadily up to a membership of about 800. In 1953 there is a tremendous drop down to only 194, a loss of 613 members! The next year the membership is given as 244 which is a slight recovery. The years 1960 and 1961 show remarkable recovery, with a membership of 584 and 603 respectively. It should be noted that in 1953, when only

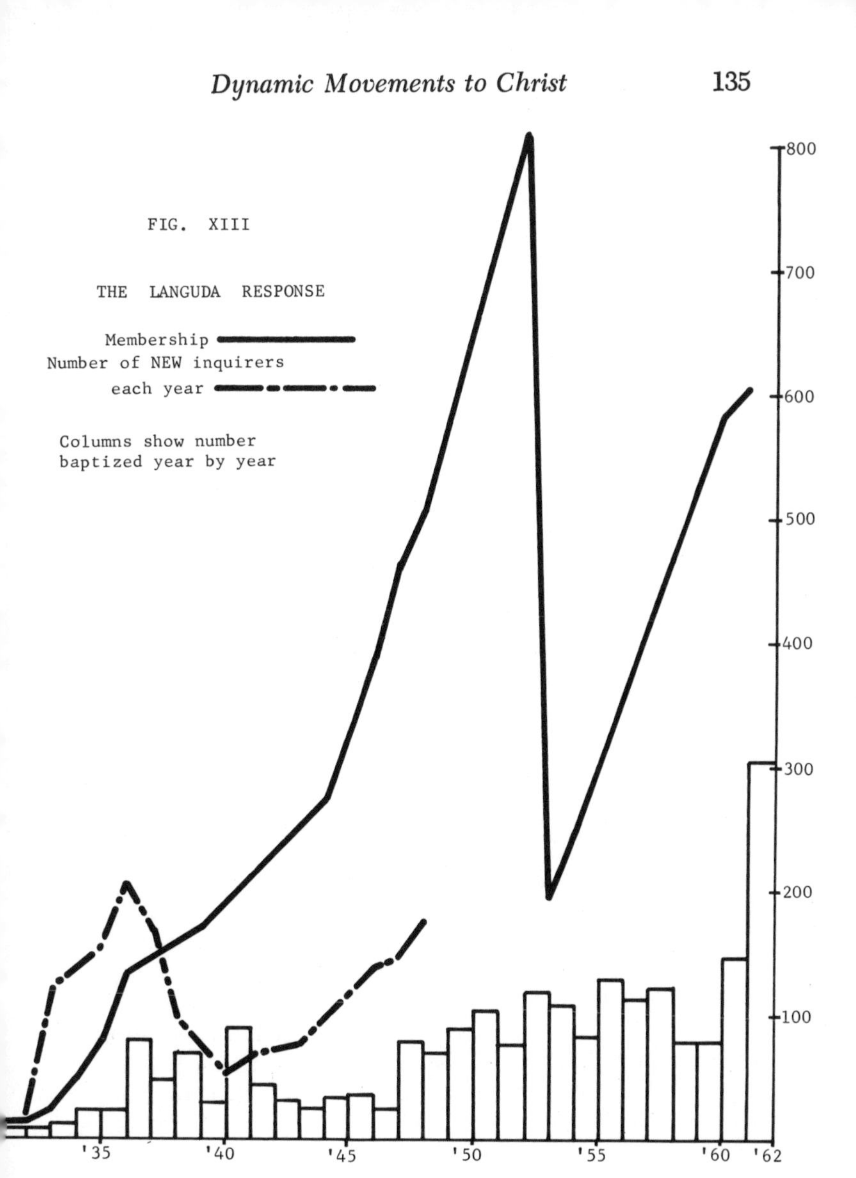
FIG. XIII
THE LANGUDA RESPONSE
Membership
Number of NEW inquirers
each year
Columns show number
baptized year by year
800
700
600
500
400
300
200
100
'35
'40
'45
'50
'55
'60
'62

194 members are recorded, according to the baptismal record the Church was then in the midst of its second strong response to the gospel. While a discouraging year as far as total membership was concerned, there were 111 baptisms; and 121 the year before!

The great discrepancy between those baptized and the church membership figure is related to natural deaths, infant baptisms,[6] the loss of Christians through reversions, and the disfellowshipping of others; and perhaps most important of all, the introduction of membership cards.

The introduction in 1953 of church membership cards with a fee payment was responsible for the great drop. Only those who paid the fee and received membership cards were counted members. The introduction of cards, as in other parts of TEKAS, had a disquieting effect. Many who were not opposed to the cards just did not get around to paying the fee. Others made their payment the first year and then did not renew it the next. The increasing mobility of church members makes a membership card a valuable key to other TEKAS Churches. Beginning with 1961, TEKAS membership is reported in two ways: total membership and active membership. The "active" members are those who have paid their church fee and attend church regularly.

In 1954 Languda membership began a slow climb back – initiated as much by the continuously good yearly baptisms as by persuading Christians to pay church fees. There were 584 who renewed church cards in 1960, and 603 in 1961. Considering that there were 303 baptisms in 1961 alone, and that most of these likely paid their fees, the total membership in 1961 of 603 was made up of 50% new members! Thus, when we remember that there had been more than 2,300 baptized from the beginning, it is reasonable to suppose that there were more than 1,000 other baptized believers who had not paid fees, and did not, therefore, have membership cards, and in the Lutheran Church did not commune, but who in every other way were convinced

[6] The infant baptisms are rather substantial in number, being 487 out of 1,643 from 1946 to 1961. Hojvig, E., Correspondence, Mar. 11, 1963. Also, infant mortality is still very high in the Central Belt.

Christians and were living a life according to the precepts of the Church.

At any rate, in 1961 there were 603 card-bearing Christians, at least 1,000 other baptized believers, and 8,108 attending church each Sunday morning in 29 organized congregations and many other meeting places. The responsiveness of the Languda tribe has been outstanding.

Dynamic Influences in the Languda Response

Probably the first influence has been the energetic free preaching of the gospel everywhere. The youth who first heard the gospel at Shellem went back on vacations to preach it. Though Dawuda was a paid preacher, the mission when it arrived did not pay the young men who were evangelists.[7] In 1936 there were nine such evangelists, in 1946 eighteen, and in 1961 thirty. An unpaid lay leadership that looked after the congregations and preached the Word to all was an important part of the church growth picture. The missionaries and two ordained Languda pastors were the only full-time paid leaders.

Missionary leadership was another influence. The tribe was responsive and was hence kept occupied. However, Gwuyok did not become a large institutional station. It was staffed through the years at the rate of only 2.2 missionaries. Languda initiative was encouraged, not smothered, by missionary supervisors.

Junior primary schools were also an important part of the church growth picture. The first was opened in 1933 with an attendance of 66. Later three more schools were opened and, despite the fact that only two survived, played a crucial part in creating the Church, though they never outshone the churches. There are two junior primary schools today and 29 churches. Most persons have not become Christians by way of the schools. Yet the Church was strengthened by the school, which was an evangelizing agency among its students and others, but the Church grew above and beyond the school. (In the Central Belt as a

[7] Jorgensen, A., Correspondence, November, 1963.

whole schools have been a doorway into the Church in most places, but since World War II some churches have extended widely beyond the realm of the schools. All of them must.)

If there is close enough cooperation between the pastors, evangelists, and school teachers, the Languda have an evangelistic team that, coupled with the increasing responsiveness of the tribe, should produce exceptional growth.

The Languda, as well as other tribes in the Lutheran Church area, are ready for great turnings to Christ. In the past Malam Taddawus Jameta said there has not been much clan or family response. But the great turnings, when they come, will likely bring in chains of families and groups of households. Thus village after village and hamlet after hamlet will become Christian. The Lutheran G. F. Vicedom in *Church and People in New Guinea,* already mentioned, has a message for all the Churches in the Central Belt. Could not the Languda move to Christ by clans and hamlets, with Lydda and Sharon as New Testament precedents and Vicedom's New Guinea churches as comtemporary examples?

2. The Yedseram River Valley Expansion[8]

Between 1945 and 1962 a small but enthusiastic mission church at Lassa of eighty-one members living in two villages and several neighboring hamlets grew to a constellation of fifteen churches, 146 preaching points, ninety-six classes of religious instruction directed by as many church-supported evangelists, a total communicant membership of 4,619, and a Sunday attendance of 9,725. An extended study of this expansion should be a profitable experience for all who are concerned for the growth of the Church. How did it occur? How did the Spirit lead the Church to grow in such New Testament fashion?

To answer these questions adequately I describe the Yedseram Valley expansion in detail. This is the area I know best, having spent ten years working with the church at Lassa, at Gulak, and since 1955 at Uba. The same sort of conditions exist in many parts of the Central Belt. The

[8] See Maps A, B, C, D of Fig. XIV.

topography differs from place to place, but the tribal situation and the move out from isolation and the desire for change and the opportunity for great growth are the same. I am convinced that there are many places in other parts of Africa and in the world in general where similar conditions exist favoring great spontaneous growth. I am also convinced that many missionaries as well as national leaders of the Church are not as aware of the opportunities before them as they should be. Too often the emphasis upon the primacy of indigenous leadership causes the mission involved to relax and hesitate to initiate new creative programs of outreach; likewise the attainment of leadership by nationals brings such an involvement with the Church and its problems that outreach takes a second place. In the Yedseram expansion the Church and mission went hand in hand extending the Kingdom of God. Missionaries were integrated into the life of the expanding Church.

The story of church expansion in the Yedseram River Valley of the Eastern Church begins in 1927 when the first Church of the Brethren missionaries trekked from Garkida to establish a station at Dille Mountain, an important Margi center. Sufficient water was not found and the station moved to Lassa on the banks of the Yedseram River. Water was plentiful for all future developments of hospital, school, orchards, and agricultural experimentation. The triad of missionary penetration – evangelism, education, and medicine – were enthusiastically begun and carried on through the years. While there were periods when education lagged and the hospital staff was meager, there was always at least one missionary at the station whose primary concern was the establishment of the Church.

Education and evangelism went on hand-in-hand, both in the classroom and in the out-village itineration. A magnificent job was accomplished in this respect by Rev. Bassey Minso, a Nigerian "home missionary," who, with his family, came from Calabar in Southern Nigeria to help the mission and church in Lassa. He was the principal of the school and exceptionally active in the work of the local church. His wife was active as a women's leader and Sunday school teacher. His contact with schoolboys who had come in

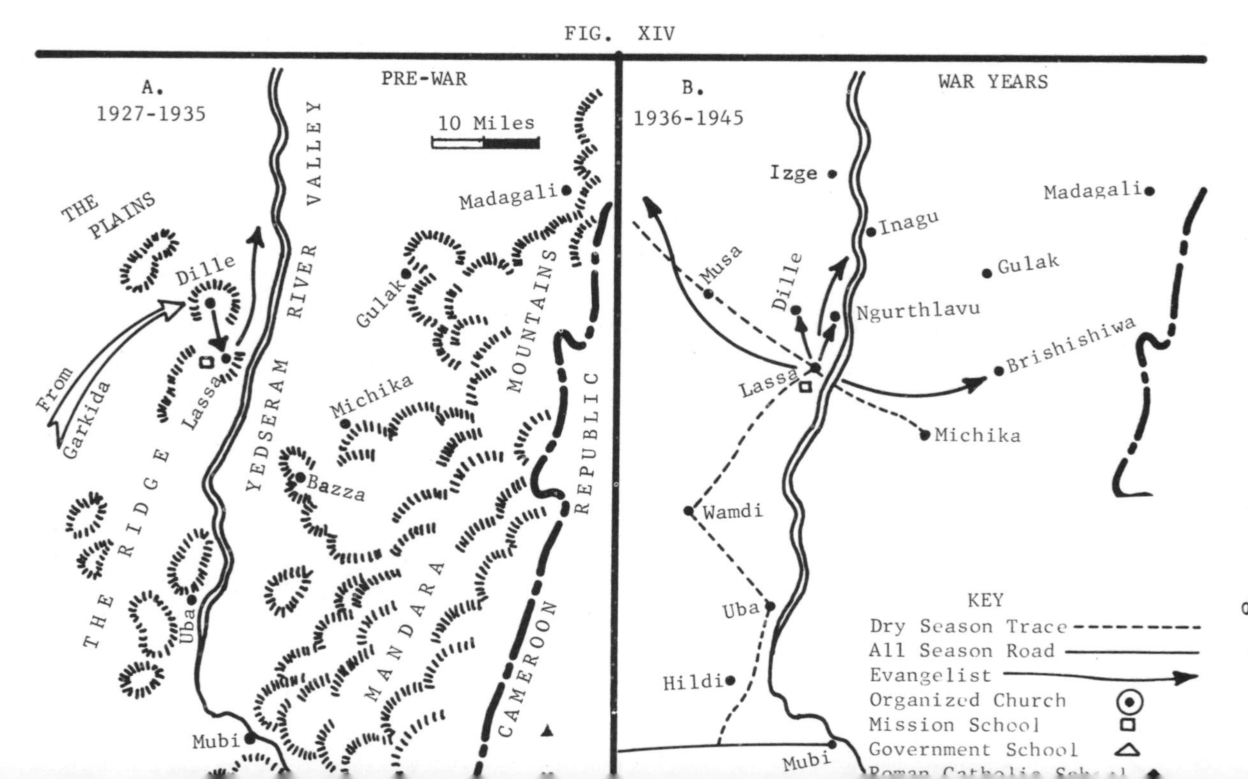
FIG. XIV
A.
1927-1935
PRE-WAR
10 Miles
THE PLAINS
Dille
From Garkida
Lassa
THE RIDGE
Uba
Mubi
YEDSERAM RIVER VALLEY
Madagali
Gulak
Michika
Bazza
MANDARA MOUNTAINS
CAMEROON REPUBLIC
B.
1936-1945
WAR YEARS
Izge
Inagu
Madagali
Gulak
Musa
Dille
Ngurthlavu
Brishishiwa
Lassa
Michika
Wamdi
Uba
Hildi
Mubi
KEY
Dry Season Trace
All Season Road
Evangelist
Organized Church
Mission School
Government School

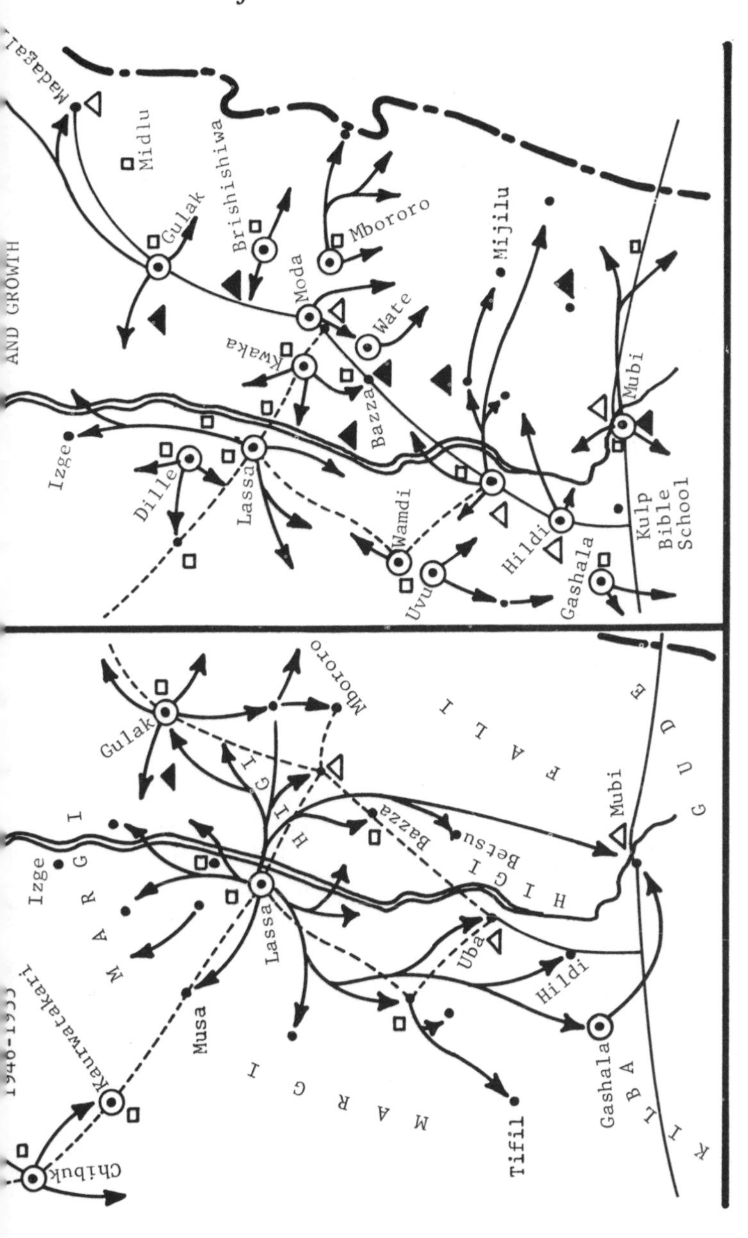
AND GROWTH
Madagali
Midlu
Gulak
Brishishiwa
Mbororo
Moda
Wate
Kwaka
Mijilu
Bazza
Mubi
Izge
Dille
Lassa
Wamdi
Hildi
Uvu
Gashala
Kulp
Bible
School
Gulak
Mbororo
Bazza
Betsu
Mubi
Izge
Lassa
Uba
Hildi
Musa
Kaurwatakari
Chibuk
Tifil
Gashala
M A R G I
H I G I
F A L I
G U D E
H I G I
M A R G I
K I L B A

from neighboring villages led him to visit them in their homes. He carried on a heavy schedule of village visitation in both the Margi and Higi tribes. It is beyond question that this dark-skinned missionary, though struggling against the handicap of being a "Southerner," had a great deal to do with laying the foundation of the Church in the Yedseram River Valley.

Let us turn our attention to the environs of the Lassa Church. Map A, Figure XIV, presents a somewhat stylized drawing of the country under consideration. It should be noticed that there are four geographical regions.

(1) The Mountains

The Mandara Mountain region is exceedingly picturesque. The expanse of river valley, ten or more miles wide, thinly covered with trees and extensively farmed, is bordered by the wall of the Mandara Mountains to the east. These mountains vary from high hills to five-thousand-feet projections above sea level. Evidence of ancient volcanic action is seen in the many pillars of rock. These mountains are of special significance in our study because they are inhabited by the Higi tribe in which the Church is growing very rapidly. There are no permanent roads into the mountains, only a few traces that may or may not be opened to motor travel during the dry season, depending upon the enthusiasm of the local people and the state of the district treasury. The mountains are like fingers of rock projecting out on to the plains with a spread of a quarter mile between them. Other valleys unexpectedly open up on either side. "Exploration" by motorcycle can get one around through these fascinating labyrinths of valley-upon-valley. But walking is the only way to reach the villages on the tops of the mountains, where, amazingly enough, thousands of people live. The slopes are terraced, and on the tops are large areas suitable for farming. The generation that is passing maintains the ancient traditions in these mountain fastnesses, but many of the youth are impatient with the isolation. The open land below symbolizes the new freedom for body and mind that beckons to them.

(2) The River Valley

Peace in Nigeria, coupled with a desire for better farm lands, and a government resettlement program that carries with it the benefit of free, government-built homes, has brought a steady movement down from the mountains, and much of the arable land is being taken. In 1945 there were very few farms in the river valley between Lassa and Michika, but now clusters of Higi farming homes are scattered over the entire area, so that in driving the nine miles across the valley a Higi home is never out of sight. This type of scattered, farming-family settlement is found to a somewhat lesser extent throughout much of the Yedseram Valley between Mubi and Inagu.

The Yedseram River, flowing one hundred feet wide and three to eight feet deep in the rainy season, dwindles to a few feet wide and a foot or less deep in the dry season. Its flow ceases completely above Uba, where it shrinks to a series of stagnant pools in the sandy river bottom.

During most of the year the valley is ideal for all sorts of farming development: guinea corn, peanuts, cotton, sweet potatoes, vegetable gardening, and citrus orchards. At most places, even in the dry season, water is only a few feet below the surface. Irrigation to a limited extent may be used for vegetable gardens, especially in the areas of small pools surrounded by jungle-like vegetation which dot the area.

(3) The Plains

The Bornu plains roll on to the north and west of the river valley. Very recently these plains contained many roans, hartebeests, and elephants. But now, as the result of the increase of Nigerian hunters and the large herds of Fulani cattle that graze the area, the large game is practically gone. The "orchard bush" has great possibilities for the development of peanut and cotton farmers, and Chibuk is known for its good guinea corn. The nomad herder and the settled farmer have their conflicts in this wide-open country.

The Chibuk people have a proud history of resistance to the Fulani invasions that culminated in the "Chibuk Wars." They speak a language related to both Bura and

Margi, being so similar to the former that missionaries have used this language almost entirely in their work at the Chibuk station and in the surrounding countryside.

To the north and west of Chibuk is an extension of the Margi tribe often referred to as West Margi. These people have been Moslemized and Kanurized by their close contacts with the large Kanuri tribe of Bornu Province.

(4) The Ridge or Watershed Area

This area is characterized by a heavy bush cover of tall grass and low trees. The ridge turns the water into the Yedseram to the east and into the Hawal on the west. The rain that falls on Hilde, for instance, divides partly to Lake Chad and mostly to the Atlantic by way of the Hawal, Gongola, Benue, and Niger Rivers.

This area is populated largely by the Margi, but because of its excellently drained land the Higi, pressing west from the river valley, have entered the ridge area between Lassa and Wamdi. The northeastern tip of the Kilba tribe reaches into the southern part of this area. Both Gashala and Tiful are Kilba villages and part of the Eastern Church.

It is characteristic of this ridge area that villages are located about the base of granite outcroppings that project several hundred feet above the level of the surrounding countryside. Such villages are Hildi, Tilful, Uvu, Wamdi, Uba, Musa, and Dille – each with its own private mountain. Scattered between these villages, and having gone out from them, are numerous farming hamlets.

The Tribes (Map C)

In the preceding section the various tribes have been mentioned in connection with the four topographical regions. The tribes are as follows:

Tribe	Estimated Population in the area of responsibility
A. Margi	80,000
B. South Margi	
C. West Margi	30,000
D. North Kilba	2,000

E. Higi	112,400
F. Waga and Mandara Hill Tribes	50,000
G. Fali	30,000
H. Gude	30,000
I. Chibuk	25,000
	359,400

There are approximately 360,000 people in this area of the original Lassa Church responsibility. The three Margi groups have close language relationships through South Margi to Kilba. Fali and Gude are also closely related. Waga lies between Higi on the south and the Gwoza Hill tribes to the north and is likely related to both. Higi is the western arm of the Kapsiki of the Cameroon Republic and is of the same language family with Margi, but the two are mutually unintelligible as are South Margi and Fali. Also Chibuk, though it comes together with Margi in Kaurwatakari, is not understood by the Margi, nor is Margi understood by the Chibuk, but West Margi and Chibuk are mutually understandable.

The socio-religious life of each tribe shows variations of one animistic pattern. The governing chief of the tribe tends to be distinct from the religious-rites leader. Ancestor worship takes second place to the worship of spirits housed in sacred groves, oddly shaped trees, piles of boulders, or pools. Sacred earthenware pots are prominent as personal shrines. Yearly festivals relating to the farming cycle such as the Yawal and Ladir of the Margi are characteristic of the wider religious life of the community. Witchcraft also plays an important part in the life of the average person, and many are believed to possess familiars of leopards, wart hogs, hyenas, and other animals.

Subsistence farming with the most primitive of methods still predominates, though ox-drawn plows have become greatly desired and are being used by a scattering of farmers. There are numerous traders of local products and imported rock salt and dried fish from Lake Chad. There is, in recent years, a growing trade in all sorts of "western" articles: cloth, with the accompanying tailor and his Singer sewing machine, the bicycle and its "makaniki," kerosene lamps, flashlights, soap, vaseline, matches, mirrors, combs, sunglasses, padlocks, and a host of other such items. This trade moves from the major Wednesday market of Mubi out among the other market towns: market at Uba on Thursday, at Wamdi on Friday, at Betsu on Saturday, at Michika on Sunday, at Lassa on Monday, at Bazza and Hilde on Tuesday. These markets afford an informal meeting place for Christian friends.

Other Background Factors

After World War I the German Cameroons had been divided between Britain and France. The British Cameroons later became United Nations Trust Territory administered by the British. This Trust Territory became Sardauna Province of Nigeria in 1961. In 1927 when the first missionaries reached Lassa there were no Christians in the Yedseram area. The whole country was practically untouched by outside influence, and the Moslem overlord, Hamiaji,* was still raiding in the Gulak area. At this early date there was only one dry-season road into the southern part of the area, to Mubi (Map A) where a government Touring Officer was stationed. Most of the mountain area including all of Higi and Waga was "closed territory"[9] until 1951, and thus very little missionary touring was done in that area.

On Map C, "Post-War Expansion," 1946-1955, we see that the all-season road had reached Uba, and there was a dry season trace through to Michika and on to Gulak and Madagali. In 1955 the Mission opened a new station at Uba, and the government began work on an all-season road to Madagali and on to Gwoza. By 1963 the difficult stretch of low swampland from Gwoza to Bama had been completed, thus making a link with the Bama-Maiduguri-Jos road.

The Mission, however, did not wait for the building of

* Or, Hamman Yaji.

[9] Areas in which travel by nonofficial Europeans was not allowed except by special permit, and then only when accompanied by a government officer. This restriction was due to the British government's regard of certain areas as unsettled and in which a traveler's safety could not be guaranteed.

roads to establish itself in strategic places. Chibuk is still forty-five miles from all-season road, and Mbororo is five miles off behind the mountains of Michika. Gulak was opened ten years before it was reached by the new all-season road.

One last factor, and an important one, is that of the position of Islam in this area. The maps locate four largely Moslem towns: Mubi, Uba, Michika, and Madagali. Mubi, the government center and largest town in the area, numbers over 14,000 and is largely Moslem. Uba is a town of 4,000 with only 700 non-Moslems. Michika and Madagali would be rather similar in size and makeup to Uba. Most of the villages of the area have small Moslem communities attached to them. Such communities vary in size. There are only six Moslems living in the Margi village of Ngurthlavu, fifty in Hildi (one-fiftieth of the population), 154 in Musa (one-twentieth of the population) and 345 in Lassa (one-fourth of the population).

Islam has had a subtle influence for many years through its mallams, who instruct Moslem children and converts around flaming bonfires several evenings a week. A less subtle influence has been exerted by the Moslem District Heads upon village chiefs. Any village chief turning Moslem has been looked upon with special favor. However, as far as the general tribal populace is concerned, Islam has been under a disadvantage in that most adults still remember that it came in with the raiding Fulani. The British government officer and missionary have been looked upon as the saviors of the tribal populace. This has played an important part in the friendly attitude shown by most tribal chiefs throughout the whole area.

The Vigorous Expansion of the Lassa Church

In 1927 the Kulps had located at Dille (Map A) and the following year the Dr. Burkes arrived and the station was moved to Lassa. During these early years the medical doctor, in order to acquaint the surrounding populace with the blessings of modern medicine, made many trips north through Ngurthlavu and toward Izge. These trips were combined with evangelistic preaching. Interest was aroused to the extent that youth began to turn up at the newly opened Lassa Junior Primary School, which was destined to grow to over one-hundred pupils in the 1950s, and expanded to include Senior Primary with a total attendance of 500 pupils in 1960.

Map B, "The War Years," 1936-1945, shows that in spite of reduced missionary staffs at Lassa the Mission continued to reach out into the surrounding areas. In 1938 a Nigerian Bura evangelist from Garkida began work at Chibuk, and in 1941 a missionary family located there. The evangelistic thrust had reached Inagu to the north and Brishishiwa in the closed area of Higiland. Adam, a blind Higi lad from Brishishiwa, came to Lassa and soon was sent to the Sudan Interior Mission School for the Blind in Kano. He learned to read Braille and returned to his own area, where, in the "Post-War Expansion Period" (Map C) he played a major role in reaching the Higi people for Christ.

Preceding World War II the response had been very slow. The first three Margi young men were baptized shortly following the arrival of the Mission, but during the next ten years there were only about eighty-two baptized. Then, in spite of the fact that thirty-two were baptized during the years 1941 to 1945, the communicant membership in 1945 was only about eighty-one, and these Christians were located mainly in Lassa and Dille. About thirty-three had been lost – most of them as a result of church discipline.

In the early 1940s there were many decisions for Christ at Dille, but few succeeded in becoming baptized members. In 1941 there were ninety-one decisions for Christ ("covenants"), but only about twenty-nine of them were later baptized. During the period 1936-45 there were only about fifty baptized.

Map C, "The Post-War Expansion," 1946-1955, shows the way in which the Lassa Church pushed out into the river valley and ridge regions. The mission established stations, and the Church chose and sent out Nigerian evangelists. Each arrow on the map represents one or more evangelists. The main mission thrusts were to Gulak in 1948, to Mbororo in 1954 (which extension had been preceded by the work of "Blind Adam" mentioned above), to Uba in 1955 (preceded by a Lassa Church evangelist as of 1952), and also to Mubi in 1955. The opening of this last station had been preceded by missionary and Nigerian evangelist visits by horse and cycle via Bazza and Betsu, by the enthusiastic encouragement of Christian students, by Principal Jack Spicer at the newly opened Government Teacher Training Centre at Mubi and also by groups of Christians from Southern Nigeria, Anglican and Baptist, and from the neighboring Cameroons, Lutheran Brethren, who had come into Mubi in search of work on the expanding government projects of schools, hospital, and community improvement, were anxious for spiritual guidance. All of these groups received pastoral care from the visits of the Lassa churchmen. The Lutheran Brethren from the Mundang tribe in the Cameroon Republic became members of the Eastern Church. The other denominations founded their own congregations.

The arrows indicate that there was a wide expansion on the part of the Lassa Church through its evangelists working in fellowship with the missionaries. Blind Adam was pushing east from Brishishiwa with the help of an additional Higi evangelist, Madi, from the Garkida Leprosarium. All the other areas of advance were likewise carried on by the evangelists of Lassa Church under the direction of the Church Committee. At this time Risku Madziga traveled far and wide encouraging other evangelists and reaching out into places such as Izge, Gulak, and Higiland. All evangelists were supported cooperatively by the Mission and by the Lassa Church and the villages in which they worked. The Mission has not been handicapped by a false application of the indigenous-church principle, which would prevent mission aid. Under the direction of the Church Committee, it has paid the evangelists a token salary of two to four dollars a month, and the villages in which they worked helped them to build their homes and hoe their farms. These evangelists were always married men.

Beginning about 1958 evangelists and all pastors were paid by the Church itself. The small subsidy available to the Church from the Church in America could be used only in opening completely new evangelistic work, such as the three extensions into Izge, Waga, and Mijilu (Map D).

An important development during this period was the return of many soldiers to their home communities. They had been to Burma and had a broadened view of life and a desire to see their home communities progress into the new world of the future. Most of these men were quickly disillusioned, finding their home villages unmoved by their unbelievable tales and their hopes for a better way of life. However, Audu of Gashala found an encouraging response. After returning home he told the youth of his village, "I'm going to go to Dzongola (near Garkida). There are Christians there and I want to become a Christian." They responded by saying, "Don't go! Stay here and we will all become Christians." A Kilba man named Bauchi, who had been a Garkida Church evangelist, was called by the Lassa Church to go and settle at Gashala. Special gifts from a Methodist in America paid his small salary. By 1956 Gashala was able to pay for its own pastoral care. In 1951 Audu alone was baptized at Gashala, but since then the Church of Gashala has grown to 372 communicant members in 1962 with an average Sunday attendance at its several worship centers of 910, with Audu as schoolteacher and ordained pastor.

Gulak and Gashala were organized as congregations in 1951 and 1953 respectively. The Chibuk Church was organized in 1952 and Kaurwatakari shortly after.

By the close of this expansion period the Lassa cluster of churches had a membership of 839 with a Sunday morning attendance of 2,644. There were now five organized churches. The next period, 1956 to 1962, saw still more growth in numbers of Christians and of indigenous churches.

Turning to Map D, "The Years of Church Establishment and Growth," 1956-1963, we note that arrows showing direction of extension have become shorter. Only a few long arrows are seen – one from Lassa to Izge where the Lassa Church determined to evangelize this heavy population area, and another the advance of the Gulak Church into the Waga mountain tribe north of Madagali. The South Margi Church at Uba and the Mubi Church also began a cooperative effort to enter the Fali tribe.

All the other arrows are comparatively short, for they are extensions from newly organized churches into neighboring environs. Following is a list of the churches organized:

		Communicant members at time of organization and in 1962	
Period I:	1927-1935 — No churches organized		
Period II:	1936-1945 — No churches organized		
Period III:	1946-1955 — Five churches organized		
1947:	Lassa	100	608
1951:	Gulak	35	82
1952:	Chibuk	28	205
1952:	Kaurwatakari	20	62
1953:	Gashala	100	372
Period IV:	1955-1962 — Ten (plus one in 1963) organized		
1957:	Dille	82	182
1958:	Kwaka	140	708
1958:	Mbororo	102	510
1958:	South Margi (Uba)	286	248
1958:	Mubi	56	252
1959:	Wamdi	403	240
1960:	Brishishiwa	112	173
1960:	Moda	302	493
1962:	Uvu	239	239
1962:	Hildi	245	245
1963:	Wate	247	1963: 247

During the expansion of the 1946-1955 period the Church grew in numbers primarily through direct evangelism. However, junior primary schools were also being established at Gulak, Chibuk, Kaurwatakari, Bazza, Wamdi, Gashala, Dille, Kwaka, Uba, Musa, Brishishiwa, and Mubi.

Thus, while most of the organized churches are not at mission stations, most of them have a mission-sponsored school. Yet Christians are scattered far and wide in the many villages and hamlets of the area. Moda, with a membership of 493 in 1962, has never had a junior primary school, but has always had an active class of religious instruction. The newly organized church centered at Wate includes the Bazza Junior Primary School within its bounds. This school was begun many years ago, and is two miles from Wate. The teachers of these schools, paid by the government during the last period, have played an important role as literate church leaders in preparing converts for baptism.

It is difficult to estimate the influence of the school upon the growth of the church. Certainly it has been very great. However, the majority of church members have not completed even the four years of education made available by the junior primary schools. Only 10% of the average Sunday attendance of 3,214 (1962) of the Higi churches is made up of junior primary school children. In addition there are 927 pupils enrolled in village classes of religious instruction, and perhaps 50% of these are children, so that the Sunday attendance is 25% children who are enrolled in some sort of "school." The rest are mostly young adults with a good scattering of old people, especially older women who have responded enthusiastically to the gospel message. It is not uncommon for several of these older women to rise in a worship service and express their joy by doing a few dance steps as they raucously "line" a Higi Christian song, punctuating it with the traditional Higi woman's salutation of a high-pitched scream staccatoed by rapidly flapping the tongue in the open mouth. In two of the fastest growing churches, Kwaka (Higi) and Wamdi-Uvu (Margi), and now also Wate (Higi), the great majority of members have never attended school. In the whole area, only at Lassa have girls responded to education in any significant number, but in all of the churches there seems to be an equal response to the gospel among females as among males.

The Mbororo Church in 1963 had only fifty-two members who had completed fourth grade or higher out of a communicant total membership of 686. The low level of literacy brings memorization and the need for Biblical preaching and teaching to the fore.

A second aspect of the Church's growth is that of the wide influence of the Lassa Hospital and numerous out-village dressing stations. Church evangelists take short courses at the hospital that enable them to dispense medicines along with their evangelistic work. All the medical doctors (up to 1962) who have served at the Lassa hospital have been ordained ministers of the gospel and have done evangelistic touring, making church supervision a part of their weekly program.

Growth Through Cell-Like Division

The Yedseram Valley Church has grown through a series of cell-like divisions. Each arm of the Church, whether Gulak, Uba, or Mubi, was part of the Lassa Church until its actual date of separate organization. Until then the Church Committee and elder of the Lassa Church dealt with all aspects of church life in the new area, giving the new group of Christians historic and geographic roots. At the time of organization it divided from the mother church at Lassa with a feeling of accomplishment and challenge. In 1951 Gulak divided off from Lassa, reducing Lassa membership by 35, and later Mbororo (1958) divided off of Gulak to form its own church. The whole South Margi area divided off in 1958, thus reducing the Lassa membership by 286. The various preaching centers where Christians grew in numbers then planned to organize their own churches and accomplished it by dividing off from the South Margi church, and forming first Wamdi, which included Uvu, thus reducing the South Margi membership by 286. Shortly Uvu divided off Wamdi, forming its own church in 1962, and reducing the Wamdi membership by 239. On the same day Hildi also divided from South Margi, forming a church that included the new Bible school at Kwarhi. This again reduced the South Margi membership by 245. Even so, it still had a membership of 248 in 1962, and grew to 462 in 1963! Kwaka also divided from Lassa in 1958, and Lassa's membership was again cut by 102. Brishishiwa divided from Mbororo in 1960, and then Moda divided from Mbororo, taking 302 members with it. In 1963 Wate divided from Kwaka. The new Wate church then agreed with Kwaka on a shift of boundaries that brought Bazza in as part of Wate and gave Wate a beginning membership of 247.

This cell-like division is made possible by strong evangelistic outreach. The "loss" of members from one church when its outreach forms into a separate church is no real loss, for each "mother cell" continues to grow apace, replacing its "lost" membership with new converts locally or in another outreach area. Thus membership of a church suddenly drops as the areas of greatest growth divide off, forming new churches, but enthusiastic outreach causes it to swell quickly again.

Growth is due to the increase in the number of Nigerian evangelists in the field. The Lassa mother church continues to increase, in spite of geographical loss, by keeping evangelists in the field. In 1963 it still had ten evangelists in as many villages. In the whole Eastern church in 1945 there were only thirty-four evangelists; in 1951, sixty-eight; in 1955, ninety-six; and in 1961, 172. In 1962 these evangelists were conducting Christian worship in 277 different places. The great growth of the Lutheran Church is also related to the number of evangelists in the field, and if the Eastern and Lutheran figures are compared it can be seen that the larger number of Lutheran evangelists (450) correlates well with its larger membership.

Rev. Robert Bischof's report on the founding of the newest church of the Yedseram Valley illustrates both the vitality and the method of these growing churches.

> On March 3, 1963 the 5th church among the Higi people was organized. Six villages make up this church. At Bazza, which is the southernmost point of the church, we have a junior primary school where the work has been going on for a little over ten years. Then about two miles north of Bazza to the east of the road is the village of Wate. The work was begun there in 1960, and in Yambila, a village just a little west of the road and between Bazza and Wate, in 1961. Two other villages located east of the road are Yammu and Vii. The sixth village, Dlimi, is located on the top of one of the mountains several miles to the east.
>
> The following gives some indication of the church growth in this area:

Village	First Baptisms	Communicant Members March, '63
1. Wate	8 baptized April 27, 1960	91
2. Yammu	3 baptized April 1961	37
3. Dlimi	3 baptized Oct. 21, 1961	45

4. Yambila	1 baptized April	1962	11
5. Vii	1 baptized April	1962	6
6. Bazza	several in 1953		57[10]

> In October 1962 this area asked to be organized into a church. The District Council gave its permission. At the time of requesting organization there were 145 church members in the area. Since that time others have been baptized so that when the church was organized it had a membership of 247.
> 652 people attended the service of organization. It was a great day for Daniel Moda and Bulus Kwallia, two former leprosy patients who had done much to take the Word of God back into the area. The church supports its own work. All of the villages have church farms, and have contributed to the work of the District as well as supporting their own work. A total of $50.00 was raised through their church farms last year.
> The first church among the Higi people was organized in May, 1958; the fifth church, March 3, 1963 – not quite five years later, thus showing a steady growth and outreach.
> We thank God for giving the increase. Already this church is seeking three evangelists to send back farther into the valley.[11]

The Yedseram River valley expansion from 81 to 4,619 communicants, with a community of perhaps 8,000 and a Sunday attendance of 9,725, is a sign of great things to come. Here the hospital at Lassa and the several dispensaries at Chibuk, Gulak, and Mbororo have broken through the hard crust of fetishism and established a friendly relationship. The schools have served as both a launching pad and a continuing supply of energy for the Church. Converts have not been confined to schoolboys and ex-schoolboys and their wives. The Church itself has persuaded a goodly number of mature men and women, as well as throngs of unschooled youth, to become disciples of Jesus Christ and members of His Church. Churches are multiplying rapidly

[10] At Bazza a total of ninety-three have been baptized, but many of the young men have gone off to school and to the large cities for work.
[11] Bischof, R., Correspondence, March, 1963.

as the cell-like division continues at an increasingly rapid pace. The Church in the Yedseram Valley is directing its own church life and extension with the aid of only four missionary advisors among its sixteen churches.

Yet this must not obscure the fact that the evangelization of the Yedseram Valley is only just well begun. The 10,000 Sunday attendance is only 2.7 per cent of the area's population of 360,000! The question that faces the Church now is: how can the total population be won? Considering the strategic covering of the Church (note the location of the churches on Map D), greatly increased growth can be expected in the immediate future even though no changes in method are made. However, I believe the individualistic approach of evangelists and convinced Christians meeting non-Christians one by one, usually causing social dislocation for the new convert, must be shifted to a broader base (to be discussed in Chapter IX) that will bring whole families, clans, hamlets, and villages into the Church through multi-individual decisions for Christ (referring to the type of decision where each individual in a group makes a decision based upon his own conviction *in fellowship with others of like conviction*). A kind of multi-individual decision has already been very prominent among the youth of various communities. However, it has separated them from the older generations and caused social dislocation, which the Church has found very difficult to alleviate. A way must be found to bring multitudes of men and women to Christ within their social structure. The Spirit of Christ may then bring *from within* an evolving of social patterns that will liberate from fear, fetishism, sexual promiscuity, and polygamy. As early as 1930 Malam Risku, the first evangelist in the Yedseram Valley and now Government District Head at Gulak, dreamed of such a Christian redemption of society. From Lassa he returned to his home people of Waga expecting that there would be a great turning to Christ. But his people rejected him and the message of Christ that he brought. He returned to Lassa singing the first Margi Christian song: ["Jilirya anggerdari . . ."] "Our people have forsaken me:

my father has forsaken me; but Jesus has received me." Such was a discouraging beginning, but times have changed. The expansion in the Yedseram Valley is significant in that it gives promise of movements to Christ flowing along the web of social relationship.

Chapter VIII. Some Dynamic Factors in Church Growth

THERE ARE MANY FACTORS THAT MAY AID OR HAMPER THE growth of the Church. Some of them are: church-mission relationships, tribal relationships, polygamy and pagan ways of life, Islam, mission auxiliaries, and Sunday attendance at worship services. Through these and others the Holy Spirit works, bringing a community to a fullness of time. Yet the Church grows only as individuals come into its fellowship. It is a deeply personal matter. I asked every church leader I met during my tour of the churches in March, 1962, "What first influenced you to become a Christian?" The answers give a glimpse, by way of introduction, into the factors that lead to church growth.

The question was asked of 339 adult Christians, 317 of which were distributed as follows:

Those questioned

The Church	**Place**	**Number asked**	**Who they were**
Tiv	Mkar	10	Pastors and lay workers
Plateau	Gwoza	13	Lay workers and wives
Muri	Bambur	14	Pastors in training
Lutheran	Shellem	16	Evangelists and lay workers
ECWA	Zalanga	17	Pastors and wives in training
Benue	Lupwe	20	Evangelists in training
Plateau	Panyam	24	Evangelists in refresher course
Tiv	Zaki Biam	26	Wives of evangelists in training
Mada Hills	Alushi	28	Pastors and evangelists
Eastern	Lassa	149	Evangelists in refresher course

Some of the answers were of homely incidents that caught fire in the heart, as in the case of one who answered, "Another man and I were taking a cow to market and he told me that the Word of God preached by the village evangelist was very important and I should take care to listen." And another who said, "I saw a man holding a Bible in his hand and I wanted to hold one too." Or the sick man who was taught about God by another sick man in the hospital bed beside him. Or again, the man who was attracted when he heard a Christian singing a Christian song while he worked.

Some answers were touched with humor as in the case of the Panyam evangelist who said he first became interested in Christianity when he went with friends to the river to bathe. His friends began reciting the A B C's. He thought, "How can I keep up with this?" So, to keep up, he went to the church literacy class. Or, the case of another who, having five wives, noticed that there were some very nice girls in the Church. So he became interested in Christianity, hoping to increase the number of his wives. "But," he said, with a broad grin, "here I am now with only one!"

In other answers there were overtones of terror as of one who said, "I dreamed a fire burned all the village. I ran and jumped into the river and even the water burned up. Later I heard a missionary lady say, 'If you don't repent you will one day be in a fire.' I remembered my dream and was afraid, so I became a Christian."

When the 339 answers were classified, fourteen main influences appeared.

133 were first moved to Christ by some aspect of Christian education, either the junior primary school or class of religious instruction.
54 were first influenced by direct preaching
26 by a friend
23 by personal contact with an evangelist
20 by Christian songs
20 by a brother, sister, or uncle
18 by a wife or husband
18 by experiences at a hospital or dispensary
15 by a mother or father
10 by Christian pictures and plays
9 by leprosy care
5 by "hearing a call"
3 by the Boys' Brigade
3 by the desire to get a wife

(This list adds up to more than 339 questioned because there were forty who were moved by two equal influences and both were recorded; hence the figure is actually 379.)

This list reveals the primary influences that directed 339 people who are now stable adult church leaders into the way of Christ.

It is significant that Christian education is foremost and that preaching (mostly, but not entirely, by Nigerians) ranks second. The personal and friendly contacts rank high. "A friend first told me about Jesus" is commonly heard. If the twenty-six influenced by a friend were added to the other personal contacts made by evangelists (23), a brother or sister or uncle (20), a wife or husband (18), and a mother or father (15), the person-to-person influence would total 102, only thirty-one short of equalling the influence of education. Person-to-person contacts are very important and must be kept in mind as we describe other relationships that aid or deter church growth in the Central Belt, and that may lead to a broader, less individualistic type of church growth.

A. CHURCH-MISSION RELATIONSHIPS

These are very important to church growth. They may lead toward creative growth and development, or bind and stifle either or both parties. Some churches and missions are moving forward together; but in other cases, the church is rushing ahead, feeling that the mission is a hindrance, an unnecessary encumbrance.

Every church-mission situation is different depending on a variety of circumstances. The type of mission that brought the gospel, whether interdenominational or denominational, makes a difference. Every denomination has a different historic background out of which grow as many different approaches to church establishment as there are denominations. The circumstances also include the length of time the mission has been in an area. Conditions are different where a mission has been established for 100 years from those where a mission has begun work as recently as 1960. In these days when the Church is in fact established in so many countries throughout the world, it is a temptation to judge all situations on the basis of the best and longest established younger Churches. The Church in India, for instance, is a very different matter from the Church in the Central Belt of Nigeria. And a church in metropolitan Lagos is a very different matter from a church in remote Gwoza.

The particular approaches of the various missions have brought about different rates of development, both in the general situation within a tribe and in the existence of indigenous leaders. The variety of tribal customs also brings differences in speed of response. Churches and missions working among Moslems cannot be judged on the same basis as those working among the animistic pagan tribes. Nor does a mission in a tribe of one million population appear the same as a mission among hill tribes numbering a few thousand. Also, culturally there is a great variation today as a result of the spotty way in which church and national influences have penetrated the Central Belt. Tribes of the Mandara Mountains or the Mumuye along the Benue, both in their pristine state, can scarcely be compared to the Bura or Bachuma in neighboring areas, or with the Yoruba of southern Ilorin Province.

One of the most important areas of church-mission relationship is that which has to do with mission representation in the Church. In the Eastern Church (in 1962) one missionary – the Church representative – was a reporter between the Church and Mission organizations, and the Field Secretary was a voting member of the District Council.

In the United Missionary Church the mission is officially represented by missionary delegates, apparently on a par with the church delegates of the three regions with which they meet in a joint council once a year. The mission *appears* as a fourth region of the Church.

The Muri Church also meets in a joint council with mission representatives and with co-chairmen, one of the mission council and the other of the church council.

The Christian Reformed Church Mission and its two Churches (Tiv and Benue) all come together in their Nigerian General Conference, making the unique situation of two autonomous Churches meeting in the same council with the "parent" mission of both.

Another very important area is that of Churches sending representatives to the mission councils. Missions have not questioned the value of missionary advisors to the Churches, but the value of Nigerian churchmen as advisors to missions needs to be more widely appreciated and exploited to the advantage of all. The Christian Reformed Church Mission has Nigerian churchmen as advisors on its mission councils and most missions have some plan for receiving advice from nationals. Two paths being traveled by various missions bring the Nigerian into advisory capacity: 1) bringing the Nigerian into the mission councils, and 2) transferring "mission activities" into the Church, thus confining the "mission" to problems revolving about the missionaries' residence in Nigeria.

Since the Church is now indigenously organized, one question that has received a great deal of attention is, "What is to happen to the social services that missions have sponsored and maintained with funds and staff from outside Nigeria?" Can they be transferred to the Church? Should they be? Most missions are now receiving very substantial grants from the government and most of the staff members of the schools and hospitals are Nigerian. For the Church to administer schools and hospitals would be equitable and just in that a high percentage of the money for those institutions comes from Nigeria, but it is realized that the time is not far off when primary schools may be taken over by the government, and so whatever arrangements are made now are temporary.

But these relationships have little to do with the actual possibility of more or less church extension. There are other aspects to church-mission relations that do have a very definite bearing upon the growth of the Church. These are the personal relationships and the interplay of ideas.

With the indigenous Church as an actual reality, the missionary has taken a less conspicuous position than that previously held. He is urged to put the burden of responsibility onto national shoulders. The Church's leadership may, however, indolently bask in new-found freedom without accepting the responsibility that should come with authority. How much can a missionary do and still have primary leadership in the hands of Nigerians? It may be true in certain cases, that it is better for an indigene to do a job poorly than for a missionary to do it well, but our intention is to achieve the greatest possible amount of growth within the context of the changing conditions of our time. When souls are at stake, it is not for the missionary to sit back just to preserve the idea of the indigenous Church. To separate ourselves from those to whom God sent us, as though we were some different type of being, unwilling, or unable to fellowship in creative relationships and join our personalities and resources with theirs, is to introduce a new type of superiority just as devastating to the Church as the old superiority which said, "Stand back. I am the only one who can direct this enterprise."

The self-directing position of the indigenous Church must be safeguarded, but the interplay of Nigerian and missionary minds should be encouraged, not discarded. The actual position of the missionary in the Church is very important and there is a variety of ideas as to just what this should be. However, I am convinced that a missionary must be an integral part of the church. Though his roots are in another country he must live as part of the body of Christ where he is. He receives his spiritual nourishment and inspiration along with his Nigerian brethren – in the same worship services, at the same table of the Lord. The integration is for every missionary – lay as well as ordained. Integration is important. Much more is involved than the accomplishment of certain ends through giving of financial and staff resources. The spiritual encounter between Nigerian and missionary leaders must in these opportunity-filled days be mutually constructive. The outcome of such an encounter is not predetermined by the greater Christian experience and knowledge of the missionary, for the Nigerian leader brings valuable new insights as well as a fresh experience of Christ. His contribution is unfettered by historic denominational controversies and attachments. It is thoroughly Nigerian.

Dr. Harry R. Boer, missionary of the Christian Reformed Church and principal of the Theological College of Northern Nigeria, writes:

> The Church in Africa has lying before it the great opportunity of following new paths that are unencumbered by the antipathies engendered by theological debate, religious wars, and ecclesiastical splits and schisms. That she should explore these paths is not only a clear command of Scripture; it is no less a requirement of her present situation.[1]

If the Nigerian Christian and the missionary can explore these new paths together it will bring mutual benefits beyond our present expectations, benefits that I trust, would reach to other Churches around the world. The interaction of socio-historic features from the backgrounds of both should produce a synthesis much more able to meet the spiritual needs of the new Nigeria than that of a purely indigenous development.

On the commercial, educational, engineering, medical, and other technical levels there is no indication that Nigeria desires to start from scratch nor to proceed on purely indigenous lines. On the spiritual and eccelesiastical level, while Nigerians rightly desire Nigerian ways of doing and thinking, yet Nigerian Christians can hardly be satisfied with less than the fullest, truest, and most universal Christianity. Christianity is not provincial or national or bound to any culture – West or East – but meets the needs of man everywhere. Western missionaries, because of the universality of the Christian faith, need to be aware of the danger of Americanisms or Englishisms, but Nigerians must surely wish to assimilate truth regardless of origin into the indigenous pattern of church life.

Strangely enough, the missionary who has carried the message of Christ around the world is too apt to be the first to show provincialism and particular viewpoints that mar the image of universal Christianity. Dr. Boer writes:

[1] Boer, H. R., "The Year of the Elephant," *The Reformed Journal*, November, 1962, p. 4.

> The big issue in Nigerian Christianity is not whether the Church will be predominantly Lutheran or Reformed or Baptist or Anglican, but whether it will survive as Christian. The first duty of missionaries is to found the Church. The second duty of missionaries is to nurture the Church. This nurture must always take into consideration the nature of the Church's situation. The missionary message should not be a colorless, creedless Christianity. It should come in the form of a convinced and convincing presentation of historical Christianity in which the missionary and his Church grew up. But this type of presentation must never go off the deep end so that the Church's unity in Christ is endangered. Any pressing of viewpoints that tend to undermine the life of the Church as a whole is by that fact suspect, is by that fact contraband. The Church comes first. The Church must always come first. The Body of Christ, the place where the sacraments are administered and the Word is proclaimed, the place where the communion of saints receives its highest expression — the Church, always the Church, comes first. And not just *my* Church, *our* Church, but *the* Church, the *whole* Church, the Church of *Christ,* comes first. . . . Within the one Church there must be room for many viewpoints, but these viewpoints must be held within the one Church. If this tension between unity and diversity is observed, as it was so markedly in the Church of the New Testament, the future of the Church in Nigeria will be bright with promise.[2]

The Nigerian Christians' feeling for unity and oneness of fellowship is heightened by being faced with a powerful Islam and paganism. The missionary does not feel a challenge to his Christian existence as does the Nigerian of the Central Belt. Certainly the unity of Islam is a great attraction to those determined to leave animistic paganism, as was so well pointed out by Rev. R. K. Macdonald at the All-African Conference at Ibadan in 1958.

> He (the African on the move) sees the piety of the Muslims, the strict discipline of the Roman Catholics, and he knows many keen and enthusiastic Anglicans, Methodists, Presbyterians, Baptists, Congregationalists, Brethren, Seventh-Day Adventists and Jehovah's Witnesses. Church history means

[2] Boer, H. R., *op. cit.*, p. 5.

> nothing to him. To whom shall we go? With all this bewildering competition will he not prefer the unity of the Muslim faith to the divided Christ? Every reunion of our divided ranks makes the call of Christ clearer to him. . . . Dare we continue to let him hear a confused mumble when we presume to call ourselves heralds of Christ?[3]

The oneness of spirit and unity of the Church may well be the primary dynamic of Church life. Christ in His prayer for oneness in the seventeenth chapter of the Gospel of John emphasizes the dynamic part this oneness is to play: "so that the world may believe that thou hast sent me" (John 17:21).

Mission and Church relationships have usually developed through an evolutionary process. Few developments have been revolutionary in character in the Central Belt. Changes have come slowly and peacefully, but patience on the part of all concerned is needed.

In the Tiv Church, we see evidence of this evolutionary character of developing relationships drawn in exceptionally bold lines because of the situation caused by the turnover of one mission's work into the care of another. A rather unique "step-parent" relationship has emerged that calls for a shifting of loyalities not always accomplished smoothly. The opportunity created for the emergence of strong, independent, indigenous leadership is very desirable, but the attendant tendency to ignore the "step-parent," while natural enough, may prove detrimental to the Church.

Attitudes and procedures learned over a long period of time from a conservative and paternalistic "parent" cannot be changed in a moment of time, especially when this conservatism strengthens the traditionally conservative tribal position.[4]

The conservative, easy-going attitude of the indigenous Church relieves tensions and mitigates revolutionary impulses, but at the same time this conservatism may deaden the life of the Church. "What is once tied must remain tied" is not the spirit of modern Nigeria, but this attitude may

[3] Northcott, C., *op. cit.*, p. 87.
[4] Rubingh, E. R., Correspondence, December 10, 1962, p. 3.

plague the indigenous Church. Here is another area in which close fellowship of missionary and Nigerian leaders can be most propitious. A friendly, vital church-mission relationship must help break through this natural conservatism, which, while harmless enough on the surface, may stagnate into a self-centered and self-righteous outlook that could stifle all evangelistic outreach. Thus, if the evangelistic consciousness of the Church is to be wakened, creative and dynamic relationships between church leaders and missionaries who have evangelism at heart are very important. Religious conceptions inherited from conservative, animistic background may hinder a compulsion to win lost tribesmen. Spirits and gods confined to stones, trees, pots, or mountains, concerned only with the people of the tribe or clan or village in the immediate area, give no impetus to extend the faith in a particular god or spirit to other tribes or even neighboring villages. The other tribes already have *their* gods and spirits in their own mountains, trees, or pots. Animistic religion is totally tribal and self-centered and concerned with only the basic material needs of life: fertility of wives and fields, the welfare of the village, and protection from evil spirits. It is not only materialistic, but also fatalistic. It is not dynamic. It never contemplates extending its faith to others.

With this animistic background, a self-centered conception of Christianity is natural to individual Christians and to their Churches. Only in close and sympathetic fellowship can the mission and its missionaries demonstrate and interpret the New Testament command and joyous experience of evangelistic expansion. For it is true that ". . . only an indigenous, missionary-minded church will be capable of meeting Africa's needs and of providing soul and substance for a people in revolution."[5]

At this stage in the history of the indigenous Church in the Central Belt, the missionary must play a strategic role in bringing missionary zeal to full power. Whether the missionary be an advisor to a local church, an officer in a district church council, a teacher in a Bible school or theo-

[5] Northcott, C., *op. cit.*, p. 68.

logical college, a medical worker, educationalist, agriculturalist, sociologist, or anthropologist, his primary concern must be to witness to the *mission* of the Church. This cannot be less than the multiplication of churches – the multiplication of true followers of Jesus Christ, not only *in* every village, but to the end that *whole* villages "confess that Jesus Christ is Lord, to the glory of the Father" (Phil. 2:11). This is the most important aspect of church-mission relationships.

B. TRIBAL RELATIONSHIPS

In the Central Belt of Nigeria where there are 110 tribes, twenty-nine of which are not being reached at all by the Church, the tribal factor in church growth or nongrowth looms very large. What aspects of the tribal complexity bear upon church growth?

First, strong animosities often exist between tribes as a result of struggles for land and prestige. It is not uncommon to find that a tribe calls a neighboring tribe by a name of derision and that its own name simply means "the people" – as though there were no other people. Even within tribes, clans are extremely antagonistic toward each other. Villages two miles apart may be deeply suspicious of each other and exceedingly competitive. It was this ill will between tribes that made the populace of the Central Belt such an easy prey for the raiding Fulani of the nineteenth century. Very seldom were neighboring villages, much less tribes, willing to join forces against the common enemy. Thus internal discord and external pressure tended to greater and greater isolation.

Tribes overrun by the Fulani often turned upon neighboring tribes and became middlemen in the slave trade. The Fyem tribe (number 30 on the map, Figure III) is a case in point. A mixture of the pagan Angas (number 18) with the Fulani of the North, they made ideal go-betweens for the slave-traders. The tribes of Angas, Sura, Birom, Jarawa, and Kwanka have not yet forgotten the Fyem slave raiding.

It is no wonder then that the church in Gindiri, a predominantly Fyem town, should find a rather cool response in the surrounding tribal area. After twenty-eight years of preaching the gospel, the 1962 membership had reached only eighty-five. The total attendance of thirteen places of worship was 700. There had been so few baptisms yearly that the possibility of twenty for 1962 was to them very encouraging. This lack of growth is especially noticeable when it is remembered that the Gindiri town church is part of the Plateau Church, with the fast-growing Churches of Forum (Birom, number 31) to the north and Panyam (Sura, number 14) to the south. These animosities will best be overcome by establishing churches directly among the surrounding tribes, which are in no way dependent upon the Fyem. Counting on the Fyem Church to spread the Gospel is not wise.

Tribal hatreds, while fast cooling, are to a certain extent being perpetuated through the legitimate development of political parties. Most church leaders interviewed in the Central Belt, while tremendously enthusiastic about Nigerian independence, reported that the activities of political parties not only stirred up old tribal loyalties on a different level but also set brother against brother. The church leaders of the Benue, Muri, and Eastern Churches in particular said that political activity in reviving clan and tribal animosities was detrimental to the growth of the Church. In the Benue Church the Jukun (number 78) had taken the gospel to the Kuteb (number 69), developing a splendid intertribal relationship – until politics arrived. Now the two tribes vote for different political parties. That the members of the church are divided in their choice of political parties is a healthy situation from the point of view of Christian freedom, but that the vote should be divided along tribal lines is a matter of concern.

Another aspect of the tribal complexity that affects church growth is that of language. The Kuteb had spoken Jukun in addition to their own language. This made it possible for the Jukun to take the gospel to their Kuteb neighbors. Now that politics has driven them apart the Kuteb have determined not to use the Jukun language. Of course the leaders of both may still communicate by using Hausa.

On the whole, language has only been a barrier when the people themselves wanted it to be. It is amazing at what speed members of one tribe can learn another language when they really want to do so. However, Central Belt people are reluctant to learn the language of an "inferior" tribe.

Because of the prestige considerations – as well as the desire to communicate – Hausa is usually willingly accepted by the tribes of the Central Belt. It is the only language that can be used to communicate to all of the various tribal groups represented within the Church. Of course there are many older people who have not had the opportunity to receive classroom instruction and do not speak Hausa. However, the popularity of Hausa in the marketplace has given opportunity for most people to become familiar with it. Certainly the Hausa Bible is a great unifying force in the life of the Central Belt.

And yet, for local church worship and study, the tribal language or dialect is unquestionably the best medium of communication. Church leaders of the Mada Hills Church were disappointed that only three missionaries had ever learned Egon (number 11). They estimated that only about half of the people in the Church understood Hausa, and that outside of the Church most did not. The church leaders said fellowship between their numerous tribes was easy with Hausa, but that even so they still valued their own language. Gwoza (number 99) leaders said much faster progress could be made if missionaries and evangelists would learn the hill languages. Even in the Benue Church, where good church growth is being obtained with the use of Hausa, leaders stated that the use of tribal languages would enable better and more natural extension.

While there are three main difficulties in the Central Belt tribal complexity (tribal animosities, political revival of tribal differences, and the language complexity) none of these is an insurmountable obstacle in the growth of the church. Intermarriage between tribes is increasingly common, and through the years this has tended to blend the edge of one tribe into another. An excellent illustration of this is found in the Yedseram-Hawal River areas of the Eastern Church. The Kilba and the Margi blend into South Margi, but the South Margi could just as well be called North Kilba, the similarity is so marked. Bura blends into Kilba in the Dzongola area. Margi and Higi, while having few obvious similarities, are being fused through much intermarriage. These tribes are not obstacles to each other, but rather stepping stones.

In the Eastern Church area the Christian message won its first followers among the Bura tribe. When missionaries moved from Buraland to Margiland they were accompanied by Bura Christians, and Bura teachers taught in the first school in the Margi tribe. Soon the Higi across the river received the gospel from two avenues. Their youth attended the school in Lassa, and their lepers went to the leprosarium in Buraland. These intertribal relationships meant that Margi and Higi people learned the Bura language in a friendly atmosphere, which presaged the founding of the intertribal Eastern Church, with the three main language groups of Bura, Margi, and Higi.

At Numan the Lutheran Mission was greatly encouraged through its girls' school in the mid-twenties. At first it was restricted to Bachama girls with the hope of encouraging Bachama (number 88) families of good standing to take pride in it. But it was so successful that it had to be expanded to include many others[6] and through the years girls from many different tribes have found the Christian message both enlightening and uniting. In the great expansion of the Lutheran Church of the last ten years, the thirteen tribes of that area have not been a hindrance to church growth. Likewise the Benue Church has prospered in the midst of the seventeen tribes of the Baissa area.

When responsiveness is high and tribal exclusiveness among the youth is low, the Christian faith grows rapidly in an intertribal situation. This has been particularly true when youth of different tribes rub elbows in the mission schools. But it is more difficult to break through into the adult strata of the population. A more tribal approach is then needed.

In the United Missionary Church two tribal groups were large enough to warrant a special division of the Church into tribal regions: the Nupe Region and the Yoruba Region. And in one town, Share, two mission stations have been built: one for the Nupe and one for the Yoruba.

[6] Kirk-Greene, A. H. M., *op. cit.*, p. 122.

The advisability of divisions on tribal lines might be denied on the basis that all divisions of the Church on racial or tribal lines are sin. However, our question cannot be thus answered negatively by general insistence upon Christian unity, which we noted to be so very important in the first part of this chapter. Divisions that are not based upon racial theories or feelings of superiority and inferiority but upon practical considerations of homogeneous units are not contrary to the doctrine of Christian unity. The name United Missionary Church proclaims unity, but there is a diversity in this unity. The tribal divisions lend themselves to practical benefit for all concerned. It may be that Yoruba people feel superior to the Nupe and vice versa, but it is of no practical value to insist that both must worship together simply because the Church is one in Christ and in it there is neither "barbarian, Scythian, slave, freeman, but Christ is all and in all" (Col. 3:11).

Worshiping separately has advantages in that no "trade language" needs to be used and the literature of worship and Christian instruction may be in the mother tongue of the people. On the other hand, the third region of the United Missionary Church is the Hausa, so named because the Hausa language is used to bridge the language gulf between five tribes – in none of which is there a large enough Church to warrant organizing separately. Perhaps in the future this will be called for. However, in linguistic complexes the original need for a *lingua franca* makes the use of tribal languages in the future more difficult. Usage produces usage, and those using the "foreign language," Hausa, become more and more at home in it – not only in church life, but in the market and local government as well.

While the use of several interpreters in a worship service may be illustrative of the unity of the spirit, in spite of differences in language, it is not conducive to a truly spontaneous worship experience. Unfortunately the interpreters direct attention at least as much to the divisions in the congregation as to the unity of all in Christ.

The answer does not lie entirely in the use of Hausa as a unifying means of communication. Communication includes more than just language. The total life situation and the feeling of God speaking to men in that life situation – not from without it or from over a barrier, but from within it – is very important. The Tiv Church has a tremendous advantage here in having one cultural background, one language, one "life-way." Each person understands every other within the context of one pattern. The hopes and fears, the temptations and the victories – all are in similar patterns for all. Preaching, Bible, songbook, Christian literature and study courses, all in the Tiv language, enhance the Tiv Christian's feeling that the Church is *his* Church. All of this is a powerful attraction to Tiv people not yet in the Church.

Nigeria stands in the midst of a vast linguistic revolution. Since she is made up of several regions, each with many large primary linguistic groups, English will continue to make rapid headway as the *lingua franca.* However, for many years to come the best known language of "everyman" will be that of his ancestors – the language in which he mourns and laughs and loves. In such a language he can also worship most meaningfully.

The United Church of Christ in Kaduna, born out of a multi-tribal city immigrant complex, is a dynamic illustration of unity and diversity. 700 attend the service in Hausa, and 150 attend the service in Tiv, with a total communicant membership of 360. These two services are not a hindrance to the growth of the church, but an opportunity for freer and more creative worship. The church maintains two other "communion centers" in the capital territory of Kaduna, and is expanding through several other places of worship.

It is my considered opinion that while Hausa will continue to be the primary language of worship in the cities, and English in educational centers and schools of the Central Belt, the coming expansion, where three-fourths of a tribe becomes Christian and there is a church in every village and hamlet, will rest primarily upon the mother tongue. Such movement to Christ will be greatly assisted by the Bible, hymnbook, and liturgy being in the mother tongue.

There is one other very important aspect of the tribal factor in church growth. It is that of the web of relationships emphasized by Dr. Donald McGavran as of primary importance to multiplying churches. These webs of relationship through family and clan are closely related to the feeling of "we, the people." The strands of the web must be followed in the discipling of any tribe.

Homogeneous tribal units, held together by the web of clan and family relationships, present natural pathways for the spontaneous growth of the Church. In spite of three different dialects within the Higi tribe, its overall homogeneity is largely responsible for the rapid growth of the Church in its midst from 656 in 1958 to 2,110 in 1962. Much should be made of the web of relationships in an attempt to disciple whole segments of a tribe from the outset, including the chiefs and elders. Would the "Sevav Plan" (to be described later) work in any tribe? It is being introduced in Tivland, and I am convinced that it could be used in any responsive population.

C. ISLAM

From the days of the Fulani raids Islam has increasingly made inroads among the tribal peoples of the Central Belt. This is especially true in areas where the Fulani were successful in conquest. As a result some tribes have, outwardly at least, turned to Islam. In many areas the village chiefs have become Moslem in order to keep their position or to enhance their prestige. Through the years many pagans, honestly seeking a better way, have turned to Islam. In the Moslem towns scattered throughout the Central Belt one can find many who now appear to be truly Moslem, but who were born in the pagan villages of the nearby tribes. Recently a Fulani man was won to Christ in the village of Lassa. He was an old man, and such a conversion is very uncommon. But this Fulani had not been born a Fulani. He had been born a Higi. Years ago he had become part of Islamic culture. For him to make a second change of faith was indeed a miracle of God's grace! Most tribal people who become Moslem are not persuaded to make a second change.

Moslem communities grow up on the edge of pagan villages. They are made up of pagan converts gathered about a Moslem teacher who has unobtrusively moved into their midst "on his way to Mecca." This new community, separated from the pagan populace by its being grouped together in one place, is freed from the demands of pagan village life. In an attempt to get this same freedom the Christian has often taken his family and, joining himself with other Christians, has created a Christian village, either on the edge of his pagan village area or at the site of a mission station. However, the pagan relatives do not as readily free the convert to Christianity from village responsibilities as they do the convert to Islam.

While the lower standards of Islam (maximum of four wives, use of God's name "in vain," wearing of amulets and charms, use of "medicine men," etc.) opens an easy way into Islam for an animistic tribesman, yet the convert to Islam must make a complete break with "pagan" relatives, even though pagan ways are incorporated into his new religion. The Christian convert is not duty bound to break the ties that bind him to his original community to the extent that is demanded of the convert to Islam. The latter cannot eat with his pagan relatives; the Christian can, and does. The Moslem despises those who are uncircumised, eat pork, and are "pagan." The Christian, on the other hand, is urged by his faith to love those without Christ and to speak of no man as ignoble or "pagan." So the way is open for a Christian to bring influence to bear upon his own family and the total pattern of paganism in his village. The "web of relationship" need not and should not be broken. At the same time, if the web is unbroken it makes it possible for pagan influences to flow toward the Christian, perhaps even more readily than for his Christian faith to flow outward to his pagan friends and relatives. By breaking the web of relationship, Islam makes it less possible for converts to revert again to tribal patterns of animistic paganism.

In addition to breaking the web of relationship, the convert to Islam also enters a culture that has for hundreds of years been formed within the African setting. There is no uncertainty about the requirements or his place within that culture. The convert to Christianity, on the other hand, enters a culture that is in the process of forming. There are many uncertainties in areas where his animistic upbringing clashes with the new Christian way. Where hard lines should be drawn and where there should be a synthesis of the two is not always clear. The former has often been done, the latter is in the process of evolving with more or less satisfactory progress from place to place. However, the Christian culture has now formed sufficiently in some areas so that when an individual slips into pagan practices, the tendency is not to disfellowship him and thus force his reversion to paganism but to deal with the error within the Christian community. As a result, what often seems to western observers like deplorable laxity in the Church is only evidence of progress in Christian orientation and the slow but sure formation of Christian culture in the African setting.[7]

Both Christianity and Islam have helped bring about a deterioration of the village sacred places. Yet, the "life way" of the mass of the pagan population has not changed. In most places outside influences move along in streams – parallel with paganism – here and there breaking into each other to intermingle and then separate again.

Maps such as Trimingham's in *Islam in West Africa,* which show percentage of pagan, Moslem, and Christian in the population, while giving a largely correct overall impression, may go astray in particular areas. Since reliable population figures on religious affiliation are difficult to find, such maps are merely estimates. From my observation the number of Moslems in the eastern part of the Central Belt of Nigeria is exaggerated in Trimingham's map. The area from Wukari north to Biu and from Bauchi east to the border of Nigeria should be represented in clear white as pagan rather than 25% to 50% Moslem. While the Church is growing rapidly in this area it is also far from reaching 25% of the population. Also, in the Tiv area south of the Benue River the Christians have not yet reached 25% of the population. In fact at the present time 10% would be a very high estimate. Likewise, Moslems are very few in the Tiv area.

The representation of 50% to 75% Moslem in the western part of the Central Belt is certainly correct – perhaps even higher in the Nupe tribe. But there are many large pockets

[7] Kulp, H. S., Personal interview, August, 1963.

of pagan people throughout this area. In such pockets the Church today must exert its strongest witness.

The concentration of population geographically is very significant when considering a map of religious distribution. The results of the 1964 Nigerian Census may throw some light upon this, but these figures are not available at the time of my writing. It is evident, however, that the concentration of population becomes increasingly lighter as one leaves the coastal areas and moves toward the more arid country to the north. Thus a comparison of percentage of population is not necessarily a clear comparison of size of religious constituency. 50% to 75% in the north of Nigeria may not represent as large a constituency as 25% to 50% in the coastal areas. The high concentration of population in the Central Belt is a factor that must not be overlooked. The faith that wins the millions of people here will largely guide the future tides of Nigeria.

The value of Trimingham's map is that it shows the dynamic confrontation between one faith and another — a confrontation that is vital to the growth of the Church today. That Islam is increasing is obvious to those of us here in the Central Belt today. But that the day has already been won is not a foregone conclusion at all. Yet I am certain that a much more rapid movement to Christ is a prerequisite to a church growth that will forestall the tragedy of a Christianity restricted to the coastal areas. A tragedy indeed it would be, not for the Church itself, but for the millions that would then be cut off from the blessings of life in Christ.

D. POLYGAMY

The practice of polygamy and the churches' stand against it has had a negative effect upon the numerical growth of the Church in the Central Belt. In all areas of TEKAS, and the several of ECWA I visited, Nigerian leaders, evangelists, and pastors expressed concern about the difficulties polygamy brought to the life of the Church. Christian leaders stated that many among the 100,000 non-Christians attending Sunday worship in Tivland would become Christians very readily if it were not for the monogamous position of the church.

At Panyam (Plateau Church) a group of twenty-two evangelists felt polygamy was "not a great problem." Even so, when they drew up a list of six hindrances to the growth of the church they listed it as third. Number one was beer drinking; number two, adultery; four was that educated teachers lose interest; five emphasized the strength of paganism; six, that evangelists too often do what they like. This last was a touch of self-judgment, which is commendable in a group of evangelists and is likely prophetic of spiritual growth and practical improvement. If "politics" were added in about fourth place in this list, it would complete the primary hindrances given by the TEKAS church leaders.

The evangelists thought that the primary reason so many Christians are tempted to take a second wife is that in a pagan and Moslem society a plurality of wives brings adult status. Youths who at the time of baptism are not yet married or have only just recently taken their first wife do not face the issue seriously. They may answer the question, "Do you understand that the Christian way is one man and one wife, and do you intend to follow that way?" with a glib, "Yes." Or, answering it sincerely, they do not yet realize the social pressures soon to come from parents, relatives, and community to take a second wife. It was stated that when a man gets a good-paying government position he is tempted to put his money in a second "bride price" rather than give it to the church. This temptation comes very strongly to school teachers who, receiving good salaries and being in positions of community leadership, feel that the one blot upon their social status is that they have only one wife. In the new Nigeria, however, polygamy tends to mark one as less than "modern." Thus the element of status through polygamy is in the process of significant change.

At Zaki Biam a group of twenty-six women, nineteen of whom were wives of evangelists, were very vocal about monogamy being the only possible Christian way. They said, "Polygamy is not the desire of women. Every woman desires freedom, living with her own husband." Out of these twenty-six, fifteen said their husbands had persuaded them to become Christians.

It must be realized that the question of monogamy or polygamy concerns the extended family, and is not only a matter of status for the husband. It is also a matter of progeny. The traditional attitude toward the family in the Central Belt is such that a childless marriage is an invalid marriage. Separation and taking a new husband, or taking a new or second wife, in order to try afresh for children, is a common practice in pagan life, but it brings deep spiritual and practical problems to the Christian.

In the recent past, polygamy has been related to the need for increased labor in the fields, but with improved agriculture and the reduction of infant mortality in Christian communities this is not as important as it once was. In fact, the higher standards of living striven for by many Christians tend to eliminate the possibility of sinking large sums in the bride price and upkeep of another wife. With infant mortality on the decrease, the possibility of having too many children to feed, clothe, and educate – even with only one wife – is already an increasingly difficult problem for some Christian families.

It is clear from conference with Nigerian church leaders that the exclusion of polygamy from the church is not based primarily upon sexual considerations, but first of all, Biblical. Paul wrote, "Because of the temptation to immorality, let every man have his own wife and every woman her own husband" (I Cor. 7:2). He makes this statement reluctantly, as though even one wife is more than ideal. However, we of European and American culture know that monogamy does not create a moral man, and neither does polygamy. The Nigerian Christian also knows this. A Nigerian pastor said to me, "If you have one wife and are running around the village, ten wives will not stop your running around the village!" This same pastor was asked, "But, considering your tribal taboos, would it not be difficult if you had only one wife and she were pregnant?" He answered, "Suppose you have three wives and they are all pregnant?" It is not the marriage state, whatever its form, that creates morality. Morality is a matter of the inner man.

A strong Christian argument against polygamy is given by Rev. C. O. Ogan, Methodist, of Umahia, Nigeria, in a paper he delivered at the meeting held in May, 1960, of the Christian Council of Nigeria. He said, "In the final analysis, the argument against polygamy is an argument against using another person wholly and solely for one's own interests, and the old conception of marriage made women to be so used."

In a Christian family where the husband accepts his wife as a human being, as valuable as himself in the sight of God and in daily life, and a companion to whom he has certain responsibilities, monogamy is not a difficult way. Since status and self-aggrandizement are the primary problems, and pagan marriages, both polygamous and monogamous, break up very often under ordinary life conditions, most church leaders in the Central Belt feel that it would not be too difficult for polygamous men to arrange a monogamous family situation for themselves if they really wanted to. Though few women in the pagan community have had only one husband in their lifetime, a woman finds it difficult to leave a polygamous relationship and enter a monogamous one because family and clan relationships might not allow her to go to one of the adult wifeless men usually plentiful in the villages. But she would have no difficulty in entering another polygamous relationship.

While polygamy as a continuing system of family life in the new Nigeria is doomed, its death will not come quickly. The excess of women to men is against its quick death. While most population statistics give only a slight edge to the females, in certain parts of the Central Belt, the female population is, in fact, significantly larger than the male.

The 1962 tax figures of the Cubanawa and Uba Government Districts of the Eastern Church give a total figure of 114,728 Higi people. Of these, 43,064 are males and 71,664 are females! This means that, speaking statistically, there are 1.6 Higi women to every Higi man, or about half the men could have three wives each, if the other half had none. As a matter of fact, however, a good portion of those people are still unmarried. Also, there are quite a few men who have five or more wives, as well as a surprising number of adult men in every village with no wife at all at the moment and, of course, many who have only one wife. Tribal wars once reduced the number of men and increased the number of women through capture, but it is significant to note that after thirty-five years of peace the female population is still so much in excess of the male in the Higi tribe. The large number of Higi men who have gone away from their homes to join the army and the police and into the large cities looking for money-paying jobs has accentuated this excess of women in their home communities.

Yet in the Higi tribe, where men and women are so disproportionate and where polygamy is deeply ingrained, the Eastern Church has had its fastest growth. In seven years it jumped from approximately 120 communicant members to 2,110 in 1962! Apparently the monogamous stand of the church has been no serious drawback as yet. But many of the members are young married people who have not seriously faced the possibility of a second wife.

However, polygamy is not the only problem, nor necessarily the most serious one, that brings trouble as Christians attempt to make a home in the midst of a pagan culture. The total pattern of marriage customs is involved. There is the relationship between the two families, which is symbolized by the bride price and dowry. There are matters of inheritance and of levirate and sororate marriages. Where the Christian congregation is made up largely of young men, many of whom are ex-schoolboys, the finding of Christian wives is difficult, and so is marrying a pagan girl without entering into the pagan rites. Developing an affectionate fellowship between husband and wife is also a primary difficulty. Each party to the marriage is usually more strongly bound to his and her own people than to each other. All sorts of problems arise, ranging from separate farms, separate money bags, separate clan responsibilities, to paternal ownership of children, sexual incompatibility, beatings, and infidelity. Some men are pressed into polygamy as a result of their sins of infidelity, preferring to take their pregnant "girl friend" as a second wife to all the problems involved in an illegitimate child. These problems will afflict the Christian Church long after polygamy is dead. Church leaders agree that situations growing out of the above marriage relationships are every bit as great a hindrance as is polygamy.

It is urgently important that young people have a deep

and vital experience of Christ in their monogamous state so that the pride and status of polygamy will not be a serious temptation to them. Also, considering the Christian ideal of faithfulness to one wife, which eliminates promiscuity so prevalent in Central Belt pagan life, it is of highest priority that young Christians learn "to be happy with the wife of their youth" and that both the man and the woman find physical, spiritual, and intellectual satisfactions in each other that are so complete that neither will be tempted by others.

How disruptive are the tensions due to the Church's stand for monogamy? As far as I have been able to determine there have been no serious breaks with the Church over this problem. In two areas in the Central Belt I found that polygamy had become an open issue. In one part of the Eastern Church it had been aroused by a missionary, and at Kwalla in the Plateau Church a small group had partly broken away over this issue.

In Southern Nigeria there are many separatist churches and it is often thought that these breaks with the more traditional churches were largely due to the desire for polygamy. Geoffrey Parrinder in his book *Religion in an African City* observes:

> There is a further notion prevalent that the separatists all broke away from the orthodox churches on the issue of polygamy. This is an error. Polygamy was not the root cause of separation, except in a minority of cases . . . and while it is true that a greater latitude for polygamy is allowed in the separatist bodies than in the mission churches, yet there are some differences of practice on this matter between one church and another.[8]

Parrinder points out that the rise of the African Church was due to a dissension over the assignment of Bishop Johnson of the St. Paul's Church, Breadfruit, Lagos, to a new position in the north. This, and not a desire for polygamy, was the beginning of the break that brought secession and the formation of the new Church.

Yet monogamy as the only form of marriage within the church has had a slowing-down effect upon church growth, as

[8] Parrinder, E. G., *Religion in an African City,* p. 108.

well as causing a loss in membership. According to the record of the predominantly Margi Church of Lassa, Eastern Church, which in 1962 had a communicant membership of 680 with several hundred others in preparation for membership, had from its inception in the early 1930s lost a total of 226 members. Of these, ninety-seven had moved away and 129 were lost through discipline by the Church, as follows:

Cause	**Number permanently disfellowshiped from the Church**
Beer drinking	2
Stealing	4
Reversion to Paganism	5
Immorality	8
Roman Catholicism	12
Islam	21
Disinterest	23
Polygamy	54
	129

Here is evidence that in one church's records polygamy has been the cause of a substantial loss through the years. It is instructive to note that the polygamous loss of fifty-four was not all on the initiative of men taking second wives. Seventeen of these fifty-four were women who went to polygamous husbands or who took other women's husbands monogamously.[9] Also, it is of interest to note that the loss through polygamy, while substantial, is well under half of the total loss for disciplinary reasons. Loss through mere disinterest is almost 50% of that due to polygamy. Note also the twenty-one lost to Islam.

In the Central Belt I did not detect any feeling among the church leaders that the monogamous position was more strict than the love of Christ demanded for the well-being of His followers. All Churches have taken the stand that monogamy is the only form of Christian marriage. To retreat from this position would be to change the whole character

[9] That is, the first wife having been driven off.

of the Christian message, putting destructive self-interest into the place of love for God and fellow man. Certainly such a move in these fast-changing days would be doing a disservice to the members of the Christian Church, and to Nigeria. As the non-Christian world moves forward, the Church should lead in the enlightenment that is coming, not drag behind, as it has too often done in actual practice. In other parts of the world racial discrimination and denominational clashes, for instance, have been cases of such "drag."

But the bulk of the population over forty years of age, already involved in and dominated by polygamy, has scarcely been touched by the Christian message. A cross section of the population has *not* been converted. Whole hamlets have not come in. The importance of literacy looms so large in the eyes of Nigerian and missionary church leaders in some areas that to bring in the older population who cannot read seems to them a backward step. However, the older people must be reached. The great harvest is still in the future. In Higiland the 2,110 church members, with 3,700 attending church on Sunday morning, are only a very small portion of the almost 115,000 population. The challenge of the future is very great, and social factors relating to polygamy and the home will play a large part in the life of the church in Higiland. They are also very important throughout all the Central Belt.

So something must be done to open wider the door of the Church to the tribal populace still bound in the chains of polygamous practice. It is hoped that multi-individual decisions on a very broad tribal base may bring hundreds of thousands into the Church of Christ in the immediate future. While frustrated with the old fetishes, tribal groups find their leading men handicapped by difficult polygamous situations, and thus are prevented from making complete village decisions for Christ.

The Church needs a plan for facing this situation in a creative way. To say, "Believe even though the 'nails' of polygamy prevent baptism and 'today you shall be with me in Paradise,'" is not sufficient.

A significant statement has been made recently by a special

conference[10] on African independent church movements that relates to the monogamous position of the Church:

> The negative attitude hitherto adopted by the older churches toward members of polygamous homes has been no small barrier to converts to Christianity. In respect of this issue, a loveless, censorious and legalistic approach has developed which does not reflect the Spirit of our Lord Jesus. The Church is called to be a minister of Christ's redeeming power and grace, not His punitive instrument. In the judgment of many of us, the polygamous status of a new convert from a non-Christian background should be no barrier to his acceptance into church membership. However, Christians within the fold must be taught to appreciate and practice standards of home life based on the mind of Christ, which, among other things, includes monogamy.
>
> It is hoped that members of polygamous homes will be treated with such humaneness as is consonant with the spirit of our Lord, and that women will be educated to realize their status in the light of God's will and purpose. Polygamy in its traditional form is passing: the Churches must further educate their members towards stable Christian family life, while recognizing that this has to be set within the context of the increasing breakdown of all sexual moral standards.
>
> This issue is frequently a burning one between older and independent churches. We suggest that the former should consider whether in those of the latter where there has been little change from traditional African patterns of marriage, there may not be, nevertheless, a genuine relationship to Jesus Christ. By virtue of this, may they not be recognized as churches with whom possibilities of Christian fellowship must be explored?[11]

The suggestion in the first paragraph that persons coming from a pagan background be not hindered by polygamy from entering the Church, but that those in the Church should maintain monogamy, has often been suggested and sounds like a possible solution at first glance, but it is not. There are

[10] Arranged by the Department of Missionary Studies of the World Council of Churches and held under the auspices of the All-Africa Church Conference at the Mindolo Ecumenical Centre, Sept. 6-13, 1962.

[11] The International Review of Missions, April, 1963, p. 168.

few who can draw such a fine line. In one section of the Eastern Church a very liberal view was championed for a period of three years. The view presented was that monogamy is the ideal Christian position, but that Christ meets everyone *in* the culture in which he finds him. Result? Several Christians of many years' experience took a second wife and many young people in the Church were led astray from the "Christian ideal."

The suggestions in the second and third paragraphs of the quotation are worthy of serious consideration. However, if teaching concerning women's true status is given, it must be directed primarily to the men.

No complete solution to the problem has been found. However, the Eastern Church has, in addition to the register for church members, a register of those who for various reasons (polygamy, beer drinking, Moslem pressure) cannot come into full membership through baptism. Any polygamist who attends church regularly and expresses sincere faith in Jesus Christ, but who is unable or unwilling to "put away his wives," is urged to make a definite witness to his faith by having his name written in this special register and making a public statement of faith. He thereby *sets his face toward the Church and is counted as part of the Christian community.* His wives may be registered in the same way. In fact, the first of his wives may become a baptized Christian, and of course any older wives who separate from their husbands according to the tribal custom of separation after passing beyond the age of child bearing may also be baptized.

In addition to maintaining the New Testament teaching of Christian monogamy[12] this special register gives a basis for making an appeal to the older leaders of a community, who are likely polygamous, to lead their people into the fellowship of the Church. It may be used by the Spirit of God in reaching the older people and the leaders in these days of great responsiveness, for its greatest advantage is that it opens the door for complete family groups, clans, and hamlets to make decisions for Christ together. After the primary move to Christ, classes of religious instruction will bring a large per-

[12] Cf. Mark 10:2-9; Eph. 5:33; I Cor. 7:2, 3, 10, 11; I Thess. 4:3-8.

centage of the group to full membership through baptism. But from the very beginning Christian worship and Bible study will replace fetish worship, and Christian services for seed planting and harvest and child dedication will take the place of fertility rites.

E. OTHER ASPECTS OF PAGANISM

In addition to polygamy, there are other aspects of animistic pagan life that are vitally related to church growth. Pagan worship forms involving fetishism and the use of beer dominate Central Belt village life. These religious forms are disintegrating under the impact of Christian education and the changing climate. Yet it must not be thought that paganism is dead. "Great Pan . . . is not dead," writes Max Warren.[13] Some of the more vicious forms of pagan practices have long been outlawed and subdued by the government, but the revival of the Bori cult of devil possession in the Muri Church area and the tenacious hold of the practice of infanticide upon the South Margi tribe in the Eastern Church area and among the eastern hill tribes of the Plateau Church indicate how deeply rooted are pagan practices – and underline the fact that many tribes in the Central Belt have scarcely changed their customs from what they were in 1900.

The Bori revival in the Muri area brings the power struggle of Christianity and paganism to the fore. Its appeal to the youth of marriageable age is very great; for, in the context of courtship, bravery is demonstrated by self-torture. In the southern area of the church, south of the river, the Mumuye initiatory "Dodo" rites, practiced every several years, hinder the response to Christ. During a "Dodo year" both the Church and Islam lose followers to the pagan rites. One of the very few Mumuye Christians reported, "The people of my tribe think I became a Christian because I didn't want to be beaten by the other youths. The beating is part of the Dodo rites. If any one runs away or refuses to join the beatings, he is called a woman."

Beer drinking is associated with pagan rites and worship

[13] Church Missionary Society News Letter, No. 196, July, 1957.

and is used as an oblation to the spirits and also as a symbol of close relationship between the worshipers. In the Eastern Church area there is the practice of two men drinking beer cheek to cheek from the same gourd. Only the closest of friends may participate in this type of "communion." This intimate ritual relationship of beer to worship and fellowship is strengthened by the fact that for many of the older men the corn-brewed beer has become, as they say, "our food."

All the churches visited were finding drinking an increasingly serious problem. One church reported that beer drinking is "beginning to be a problem." Most found it to be a "great problem," a "temptation to both men and women," a "sad situation," a "cause for much disciplinary action by the church," and a "hindrance to people entering the church." In the Zalanga Church of ECWA, beer drinking vies with Islam as a hindrance to the growth of the church.

But if Pan is not dead, he is mortally wounded. The leaders of the churches in the Central Belt indicate that, while there is a wide variation in tribal areas, the erosion and breakup of pagan ways is the open door to church extension. Pan is fatally ill and the animist is looking for a "better way." Church leaders often reported that even older men realize that Christianity is the true way, but continue the pagan way half-heartedly. Some have left the old fetishes, but handicapped by polygamy, have not become Christians. This serious situation is the open door to Islam. The dynamic decision is not between Christianity and paganism with an infinite amount of time to think about it. The powers of Islam and materialism increase the urgency of the contest for tribes on the move.

There is yet one other aspect to the situation. When youth of any numbers have had a deep personal Christian experience, they may react so negatively to the pagan ways of their village that creative interplay between the Christian youth and the elders of the village is impossible.

A striking illustration of this was enacted recently in the village of Uvu in the Margi tribe where in 1962 a group of more than two hundred youths and young married adults were formally organized into the Uvu Church of EKAS, Eastern. The clash between these Christians and the elders of their village came to a head at the time of one of the many special days set aside for pagan rituals, which supposedly assure the welfare of the village and the fertility of fields and women. It is required that on the day the rites are performed no one puts an iron hoe to the ground. Young men of the Christian community felt such a pagan taboo had no claim upon them. Therefore they went to their fields, not quietly, but with the beating of drums as is usual for a hoeing bee, proclaiming to all, far and near, that they were breaking with the village tradition. The seriousness of such a break is that from the point of view of the elders the village is one unit in which all play an interrelated part. The offense would bring suffering not only to the offenders but to the whole village. Naturally, the chief and his elders were outraged and threatened the leaders of the church with physical punishment and court action.

As church advisor I was called to discuss the matter. I went with the Nigerian secretary of a neighboring church and met with the chief, his elders, and a half dozen local church leaders. We soon found that the Christians of Uvu were adamant in their stand to ignore all pagan taboos. We suggested that while these taboos were meaningless to the Christians, they might transform the periodic ritual days into Christian days by changing them into times of special worship and Bible study. The elders of the village showed immediate interest. We mentioned that throughout the history of the Christian church, pagan festivals had been changed into Christian festivals. "Make these days into opportunities for special prayer for the welfare of the village, praying not to the spirits of the village 'yals,' but praying to the one true God and Father of the Lord Jesus Christ. Stay home from the fields, not because of pagan taboos, but in deference to the honor due to the chief and the village elders (Rom. 13). By thus showing them honor, they will be attracted to the Way of Christ. Plan Christian worship for morning, afternoon, and evening of these days, and call in special speakers from the neighboring churches." The chief and his elders responded by saying, "And we will come to your Christian services!" The secretary of the neighboring church was enthusiastic and spoke for this suggestion to be given a try, but the Christians of the village would not yield, for they felt that by so doing they would be compromising their faith in Christ who said that the Christian way would separate between a Christian and his people (Matt. 10:34-39). No solution has been worked out. The Christians are being persecuted during these periodic days and the village elders are being estranged further and further from Christianity. The church has been growing so fast among the youth that the elders are embarassingly on the losing side – tragically lost for time and eternity.

F. MISSION AUXILIARIES

The mission auxiliaries (schools, hospitals, and rural development programs) have been an important part of the dynamics of church growth in the Central Belt. That this aspect of mission activity has attracted the eye of the educated Nigerian in positions of social and governmental leadership is clear from A. A. Nwafor Orizu's statement (page 19) as to what he believes to be the "mission" of Christianity. He is thinking of more than the social services of education, medicine, and improved agriculture, but certainly must have these predominantly in mind. The "proper light" must shine among the Africans to "regenerate their society, to emancipate their mentality, to nationalize their activities, and to secure their existence."

The mission of the Church does bring enlightenment and transformation to society, but this is not the goal. The primary goal is that man comes into a right relationship with God as revealed in Christ Jesus. The Christian Church maintains that the basic problem of mankind is not poverty, ill health, or illiteracy, but estrangement from God. When this is ended, the indwelling Spirit of God will lead to enlightenment in every other realm. Nothing will advance the Central Belt more rapidly and wholesomely than for the tribes to turn to Christ in a series of thorough-going, well-shepherded "people movements."[14]

Nevertheless, compassion and a desire to serve have made

[14] Described by McGavran in *The Bridges of God.*

Christian missions in the Central Belt responsive to the physical, mental, and social needs of the tribal peoples. From the very beginning social services were prominent in the activity of missionaries, as can be illustrated by the early founding of the Freed Slaves Home at Rumasha in 1908.

Medical services of dispensary, hospital, and medical-evangelistic touring have played an increasingly large place in the work of missions.

Complete figures are difficult to get, but an indication of the tremendous medical services being rendered in the Central Belt is given here:

	New Patients	
Sudan United Mission (as a whole)	1959: 403,927	
South African Branch	1959: 54,810	
Christian Reformed Church at Zaki Biam		1958: 33,603
Evangelical United Brethren at Bambur	1950: 8,934	1961: 26,880
British, Plateau	1946: 2,092	1960: 12,500
Lutheran at Shellem	1951: 1,905	1961: 10,552
Lutheran at Languda	1937: 885	1948: 2,000
Christian Reformed Church at Baissa	1951: 1,610	1961: 5,605
Church of the Brethren Mission at Garkida and Lassa	1927: 1,118	1960: 20,187

This is an incomplete report, but two things can be seen: (1) There has been a tremendous increase in new patients treated during the last twenty years. (2) Hundreds of thousands of new patients are treated each year by mission hospitals and dispensaries. In addition to these there have been tens of thousands of leprosy patients treated in the Central Belt. In 1961 the total number of leprosy patients under treatment in the care of the Church of the Brethren Mission alone was 6,068, and all branches of the Sudan United Mission treated 23,431 cases in 1959.

Medical service was originally begun by missionary doctors and nurses, and is now augmented by scores of Nigerian registered nurses, most of them trained in mission training courses.

The service given by missions in education has been equally

significant. A. D. Galloway, writing in the Independence issue of *Nigeria* magazine, says, "The mission school is probably the greatest single missionary factor influencing the life and culture of Nigeria."[15] The following list suggests the extent of impact in part of the Central Belt:

Enrollment in Primary Schools

	Year	Enrollment
All Sudan United Mission branches:	1955:	7,175
	1959:	14,412
Christian Reformed Church Mission:	1961:	7,265
In single station areas:		
Baissa	1949:	24
	1961:	556
Mkar	1961:	1,864
Alushi	1955:	785
	1960:	1,430
Forum	1950:	403
	1960:	1,400
Church of the Brethren Mission	1923:	26
	1945:	403
	1961:	4,198
	1962:	5,335

Figure XII gives the number of new pupils each year and total enrollment in the Church of the Brethren Mission schools. Awakening came immediately following World War II. From the beginning of this mission's schools (1926) to 1950 there were approximately 4,000 pupils enrolled. Then from 1950 to 1960 there was an average intake of new pupils each year of approximately 1,085 and a total number of individuals in school for some part of the ten-year period of 10,855, making a cumulative total about 15,000 young people taught in the schools. Note also that the number of new persons attending school in the ten years between 1950 and 1960 is more than two and one-half times the number in the twenty-seven years from 1923 to 1950. The total number of new pupils influenced by the schools, up to and including 1962, was over 19,000.

Mission schools in the Central Belt have not yet reached their peak of usefulness. The educational task for Northern

[15] *Nigeria,* Independence Issue, October, 1960, p. 63.

Nigeria has just well begun, as the following table shows. Note the ratio of children in school to the number of school-age children (6-12 years) in the various provinces.

Ratio of the Primary School Enrollment
the 6-12 Age Group[16]

Province	Population
North of the Central Belt:	
Sokoto	1 in 35.7
Katsina	1 in 22.2
Kano	1 in 22.2
Bornu	1 in 22.2
In the Central Belt:	
Sardauna	1 in 14.5
Bauchi	1 in 12
Adamawa	1 in 9.8
Niger	1 in 8.26
Zaria	1 in 5.25
Plateau	1 in 4.5
Benue	1 in 4.3
Kabba	1 in 3.1
Ilorin	1 in 2.76
Capital Territory of Kaduna	1 in 1.79

Most missions are enlarging their educational programs to help meet this ever-increasing need for education.

Pastor David Olatayo of ECWA states that the Church must be interested in the material needs of the people as well as in their spiritual needs, and he recognizes the evangelistic opportunities that newly opened schools bring. He says:

> Our people desire education. Without a concern for the material needs of the people the Christian message cannot go forward in this land as we would desire. Schools open opportunities to preach Christ. One totally Moslem town asked our church to open a school there. We told them, "But you must understand that if we open a school we will also preach Christ." They answered, "This is all right. After all, were

[16] This table is based upon 1952 census population statistics and 1960 school statistics as prepared by the Survey Department of Nigeria. Considering the increase in population since 1952, the task ahead is even greater than these figures portray.

> we not pagans originally? Our parents did not keep us from becoming Moslem and we will not prevent our children from becoming Christian."[17]

What effect does medical and educational work actually have upon church growth? Hospitals and dispensaries have not made large numbers of direct conversions as a result of the sympathetic care given to the ill, even though most carry out evangelistic visitation among the patients and have special prayer services – all of which is primarily directed by Nigerian pastors and evangelists. However, medical work has been a spectacular ground-breaker.

Immediately after the closed area of what is now Sardauna Province was opened to itineration by people other than government officers in the early 1950s, I visited the village of Kamale on the border of the Cameroon Republic. While chatting with the chief and his elders in the shade of a large tree, I made the comment that if the government regulation had not kept us out on the grounds that they were too dangerous, we would have visited them long before! This was taken as a rousing joke by all present, and after a hearty laugh one of the elders ventured, "Why, we aren't dangerous. We know you! We go to the hospital at Lassa (20 miles to the west) all the time!" Too many years passed after this first visit before an evangelist was sent to their village, but the medical service of the Lassa Hospital had opened the doors of the village to the Church. In 1961 the first twenty-four people of the village turned to Christ, and a year later about half that number were baptized. Unfortunately, there were no older people in this first move to Christ. But young and old had been made responsive as a result of the service of the hospital.

Mission hospitals have been an important element in the break-up of fetish religion. In the Tiv tribe witchcraft, as a means of physical healing, was proved untrue by modern medicine. At Takum, where there is a large new Christian Reformed Church Mission hospital, the elders of the church claimed that the hospital helps break fetish power. At

[17] Personal interview, Aug., 1963.

Zaki Biam the men in the Bible school said, "The dispensary and hospital cure more diseases than the idols. The Word of God is heard there and people find that their children live without pagan rites." The Languda, who believe special spirits cause practically every disease, were strongly attracted to the Christian faith when they found that the dispensary at Shellem could heal their leg ulcers. On the other hand, at Lankaveri in the Mumuye tribe there is little faith in the dispensary as yet. "The people would rather give the required seven goats to a medicine man of their tribe, for if the patient dies the goats are always returned!"

The big question is that of whether the actual growth of the Church is commensurate with the great resources put into medical work. Before attempting to discuss this, let us return to the school picture, for on this matter of church growth the two can be "put into one bag," as the Margi people would say.

Have the schools been an aid to church growth? In some parts of the world mission, educational work has not brought the growth and stability to the Church that was hoped for. In India no one would think of suggesting – even before the government took over the schools – that the schools were a direct evangelizing agency. In West Africa, however, the schools are a direct and effective evangelistic arm of the Church.

The Nigerian church leaders see Church and schools not so much as walking side by side but as keenly involved within each other. The mission schools are staffed with Christian teachers, and every day means at least one class period for studying a mission-prepared Christianity syllabus as a regular part of the government-approved curriculum. In addition to this, there are chapel periods and music periods in which Christian indigenous songs are sung. These are the aspects that make education an instrument of church growth.

The "Ten Year Program" of the Church of the Brethren states, "The administration of program (educational, medical, agricultural) to meet the basic objective ('To teach all . . . so clearly . . . that they will decide to follow Christ') must involve measuring every aspect of program, every institution, every investment, every assignment against its probable effect in terms of gospel proclamation and church growth."

It would be difficult to find a Christian in the Central Belt who would suggest discontinuing the social services of the mission in order to direct resources to the central task of evangelizing. Pastor Dusu of the Plateau Church said, "Such a possibility never enters our minds."

Is the Nigerian attitude justified on the basis of actual church growth? In the Central Belt of Nigeria I believe it is, though response to the Church through medicine and education has not been equally good everywhere, and in early 1963 church leaders of the Plateau Church did actually raise the question as to the advisability of church involvement in education. Yet, as of January, 1964, the Plateau Church became proprietor of all of the primary schools of its "parent" mission, the British Branch of the Sudan United Mission!

On the whole, a very large proportion of school children have become Christians. The chart of the Eastern Church (Figure XII) shows that school enrollment exceeded the membership of the Church until 1958. In that year school attendance was 4,029 and church membership was 4,371. Until about 1957 the age of youth entering the schools was much higher than after that date. Middle and even late teenagers (some married) were numerous in the primary grades. A number of them had been baptized even before any school experience. This made the school a real source of strength to the church. Now government regulations have cut out the older pupils. Thus, a higher percentage of school children were baptized Christians before 1957 than since. But with 19,000 having attended school as of 1962, as noted in the graph of new pupils (Figure XII), there is a continually growing "enlightened" reservoir in the community from which to draw new church members. Since 1958 church membership has fast left the school enrollment behind, and is drawing large groups of youth who have never attended any kind of school other than their catechism classes. Through the years, many of the "enlightened" have left the local community and gone to the large cities of the North, thus reducing the educated church membership potential, but greatly aiding the general upgrading of Nigeria. In a period of ten years one local church lost over one hundred members by this movement to other parts of Nigeria.

The following chart gives the picture of a characteristic four-class junior primary school in the Church of the Brethren Mission area, and shows the proportion of Christians to non-Christians and to those in preparation for baptism.

South Margi Junior Primary School
Church of the Brethren Mission – April 1962

Class	Age Group	Non-Christians	Inquirers	Cate-chumens	Baptized Christians	Totals in class
I	7-10	39	19	4	1	44
II	8-11	29	6	10	1	40
III	9-12	14	12	7	2	23
IV	10-13	8	4	4	18	30
		90	41	25	22	137

When a pupil finishes class four, he goes on to the senior primary classes: five, six, and seven. With forty (1962) junior primary schools in the Church of the Brethren Mission and only eleven senior primary schools, five of which were newly opened in 1963, it can be readily seen that the competition is very keen. (The government is now insisting that every primary school include junior and senior primary classes. This will be a big step forward, moving the "bottle-neck" a bit higher up.) Only those whose grades qualify them are eligible, and these must be drastically cut through interview. The pupils who enter senior primary school are only fourteen or fewer years old, and many are not yet baptized Christians, as is shown in the graph of the four senior primary schools (Figure XV). Note that at the completion of class seven only Mubi School has a 100% Christian class, including six who are catechumens. There are still six non-Christians in the Garkida Class VII, one in Lassa, and three in Marama. In Marama, where the church is large and the Nigerian leadership strong, the entrance into the Christian faith is much slower than in the other schools. This may be partially explained by a good portion of the pupils being second-genera-

FIG. XV

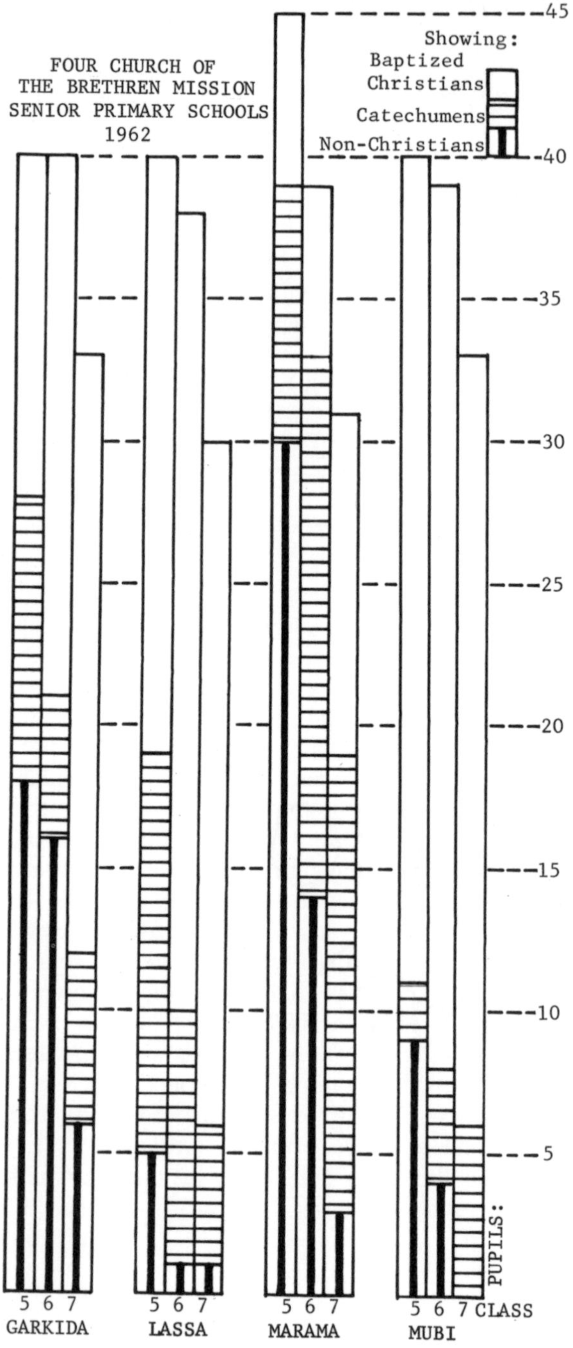

FOUR CHURCH OF
THE BRETHREN MISSION
SENIOR PRIMARY SCHOOLS
1962

Showing:
Baptized Christians
Catechumens
Non-Christians

45
40
35
30
25
20
15
10
5
PUPILS:

5 6 7
GARKIDA

5 6 7
LASSA

5 6 7
MARAMA

5 6 7 CLASS
MUBI

tion Christians. The insistence on high baptismal standards means the school children are baptized at an older age.

Dr. J. A. Faust and Rev. E. M. Westley, missionaries of the Evangelical United Brethren Branch of the Sudan United Mission working with EKAS, Muri, point out that, while missionaries entered the Muri Church area at the same time that missionaries entered the Eastern Church area (1923), the growth of the Eastern Church has far exceeded that of the Muri Church. They believe that a primary reason for this difference in growth is that the Muri area never had more than eight missionaries until 1946 and these did not stress the opening of schools, but rather felt that direct evangelism was their primary task and that Christians needed no education other than that which led to an ability to read the Bible. The Eastern Church, on the other hand, pressed the opening of primary schools from the beginning. The winds of change blowing in the Central Belt were largely ignored by the missionaries of the Muri area and the great initiative gained by the Eastern Church was lost to them. The Muri Church has, they feel, suffered through the years as a result of this shortsightedness.[18]

But most missions have considered schools as an evangelistic arm of the Church, and have sought to place them strategically in responsive areas. Of the thirty organized church congregations (1963) in the Eastern Church area only twelve are centered at mission stations, but most of the thirty have a junior primary school within the limits of their church boundaries. In some cases the church has grown up around the school, but in many others there has been no large concentration of Christians about the schools. The Christians are scattered among the villages and hamlets in the surrounding farming country. The "Mission Station Approach" described by Dr. Donald A. McGavran in *Bridges of God* was very commonly the approach in the Central Belt until the end of World War II. But the awakening and the response to the gospel could no longer be contained by so static an approach. The Christian community not only swelled out over the edge of the mission stations, but began reproducing itself spontan-

[18] Personal interview at Bambur, Jan. 17, 1964.

eously as the result of the work of numerous Nigerian evangelists; Christian groups were formed and met for Christian worship and fellowship in the most unexpected places, miles from any mission station, on the tops of mountains and in the suddenly expanding trade centers. The contacts through the mission-station approach made during the years was beginning to bear fruit.

It is of great importance now that the Church continues its growth among the adults and the illiterate community, in a way commensurate with the early preparatory work of the missions, and takes advantage of every breeze in the whirling winds of change.

There are some cross currents in the part mission auxiliaries are now playing that need careful attention if the social services are to continue their beneficent part in the growth of the Church. One cross current felt all along the way as I visited the churches was the cooling evangelistic ardor of auxiliary staff. Though church leaders everywhere are enthusiastic about continued educational and medical work by missions and churches, they are not satisfied with the witness the Nigerian workers are making through the auxiliaries. Leaders said, "Christian school teachers ought to preach the Christian message on Sunday, for Sunday belongs to God; but few of them do. When people put their mind to education they don't seem strong in the Holy Spirit." Others pointed out that the newer teachers do not take the interest in the Church that the older ones did, and concern about salary is greater than concern about the Kingdom of God. Many Christians who receive teaching positions in the Native Administration schools do not continue their Christian witness. These have opportunity to teach the Christianity syllabus in such schools, but they often fail to do so.

There were some encouraging exceptions to this disinterest. In the Mada Hills Church, National Administration teachers are active elders in the church. Also, the Takum Church leaders praised teachers highly for their interest in the church, and their teaching the Christianity syllabus in the Native Administration Schools. In the Tiv Church many school teachers take part in the work of the church, as elders and in teaching religious classes for the church. The teachers and medical workers receiving high government-paid salaries tithe in some churches, such as Kaltango and Biliri of ECWA, and in parts of the Eastern Church of TEKAS. Since such tithes in the ECWA churches go into the home mission fund, which supports many Nigerian evangelists, this giving greatly helps the outreach of the Church.

Another cross current growing out of the emphasis on schools, which unfortunately is not so well balanced on the positive side as the above, is that of the impression everywhere that Christianity is for the youth. Pastor Theodore of the Lutheran Church at Numan found this attitude very prevalent among the adult tribesmen. They said, "Christianity is for the boys, so boys go!" He answered them, "Are you older than God? Of course not! So you are boys to God!" The men all laughed and listened to his preaching, but they did not enroll as catechumens.

The attitude that Christianity is for children is very widespread and likely due in part to missionaries following Jesus' lead of "Let the children come." This primacy of the child is just as strange to the tribesmen of the Central Belt as it was to the disciples of Jesus' day! It must be remembered, however, that mothers brought their children to Jesus, and were themselves His disciples. Too often we have received children apart from their parents and separated them from their tribal patterns.

The makeup of the Sunday morning church attendance gives us some indication of the place of youth in the life of the church. In the TEKAS churches school children attending the primary schools are about 25% of the Sunday attendance. However, the estimate for the several churches within TEKAS varies a great deal from this average as follows: Muri and Lutheran, 25%; Plateau, 30%; Eastern, 15%; and Tiv, with the largest Sunday morning attendance of all, only 14%. Thus the Sunday attendance is not so heavily weighted with school children as the emphasis upon education might cause one to expect.

However, youth defined as "every one below twenty-five or thirty years of age" makes up a much larger percentage. Ralph Baker, a Christian Reformed Church missionary, gives the following estimates for the Tiv Church: the Sunday-morning attendance of 51,000 in 1961 included 5,500 mission-school children and about 3,000 additional school children from the Native Administration Schools; 6,500 youth in weekday classes of religious instruction; and 10,000 others below the age of twelve years. There are also about 8,000 older youth below the age of thirty, so that the total youth would be about 33,000 of the 51,000 attendance, or 65%. Observation confirms that the situation in the Tiv Church is fairly characteristic of the Central Belt Churches.

From 1900 to 1940 the difficulty of breaking through the paganism of the Central Belt was enormous. Every means was used as a possibility for an entrance into the lives of the people: a Freed Slaves Home, orphanages, boarding homes and schools for children. The result is that the Church of the Central Belt is largely a youth church. This may presage strength for the future, but the present foundations, resting on a small proportion of strong, stable Nigerian leaders, are neither broad enough nor deep enough. Today adults are winnable and they must be won.

The prominence of schools gives the unfortunate impression that Christianity is a new cultural achievement of youth, rather than a matter of faith in Christ. Some churches require literacy before baptism, and this heightens this impression. "I am an old man and cannot become a Christian," is too often heard from those over fifty years of age. Furthermore, the school door to the church sends Christian youth back to communities still dominated by pagan elders. The Christian convictions formed in the school may quickly crumble as a result of family and village traditions.

This study of mission auxiliaries brings us to conclude that they have been of great assistance in the founding and development of the Church in the Central Belt of Nigeria. The village chief, in giving his consent for a mission school, has in so doing acknowledged his village's desire to choose Christianity in the inevitable change from paganism.

We may raise the question, however, as to whether or not the Nigerian Church should become a proprietor of such large social services. While some churches are becoming proprietors of dispensaries, there has been little interest in church proprietorship of hospitals. The ECWA and Plateau churches are involved in proprietorship of dispensaries and schools, but most of the TEKAS churches are satisfied to let the missions continue as proprietors. However, EKAS Tiv will by 1965 have become proprietor of a number of schools. In the Church of the Brethren much attention has been given to the Nigerianization of its auxiliaries, but transfer of proprietorship to the Church has met with little enthusiasm on the part of the Eastern Church.

Since the government is bearing the largest share of the financial burden, it will probably eventually take over the schools. However, other plans are called for in the immediate future. In some cases the Church itself is becoming the proprietor of schools. In other cases it may be possible for a Community Board of Education, made up of Christians or of non-Christians, or of both, to become the proprietor.

Turnover to community agencies is provided for in the 1962 Northern Education Law, which makes provision for the establishment of Education Authorities that will take over both Voluntary Agencies (Missions) and Native Administrative primary schools. It is expected that some authorities will have been established and some schools taken over by 1964. It is supposed to be a gradual development thereafter, but the completion of takeover may come more rapidly than previously expected. The former mission schools are to have a special "transferred" relationship to the new Education Authority. Religion will be taught in the tradition of the school, and the former proprietor (the mission) will have freedom to supervise and inspect the teaching of religion and the right of approving teachers for the school.[19] However, turnover to government or local community agencies awaits the development of sufficiently trained Nigerian staff to administer such a wide and expanding program. In 1964 three Church of the Brethren mission schools were in process of being turned over to a Native Authority Agency, with religious instruction still in the hands of the mission.

19 Eikenberry, Ivan (Secretary of Northern Education Advisory Council with offices in Kaduna, Nigeria), Correspondence, January 1, 1963.

In my opinion, the takeover by community agencies with the church supervising the classes in religion will be an ideal situation for both community and church. As long as Christian teachers are in the school, and there is a Christianity syllabus, I see no reason why the school cannot continue under such a relationship to be both an evangelizing agency and a source of strength for the Christian Church. It is also my conviction that while some Churches are enthusiastic about becoming proprietors of schools, missions should preferably hold on to their proprietorship until government or community agencies can take over. In fact, as long as the government permits, this is an area of service and Christian witness that resources of the Church in Europe and America can well continue. It could be devastating to the witness of the Church in the Central Belt of Nigeria to force it to take the responsibility of this social service when, in most cases, its funds and personnel are seriously limited. It would be just as devastating for the missions to discontinue the establishment of new schools at this strategic time.

G. CHURCH ATTENDANCE

Attendance at Sunday worship is important, for it indicates the vitality of the Christian message in any area under consideration and is an indication of the potential of church growth in the immediate future. In the churches of Europe and America it is usual that the Sunday morning attendance is considerably less than the membership. It is no wonder then that churches in the West grow so slowly, for their own biological growth is the primary source of new members. Conversions from the world are difficult because the unconverted so seldom attend church. In the Central Belt, however, the Sunday morning attendance is many times greater than the church membership.

Comparison of the church membership graph (Figure XVII) and the church attendance graph (Figure XVI) reveals the tremendous difference between numbers of church members and Sunday attendance. In 1962 the Tiv Church with 4,162 members had an average Sunday attendance of

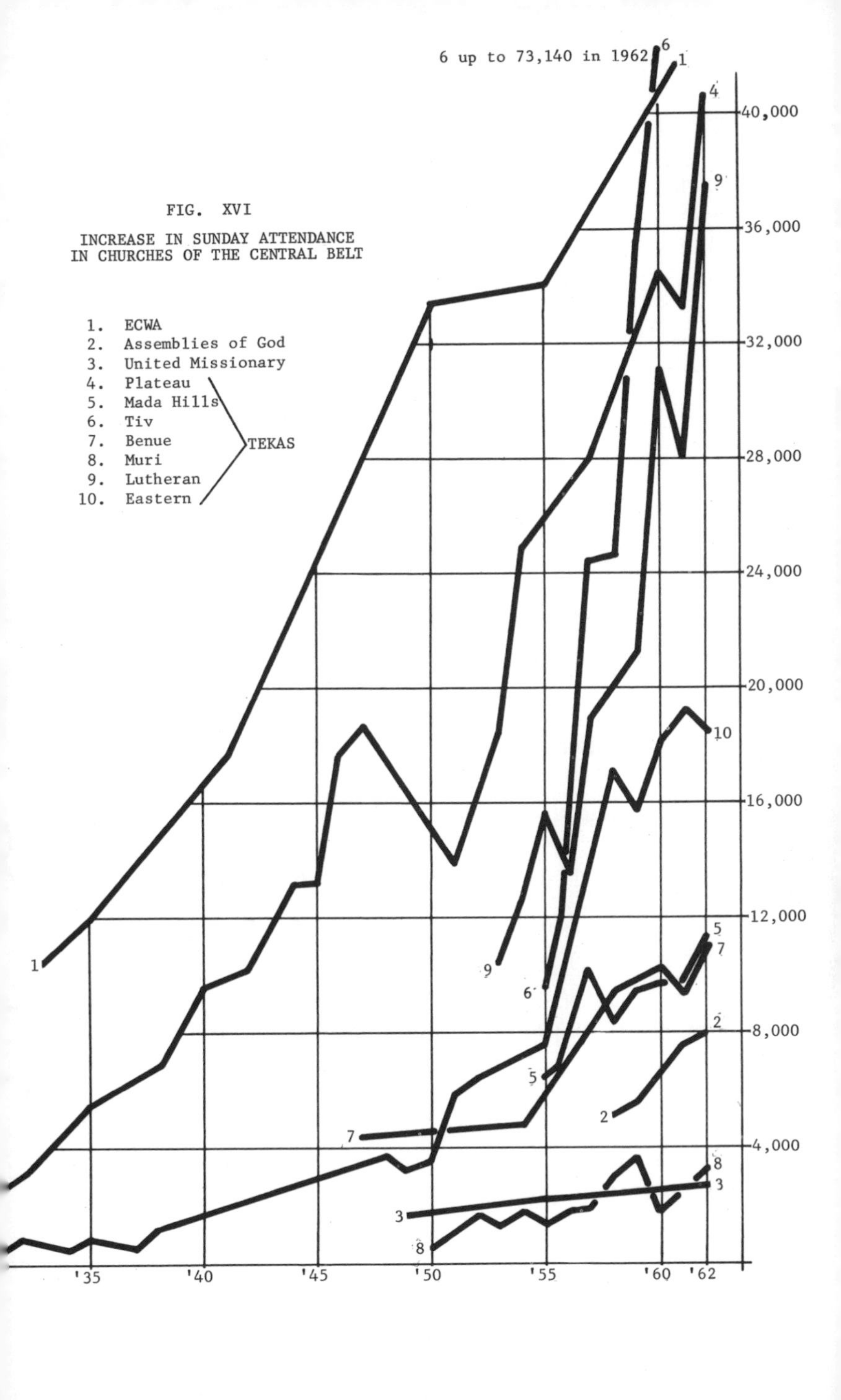

6 up to 73,140 in 1962
FIG. XVI
INCREASE IN SUNDAY ATTENDANCE
IN CHURCHES OF THE CENTRAL BELT
1. ECWA
2. Assemblies of God
3. United Missionary
4. Plateau
5. Mada Hills
6. Tiv
7. Benue
8. Muri
9. Lutheran
10. Eastern
TEKAS
40,000
36,000
32,000
28,000
24,000
20,000
16,000
12,000
8,000
4,000
'35
'40
'45
'50
'55
'60
'62

73,140. For all the TEKAS churches the communicant membership in 1962 was 44,688, with an average Sunday attendance of 201,938. For all the churches of the Central Belt (1962), with an estimated membership of 72,000, the Sunday attendance was over 257,000.

Let us look at the makeup of the Sunday attendance, for it gives insight into the dynamics of church growth.

The Makeup of the Sunday Church Attendance in the TEKAS Churches[20]

(The numbers in the chart are percentages of the total average Sunday attendance)

	Plateau	Mada Hills	Tiv	Benue	Muri	Lutheran	Eastern	TEKAS Average
(a) Communicant members	25		7	47	33	25	35	29
(b) Preparing for membership	20		16	11	10	10	15	14
(c) Members out of fellowship	8		.005	2.5	3	2	2	3
(d) Nonmembers of a Christian's family	10		40	30	8		10	19
(e) School children	30		14	23	35	35	15	25
(f) Casual visitors:								
Pagan	25		35	2	9	25	47	24
Moslem	.005			.001		1	.01	.25
(g) Polygamist nonmembers	6		30	1	2	2	2	7
(h) Percentage of (f) with strong leanings to the Church:								
Pagan	85		75	1	50	50	80	57
Moslem	1					1	2	1

(Percentages listed overlap each other, thus additions vertically will total more than 100%.)

It is seen that the attendance on a Sunday morning includes a great variety of people. Members (a) are only 29% of the total attendance.

The Plateau Church estimates the highest percentage of those preparing for membership (b): 20%. The Lutheran Church has the greatest actual membership increase in 1962, yet only 10% of the attendance is preparing for member-

[20] Estimates by missionaries at work in the churches.

ship. The Tiv Church, which had a much lower membership increase, has 16% preparing for membership.

One of the largest groups attending is that of school children (e), which, of course, overlaps the membership percentage. Perhaps 50% of the school children are already members.

Look at (f) and (g), casual visitors and polygamist nonmembers – persons who are still not vitally related to the church. The highest percentage of them attending worship is found in the Tiv Churches: 65% (35% plus 30%), which is more than double the average for all of TEKAS. The Eastern Church has 49% in this same category; and the Benue Church, on the other extreme, estimates only 3%; it, at the same time, has the highest percentage of church members attending – 47%. The Benue Church is getting comparatively few non-Christians to attend.

Perhaps the most interesting percentage is that of polygamous nonmembers (g) attending the Tiv Church. Thirty percent of the 73,000 attending church in Tivland would be about 21,000. This contrasts with the estimates for the other TEKAS Churches, three of which report only 2% in this category, one only 1% and one 6%, making an average percentage of only 7%. If the Tiv estimate is correct, and represents a common condition throughout Tivland, it reveals a situation full of both opportunity and danger. With the breakup of paganism in the Tiv tribe, Christianity has had little opposition from any other form of religious life, and as a result the many polygamous families have been willing to fellowship with the Church without any formal relationship. How long they will continue this without any recognition whatever is a question. A more creative and dynamic approach must be found. A special register, such as that used in the Eastern Church, has definite possibilities for bringing polygamist believers into a satisfying, though partial, relationship. In the Eastern Church the number of persons on such a register is small in comparison to the total membership, but in the Tiv Church this register could be very large indeed.

The situation is far from academic. It is tremendously practical. Christianity is not likely to remain unchallenged in Tivland indefinitely. If Islam does not soon become more prominent, materialistic irreligion no doubt will. Unless every opportunity is taken to lead the responsive into a satisfying fellowship with Christ and His Church, the winds of change may bring the "seven other spirits," making "the latter state . . . worse than the first " (Matt. 12:45).

Both the Tiv and Benue Churches show a high percentage of nonmembers who are part of Christian families (d). Many of these are older relatives, as well as young persons. The web of family relationship has played a major role in the life of the tribes, and must be acknowledged as the most natural way for the message of salvation to pass from one person or group to another. The Sevav plan, to be discussed in the next chapter, is built upon this primary aspect of African life: the family and the clan.

What does the large Sunday attendance mean for the future growth of the Church? First, it seems that the Spirit of God has been going before, stirring the people of the Central Belt to seek a way out of the fears and frustrations of the past into a new life. Missionaries are often concerned because a consciousness of sin and forgiveness does not play a large part in "conversion." This is due, I believe, to the fact that people coming from animistic paganism do not often feel that they have been sinners, but rather that what was right for their ancestors has suddenly, in the face of changing times, become meaningless. They vaguely feel that ancestor worship orients one to the past and stifles progress, though they are not able to put this into words. They do not realize that their past has been totally pragmatic with no solid moral basis for conduct, but they will awaken to it. They do not recognize that animism "directly and indirectly encourages many antisocial practices: fear of witches, suspicions of black magic, loss of life through initiation ceremonies . . . the use of erratic divination for making social decisions, and dependence upon emotionally unstable persons who may dominate not only the religious activities of the group, but also the political and economic areas of life as well,"[21] but they rejoice in their emancipation from them.

[21] Nida, E. and Smalley, W., *Introducing Animism,* pp. 57, 58.

The large church attendance throws out a challenge to "disciple the tribes" and to teach them all that Christ has taught in His Word. Their desire for a *new way* pushes them toward the Way.

The second thing this large Sunday attendance means is that the growth of the church has expanded well beyond the centrally located mission stations. In the age we have now entered mission stations continue to be centers for medical and educational work, but the Church will increasingly consist of vast numbers of village churches. Such churches must no longer be called "out-stations." In many cases they are larger and more growing than are the churches at the mission stations. Indeed, many of the station churches are in need of spiritual revival, for it is here that the nominal Christians are found to whom Christianity means civilization, education, good pay, and "white-collar" jobs. The broad expansion beyond mission stations is shown in that there were 2,778 places of worship and 1,557 evangelists and 145 ordained pastors in the TEKAS churches as of 1962. In the ECWA churches, there were 740 places of worship, 391 evangelists, and 179 ordained pastors. These two Fellowships of Churches total 3,518 places of worship, 1,948 evangelists, and 324 pastors. For the whole of the Central Belt there would be well over 4,000 places of worship, and the continuing potential for multiplying places of worship is great.

A third meaning in the large attendance is that there are too few organized churches. While there were 2,778 places of worship in TEKAS (1962), the number of organized churches was only 149. The Plateau Church had thirty-seven such indigenously organized churches; Eastern Church, twenty-seven; Benue, twenty-one; Lutheran, nineteen; Tiv, sixteen; Mada Hills, fifteen; and Muri, eleven. (Tiv had organized two more churches and Benue one more by May, 1963, and Eastern had organized three more by March, 1963.) In the slow-growing Churches generally the percentage of organized churches per thousand membership is very high. In the fastest-growing Churches the percentage of organized churches per thousand members is much less. One of the encouraging aspects of Central Belt church growth is the way in which churches have been organized to carry on the full life of the church at village centers far from any mission station. But this process of church organization must proceed at a much faster pace if the witness of the Church is to carry the weight it should within the tribal groups where it is founded. And this multiplication of churches must come about in spite of the leadership shortage discussed below.

The large Sunday attendance reveals, fourthly, that there are too few ordained pastors available for the nurture of the Church. In spite of numerous evangelists, 1,948 in TEKAS and ECWA combined, the few pastors (324) and few organized churches pose the problem of truly effective Christian nurture. Because of the difficulty in administering the Lord's supper in the thousands of worship places, many Christians go for long periods without the strength derived from communion, or they must walk long distances to the nearest organized church. Pre- and post-baptismal classes and literacy classes are often neglected at isolated worship centers. The shortage of pastors also means few Christian marriages solemnized and little really solid Bible teaching given. Also one of the keenest losses is the strength derived from sending representatives to the larger districts. Delegating administrative authority to an ever-widening group enhances the dignity of any church, and the self-respect of all its members.

A fifth observation on the meaning of church attendance is a sobering word by Rev. Bob Recker, of the Baissa District of the Benue Church. He writes:

> I have noticed that there is a period in the history of almost all of the villages when, for a short time, the door for expansion is wide open. After that first period of grace, it never seems to be so wide open again. The first Christians settle into an acceptance of the status quo, and it becomes unusual for a confirmed pagan or Muslim to attend Christian services. The three groups, pagan, Muslim, and Christian, become static. It is in the new villages . . . that we have fruitful contact with pagans and Muslims. There is a sort of frontier area where the situation is still fluid.[22]

[22] Recker, R., Correspondence, January 30, 1963.

In the days that lie ahead, again and again village groups will open to the gospel. Moments will come when churches can be planted. This is the essential meaning of the large church attendance. If these moments are not seized to establish self-supporting, self-propagating, and self-governing churches, the doors may shut.

Every missionary and English-speaking national should read Dr. John L. Nevius' *The Planting of Missionary Churches* (see Bibliography). Nevius was writing about China and not Nigeria, but his single-eyed devotion to planting churches, his amazing success in getting new converts to become unpaid, competent church leaders, his lay training sessions for the unpaid leaders, and his discussion of sixty widely scattered, small village churches would be stimulating reading to Christian leaders in the Central Belt facing today's large church attendance.

For the Sunday attendance really to mean growth in the immediate future certain conditions need to be met.

1. Both quality and quantity of the evangelists and church leaders must be increased. Bible study courses must take a prominent and continuous place in the program of the church.

2. More Nigerian pastors are needed. They must break away from the pattern copied from missionaries of being district supervisors and follow their own special genius in saving their people. Ordination must not be restricted to those with formal theological training.

3. Church districts must push forward to organize more self-directing churches. Such churches cannot wait to be born until a Nigerian or missionary pastor is available, but must organize with local lay elders.

4. Leadership training of adults on a large scale should be instituted immediately. When a new church is formed its lay leaders, its unpaid elders, and its chief men should be trained by local institutes at village centers. Every opportunity must be taken to use students in pastors' classes and Bible schools to lead in giving this essential training to lay Christians.

5. The missionary must not drift to the periphery of

church life. He must know the church and its adherents. He must know what is going on. It may be that he is not elected to church positions, nor asked for advice, but he must be alert to be a brother in Christ with sufficient insight and skill to help others do the job. He must be a catalytic agent getting action.

Chapter IX. Broadening the Base of Church Growth

A. REACHING THE WHOLE POPULATION: THE SEVAV PLAN

IN THE OLDER CHURCHES OF THE WEST YOUTH MAY FEEL THAT they have little part in the life of the Church. They are even delegated to a separate youth department. But in the Central Belt the youth *are* the Church.

The youthful face of the Church, however, can be a hindrance in its evangelistic extension unless the youthful members experience an awakening of deep spiritual concern for their elder generation. Older mature Christians, who have established firm, Christian homes and who are a stable part of the community, must join them in an all-out effort to extend the Church of Christ into the innumerable villages and hamlets in such a way that adults with their whole families respond.

When a pagan espouses Islam, his whole family commonly becomes Moslem. It is not our desire to use the same physical and psychological pressures often used in Islamic conversions. But the messenger of Christ is challenged to present his message in such a clear and meaningful way that it will be seen as the way of salvation for the whole family, clan, or tribe. Admittedly, the transformation anticipated in a turn to Christ is much more demanding than a similar turn to Islam.

However, a clear view of the difference between "discipling" and "perfecting" must be kept in mind. It cannot be expected that there will in all cases be an immediate, automatic transformation of all of life. (We of the older Churches, in fact, leave much to be desired in this.) But a complete change of the Center about which life revolves is the great essential. The change must be from faith in fetish to faith in Christ, from "the dominion of darkness

. . . to the kingdom of God's beloved Son, in whom we have redemption, the forgiveness of sins" (Col. 1:13). Disciples of Christ must be born anew – men and women who make Christ central and learn of Him. The tribes must be "discipled" so that they can move forward with Christ to spiritual and moral maturity. With Christ as the center the Christian life can "go on to maturity" (Heb. 6:1).

In the Central Belt about 260,000 people attend church every Sunday. This tremendous number is made up of people from responsive tribes. Adults are well represented in this Sunday morning attendance, but most of them are holding back from full commitment in church membership. There are many reasons for this, but a lack of willingness to believe in Jesus Christ as the Saviour is not usually one of them. Sometimes there is a willingness to believe in a syncretistic or pantheistic way, as in the case of the witch doctor who adds the name of Jesus to the list of deities and spirits he petitions. But at other times there is a clear realization that Jesus Christ is God and no spirits have any place before Him. The high moral code of the Church may cause some believers to hesitate to make the break that sets them apart from the other adults of their community. This is especially the case when an adult believer acts alone – as he most commonly does. Also, some adults avoid the stiff catechumen courses because they fear they will not be able to learn to read, or learn the material of the course. Most adults do not wish to attend a children's class. The length of preparation for membership in some churches may be a discouragement for many adults who feel that a long period of being neither pagan nor fully accepted as Christian is a dangerous state in which to be. If fetishes are given up, "protection" within the Christian Church is a vital necessity.

But it is not necessarily the missionary who insists upon long periods of preparation. He is likely to adapt and change according to the needs of the changing situation. The Nigerian church leaders, having become accustomed to a certain policy, will often insist that "what has been tied should not be untied."

Eugene Rubingh points out that many missionaries have asked for a reconsideration of membership preparation policy, but the Tiv Church has refused to make any significant change.[1] A reconsideration does seem in order when it is remembered that there are more than 73,000 attending church in Tivland every Sunday morning, that there are 7,500 inquirers and 3,600 catechumens, 16,400 in classes of religious instruction, and 7,800 primary school pupils, but a communicant membership of only 4,162, in 1962. Of course, from the point of view of the Tiv church leadership, length of preparation is not an important element, for they reported to me that "The long way is the right way, because those who are impatient and cannot wait for baptism would not be good Christians anyway!"

There seems to be a "bottleneck" somewhere. Since in 1962 there were only seventeen Nigerian and fourteen missionary ordained pastors in the Tiv Church, and only twenty-one evangelists, but 1,079 places of worship, the shortage in churchmen who can bring those preparing into membership has been part of the "bottleneck." Encouragingly this difficulty is recognized and a vernacular class of twenty men of pastoral qualifications is planned to open in 1964. Also, the neighboring Benue Church graduated nine pastors from a vernacular course in June, 1963.[2]

The Plateau Church has attempted to overcome the shortage of ordained pastors by temporarily ordaining catechists for the purpose of baptizing in the area where they have been working. This has many good features, but the practice is not widely lauded by the Nigerian pastorate. The term "pastor" is a technical term in the Central Belt meaning "ordained minister." It is only natural that the catechist with temporary ordination should be called "pastor" by his people in the local situation. This, however, is frowned upon by the regularly ordained pastors.

Sound policies relating to membership preparation and shortage of clergy are urgently needed. Even more impor-

[1] Rubingh, E. R., Correspondence with Dr. McGavran, December 10, 1962.

[2] Recker, R., Personal interview, July, 1963.

tant is our general attitude toward the adult population and the urgency of the task before us. Do we really desire to win the whole population for Jesus Christ? Or are we satisfied with an attitude that rejoices in a few "called ones"? This attitude, while claiming to be "Biblical," is in fact contrary to Christ's command to "make disciples of all nations."

If the Church wishes to win adults, both men and women, it must pay special attention to them. It must prepare special courses of a condensed and minimal nature for them and relax or completely discard literacy requirements. Dr. McGavran affirms:

> Literacy requirements and long-continued catechumen courses (up to three years) reflect colonial conditions when government controlled all education and intended to do educational work indefinitely into the future through the missions. Under those conditions, the Church was reasonably safe in accepting only educated youth. Old pagans would die off and educated Christians would take their places. Under those conditions, literacy requirements and a long school-catechumenate may have been common sense, though theological assumptions in literacy requirements are staggering and many of our Lord's disciples were illiterate.
>
> Today it is clear that the Church in Nigeria does not have a hundred years before it, secure in its monopoly of the educational processes. Today it must take in the illiterate and learn how they may become good Christians, organized into sound Christian churches. This is happening elsewhere in the world. It can happen in the Central Belt.[3]

The adult population can only be reached by a plan that does not depend upon the schools, as important as they are for the mature Christian community. Certainly, the Christian Church is committed to a Bible-reading fellowship and can never permit a permanently illiterate membership. Yet, schools are not essential in winning adults to Christ. A plan must be devised that will multiply sound Christian churches.

One such plan has been introduced and tested by Rev. Eugene Rubingh and Rev. Ralph Baker of the Christian

[3] McGavran, D. A., Personal interview, March, 1963.

Reformed Church Mission. It, the Sevav plan, is not the only one possible, but it is a good plan, and by their permission is presented here. It sets clearly before us the dimensions of the problem and shows one approach toward solving it. It originated at Sevav in the Tiv Church. It depends on the fact that men live in structured groups. The people of the Central Belt are not merely Nigerians. Each person is a member of some tribe, some clan, some extended family. This social structure is often ignored by missionaries who tend to minimize tribe, race, and social levels. But when these are disregarded and Christ is proclaimed "universally" we fail to take advantage of the natural structure of communication between individuals and groups. When converts come from schoolboys, thrown together in class from many different villages often unrelated to each other, the Church grows against the grain of the social structure, and in consequence grows slowly.

Messrs. Baker and Rubingh noticed that "for thirteen years of work here, there was not one baptism at Sevav." They noticed that the Christians were spread out across the countryside, one in this clan, one in that, and many clans were seen without any Christians in them at all. Following up these Christians outside the immediate neighborhood of the mission station was a difficult task. Rubingh and Baker admired the devotion of earlier missionaries, which had created in the Sevav area a Church of 165 members by 1958,[4] but they believed there was a better way of presenting the gospel to the Tiv: a way that would make an approach through the clans. Rubingh writes, "If nuclei of believers could gather together for worship according to subclan or segment lines, how much better it would be." So they devised the following plan to make it possible for Christian groups to arise in each segment.

1. In the social structure of the Tiv the smallest unit or segment is called the "ipaven u ken iyou." This normally consists of from nine to twelve extended family compounds. The segment head lives in the central compound. Mr. Ru-

[4] Rubingh, E. R., Correspondence with Dr. McGavran, September, 1963.

bingh determined as a pilot project to evangelize one segment and to obtain catechumens and eventually baptized believers who were all members of the same segment.

2. This plan was explained to the leaders of the local church and a team of men enlisted who would give one day a week for fourteen weeks to work in the chosen segment. Mr. Baker prepared a syllabus of fourteen lessons that explained the way of salvation.

3. The team on the first of the fourteen days went to the segment and there divided so that in each compound one man taught the assigned lesson, preached the assigned sermon, and told the assigned story.

4. At the close of the fourteen weeks, a three-day conference was held in the compound of the clan head. Decisions for Christ were called for.

5. Those who responded were organized into a catechumen class and began regular weekly worship. They continued working for the enlistment of other catechumens. While not an organized church they carried out many functions of a church congregation.

6. Definite plans for another visit were made previous to the team's leaving.

In December, 1962, Mr. Rubingh reported the results of his first attempt at this type of segment evangelism. Three areas were chosen and three teams were trained. He wrote:

> . . . the first segment contained nine compounds, with a total population of perhaps 350 people, and an average of forty persons to a compound. . . .
>
> At the final meeting of the three-day conference (July 1, 1962), twenty-one people arose to profess conversion. Their names were recorded and they began catechism training and regular weekly worship in the segment. At last report (Dec. 1, 1962) they were nearly all coming to the catechism classes. The number 21 represents approximately 20% of the adults of the segment. (Twelve were married and nine single). The results in the other two areas are almost exactly comparable. The total number of catechumens enrolled was sixty.

> The Christians on the teams were very enthusiastic . . . and happy to have a planned program. They felt used by the Lord more than if they had engaged in wandering, far-flung, one-shot preaching.[5]

This Sevav Plan coupled with the special register described in Chapter VIII, Section D, will make a very strong appeal to the tribal units of the Central Belt. Had the special register been used at Sevav, it might have raised the percentage of definite decisions for Christ very appreciably. In fact, while the great majority of the 350 people were not able to make the response that would lead to church membership, I can well imagine that, considering the conditions within the Tiv tribe, many more might have been anxious to be registered as pro-Christian, setting their faces toward Christ.

Mr. Rubingh pointed out that one advantage of this approach is that the gospel is proclaimed within the cultural setting of the complete family. People declare for Christ within their tribal relationships and not as lone and separate individuals. A nucleus is formed in which each believer acts as a stabilizing influence upon every other, supplying Christian support in times of persecution and increasing Christian enthusiasm in winning others and building segment churches.

The converts constantly contact their close relatives. They are the means of winning others in the family. As the percentage of Christians in one compound rises, it becomes an influence upon other compounds in the segment. And as the segment itself becomes more and more Christian, it will have a profound effect on other nearby "ipaven u ken iyous." Once conversion without social dislocation has been demonstrated, we shall see better and more rapid advance of the Church. "This group approach will produce sounder Christians and sounder churches and go far toward providing that indefinitely reproduceable pattern of church formation which the Central Belt so urgently needs in this day of 260,000 church attendants!"[6]

[5] *Ibid.*, December 10, 1962.
[6] McGavran, D. A., Correspondence, August, 1963.

Such a mode of evangelism contrasts sharply with the pre-war model, which depends so largely upon school enrollments and youth evangelism, and leaves the heart of the pagan community untouched. In setting forth this "better way" the Tiv Church is pioneering a mode of evangelism applicable to all tribes in the Central Belt. To be sure, social structures differ from tribe to tribe. Not all tribes are as clearly divided into clan segments as the Tiv. But all have webs of relationship. All have segments, clans, and extended families. The social structure may become the highway of the Spirit of God. Let us not bypass it, but use it.

A second advantage is that this method is intensive.

> For fourteen Sundays people are saturated with the truth. They can hardly shrug it off anymore at that point. The thing calls for a decision – one way or the other. True, all this is at the expense of not reaching some other areas more superficially. But, one-shot confrontations without follow-up are less effective. Even the potentially receptive scattered individuals in a wide area are not adequately reached by occasional trekking.[7]

Because of church regulations, however, the sixty catechumens could not be baptized even after six months of intensive instruction. Only those who become literate after a three-year catechumenate during which polygamists are not permitted to attend the classes of instruction, can be baptized. Mr. Rubingh writes, partly of the sixty and partly of the 7,200 church attenders in his area (a communicant membership of 400 as of 1962), the following sorrowful note:

> But after thousands have turned to Christ in their hearts, then what? After they have faced the devil and wrestled with him, they then must face all these obstacles thrown into the path of their becoming members of Christ's church. We are blanketing the area with tracts. We have a fine literature program. We have a sight-sound truck with movies and slide programs and the Tiv attend en masse. . . . Sometimes one asks, Why bother with all the tracts, movies, and conferences, anyway?[8]

[7] Rubingh, E. R., Correspondence with Dr. McGavran, December 10, 1962.

[8] *Ibid.*

If the ripened grain is not reaped, it will fall in the field and rot. A ripening is taking place in the Central Belt today, far greater than we can ask or imagine. The conversion of youth in mission schools has been, under God, part of the reason for this ripeness. We thank God for it. Now the Church must reach winnable adults while they are still available.

Mr. Rubingh's plan could be used effectively with many of the Central Belt tribes. Other plans may be devised by Nigerian pastors or missionaries that will fit particular tribal situations and churches more specifically. But let us press onward to present the gospel as a living and vital option to group after group of Central Belt Nigerians, expecting in faith that God will add many souls in many clan groups to the Church. The congregations of the Central Belt must be as the stars of the sky in multitude, each one at the center of some large extended family, some clan, some "ipaven u ken iyou," till from the Cameroons to Dahomey there is a church in every segment, a Bible in every home, and Christ in every heart.

B. FOCUSING ALL FACTORS ON CHURCH GROWTH

The opportunity for church growth is so great in the Central Belt of Nigeria that no Church should limit itself to any one approach. The Spirit of Christ has worked through many and varied methods in the past and is doing so today. The Sevav Plan and others like it must come into greater prominence. The compassion of Christ in the medical work and the enlightenment of education must continue to be felt throughout the Central Belt. Whether these institutions continue under the mission or are taken over by the church or community, the important thing is that, in both medicine and education, dedicated Christians, active in discipling, must make up the majority of the staff. Where there are dedicated Christians the gospel of Christ will continue to make its presence felt.

New institutions for the training of Christian leaders are springing up everywhere. These must be focused to training leaders devoted to the growth of the Church. The Theological College of Northern Nigeria, founded and supported by the churches and missions of TEKAS, is a two-level school of certificate and diploma courses, the better to meet the needs of the men now preparing for the Christian ministry. The place of higher education is very significant in the maturation of the Church. The Theological College has graduated nineteen men as of July, 1963. Almost one-third of these have been quickly drawn into institutions.[9] The others are working as pastors of local churches. From such men may develop the leadership that must take its place in the national and world councils of the Church.

The Kulp Bible School, a cooperative venture of the Eastern Church and its "parent" mission, is aimed to develop Christian farmers who will give greatly needed local leadership. Many of these will do evangelistic work and a few will become ordained pastors. The Tiv Church-Mission Bible School at Zaki Biam is devoted to preparing men to teach in the 600 and more literacy and religious classes throughout Tivland. The United Missionary Church has a vernacular Bible school in each of its three regions. Their value is so evident that there are plans to open an advanced Bible school and a seminary in Jebba. The students of the Bible schools have established several new churches through their weekend itineration.[10] The pastors' class at Bambur is driving hard to produce church-extension-minded men. In all the churches numerous classes for evangelists meet monthly, or quarterly, or for periods of several weeks. These must be aroused to the urgency and glory of church planting and church growth.

Bible schools for adults, such as those mentioned above, along with others at Baissa, Wukari, and Lupwe, are, in themselves, strong evangelistic arms of the Church. The students receive evangelistic training and also do regular evangelistic touring in the surrounding areas. Such visitation must be more than "training for the students"; it must be focused on planting new churches.

[9] One as a chaplain of a secondary school; one as a hospital chaplain; one as chaplain of a teacher training college; three as chaplains and teachers in Bible and evangelist schools (H. R. Boer, Personal interview, July, 1963).

[10] Brenneman, W., "A Church Is Born," unpublished paper, p. 5.

The program and possibilities of improved agriculture hold a central place in the future progress of the Church in the largely rural Central Belt. Its significance is in the strengthening of each Christian community from which the evangelistic advance proceeds. Many of the problems of the Church itself that frustrate spontaneous growth may be solved in the "Christian Rural Life Program" of church and mission.

Some of these problems may be listed as follows:

1. The discontent of the rapidly increasing group of young married people caught between too little education to go on to the professions and too much to be satisfied with the old way of doing things.

2. The temptation to get status and greater farming potential by becoming polygamous.

3. The frustration of subsistence farming in the face of the broadening material needs of a higher standard of living.

4. The debilitating effect of subsistence farming upon the financial support of the Church.

5. The inability of churches to pay pastors and evangelists even a small portion of what the government pays clerks, nurses, and school teachers.

Solutions to these problems lie in the development of a sound rural economy based upon mixed farming, orchard and vegetable development, animal husbandry, and village crafts.

Missions have varied in their views, some holding that to place emphasis here is to introduce westernisms and identify Christianity too closely with "civilizing influences." There are dangers here, but few would willingly choose the short-handled hoe in preference to the ox-drawn plow after the results of the first harvest were seen, and we can scarcely say that leaving the hoe for the ox-drawn plow is westernizing in these days of mechanization! *Primitivism must not be confused with indigeneity,* especially when improved agricultural methods in the hands of Nigerian Christians may mean the difference between a truly self-supporting, church-planting group of Christians with a pastor of their own, and that of a small, frustrated, self-centered, and unshepherded church. All activities of church and mission must be focused on the primary goal of church planting and the nurture of Christians, who, in turn, may send the message of Christ out in an ever-widening and more inclusive circle.

C. THE WAVE OF THE FUTURE

Having described the Churches of the Central Belt, observed movements of people to Christ, and considered the dynamic factors involved, let us now note the picture of church growth as a whole.

Figure XVII brings lines of growth for all Churches together for comparison. Figure XIX shows the total growth of the Church in the Central Belt. Figure XVIII emphasizes the comparative mass of Christians in TEKAS Churches between the years 1957 and 1962.

The Lutheran Church in the eastern reaches of the Benue and Gongola Rivers has had the greatest growth, making a gain of 8,451 members in five years. The Eastern Church of the Hawal-Yedseram River area ranks second with its addition of 4,771 members in the same period of time, yet it gained only a little more than half of the Lutheran increase. While the Plateau Church ranks a close third in size of membership, it does not rank third for rate of increase of members. Third place goes to the Benue Church with an increase of 4,721 in the five-year period, falling only fifty short of equaling the increase of the Eastern Church. The Plateau Church then takes fourth place with an increase of 3,657, followed by the Tiv Church with an increase of 2,662, and Mada Hills Church and Muri Church with increases of 974 and 557 respectively.

The lines and rectangles of these charts are not mere marks upon paper, but people! If there is rejoicing in heaven when one person repents and comes to the Lord Jesus Christ, how much greater the rejoicing when there are thousands! The "doctrine of the remnant" and past experience in shepherding small groups of struggling, persecuted Christians has sometimes developed a mission mind-set that depreciates numbers and claims to look for quality, not quantity. Christ, on the other hand, speaks of *fields* of *good* grain white unto harvest – and how few are the laborers! Churches that have

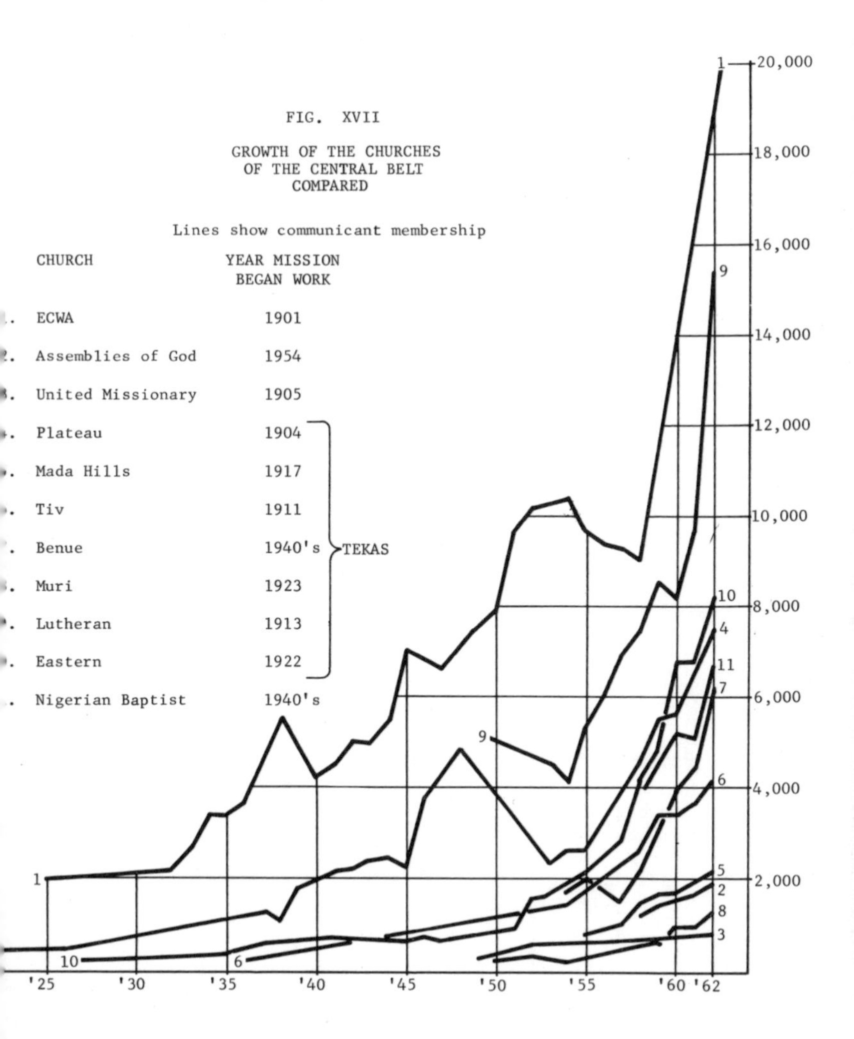

not grown significantly cannot take comfort in perfecting an elite group of believers, nor can a fast-growing Church bask in self-satisfaction when it is in the midst of hundreds of thousands still without Christ.

The causes behind lack of growth in the least-growing

FIG. XVIII
MEMBERSHIP GROWTH 1957-1962
OF THE
CHURCHES OF CHRIST IN THE SUDAN

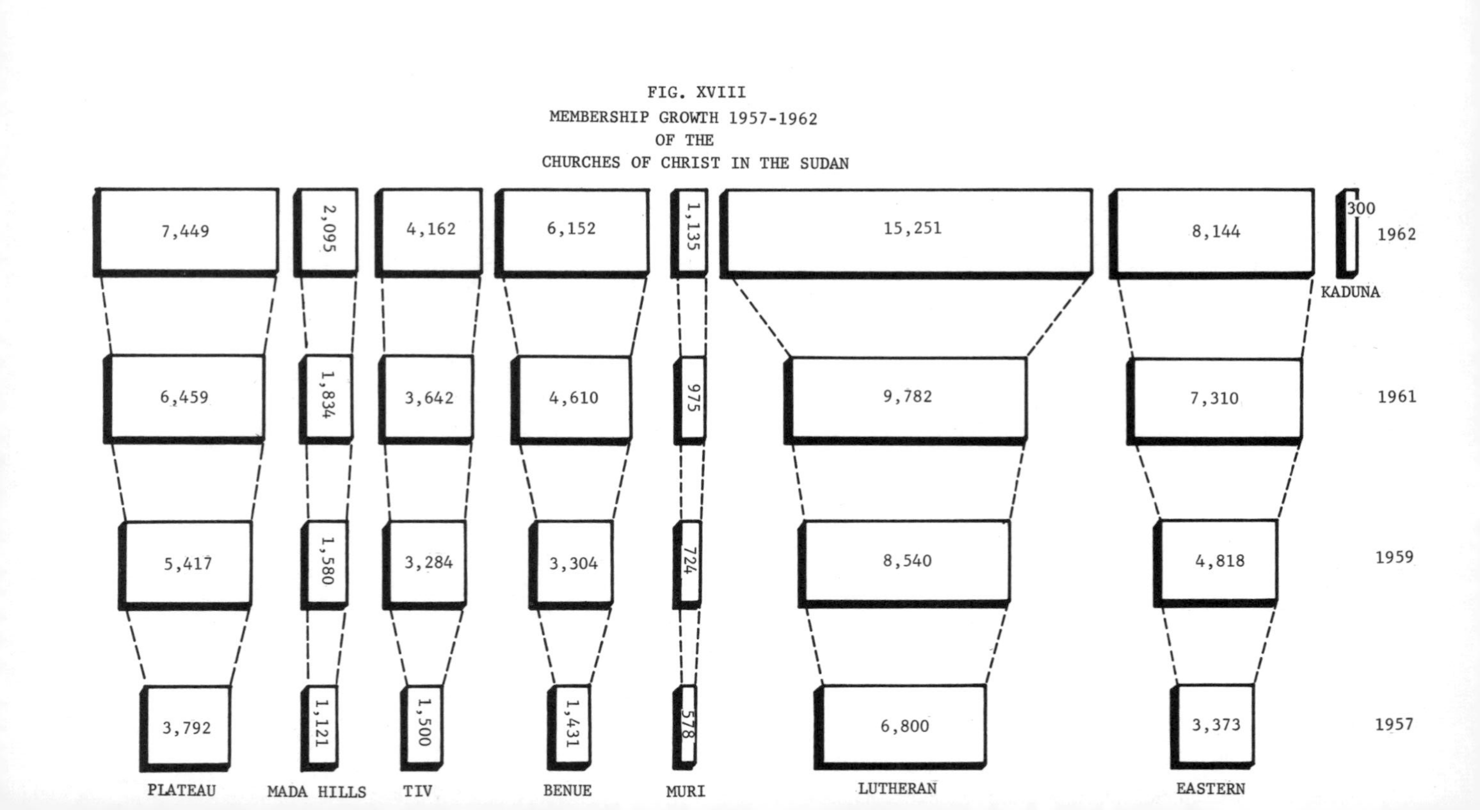

Churches – Tiv, Muri, and Mada Hills – are not easy to pinpoint. However, some specific observations can be made. In the Tiv Church slow growth is partly due to the long, strict membership procedures and also to the importance of formal education as a prerequisite to church membership. There are few, if any, places in the Central Belt where paganism has received a more devastating blow by the mission auxiliaries than in Tivland. The church elite have also made it clear that witchcraft which played the predominant role in their society, need not be feared by Christians. Thus, God has prepared the Tiv for a great revival.

The Muri Church has possibly the most difficult position in the Central Belt.[11] It is located on the bend of the Benue and is entirely cut off from the outside world during the rainy season except by air. The tribes of the Bambur area have been scarcely touched by the winds of change. Yet the immediate future should see a great awakening. Politics will awaken a self-consciousness in the most remote villages. The Bori revival in its extreme expression can hardly last. The Holy Spirit is "going before" to prepare the Pero and the Mumuye for the new day in Christ. The hospital, with its Christian staff and 26,000 patients treated yearly, and the schools staffed with Christian teachers and nearly a thousand pupils in attendance will increasingly enhance the position of the Church. A break into the Mumuye tribe is noted at the new station of Kassa, where in 1963 there were four baptized and several preparing for baptism. At Zinna there were about 80 Mumuye Christians in 1963.

To meet tomorrow's responsiveness in Muri, however, harvesting must be emphasized. All energies must be turned to increasing the number of evangelists (eighty-two in 1962). Preaching for decision must be the rule. Places of worship need to be greatly increased. The ninety-two of 1962 is a beginning. The Sevav or some similar plan should be tried immediately to reach the adults in this largely undiscipled

[11] That is, among the TEKAS churches. The Moslemized condition of the Nupe in the United Missionary Church area presents, perhaps, an even more difficult situation. The very slow growth of the United Missionary Church would substantiate this observation.

area. These are the days to thrust in the sickle and bring home the sheaves. The harvest is ripening and "its fullness of time" will come. Fortunately, all parts of God's field do not ripen at the same time, but the winds of change are blowing and the Holy Spirit is moving among these tribal populations.

In the Mada Hills Church area Islam seems more prominent and the Roman Catholic Church is strong. There is a sturdy Nigerian leadership in this Church and 216 places of worship with 220 evangelists (1962). However, the day-by-day witness of Christians is of primary importance in bringing tribal people to Christ, and this was one serious problem mentioned here. Many complained that Christians did not live up to the name Christian. As Paul reminds us, "The name of God is blasphemed among the Gentiles because of you" (Rom. 2:24).

Nineteen evangelists meeting for a Refresher Course at Alushi listed nine hindrances to the growth of the Church, and of the nine five had to do with the poor witness of Christians:

1. Christians drinking beer.
2. Christians divorcing their wives.
3. Christians taking second wives.
4. Christians being sexually promiscuous.
5. Poor moral witness causing chiefs to be reluctant to give permission for holding Classes of Religious Instruction in their villages.

These evangelists were honestly facing a problem that is very keenly felt in all of the Central Belt Churches, and emphasizes the great need for more effective Christian teaching, which will cause growth in the grace and goodness of the Lord Jesus Christ. However, in the face of the opportunities before the Church in the Central Belt we dare not stop discipling the responsive tribes in order to perfect those already in the churches. Discipling and perfecting must go hand in hand. We must trust the Holy Spirit to carry out His work of grace within the human heart when the written and spoken Word is made available. Making it available is the task of the Church, not at the expense of discipling, for this would nullify the reason for its very existence, but along with it.

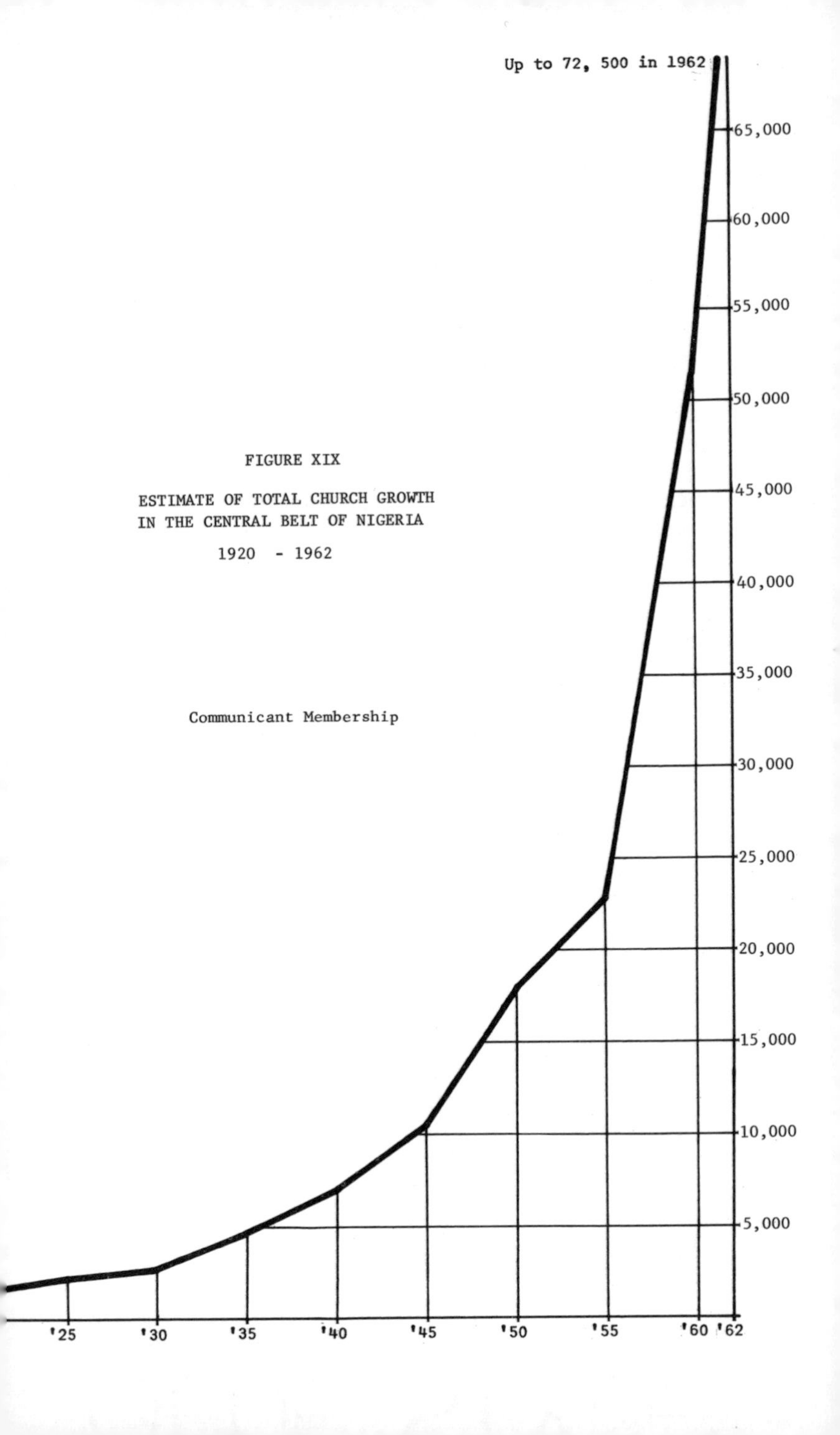

FIGURE XIX

ESTIMATE OF TOTAL CHURCH GROWTH IN THE CENTRAL BELT OF NIGERIA

1920 - 1962

The Church cannot grow in perfecting itself without continually reaching out to others.

In an attempt to disciple and perfect at one and the same time, what must the practical approach be? Mission stations and missionaries still exist, scattered throughout the area of the indigenous Church. In many places there is need for an increase of mission stations and missionaries, working within the pattern and under the direction of the indigenous Church. But it must be realized that there is a great difference between a lone mission station in the midst of 20,000 people, and a growing, multiplying Church in such a population. A station staffed by two or three missionaries who center a good portion of their time upon a school and dispensary, who only at irregular intervals itinerate among the villages, and who direct regular and formal church services in the school building or in a mission-built chapel on Sunday morning will find church growth slow and uncertain. But if the center of interest is the villages themselves with primary emphasis upon sending evangelists into those villages, the Church and not the mission station will become the center of attention and great growth can be anticipated.

The missionaries should direct attention away from the station, discouraging new Christians from building their homes near by and urging them to establish them in their own villages even though miles away. The largest Sunday attendance should not be at the mission station but at a village center, though only two or three miles away. Village church groups will then begin to feel the responsibility and blessing that is theirs without the mission or missionary at the center of their new-found faith.

In a very few years such an approach may produce church groups worshipping in ten or fifteen different places every Sunday and at least once during the week, numbering one or two hundred each. With evangelists in every center classes preparing for church membership can be held from the very beginning, and while ordained Nigerian ministers are few, the missionary can arrange with the new church leaders to take Holy Communion to the churches in the villages rather than having them congregate at the mission station. These village churches continually extend into neighboring villages and hamlets and rapidly increase the membership of the Church.

It is in this extension of the Church, in planting new congregations, that the power of Christ becomes evident in the life of the world. Small, self-centered, self-perfecting Churches are no threat to the forces of evil. The growing Church in the Central Belt is involved in a power encounter of significant proportions between the Spirit of God, made effective in Jesus Christ, and the spirits of animistic paganism, Islam, materialism, and "progress." Only as the Spirit of God permeates, enlightens, transforms, and directs the tribes of the Central Belt, moulding them into a free and creative society, can God's will for Nigeria be effectively fulfilled. God-consciousness is seen in the words of Nigeria's coat of arms, "Unity and Faith," and in the coat of arms of the Northern Region, "Work and Worship." But this God-consciousness must be directed by Him who said, "No one comes to the Father but by me." This is the encounter: the confrontation of every other way by the Way.

How effective any Church is can be judged only by the success of its encounter with the world about it. It is not enough to experience God within its own inner life. Life must be successfully communicated to those without. It is not enough to know that the Church has a mission, or even is mission; the mission must be *accomplished.* In its introduction to a ten-year program, one mission in the Central Belt gives as its objective, "To reach all the people in our area with so clear a presentation of the Good News of Jesus Christ that they will decide to follow Him." There is much more than compulsion to "witness" in this. The purpose is to witness so clearly that something will happen: that the people will decide to follow Him. Jesus said, "You shall be my *witnesses,*" and He also said, "Go, therefore, and *make* disciples of all nations." Without accomplishment, the Christian mission has failed.

Many times the Church, as a result of persecution or apostasy, retreats into caves, there to maintain a flickering light. In the Central Belt this is no time for retreat, retrenchment, or protective action! The call goes out at this strategic time in the history of Nigeria for the Church to come forth "like a strong man (who) runs his course with joy."

The Church in the Central Belt of Nigeria has been running a successful race. There have been great accomplishments, but there are many obstacles along the way. This study is, above all, a call to the Church to gird itself anew for the greater race before it, a race in which past accomplishments are dimmed by the immensity of the race before – and time is of utmost significance. The Central Belt is not content with the old way. It is rushing toward the new. The "fulness of time" is upon us, the wave of enthusiasm is rolling in, a wave of enthusiasm for the new, blown on by the winds of change. Changing situations could dissipate Christian advance in the spray of reaction, nativistic movements, communistic propaganda, or Islamic revival. But the wave is deep and God is at work. The barren land is being flooded with refreshment and life. The Church puts depth and meaning into the enthusiasm for life so rampant in the Central Belt, so that it may be for Life, the Life of God as revealed in Christ, and expressed in His growing Church.

BIBLIOGRAPHY

Allen, Roland. *The Spontaneous Expansion of the Church.* Grand Rapids: Eerdmans, 1962.

———. *Missionary Methods: St. Paul's or Ours?* Grand Rapids: Eerdmans, 1962.

———. *The Ministry of the Spirit.* Grand Rapids: Eerdmans, 1960.

Baker, Ralph. "The Evangelization of the Tiv Tribe." *Reformed Journal* (Nov. 1958).

Baldwin, Elmer R. "The Establishment of the Church of the Brethren Mission in Africa." Thesis: Bethany Biblical Seminary. Chicago, Illinois. 1953.

Bane, N. J. *Catholic Pioneers in West Africa.* 1956.

Barth, H. *Travels and Discoveries in North and Central Africa 1849-1855.* London: Longmans, Green and Co., 1857.

Bittinger, D. W. *Black and White in the Sudan.* Elgin, Ill.: Brethren Publishing House, 1941.

Brewer, Earl D. C. *Church Extension Strategy.* Committee on Missions, the Methodist Church. Atlanta, Georgia: 1962.

Buchanan, K. M. and J. C. Pugh. *Land and People in Nigeria.* University of London Press. 1955.

Christian Council of Nigeria. "The Duty of Christians in Independent Nigeria." Adopted at the Ibadan Conference, Nigeria, May 8-12, 1961.

Christian Reformed Church Publication. "The Coming of the Gospel into Tivland," n.d.

Church of the Brethren Publication. "Our Churches in Other Lands." Elgin, Ill.: Brethren Publishing House, 1952.

Coleman, James S. *Nigeria, Background to Nationalism.* Berkeley and Los Angeles, Calif.: University of California Press, n.d.

Collis, Robert. *African Encounters: A Doctor in Nigeria.* New York: Chas. Scribner's Sons, 1960.

Culberson, James O. "A Survey of Cultural Factors Relevant to Differential Reception of the Gospel in Primitive Societies." M. A. Thesis, Columbia Bible College, Columbia, So. Carolina. 1957.

Dudly, Raymond A. *The Growing Edge of the Church.* New York: Agricultural Missions Inc., 1951.

Eikenberry, Ivan. "Which Way Nigeria?" Elgin, Ill.: Brethren Publishing House, 1959.

Epelle, Sam. *The Promise of Nigeria.* London: Pan Books Limited, 1960.

Ethnographic Surveys of Africa by the International African Institute, London.

Ford, Brown, and Armstrong. *Peoples of the Niger Benue Confluence.* 1953.

Gunn, H. D. *Pagan Peoples of the Central Area of Nigeria.* 1950.

——— and Conant, F. P. *Peoples of the Middle Niger Region of Northern Nigeria.* 1960.

———. *Peoples of the Plateau of Northern Nigeria.* 1953.

Gindiri Teacher Training Centre Publication. "The Gindiri Jubilee Magazine 1934-1959," n.d.

Groves, C. P. *The Planting of Christianity in Africa.* Vol. I. London: Lutterworth Press, 1948.

Hardin, S. "The Tribal Church as an Ecumenical Problem." Thesis: Union Theological Seminary. 1960.

Helander, Gunmar. *Must We Introduce Polygamy?* Pietermaritzburg: Shuter and Shooter, 1958.

Helser, A. D. *Education of Primitive People.* London: Fleming H. Revell Co., 1934.

Hunter, Guy. *The New Societies of Tropical Africa.* London and Ibadan, Nigeria: Oxford University Press, 1962.

Hunter, J. H. *A Flame of Fire.* The Sudan Interior Mission. Aylesbury and Slough, England: Hazell Watson and Viney, Ltd., 1962.

Kirk-Greene, A. H. M. *Adamawa Past and Present.* International African Institute. London: Oxford University Press, 1958.

Knight, Charles William. "A History of the Expansion of Evangelical Christianity in Nigeria." Thesis: Southern Baptist Theological Seminary, Louisville, Kentucky. 1951.

Lewis, L. J. *Education and Political Independence in Africa.* Edinburgh: Thomas Nelson and Sons, 1962.

Maxwell, J. Lowry. *Half a Century of Grace.* Sudan United Mission, Great Portland Street, London: 1951.

———. *Nigeria, the Land, the People, and Christian Progress.* London: World Dominion Press, 1926.

McGavran, Donald A. *The Bridges of God.* New York: Friendship Press, 1955.

———. *How Churches Grow.* New York: Friendship Press, 1959.

Meek, C. K. *The Northern Tribes of Nigeria.* London: Kegan, Paul, Trench, Trubner & Co., 1925.

———. *Sudanese Kingdom.* London: Kegan, Paul, Trench, Trubner & Co., 1936.

———. *Tribal Studies in Nigeria.* Two volumes. London: Kegan Paul, Trench, Trubner & Co., 1936.

Miller, Ethel P. "Change Here for Kano." Gaskiya Corporation, Zaria, Nigeria, 1959.

Moyer, Elgin S. *Missions in the Church of the Brethren.* Elgin, Ill.: Brethren Publishing House, 1931.

Mow, Annetta C. "In African Villages." The Student Volunteer Movement, New York, 1942.

Murdock, G. P. *Africa: Its Peoples and their Cultural History.* 1959.

Nevius, J. L. *The Planting of Missionary Churches.* 4th edition. Philadelphia, Penn.: The Presbyterian and Reformed Publishing Co., 1959.

Nida, E. A. and W. A. Smalley. *Introducing Animism.* New York: Friendship Press, 1959.

Nigeria Magazine, Federal Ministry of Information Printing Division, Lagos, Nigeria: October, 1960.

Niven, C. R. *Nigeria.* London: Thomas Nelson and Sons, Ltd., 1945.

Northcott, Cecil. *Christianity in Africa.* London: S. C. M. Press Ltd., 1963.

Oliver, Roland. *The Dawn of African History.* London: Oxford University Press, 1961.

Orizu, A. A. Nwafor. *Without Bitterness.* New York: Creative Age Press, Inc., 1944.

Parrinder E. G. *Religion in an African City.* New York, London: Oxford University Press. 1953.

———. *West African Religion.* London: Epworth Press, 1961.

———. *African Traditional Religion.* London: Hutchkinson House, 1954.

Phi Delta Kappa. "Africa, Its Educational Problems and Provinces." Vol. XLI, No. 4 (Jan., 1960).

———. *The Dynamics of Church Growth.* New York: Abingdon Press, 1963.

Pickett, J. W., A. L. Warnshuis, G. H. Singh, D. A. McGavran. *Church Growth and Group Conversion.* Lucknow, India: Lucknow Pub. House, 1956.

Ritchie, John. *Indigenous Church Principles in Theory and Practice.* New York: Fleming H. Revell Co., 1946.

Rycroft, W. S. and M. M. Clemmer. *A Factual Study of Sub-Saharan Africa.* Commission on Ecumenical Missions and Relations, The United Presbyterian Church in the U.S.A., New York: 1962.

Service, E. R. *A Profile of Primitive Culture.* New York: Harper and Brothers, 1958.

Smith, E. H. "The Organization of TEKAS." Unpublished paper, n.d.

Smith, Edwin W. *The Christian Mission in Africa.* 1926.

Stock, Eugene, *History of the Chuch Missionary Society.* Volumes I, II, III. 1899.

Sudan Interior Mission, Nigeria. "Lessons on What ECWA Stands For," n.d.

Thomsen, Mark. "Evangelism-Conversion-Baptism," n.d.

Trimingham, J. Spencer. *The Christian Church and Islam in West Africa.* I. M. C. Research Pamphlet. No. 3. 1955.

TEKAS Pamphlet, "The Fellowship of the Churches of Christ in the Sudan." Jos, Nigeria: Ladapo Press, 1963.

Vicedom, G. F. *Church and People in New Guinea.* World Christian Books, No. 38. London: Lutterworth Press, 1961.

Walker, F. Deaville. *The Romance of the Black River.* London: Church Missionary Society, Salisbury Square, 1930.

Warren, J. S. "A Story of Peaceful Progress by Stages to Full Independence." Kaduna, Nigeria: Baraka Press, 1960.

Willis, J. J. *An African Church in Building.* Church Missionary Society. Southampton, England: Camelot Press, n.d.

World Missionary Atlas. Institute of Social and Religious Research, 1925.

World Atlas of Christian Missions (Student Volunteer Movement), 1911.

Church Growth in Southern Nigeria

by

Gordon E. Robinson

FOREWORD

by

His Excellency Sir Francis Ibiam, Governor of the Eastern Region, Nigeria*

The story of the growth of the Christian Church in Southern Nigeria is without doubt a story of romance and Christian fortitude. It is closely interwoven with European missionary endeavor, and brings to the arena the strong faith of men and women who had dared all and left comfortable homes to be ambassadors for Christ in far-off lands like Nigeria.

Mr. Gordon Robinson has placed before the reader the results of his careful research into the advent of the gospel to Southern Nigeria. It brings into sharp focus the difficulties and frustrations that had confronted the earliest venturers in their untiring attempts to preach and teach and heal. Much of this interesting book concerns the growth of the traditional and older Churches, especially the Anglican, Baptist, Methodist, and Presbyterian Churches, taking them alphabetically, but the author has also touched on the beginnings of the newcomers to the field, the progress of church union in Nigeria, and the establishment of the Christian Council of Nigeria. Some are dealt with in full measure because the author was able to get records of the work of the missions affected. This, unfortunately, is not so, as far as the Presbyterian Church (the offspring of the Church of Scotland, Calabar Mission) is concerned, but it is hoped that some further research will be undertaken in this respect so that the full history of the Presbyterian Church in Southern Nigeria may be brought in line with her sister churches.

One failure of the missionary bodies in the early days of

* This foreword applies most directly to *Church Growth in Southern Nigeria,* the section of this book authored by G. E. Robinson. But much of what Sir Francis says applies equally well to the central part of the country.

their evangelism was the sad neglect of the training of ordained ministers in a proper setting. One got the impression that the authorities had no idea that the missions should metamorphose to living churches and that these churches should grow to such heights as would require Nigerians in turn to be the evangelizers of their own country. Then there was the agreement among the missions to stay and give service in definite areas in order to avoid overlapping and unnecessary confusion. This policy, though good and useful in a way, was unfortunately responsible for vast sections of Southern Nigeria (e.g., certain parts of present-day Abakaliki and Ogoja Provinces) to be overlooked or neglected because the missions concerned had not enough personnel or financial competence to take care of these areas. It is encouraging to observe that the stage is well set today for a growing up of all the churches together in deep spiritual fellowship and unceasing prayer so that they may all be one in Him.

In the last chapter of the book the author has dwelt upon the future church growth, laying emphasis on those factors that make for progress and how best to employ them. Christian evangelism, if it is to be effective, must include all Nigeria – Southern and Northern Nigeria, East and West – and reach and extend into the farthest corners of the country. It is incumbent upon the church in Nigeria to plan wisely and execute in faith such plans so that Nigeria, all of it, may eventually be won for Christ. That is the church's commission from her Lord and Master.

The author has taken infinite pains to present *Church Growth in Southern Nigeria* to his readers. Graphs, statistical tables, and maps which form part of the book show evidence of his careful research and analysis. I have no doubt that *Church Growth in Southern Nigeria* will make a welcome debut with the general public and find an honorable place on the book shelves of priests, laymen, and students of history. Theological libraries in Nigeria and elsewhere cannot be complete without *Church Growth in Southern Nigeria*, which will greatly appeal to the theological student.

State House
Enugu, Nigeria

—Francis Akanu Ibiam

Introduction

Many books have been written on mission methods, history, theology of missions, and related subjects. But a study of the multitudinous factors that go together to produce church growth in Southern Nigeria has not been published before. Such a study is the purpose of this book. In discussing this project with numerous colleagues the author has met various reactions. Some have been most encouraging and suggested that such a study ought to be made. Others have expressed an opinion that such a study would be fruitless. The Bible says some plant and others water, but God provides the increase. This study does not in any way seek to diminish the spiritual factors involved in church growth. Every Christian will acknowledge that God does provide the increase and His marvelous ways among men are beyond our full comprehension.

At the same time most Christians recognize that God uses people to win people. He told Peter, "Follow me and I will make you a fisher of men." While God gave the increase, Paul did plant and Apollos did water. The planting and the watering are important and the methods used in cultivating employ many human and material factors. In studying these factors we seek through added knowledge under the leadership of the Holy Spirit to increase our usefulness to God in His redeeming purpose.

Because of the wide scope of this study among a multiplicity of ethnic groups with varieties of social patterns and among a large number of Christian denominations and communions, this book is in the form of a survey. One function that it should serve is to inspire further detailed study among the populations in local areas as the value of such studies becomes known.

One of the problems encountered in any study including Churches of several theological positions and organizational structures is that of terminology. The terminology employed in this book is not intended to have theological implications and does not reflect the author's theological views on the doctrine of the Church or other doctrines. The following terminology will be employed solely for the purpose of being understood by all and giving the least offense possible.

(1) Church with capital C will be used when referring to a denomination or communion, such as the Baptist denomination or the Anglican communion in Nigeria.

(2) Church with a small c will be used when referring to a local congregation, or when the word is used as an adjective, i.e., "church policies."

(3) Traditional Church will be used when referring to a Church that was begun or has established affiliation with an older Church or mission board in Europe or America.

(4) Independent Church will be used when referring to a Church born in Nigeria and without such outside affiliation.

Certain terms (i.e., native, tribe, and others) have, through improper usage in the past, taken on pejorative implications. This is very unfortunate because sociological descriptions necessitate some use of these terms in their true meaning. It is hoped that the author's use of these terms, as well as quotations from others using them, will be thus understood.

American and British spelling differs in certain words. Anticipating that this book will be read in several countries, the author has chosen to use American spelling, with which he is most familiar, except in quotations, where the spelling used in the original source is retained.

While the author does not claim complete accuracy in the statistics used in this book, great care has been exercised in gathering them, using the most reliable sources available. Efforts have also been made to refrain from using statistics of questionable accuracy as the sole support for conclusions.

Acknowledgments

Throughout this book acknowledgment for published and printed matter used is listed under References at the end of each chapter. I am indebted to the publishers and authors for use of this material.

I am indebted to Dr. Donald McGavran, my professor and consultant, for advice and inspiration, and to the Institute of Church Growth and Northwest Christian College for the Research Fellowship that provided the resources for this venture. I also acknowledge my gratitude to Dr. Cornell Goerner and to the Foreign Mission Board of the Southern Baptist Convention, who granted me time from other responsibilities to complete this work and encouraged me along the way.

I wish to extend my thanks to the Rt. Rev. Agori Iwe, Bishop of Benin (Anglican), to the Rev. J. E. Mills, Secretary of Missions and Evangelism for the Nigerian Baptist Convention, to other church leaders, to my fellow missionaries, to many pastors, teachers, and others too numerous to list individually, for help in gathering information in my research.

I am also grateful to His Excellency Sir Francis Ibiam, Dr. I. N. Patterson, Archdeacon George Barnard, and some of those listed above, who have critically read my manuscript and offered helpful suggestions, several of which I have incorporated in this book.

Finally, I wish to thank Nan Owens and my mother, Anna Robinson, for proofreading and correcting errors in the manuscript. And special thanks go to my wife, Maxine, whose constant help and encouragement throughout the preparation and writing has made this book possible.

G. E. R.

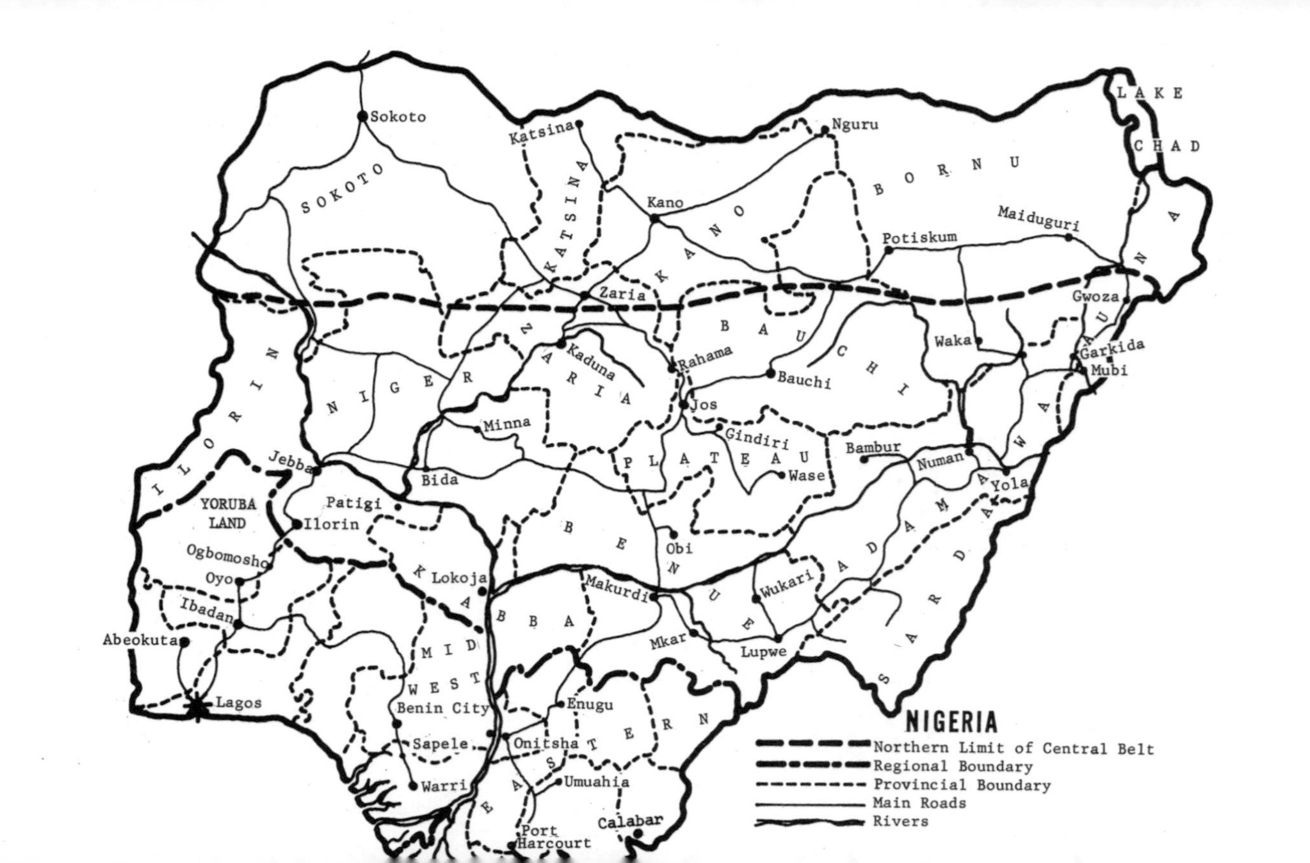
NIGERIA
Northern Limit of Central Belt
Regional Boundary
Provincial Boundary
Main Roads
Rivers
LAKE CHAD
SOKOTO
KATSINA
KANO
BORNU
ZARIA
BAUCHI
ADAMAWA
SARDAUNA
NIGER
ILORIN
PLATEAU
BENUE
KABBA
MID WEST
EASTERN
YORUBA LAND
Sokoto
Katsina
Nguru
Kano
Maiduguri
Potiskum
Zaria
Gwoza
Waka
Garkida
Mubi
Kaduna
Rahama
Bauchi
Jos
Gindiri
Minna
Bambur
Numan
Yola
Wase
Jebba
Bida
Patigi
Ilorin
Obi
Ogbomosho
Oyo
Lokoja
Makurdi
Wukari
Ibadan
Abeokuta
Mkar
Lupwe
Lagos
Enugu
Benin City
Onitsha
Sapele
Umuahia
Warri
Calabar
Port Harcourt

Chapter I. Southern Nigeria and Its People

It is not the author's purpose in this first chapter to give a detailed ethnographic study of Southern Nigeria. Indeed space would not permit it in one chapter or in one volume. The purpose is rather to show briefly both variations and complexities of the social structures found in Southern Nigeria. It is in this ethnic setting that various Christian bodies have planted churches. It is in this setting that in different times, places, and circumstances wide variations in church growth have occurred. The extent to which church growth is affected by the factors of social structure and patterns as well as methods and policies of missions and Churches is the problem set before the reader.

Nigeria in 1963 was an independent nation within the British Commonwealth. The federal government and each of the three regional governments operated under the parliamentary system. (Since this book was written a fourth region, the Midwest Region, has been constituted, embracing Benin and Delta Provinces, formerly in the Western Region.) The political division between the Eastern Region and the Western Region roughly follows the Niger River, though at some points the boundary lies several miles east or west of the river. The Eastern Region extends from the river east to the Cameroons. The Western Region extends from the river west to Dahomey. The southern boundary of the Northern Region lies about 150 to 200 miles north of the coast (see Map 1).

The Northern Region (including the solid Moslem belt and the pagan central belt) embraces 281,782 square miles with an estimated 1961 population of 18,000,000. The Eastern Region includes 46,065 square miles with an estimated 1961 population of 7,967,975. The Western Region includes 45,376 square miles, with an estimated 1961 population of 6,087,000. These population figures are sometimes challenged and may not be correct. The Nigerian Government is attempting in 1963 to get the first accurate national census. Figures from this census were not yet available at the time of the writing of this book.*

Region	Population
Northern Region	29,758,875
Eastern Region	12,394,462
Western Region	10,265,846
Midwest Region	2,535,839
Lagos	665,246
Total	55,620,268

East of Yorubaland the coastal swampland widens to a thirty- or forty-mile depth where the great Niger River fans out to form the Niger Delta. North of the delta a plain gradually rises to a plateau. The plain is heavily forested. The northern part of the plateau is grassland, especially in the extreme east. The soil is only moderately fertile and is very poor in some areas.

Economy

Throughout Southern Nigeria the basic economy is subsistence farming. The main crops are yam, cassava, cocoyam, maize, rice, peppers, beans, okra, melons, and gourds. In Yorubaland farming is primarily men's work. East of Yorubaland it is usual for both men and women to have farms. Among the tree products are citrus fruits, bananas, plantains, papaya, palm oil and kernels, cocoa, kola, coconut, and rubber.

The main cash crops are cocoa, mainly in the West, and rubber, palm products, and timber in the East and Midwest. Extensive plantations are owned by some wealthy men, who hire labor forces to help care for and harvest the crops. Others own a few trees and care for them without paid help.

Because of the prevalence of the tsetse fly there are almost no horses. A few West African dwarf cattle will be found in various localities. Sheep, chickens, guinea fowl, ducks, turkeys, goats, pigs, dogs, and cats are numerous in most villages. These are used for food, trade, and sacrifice at different places and times. A small percentage of the population, mainly in the Niger Delta area, are fishermen.

* The official government population figures from the 1963 census have since been obtained.

The hunting of small game is widespread. Most men set traps on their farms and in the bush to catch small animals, birds, and snakes. This serves both for the protection of crops and to supplement the food supply. Many have guns, often of local manufacture. There are a few hunting specialists who hunt larger game, usually on a part-time basis. The larger game consists mainly of several varieties of the antelope family, elephants, "bush cows" (close kin to water buffalo), wild pigs, crocodiles, hippopotami, and hyenas. These larger animals are mostly found in the Niger Delta area and the northeastern part of the Eastern Region. They are less common in more cultivated areas but were much more widespread fifty years ago.

Trading occupies a large part of the time of most women. Many men are also traders. Markets are held every five days at various centers in or between villages. These markets are spaced so there is a market every day within traveling distance of most villages. Thus there are professional traders who travel from market to market as well as the local villagers who carry their surplus products to market to trade. This is significant to church growth because it establishes frequent contact between the people of different villages.

Nigeria's main exports are cocoa, palm kernels, palm oil, groundnuts, benniseed, columbite, tin ore, coal, timber, plywood, bananas, goatskins, cattle hides, and cotton. The income from these exports provides the capital for imports such as sugar, confectionery, salt, wheaten flour, fish, milk, ale, beer, gin, whiskey, cigarettes, unmanufactured tobacco, sewing machines, corrugated-iron sheets, tools and implements, cycles, cars, commercial vehicles, cotton and rayon piece goods. The greater part of the foreign trade is with the United Kingdom, but there is also considerable trade with the Netherlands, Germany, Japan, Norway, the United States, and other countries.

Crafts, Local Industries, Native Arts

A high quality of weaving, dyeing, pottery, metal work, woodcarving, calabash carving, bead and leather work is found in Yorubaland. Regional variations in style can be recognized, so it is possible to identify certain arts and crafts as coming from certain villages or areas. This is true also in the Eastern Region where woodcarving, blacksmithing, weaving, pottery making, and carpentry are found. The Midwest is known for highly developed skills in brass casting, woodcarving, ivory carving, blacksmithing, leather work, potter work and weaving of special embroidered cloth. These crafts are largely in the hands of special guilds – another feature significant to church growth. Guilds and modern day trade unions establish close relationships between people, through which church growth can either take place easily or be severely hampered by group pressure. There has been considerable decline in many of the crafts and arts of Southern Nigeria with the growing Western influence, but many of these are still carried on.

Ethnic Divisions

After an analysis of the various racial groups and mixtures in Nigeria, K. M. Buchman and J. C. Pugh conclude "that the importance of race as a dividing factor in modern Nigeria is negligible; the great human groups, such as the Yoruba, the Ibo, or the Hausa, are linguistic and cultural rather than racial groups, and indeed each may contain a variety of racial strains."[1]

James S. Coleman goes the next step by adding: "For descriptive purposes ethnic distinctions have been drawn on the basis of language, aided to some extent by evidences of similarity in customs or other criteria. Ethnographical and anthropometrical surveys have been too limited in scope to provide a more accurate criterion of group demarcation. But language is frequently misleading; for example, the majority of those listed as Fulani speak the Hausa (not the Fulani) language as the mother tongue. It would be inaccurate to give ethnic and political attributes to all linguistic categories."[2] It will be noted that Coleman's example of the Fulani is from Northern Nigeria and is not exactly duplicated in the South,

[1] Buchanan, K. M. and Pugh, J. C., *Land and People in Nigeria,* p. 82.

[2] Coleman, James S., *Nigeria Background to Nationalism,* p. 13.

but his point, that language similarity does not always indicate a strong ethnic tie, is well taken.

It must also be noted that within each of the major language groups there is considerable fragmentation resulting in as many as 248 distinct dialects. Both Yorubas and Ibos commonly recognize one of their several dialects as the purest form of their language, and these are understood by most of those who speak one of these major languages. The area where language differentiation is greatest is among the many small tribes found in the Niger Delta area, both in the Midwest and in the Eastern Region. Here there is no common language for the various language units, a fact that has had negative bearing on the spread of Christianity.

In the twentieth century the language used in the schools, most newspapers, government documents, and notices for the general public is English. Thus a very widespread knowledge and use of the English language is found, especially among the literate and semiliterate population. But English has not yet taken the place of the mother tongues of the various peoples of Nigeria. Whether or not it ultimately will remains to be seen.

The principle of recognizing ethnic divisions according to language affinity categorizes the ethnic divisions of Southern Nigeria, as seen on Map 2 and Map 3. This does not imply that all the inhabitants of any one ethnic division can speak to or understand each other. It only shows areas where the dominant languages are closely related. There is considerable overlapping within these boundaries. For example, the Itsekiri (Jekri) people, identified linguistically with the Yorubas, live in an area where Urhobos (Sobo) and Ijaws also live. Nevertheless, Maps 2 and 3 give a good general picture of the broad ethnic divisions of Southern Nigeria.

Table I shows the population distribution, using estimates during the early 1950s. This illustrates some of the overlapping of the home ground of the different linguistic groups. It also shows that large numbers of people have left their home country and moved to other areas. This is done primarily on an individual basis either by migrants in search of work or through the transfer of workers by employers. It is

Map 2. PRINCIPAL ETHNIC GROUPS IN EASTERN NIGERIA

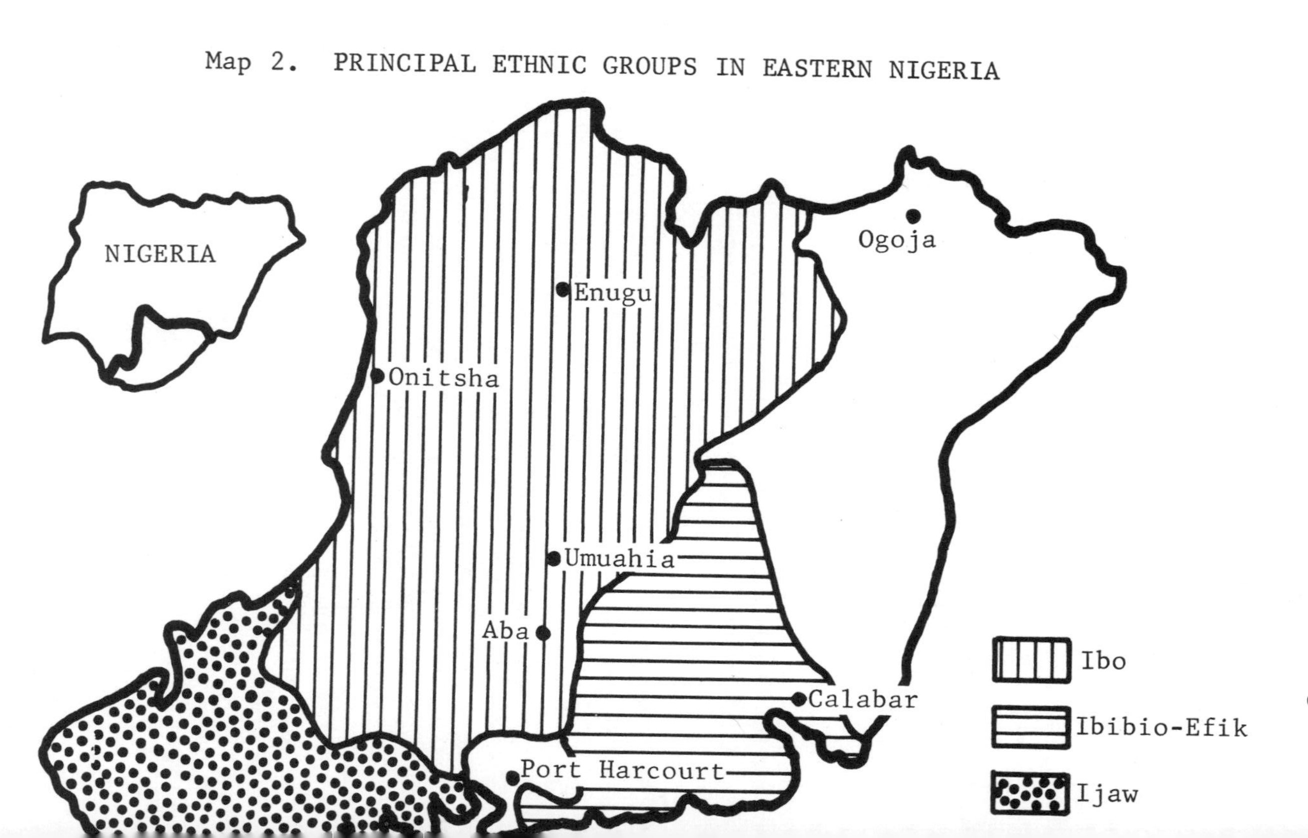

NIGERIA
Oyo
Ife
Ibadan
Abeokuta
Lagos
Benin
Sapele
Warri

Yoruba (including Jekri)
Edo (including Sobo & Etsakor)
Ijaw minority
Ibo minority

Ethnic Group & Region of Origin	Lagos Township	Western Region	Eastern Region	Northern Region	Total	% of Population of Nigeria
Western Groups:						
Yoruba	195,974	4,302,401	11,377	536,109[b]	5,045,861	16.6
Edo (Beni)	5,708	446,444	4,027	11,938	468,117	1.5
Others	5,051	486,902	a	a	491,953	
TOTAL	206,733	5,235,747	15,404	548,047	6,005,931	
Eastern Groups:						
Ibo	31,887	342,335[c]	4,916,736	166,910[d]	5,457,868	17.9
Ibibio-Efik	4,505	5,265	809,387	12,759	831,916	2.7
Ijaw	3,925	79,079[e]	258,962	a	341,966	1.1
Others	a	a	1,038,117	a	1,038,117	
TOTAL	40,317	426,679	7,023,202	179,669	7,669,867	
Northern Groups:						
Hausa	3,847	41,374	10,288	5,488,446	5,543,955	18.2
Fulani	285	6,858	757	3,022,581	3,030,481	9.9
Kanuri	148	1,170	2,151	1,298,306	1,301,775	4.2
Nupe	444	6,980	2,811	348,979	359,214	1.1
Tiv	805	2,428	5,121[f]	772,771	781,125	2.5
Others	202	4,110	a	5,051,380	5,055,692	
TOTAL	5,731	62,920	21,128	15,982,463	16,072,242	
Other Groups:	14,626	356,680	151,228	101,874	624,408	
GRAND TOTAL	267,407	6,082,026	7,210,962	16,812,053	30,372,448	

a-Exact number not known; included in "other groups."
b-Of this number, about 480,000 constitute a border minority in Northern Nigeria.
c-Of this number, about 285,000 constitute a border minority in Western Nigeria.
d-Of this number, about 40,000 constitute a border minority in Northern Nigeria.
e-Of this number, about 65,000 constitute a border minority in Western Nigeria.
f-Of this number, about 4,500 constitute a border minority in Eastern Nigeria.

Sources: Population Census of the Western Region of Nigeria, 1952 (Lagos: Govt. Statistician, 1953-54); Population Census of the Northern Region of Nigeria, 1952 (Lagos: Govt. Statistician, 1952-53), pp. 26-29; Population Census of the Eastern Region of Nigeria, 1953, Bulletin No. 1 (Lagos: Govt. Statistician, 1954), pp. 18-19.

important to note that though these people often move individually they usually settle in the section of town where those of their ethnic group who have preceded them reside. Thus in many places there are pockets where a minority ethnic group resides surrounded by another ethnic group or groups. There are certain interrelationships between these ethnic groups. Ties are also retained with the home country by those who emigrate. Thus bridges of contact are available through which Christianity can spread.

The following outlines of social and political structure are the traditional forms, but they are never static. The continuous changes and adaptations that occur are important but are far too numerous to be described in this work.

Social Organization and Political Structure: Yoruba

The social organization and traditional political structure are so interrelated that we can best view them together. "The Yoruba peoples might rightly claim to be the largest cultural aggregation in West Africa with a history of political unity and a common historical tradition. . . . Despite political fragmentation and regional dialectical differences, regional variations in religious and ceremonial forms, and tensions produced by former slave or trade wars and struggles for independence or by current land and chieftancy disputes, a comparatively strong Yoruba-consciousness has persisted."[3] All Yorubas believe they came from common ancestry at Ile Ife, and through the nineteenth century gave at least nominal allegiance to the Alafin (king) of Oyo. As a rule, the further removed from Oyo geographically, the more nominal the allegiance. "The whole of Yoruba country is divided among the traditional kingdoms, each of which has had, from time immemorial, a definite (though not necessarily unchanging) boundary with its neighbors. . . . All members of the kingdom may claim as much land as they need for farming and housebuilding."[4] So local autonomy in Yoruba land is considerable,

[3] *Ibid.*, p. 25.
[4] Lloyd, P. C., *Yoruba Land Law*, pp. 62-63.

with authority divided and subdivided among the smaller political and social units within the tribe.

The bearing of social structure on church growth is tremendous. However, social structure makes heavy reading. Any reader allergic to such description may skip to Chapter II and pick up the story there. It is probable, however, that if he is seriously desirous of church growth, he will later make a detailed study of social structure among the people with whom he works.

The following description of Yoruba social structure is based mainly upon Daryll Forde's *The Yoruba-Speaking Peoples of South-Western Nigeria.*

The smallest social unit among the Yorubas is the domestic family. It usually consists of a man, his wife or wives, and his unmarried children, and others such as his mother or a younger brother who may be included in his basic economic unit. This unit occupies part of a house and its senior male member is recognized as its head.

A larger household or extended family is formed by several closely and, for the most part, patrilineally related families. This household occupies all or part of a unit of adjacent apartments and will include most of the following: an old man and his sons, his younger brothers and their sons, his father's younger brother's sons, together with the wives and unmarried children of all these. The old man has moral authority over this household and performs rituals on its behalf, though it is not usually an economic unit for production or consumption. There is considerable cohesion within this household with the bonds of both kinship and common residence.

The next larger social unit is often referred to in English as a "compound." It is a wider cluster of extended families for which a common head is recognized. It may occupy more than one set of dwellings and the members need not be members of a single patrilineage. The oldest male member is recognized as compound head. He consults with other elders of the "compound," heads of the component extended families and their senior wives. His functions include authority over every member of the group, responsibility for settling disputes among members and for their general welfare, and the management and allocation of land for farming. "His rights often include the assistance of young men for work on his farm, gifts of farm produce from members and, in the past, a leg of every animal or fowl offered at any sacrifice in the 'compound' "[5]

Within these primary social units, individuality is limited. Important decisions, such as changing religious affiliation, are rarely made without the knowledge and consent of the head of the unit. It is sometimes easier for an entire domestic family or larger social unit to embrace a new religion than for an individual to do so alone.

"There is a system of rank according to seniority, as defined in terms of a person's affiliations, by birth or marriage, with the *omole* (descendants of the compound). . . . Seniority of status depending on seniority of birth or marriage does not necessarily correspond with age, and the advancement of a man to the rank of elder (*agba*) depends, apart from his age, on his having reached an accepted seniority in the group. Status in this system is often expressed in the term by which a person is addressed by others and there are many subtle differences in naming between fathers and children and between a man's different wives, depending, for example, on whether they have children or not."[6]

When the residents of a "compound" increase to the extent that there is no longer sufficient housing or land, branch "compounds" may be formed. The head of the branch "compound" is subordinate to the parent "compound." Sometimes conversion to Christianity of a part of a "compound" results in its fragmentation. Fragments of a "compound," which act independently of the main body at home, may also be found in other towns, particularly in larger cities. The various fragments of these extended families, even when widely scattered, still maintain family allegiance and are often

[5] Forde, Daryll, *The Yoruba-Speaking Peoples of South-Western Nigeria,* pp. 10-13.

[6] *Ibid.,* p. 15.

open avenues through which Christianity can spread.

The major patrilineage is an important unit among the Yorubas. Within this group descent is traced for succession to chiefly offices, for the control of land and the inheritance of property. Descendants retain collective rights to land or property until segmentation occurs, when the property is divided among the segments.

Relationships through women are not traced back or known for more than a few generations. However, a person regards as his kin (i.e., those whom he may not marry) not only all members of his patrilineage but also the patrilineage of his mother, his mother's mother, his father's mother, and so on, as far as they are known.

In larger settlements "compounds" are grouped into wards, which are sometimes divided into precincts composed of several "compounds." These units are based on common residence and are not usually limited to a single patrilineage.

"The larger territorial groups of 'town,' sub-tribe and tribe are, according to Fadipe, compact groups of larger settlements with dependent villages, the inhabitants of which have common peculiarities of speech, common traditions, and ascribe their origin to the same founder. The larger of such aggregations may be regarded as a tribe, or in the case of more particularist groups, of which some of the Ijebu and the Egba in pre-Abeokuta days are examples, a subtribe. According to Talbot the divisions between and within tribes are clear, and a Yoruba is usually in no doubt as to his affiliation."[7]

"The Yoruba are probably the most urban of all African peoples. Almost one-third live in the fifteen Yoruba towns with populations of over 20,000 inhabitants, while there are some 250 Yoruba towns and villages with populations greater than 1,000."[8]

A few of the Yoruba tribes have age-sets (in which the people in each village are organized in age groupings for communal work and play), but it is not widespread in Yorubaland. Volunteer associations are much more common.

[7] *Ibid.*
[8] *Ibid.*

A person can often choose from several societies organized for recreation, consisting of about fifty persons of the same sex and about the same age. These societies are usually formed during childhood and continue until the members have died. Members meet for social purposes, usually dress alike, and enjoy rather ostentatious fun. Mutual-aid associations are also common. Members contribute fixed amounts for fixed periods and upon special need can ask to draw their share from the pool, though they have not yet completed payments of their share. The members of societies and associations have a distinct relationship with their co-members, which affords further opportunities for spreading Christianity.

"In most Yoruba communities craft specialists, both men and women, are organized into guilds with recognized heads. Such crafts are often quasi-hereditary in certain *idile* or 'compounds,' a large proportion of the members of which practice the craft in question. In some chiefdoms all the principal guilds, including women's were represented on the State Council. No one is allowed to practice any craft unless admitted as a member of the appropriate guild, and an entrance fee is demanded, usually in the form of kola nuts and drinks consumed by members. Where the guild has a special *orisha* (i.e., deity) the admission ceremony is performed at its shrine. In Abeokuta a new entrant to the blacksmiths' guild is still taken to the granite-anvil block, which serves as a symbol of the god of iron and war. The guilds protect the interests of their members and also meet for purely recreational purposes."[9]

Several "secret societies" exist throughout most of Yorubaland. They are usually connected with some *orisha* but often fulfill more of a social function today than any other. At least one, the *Ogboni,* has considerable political power among some of the tribes. The most widespread of these societies are *Ogboni, Oro,* and *Egungun.*

Yoruba rulers are strictly ranked according to importance and area of authority. Various apparel, types of crowns, footstools, and other objects signify rank. These traditional

[9] *Ibid.,* p. 16.

rulers still retain considerable importance, though much of their former authority has been assumed by the Federal and Regional governments.

"Everywhere the sacred chief was held in great respect as the possessor of ritual as well as political power. His person was regarded as sacred and as embodying the succession through the preceding chiefs from Oduduwa, founder of the Yoruba people. This is the significance of features in the elaborate installation ritual that are directed to maintaining a new chief's continuity with his predecessor, such as eating his heart or retaining and worshiping his head. Other rituals sought to ensure that a new chief was endowed with the magic of the numerous *orisha*. . . ."[10]

The chiefs preside over councils representing the various lineages, and cannot act without their authority. In some chiefdoms the principal guilds were represented in the council, including hunters, traders, and often the women's guilds. Also in some chiefdoms a strong *Ogboni* society has very extensive control over the chief. A tyrannical or unpopular chief can be deposed.

Each chiefdom is divided into districts, towns, villages, wards and even compounds. Each unit is largely autonomous apart from tribute, external relations, or disagreements between units.

The administration of justice begins with the smallest unit with the head man responsible for settling disputes between members. If there is dissatisfaction with the judgment, appeal can be made to the court or head of the next higher unit. When British rule began the judicial system was reorganized. A system of courts now exists, graded according to the status of the community, with fixed areas of authority and rights of appeal. Each court has a bench of judges.

Formerly inheritance rights were from the deceased to his full brothers and sisters, children having only residuary rights to their father's personal property. During the past generation the practice is more and more to distribute the deceased man's goods equally among his sons by different wives and in some cases to his daughters as well. Funeral

[10] *Ibid.*, pp. 19-24.

expenses are distributed among certain members of the lineage, and those contributing have a share in the deceased's property. Those who inherit have the responsibility of providing for widows and children.

> Land was formerly held by patrilineages and control was exercised by their heads who apportioned plots according to need, no adult member of the community being left without land. Occupiers could not alienate any of their portion without the consent of the whole group. According to Fadipe, however, the holder had exclusive rights of use, could pawn crops and transfer, temporarily or indefinitely, a portion of his land to non-members of the lineage. Land could neither be sold nor taken away for debt, though a man could pawn or pledge the use of his land. . . . Permanent crops and trees belonged to the person who planted them and could be inherited. . . .
>
> This traditional system of land tenure still persists to a great extent but, with increase of commercial agriculture, land has come to have a monetary value, especially in the forest belt and good cocoa soils. Land sales began in and around Lagos and were recognized in the native courts at the beginning of this century. But the rights of parties are often uncertain, as a mixture of British Law and Native custom has prevailed in the Supreme Court. The transfer of title to land to non-kin is generally looked on with disapproval, for in principle land may not be disposed of as personal property. In some places, however, outright sale is generally recognized. . . .[11]

Social Organization and Political Structure: Midwest

The Midwest is made up of many tribes much less culturally alike than the several tribes of Yorubaland. The social and political patterns vary so widely in the Midwest that it is impossible to generalize satisfactorily. Certain features will therefore be noted and the areas where they apply identified. The patrilineal line dominates in all these tribes as to settlement, inheritance of moveable property, common objects of worship, and authority. Unlike the Yoruba, intermarriage between tribes is not uncommon. Thus there are numerous bridges of contact between villages and tribes,

[11] *Ibid.*, pp. 25-26.

creating ready avenues for the spread of Christianity. Every person knows his heritage from two to seven generations back on both his mother's and father's side of the family.

A hierarchy of authority within the partrilineal lineage is common here as in Yorubaland. How this hierarchy of authority can be made a vehicle of the Spirit instead of an obstacle to the spread of the churches is one of the most important questions in church policy in Nigeria. The senior man of the nuclear or compound family is responsible to the senior man of the extended family, who is in turn responsible to the head of the ward or quarter of the town and so on. Among the Bini the village is the basic political unit.

> The widest unit for age-grade organization, the minimal land-holding unit, the smallest group which can have an hereditary chief, the smallest tribal unit, and also the co-operative unit for house building; most villages unite in worship of a common deity. Each village is a compact settlement though most are divided into wards which may be separated from each other by small patches of bush. . . . . Each ward consists of one or more extended families living in close proximity and recognizing the authority of the oldest man. . . . Order of precedence between wards is recognized on the basis of antiquity and other factors.[12]

The basic political unit of Ishan is the chiefdom, consisting of from one to twenty villages.

All land in the Midwest belongs to particular villages or chiefdoms. There have been many instances of families or groups of families settling (with permission or otherwise) on land that was not their own. In the past this often led to war. Now it frequently leads to court cases.

Age grades among the male population are important, except among the Itsekiri. The Urhobo and Isoko also have age grades for females. While there are differences in detail, there seem to be three main divisions in most places. The younger divisions have communal work responsibilities in accordance with the ability of their age group. The older division is primarily the organizing and ruling group.

[12] Bradbury, R.E., *The Benin Kingdom and the Edo-Speaking Peoples of South Western Nigeria,* p. 31.

The Benin Kingdom is very highly organized with a graded hierarchy of chiefs in separate categories for administrative, judicial, military, and other specialized functions. Under these chiefs are specialized associations, each with a particular function. The *Oba* (King of Benin) traditionally has very far-reaching power and authority. He and to a lesser degree the subordinate chiefs hold both secular and sacred position and responsibility. This sacred kingship is the focal point of the Benin political system. The senior kings and chiefs of the Ishan, Urhobo, Itsekiri, and some other kingdoms trace their lineage back to some descendant who received his appointment and authority from the *Oba*. Hence they, too, are sacred as well as temporal rulers. However, this does not prohibit them from becoming Christians, as many of them have done.

Among the Urhobo, Isoko, and some Northern Edo and Western Ibo tribes, title associations (clubs of title holders) are an important part of the social organizations. In most cases membership is open to any freeborn man who can meet the expenses involved, and often good reputation is required. Title associations have social, religious, and sometimes political functions. Membership is achieved by payment of fees that are shared by the existing members. Some of these associations are limited to a single village and some seem to be common throughout a given tribe. There is usually only one title association in any village. Seniority is according to length of membership rather than age.

Social Organization and Political Structure: Eastern Region

As in the Midwest, the large number of distinct tribes in the Eastern Region, each with its own social and political patterns, makes it impossible to describe a median applicable throughout this area. The following description will, therefore, be limited to the two largest ethnic divisions in the Eastern Region, the Ibo and the Ibibio-speaking peoples. Even within this limitation it will be necessary at times to generalize because of variations within these divisions.

Among the Ibo the basic social unit is the local patrilineage, often occupying a single hamlet of scattered homesteads.

This group may include only male siblings, their wives and children, or larger groups embracing several such units related patrilineally. Each lineage of whatever scale is subject to the moral authority of the head of the senior branch in larger lineages. He arbitrates in internal disputes and represents the group in external relations. His authority is strengthened by his priestly role as intermediary between the lineage and its ancestors. Wives of the members of a lineage are subject to his authority, but the heads of their lineages may intervene on their behalf. This tight social grouping can either help or hinder church growth within the unit.

Territorial and kinship relations between patrilineages are not stable over long periods. A lineage may dissociate itself from its previous village and join another. When exogamous lineages increase considerably in size they tend to split into intermarrying groups.

> Lineages generally tend to be aligned in pairs, each being a distinct group only in relation to the other, i.e., collateral lineages of the same branch are fused in relation to a more remote collateral branch, and a small lineage which leaves one village group and joins another often fuses with an existing lineage in the new group. The definition and cohesion of lineage is thus relative and can only be described in terms of the wider social structure. . . .
>
> A number of lineages which may or may not claim ultimate common descent, usually occupying a cluster of hamlets, constitute a territorial unit which may be called a village in the sense that there is some considerable solidarity based on neighborhood and that the farmlands of the various lineages or their sub-divisions occupy contiguous areas to which other sections of the villages have reversionary rights. . . .
>
> For most purposes the highest political unit, at least among the Northern and Southern Ibo, is the 'village group,' consisting of a cluster of villages sharing a common meeting place, which is at once a ritual, political and marketing center. [These are also potential centers for the spread of Christianity]. Ties are often expressed in traditions of common descent, despite the fact that accretions from other areas have occurred, and also in the possession of a common shrine of the earth or other nature deity. These groups or clusters

> of local communities are themselves sometimes organized into larger groups, again usually expressed through assumptions of common ancestry.[13]

However, these larger groups seldom act together except in extreme circumstances, such as threatened invasion, settlement of disputes between groups, or other occasions of common disturbance. The president of such a meeting would be the head of the senior lineage of the senior village.

The common Ibo settlement pattern is a loose cluster of homesteads scattered along paths radiating from a central place that contains the shrines and groves of local deities and also serves as the market place. Larger communities often consist of two or more such units, each with its own center. Most communities include from forty to eight-thousand people and their settlement may extend over an area of up to three square miles. Often the homesteads along a given path are from one patrilineage.

Individuals may become Christians among any of these settlements, along any of these paths, or among several of them. But great growth of the churches will only occur when chains of individuals in settlement after settlement become Christian. If the churches grow greatly they will soon claim most of the members of many interrelated communities.

The Ibibio settlement pattern and territorial organization are similar to those of the Ibo. Except for the Anang, the Ibibio have a stronger feeling of tribal and subtribal unity than the Ibo, but this does not imply central political authority. Neighboring villages are more likely to join together for a common purpose than those with a tradition of common origin, but who are not close neighbors. A settlement may include from one to eight lineages. The lineage head has ritual obligations and moral authority over his lineage. Settlements are usually small and scattered.

The Sevav plan of clan evangelization, described by my fellow research scholar John Grimley in the first half of

[13] Forde, Daryll, and Jones, G. I., *The Ibo and Ibibio-Speaking Peoples of South-Eastern Nigeria,* p. 16.

this volume takes full advantage of the close Nigerian social structure, which has great significance for church growth.

Age sets are common among both Ibo and Ibibio but with varying degrees of prominence. They are most strongly developed among the Cross River groups. They are organized on a village basis sometimes having loose ties with the corresponding sets in neighboring villages. They are organized in childhood, take a name, and appoint a senior man as leader. Their activities and responsibilities vary from village to village and according to their age. Such things as initiation ceremonies, communal work, police and sometimes military duties, and self-discipline are included. In the Cross River and some other areas, women are also organized in age sets.

> Ibo titles, except some of those among the Western Ibo where the influence of Benin prevailed, differ from titles found in other parts of Nigeria in that they are not honours or marks of rank and authority conferred by an external ruler nor are they in principle hereditary or the privilege of particular descent groups. They have to be secured by payment of fees to the community or to an organization of existing title-holders; in return for admission payments members can anticipate a substantial income from fees paid by later entrants.[14]

Title associations are common in both Ibo and Ibibio villages. Membership is open to freeborn men by appropriate payments. Where membership is graded, payments are scaled accordingly and one cannot receive a higher title until he has first passed through the lower ranks. A person cannot normally hold a rank higher than his father during his father's lifetime. To a lesser extent women's title associations are found in both Ibo and Ibibio villages.

Title holders have considerable political authority and social status. Among Ibos, title associations were in times past the principal unifying agency operating on a large scale between villages. Some of these associations are secret societies and some have considerable religious function.

[14] *Ibid.*, p. 20.

Legal procedures are usually in the hands of household and lineage heads. Serious offenses are dealt with by a council of elders in an Ibo village and the town head (or sometimes the elders) in an Ibibio village. Oath-swearing and trial by ordeal are often used to establish guilt.

Property inheritance is largely to the eldest son, who is responsible for his junior brothers. If the eldest son is a minor, the paternal brother usually takes charge of the property and the deceased brother's son.

Among the Ibibio, rights are attached to all land. Within a local community six categories of land may be recognized: sacred land, lineage land, community land (belonging to the village or village group), individual holdings (by inheritance or purchase), borrowed land, and pledged land (security for a loan). Individual holdings may be sold or bequeathed to any person, but usually pass to the eldest son.

Land tenure among the Ibo is considerably more varied. Most land other than sacred land is held by lineages or villages. However, the use of land is permanently assigned to individuals and is inherited by their eldest sons in most cases. New personal rights can be obtained by securing pledged land or by purchase. Outright sale of land is permitted only in certain areas. Short-term transfers, usually for one farming season, are much more common and involve rentals. Women normally have no independent rights to land, but a wife, so long as she helps to farm her husband's land, has a right to space for her own crops. Women may acquire land through male proxy by purchase or by securing pledged land.

Religion, Magic, and Cults

The religion of all of Southern Nigeria has may similarities and will be dealt with in one section. Some of the common features are the following.

(1) Most, if not all, tribes recognize a supreme but remote god who is Lord of Heaven and the Creator. He is known by separate names among the various tribes: Olorun by the Yoruba, Oghene by the Urhobo, Chineke by the Ibo, and so on. His functions vary. In some places,

such as Northern Edo, he is seen in the form of a mud or wooden figure and placed outside the doors of houses to keep out evil spirits. At other places, such as Isoko and Urhobo, he is said to be indescribable, but in some way connected with the sky, and is by nature good and kind. Among various peoples of the Eastern Region he is variously equated with the father of the sun, the sky, lightning, the earth, and the fertility deity. In Isoko there are no shrines or sacrifices made to him, but prayers of submission are addressed to him. Among the Itsekiri his symbol is a bamboo staff whitened with chalk, with a yam in the forked end and a string of cowries and wooden cross draped with a white cloth. The Beni picture him as a king, living in splendor with many wives and children. Among his offspring were the first kings of Ife, Benin, and the Europeans. Any person may pray to him for health, children, and other benefits. Thus can be seen the wide variety of thought concerning this god among the tribes of Southern Nigeria. As did Paul at Athens, early missionaries in Nigeria began from this god and preached the God of the Bible.

(2) The various tribes and subtribes also have a multitude of lesser gods and spirits (400 among Yorubas alone), many of them with their own priests. An individual may worship more than one such deity at a time. In some places one or more of these deities are worshiped commonly by an entire lineage or even a whole village.

(3) The Yoruba oracle of divination is called Ifa and is worshipped by many non-Yoruba peoples of Southern Nigeria as well. It must be consulted before any major decision. The priests of Ifa may come from any lineage, have a three-year training period, and are also considered "skilled physicians."

(4) Ancestor worship is prominent among most if not all tribes. It includes several distinct categories: individual, genealogically defined ancestors, deceased title holders, ancestors of the king, collective ancestors or predecessors of a group, and sometimes the deceased mothers of household heads. Perhaps related to ancestor worship are hero-deities, mythical figures of the past who have become gods. In-

dividuals often worship personal spirits as well. The Beni consider that each person consists of two parts, the living person in this world and the spiritual counterpart. Some say the two alternate at each incarnation. The head, recognized as the seat of judgment, and the arm, recognized as the seat of power to accomplish things, are of special importance. People of high rank often have altars dedicated to the head or the arm. At Olomoro the crocodile and at Emevo the monitor lizard are specially revered. These are associated with the ancestors.

Closely associated with this also is the Ibibio belief in a great variety of spirits associated with animals, sacred places, and objects. These are often identified with local groups and certain food prohibitions are observed in connection with them.

(5) Charms or "medicines" have wide use for both good and evil, with no clear dichotomy between what is commonly called "black magic" (evil) and "white magic" (beneficial) in many other parts of the world. Magic may be either curative or protective. It is practiced by diviners and other specialists as well as by individuals. These charms and medicines number in the thousands. Belief in charms and magic presents very real dangers of syncretism for those who superficially accept Christianity. Christian forms and objects used in worship are easily misinterpreted when not understood.

(6) Belief in witchcraft is strong in the Midwest and among the Ibibio in the East. It is less strong among the Yoruba and the Ibo. In general witches may be of either sex and any person may be made a witch, with or without consent. The witches are organized into corporate groups and perform all sorts of evil, especially capturing and killing others. Protection from witches is possible through certain medicine, purchased from "doctors." Witches are often propitiated by sacrifices and offerings. Trial by ordeal is practiced to determine who witches are. Witches are thought to have full knowledge of their powers and are able to recognize and communicate with each other without revealing themselves to outsiders.

(7) In some places oracles or shrines are erected both to major and local deities where appeals can be made to a god and responses obtained after propitiatory offerings. These were formerly used extensively for settling disputes and gaining divine favor. They have been important in the integrating of local communities among the Ibo.

(8) Shamans among the Yoruba are said to be possessed by the spirits of former chiefs and act as mediums between the departed spirits and the living. They alone can defend against evil spirits.

(9) The feature of religion among the peoples of Southern Nigeria that is most significant to the Christian Church is the complete integration of religion with all aspects of life.

> For the African there is no "secular" and "spiritual"; the two worlds are one and the same. The spiritual motivates the whole life; it is not a fuzzy, emotional pervasion. It is reality. If the Christian Church is to be in Nigeria, it must do justice to the African mind and its heritage. Everything that is good in the African's heritage should be conserved, enriched and ennobled by contact with the spirit of Christ. It is the prayer of consecrated missionaries that African Christians will build up a body of Christian custom, true to their genius, and covering the whole of their life.[15]

[15] West, Ralph L., "A Study of Indigeneity Among Nigerian Baptists" (Unpublished doctoral dissertation), p. 25.

Chapter II. The Beginnings of Christian Missions in Southern Nigeria

EVIDENCE IN SOME OF THE ANCIENT ART FORMS INDICATES THAT Christianity was known many centuries ago in Nigeria. Historians speculate that Nigeria was originally settled by waves of immigrants from the Mediterranean area, who brought the Coptic or some other form of Christianity along with them. In time any Christianity that might have been known completely died out, to be replaced by the animistic religious beliefs described in Chapter I.

Roman Catholics were the first to send missionaries to Southern Nigeria.

> As far back as 1487 Portuguese missionaries laboured in Benin City and in what is now called Old Warri. Owing to climatic conditions and two wars in Europe their missionary work was discontinued and their converts lapsed into paganism. They are said to have had three churches in Benin City, one called Holy Cross near the site of the present Holy Cross Cathedral, another at what is now a pagan shrine called Afa-Osa, the Altar of God, and a third near the present Government School.
>
> At Old Warri a mound of earth remains of what was once the church or "Capello" by which name the place is known to this day. A part of the village is known as San Ton, which was formerly St. Anthony's quarter (area). The chief (the Olu) of the Jekris (Itsekiris) has a silver crown with a cross in front which was sent his forefathers by one of the kings of Portugal. He wears a garment resembling a Dalmatic and round his neck a chaplet (rosary beads) with a crucifix attached. It was reported by the English who came to Warri in 1897 that they saw people with beads like Roman Catholics. Apart from these things there are no remains of the Christianity planted by the Portuguese.[1]

[1] *The Nigeria Catholic Directory,* 1962, p. 68.

So although Christianity had twice been introduced to Southern Nigeria, there was very little evidence of it remaining by the nineteenth century.

Factors That Opened Doors to Christianity in the Nineteenth Century

It is rather ironic that Christianity was again introduced to Nigeria as a direct result of the slave trade that became so notorious along the west coast of Africa from the seventeenth to the nineteenth centuries. Slavery was not introduced to Africa by Europeans. It already existed because of intertribal wars and war captives. Slavery increased enormously, however, when European ship owners began to purchase and transport slaves to America to sell to American plantation owners. Slave trade became a source of wealth, and it did not take much encouragement for warlike chiefs to increase their raids and warfare on their neighbors in order to capture people to be sold or traded into slavery.

But "there was a strong feeling of guilt among certain Christian groups in America and England over the cruelties against the African slaves during this period of slave trade. This conscience beckoned for the extension of Christianity to these people as compensation."[2] In the early nineteenth century England led the way by passing laws against slave trade. They were joined by other countries until only Spain and Portugal continued to ply the trade. British warships were stationed along the coast where British interests were involved to intercept slave ships and free the slaves. Most of these freed slaves were taken to Sierra Leone and put down in a strange but free land.

The slave trade scattered tribes and the breaking of this trade brought together at Sierra Leone a mixed population from numerous places and tongues. Mission work was begun early among these people by the Wesleyan and Church Missionary Societies from England. It is quite likely that the unusual success in converting these displaced refugees was due partially to the fact that here they were separated from group pressures of their society and were free to make in-

[2] Southon, A. E., *Gold Coast Methodism*, p. 20.

dividual decisions without loss of position or even more severe sanctions from their kinsmen and fellow villagers. This plus the contrast in the treatment given them by the slave traders and that which they found among the missionaries resulted in a more ready response to the gospel than would have been likely had their lives not been interrupted in this manner. Thus many were converted to Christianity and some attended mission schools.

In the following years some of them returned to their homes in Nigeria bearing witness to the generosity and kindness of Britain and Christian missionaries who were responsible for rescuing them, teaching them and making it possible for them to return to their homes in even a better condition than they had left. Some were sent as agents of the missions, the most notable of whom was Samuel Crowther, who was later to become Bishop of the Niger. Others went on their own initiative, impelled by the desire to return to their homes and their people. By about 1840 Southon writes,

> So it happened that some of these freed slaves sailed one day into the lagoon of Lagos – and knew it immediately as the port from which they had been taken on a slave dhow to Badagry. Their home was at Abeokuta, so leaving the boat at Lagos they travelled through the forest and once again rejoined their relatives. Somehow the news of this joyful homecoming found its way to Freetown, and at once there began a movement among other Egbas settled there to return to Abeokuta. The missionaries stationed in Freetown wrote home to the Committee an account of what was taking place and urged that something be done to help these poor people.[3]

The "Committee," British Wesleyans, asked Freeman, their missionary in Accra, Gold Coast, to visit Abeokuta, some 400 miles away. Freeman realized that if his visit was to accomplish anything he would have to take with him a man to settle and work. He looked over his field and chose William DeGraft as the man for the job because of his ability, dedication, and success in Gold Coast. They sailed in 1842 and journeyed on from Badagry to Abeokuta after

[3] *Ibid.*, pp. 75-76.

sending a message to Shodeke, the king, and receiving an invitation in return. He was the first missionary there and was pressed by Shodeke to send a resident missionary. He asked that DeGraft remain but Freeman decided DeGraft could best serve the returning ex-slaves by living in Badagry. Southon says, "His judgment was proved right, for on their return to Badagry on Christmas Eve they found Rev. H. Townsend of the Church Missionary Society waiting there. He had recently landed, and was on his way up to Abeokuta to care for the returned ex-slaves who had become members of the Church Missionary Society in Freetown."[4]

"After having visited Nigeria from Jamaica in the spring of 1846, H. M. Waddell, of the United Presbyterian Church of Scotland, returned home, and in 1847 brought back several missionaries to help him with his work among the people there."[5]

And in 1850 Thomas Bowen, Southern Baptist missionary from America, arrived in Badagry and proceeded up country to establish the first Baptist work in Nigeria. Bowen wrote in 1856, "The people of Sierra Leone consist of re-captured slaves from almost every part of Africa, and if missionaries were going to any point of the east, west, south or interior of the continent, there would be an a priori probability that they could obtain interpreters if not Christian schoolmasters, and other assistants at Freetown."[6]

Thus the slave trade brought to the shores of Nigeria both missionaries from Britain and America and Nigerian ex-slaves who had found and embraced Christianity in Sierra Leone and Jamaica. Other factors at various times and places also helped to open doors in Southern Nigeria to the introduction of Christianity during this period. These factors sometimes acted jointly and sometimes singly. Few general rules can be applied, for results were not always the same even when the circumstances were similar. However, some trends can be observed and supported with experience.

[4] *Ibid.*, pp. 76-77.

[5] Green, C. Sylvester, *New Nigeria, Southern Baptists at Work in Africa,* p. 63.

[6] Bowen, T. J., *Central Africa: Adventures and Missionary Labors in Several Countries in the Interior of Africa from 1849 to 1856,* p. 218.

For many victimized tribes and villages who had been plundered by the slave trade, the British and the missionaries became the heroes of protection. This happened in Abeokuta in 1845. Domingo, a notorious Porto-novo slave dealer, sent gifts to Sagbua, the king, promising to clear out the robbers if Sagbua would allow slave traffic to be established. Sagbua's response to Domingo's messengers was, "We can ourselves tell who are our best friends – those who rescue our children from captivity and send them freely to us again, or those who bring goods to purchase them for perpetual slavery and misery. The English are our friends, and you people at Badagry take care, for if any wrong is done to them in your town, you must answer to us for it."[7] His reference to "those in Badagry" referred to Rev. Townsend of the Church Missionary Society and his co-workers, who were proposing to proceed to Abeokuta to continue the work of the mission that had opened a few years previously. Unfortunately this preference for the missionaries over the slave traders sometimes existed only in one village surrounded by hostile forces. And sometimes the village that was friendly to the missionaries at one period completely reversed its position as quickly as from one day to the next.

Another important factor was the Church Missionary Society approach of introducing commercial trade simultaneously with Christianity and on condition that slave trade and human sacrifice be stopped. The idea was in part to prove that legitimate commercial trade was more beneficial in every way to the Nigerians than the slave trade had been and brought much desired peace as well. This approach was successful in some cases. From the beginning when British commercial interests began to make exploratory trips up the Niger River with a view to establishing trade, the Church Missionary Society asked and was granted permission to send missionaries along to investigate the possibility of establishing mission stations.

Crowther was wisely chosen as one of those to make several such journeys. His approach can be seen in an ex-

[7] Page, Jesse, *The Black Bishop,* p. 92.

ample of his conversation with Chief Rogang of Egga on one of these journeys. He said,

> The Queen of the country called Great Britain has sent the king of the ship to all the chiefs of Africa to make treaties with them to give up war and the slave trade — to all their people in the cultivation of the soil, and to mind all that the white people say to them, as they wish to teach them many things, and particularly the Book which God gives, which will make all men happy.
>
> I added likewise that there are many Hufi, Hausa, and Yoruba people in the white man's country who have been liberated from the Portuguese and Spanish slave ships, that they are now living like white men, that they pray to God and learn His Book, and consequently are living a happier life than when they were in their own country, and much better off than their country people are at present. To this many of them said that they could judge of their happy state merely by my appearance. I added, moreover, that our country people in White Man's country had written a letter to the Queen who lives in Great Britain, expressing their wish to return to their country if she would send white men along with them; but the Queen who loves us all as her children, told them to stop till she had first sent her ships to the chiefs of Africa, to persuade them to give up war and the slave trade; and if they consented to her proposals she would gladly grant the request of our country people.[8]

A few years later Crowther saw that the growth of commerce would soon supplant the slave trade and did much to help develop legitimate commerce. He writes,

> The advantage of the increase of palm oil trade over that of the slave is so much felt by the people at large that their head chiefs could not help confessing to me that they — aged persons — never remembered any time of the slave trade in which so much wealth was brought into their country as has been since the commencement of the palm oil trade, the last four years; that they were perfectly satisfied with legitimate trade and with the proceedings of the British Government.[9]

[8] *Ibid.*, p. 62.
[9] *Ibid.*, p. 141.

Also in this early period a few Nigerians visited England and credited Christianity with the vast resources and benefits of civilizations as they saw it there. This proved most helpful in establishing the Church Missionary Society. King William Pepple of Bonny visited London and lived there from 1858-61 during a time of exile. When he returned to again rule in Bonny, his impressions from England and his desire for his people's welfare and progress inspired him to send word to the Bishop of London requesting missionaries. The request was relayed to Bishop Crowther, who visited in 1864, was welcomed and opened a station. Very great immediate success was recorded in Bonny largely due to the active support of King Pepple.

The early missionaries found that the animistic beliefs of the people with a strong inclination toward any teaching that deals with spiritual and supernatural affairs was sometimes a help and sometimes a hindrance. In many places the people readily received Jesus as an addition into their own system of gods and spirits, but to receive Him as the only true and living God was quite another matter. It is important to note that the idea of a Supreme Creator and Controlling God was neither new nor foreign. Speaking of the Yoruba people, one missionary of this period gave this analysis:

> God the Creator, under the name of Olorun (the possessor of heaven), is recognized as the giver of life, and the judge of all men, and is never confounded with the numerous idols. . . . God occupies the place of a world Emperor, and the idols are so many subject kings who act as mediators between the common people and the mighty potentate. The principle of mediatorial worship would suggest the appropriateness of proclaiming the "one mediator between God and men, the man Christ Jesus." But this common ground on which we stand is not so helpful as it appears, for they take the analogy so literally that it is difficult to convince them that *our* mediator is *their* mediator. They conclude that each branch of the human family, or each kingdom of the great empire, has its own mediator or ruler.[10]

[10] Pinnock, S. G., *The Romance of Missions in Nigeria*, pp. 39-40.

Nevertheless the name Olorun, the Yoruba name for the Supreme God, was immediately adopted for the Christian God, Jehovah. The same is true with the use of the name Chineke among the Southern Ibo people, Oghene among the Urhobo, and so on.

There were also occasions when British law protected Christians from persecution and death but British law was not sufficiently enforced in the nineteenth century to be of very wide-spread significance to the Christian witness. The persistent and consistent witness of many early converts in the face of persecution bore strong testimony to the truth of the Christian message. This was probably more often interpreted as obstinacy, however, and did not always serve as an instrument in attracting converts or easing the persecution.

The introduction of education, medical help, and other benefits of western civilization in the first stages of mission work in Nigeria sometimes lifted the converts rapidly in ability, influence, and prestige. "The school was Crowther's chief method of evangelization. He introduced the mission into places by getting rulers and Elders interested in the idea of having a school of their own. And usually it was to the school he asked the senior missionary to give his chief attention."[11]

Mary Slessor of Calabar is said to have declared, "Schools and teachers go with the Gospel. You can't have one without the other."[12] Another of Mary Slessor's mission methods is seen in the following quotation: "Always she carried medicine for sick bodies as well as Christ's medicine for their sin-sick souls. She found that human ministrations did far more to break down the wall of heathen opposition than her talks given at Sunday meetings."[13]

Pinnock wrote in 1917 of

> direct results from school work – In this work we have the sympathy of the parents, for Mohammedans and pagans bring their children to the missionaries to be educated under

[11] Ajayi, J. F. Ade, "Christian Missions and the Making of Nigeria 1841-1891" (Doctoral dissertation, 1958), p. 503.

[12] Miller, Basil, *Mary Slessor, Heroine of Calabar,* p. 134.

[13] *Ibid.,* p. 35.

> Christian influence. A notorious medicine man at Ilora, who was beyond all hope of conversion to Christianity, brought his four sons to the native preacher and expressed the wish that they might become Christians. His wish was granted, for all became followers of Jesus, and two of them, James Aloba and David Tade, are today students in the Seminary at Saki.[14]

Hindrances to the Introduction of Christianity in the Nineteenth Century

There were also many factors that acted as hindrances to the introduction of Christianity into Nigeria during this period.

Slavery and the slave traffic were among these factors and were interrelated with other factors. Livingstone wrote, "Naturally it was the divorcing of superfluous wives, and the freeing of slaves that formed the greatest difficulty for the missionaries – it meant nothing less than breaking up a social system developed and fortified by long centuries of custom."[15] The practice of slavery in Nigeria was a part of the problem. The capture and sale of slaves for commercial purposes was a more publicized problem. But both were condemned by early missionaries as being unchristian and this posed both a cultural and an economic problem. Livingstone may have overstated the case in that a solution may have been possible for this problem without breaking up the whole social system. This will be dealt with in a later chapter. Suffice it to say here that this was a considerable hindrance to a ready acceptance of the gospel.

Associated with the slave traffic was constant intertribal war and distrust, though slavery was certainly not the only cause of this. The sources of conflict were many.

> The Fulalas had been victorious in the Eleduwe War (1830) which opened the Yoruba country of Nigeria to Islam. . . . The Fulalas brought the Koran and the Prophet of the Sword. . . . The War of 1830 reduced to dust and ashes many beautiful towns in the Yoruba country. It brought several new kings and warriors to Yoruba towns – Kumi to Ijaiye,

[14] Pinnock, *op. cit.*, p. 161.
[15] Livingstone, W. P., *Mary Slessor of Calabar*, pp. 26-27.

> Ayo to Aberno, Oluyole to Ibadan, and Atiba to the new Oyo. Jealousies among the Yoruba warriors led the country into intertribal combat more bitter and destructive than the Fulala War.[16]

For fifty years or more after this war traveling was often perilous and difficult.

> Because the Baptist mission staff was small and wars were almost constant in the interior, the work at Ogbomosho had not been visited for a long time, but now, on account of some trouble in the church there, Brother Smith towards the end of 1885 made a visit to that city. . . . To get permission to travel and protection on the way for the first twenty-five miles he had to pay £5 ($25) in goods to the Abeokuta chiefs. The rest of the two hundred miles was free with the exception of paying tolls at various points along the road.[17]

This sometimes made it impossible to carry the gospel to new places as well as to revisit villages where small Christian groups had been established.

Crowther and others found that through wise and diplomatic approaches it was possible to gain permission from even the Moslem ruler to witness among his people, but the response to the Christian message in the Moslem area of northern Yorubaland was far short of encouraging.

Alongside the slavery issue Livingstone listed polygamy as the greatest difficulty of the missionary because it was a basic part of the social system. Some have suggested that perhaps the missionaries should have used a different approach than they did on this problem. Whether right or wrong almost all missionaries of all denominations in Nigeria during the nineteenth century stood firm in not accepting either husband or wife in a polygamous union as members of the church. This in effect said to the wealthy and influential people in each village, "You cannot be a member of the church."

[16] Howell, E. Milford, "Nigerian Baptist Leaders and Their Contribution" (Doctoral dissertation, 1956), p. 20.
[17] Duval, Louis M., *Baptist Missions in Nigeria,* p. 112.

Tied in with the problem of polygamy were other factors, both Nigerian and missionary, that made it exceedingly difficult to win older people to Christ. The Wesleyan missionary J. T. F. Halligey visited Ogbomosho and got permission to open a mission station. In his conversation with the chief he tried to persuade the chief, himself, to become a Christian and got the following response, "When we get old we do not care to change our religion, and I shall die believing in the gods my fathers trusted. But my children and my people, they are young, and will like a new religion, and will do as you say. Let them follow the white man."[18] Lifelong religion, loyalty to forefathers, polygamy, requirements of education, or training in the catechism before acceptance into the church, tribal unity, and other things may have been involved in his negative response. His willingness for his children to become Christian was remarkable. Such a stand is unknown in many lands, though in Africa this is not an unusual position for older people to take. This response is not uncommon in Nigeria even today.

Various circumstances frequently led to changes in attitude from friendliness to antagonism on the part of kings and chiefs toward missionaries and Christianity. The death of a friendly king was sometimes followed by the ascension of an equally unfriendly king. Crowther found this true at Onitsha and several other towns. The British occupation of Lagos led to very strong feeling among the chiefs at Abeokuta that resulted in driving the missionaries out of Abeokuta in 1867 and severe persecution of Christians, plundering and destroying of churches. That same year Bishop Crowther was kidnapped at Oke-Okein by Chief Abokko when he stopped to pay respects to the chief, whom he thought he knew as a friend. Abokko's grievance was that he had not received what he felt was his rightful share of the profits in trade and gifts from the British merchants. He mistakenly assumed that Crowther could control the commerce on the Niger since he had seen him on several of the British ships and in the company of the white traders. He was held for ransom and escaped only when rescued by

[18] Page, *op. cit.*, p. 238.

force. These experiences illustrate the uncertainty of help or even cooperation from the local authorities in establishing the Christian witness and seeking for its spread among the people.

Nigerians acted as units: a clan, village, family, etc. They considered all white men to be "brothers." Hence, the fact that white traders were by virtue of their color identified with missionaries was often in itself detrimental to the spread of Christianity, because few of these white men were Christian nor did they attempt to follow Christian behavior. One result of this was the use of European liquor in trade with the Nigerians. Intoxicating drinks were used in Nigeria before the white man brought his more potent varieties, but addiction to alcohol and related problems were greatly increased with the importation of large amounts of European liquor. When missionaries preached against this, it produced both confusion and opposition, because white men brought it in and now white men opposed it.

Pagan priests were sometimes quite willing for Christianity to exist side by side with them and their beliefs and practices. More often, however, they used their considerable influence to oppose and stamp it out. Sometimes this opposition sprang from jealous and dishonest priests who saw their means of livelihood and their position of importance in danger of being lost. No doubt there were others who were sincere in their beliefs and thought Christianity to be somewhat heretical to their animistic religion and certain teachings of Christianity to be in conflict with their culture. These pagan priests played no small part in stirring up enmity and bringing about persecution of the Christians in many places.

It was often difficult for these animistic people of Nigeria to understand a religion that opposed charms and fetishes. "At the foundation of all their religion there seems to be a dread of evil; that there are spirits everywhere and in everything; and it is necessary to appease or counteract the influence of these for fear they will do some harm. Thus at the bottom of their religion is the idea of sacrifice or charms."[19] It was not uncommon, therefore, for these animists

[19] Duval, *op. cit.*, p. 34.

to look upon the Bible and other objects connected with Christian worship as fetishes or charms having special powers. They often considered baptism, the Lord's Supper, and other forms as magical.

Sometimes completely unrelated events were connected in some way in the minds of the people, and this led to associations that were difficult to overcome. Bowen experienced the result of this in traveling from Abeokuta to Iketu in 1850. Some of the villages would not allow him to set foot within their gates, and others allowed him to pass through only after much argument and persuasion. In previous years a white man had visited this area and, shortly after, war had come. Some of the villages had been attacked and destroyed. Their conclusion was that if they allowed a white man to enter their village, war and destruction would follow.

Language barriers and custom variations from place to place also presented a problem to early missionaries. This was particularly exaggerated because of the brevity of the service of most of the missionaries in this period. "The Rev. A. Scott Patterson gave the following estimate in his address at the Association Conference (the forerunner to the Nigerian Baptist Convention) in 1915: 'During these 65 years Southern Baptists, in obedience to Christ's commands, have sent about 60 missionaries to the African field. . . . Of the 60 missionaries some 24 have died on the field or after leaving the field from the effects of the climate; 22 have had to leave the field on account of ill health due to the climate, and today we have about the same number of missionaries on the field as in 1855.' "[20] The average length of service on the field for these missionaries was less than six years. This lack of continuity in the mission staff was of major importance. Gaining a knowledge of the language and customs of the people occupies much of the time and attention of a missionary during his first one-to-three years on the field. Lack of continuity in personnel also means lack of continuity in plans and procedures.

Christian morals and ethics as taught by the early missionaries were often unnecessarily in conflict with beliefs and

[20] Pinnock, *op. cit.*, p. 149.

practices of the people. Mary Slessor learned from a king what happens when outsiders taboo a part of their tradition. She was pleading for leniency in the punishment of two of the king's wives, who had broken the law by entering a room where a young boy slept. The prescribed punishment was public flogging to which Miss Slessor voiced great objection as harsh and cruel. The king told her, "If you say we must not flog, we must listen to you as our guest and mother. But they will say God's Word be no good, if it destroy the power of the law to punish evildoers."[21]

This conflict between western Christian ethics and the traditions and customs of the people frequently led to discipline of church members. Such discipline was sometimes correctly interpreted and sometimes not. There were also occasions of falling away or serious offenses committed by agents of the Church. This occurred soon after Onitsha was opened by Bishop Crowther. Immorality led to the dismissal of an agent and thus weakened the staff and struck a strong blow to native confidence in the church.

Also related to this conflict between Christian ethics, as understood by the missionaries, and traditional ethics is the problem that sometimes arose over secret societies. Secret societies were often a sign of influence and status. Some of their practices were not acceptable to the Christian concept of right and wrong. This made it necessary for some to choose between being a Christian and accepting the honor of belonging to such a society. Others attempted to live a dual life with inner conflicts.

These were the conditions in nineteenth-century Southern Nigeria that brought both positive and negative influences on the work of missionaries who sought to win Christian converts and plant churches.

[21] Miller, *op. cit.*, p. 39.

Chapter III. Division and Church Growth

BEGINNING NEAR THE END OF THE NINETEENTH CENTURY A SERIES of divisions occurred affecting the growth of all the Churches. The following account of these divisions shows that the immediate causes were not all the same, but the fact that all of the traditional Churches experienced divisions reveals a general restlessness and dissatisfaction within the Christian community. Several factors should be noted in connection with this.

First, gradual extension of British authority over all of Nigeria in the last half of the nineteenth century had numerous effects. Slave raiding and tribal wars gradually came to an end. This necessitated considerable social adjustment. The expression of hostility and suspicion had to take new forms and sometimes new directions. Nationalism beyond tribal lines had its beginnings here. Though the British chose indirect rule through traditional authorities to a great degree, many Nigerians developed some suspicion toward white-man rule. This feeling was not limited to government relations but also found expression between Nigerians and missionaries at times. Nigerians were used to self-rule within their cultural units and naturally rebelled against outside authority that was not maintained by force. This made the missionaries particularly vulnerable, for within the local churches they wished to maintain strict Christian standards, according to their interpretation, and had only persuasion and sometimes financial assistance to support their authority. In cases where the missionaries were seeking to develop self-support within the churches, they lost the authority that came from their financial assistance to the churches, and became subject to suspicion of being selfish for withholding funds. Also in the administration of foreign funds to a "needy people" there is always the danger of implied superiority of the administrator. He may develop feelings of superiority himself. Whether or not he does, he may be suspected of them.

A second factor in this restlessness was the development of African leadership. Early in the mission enterprise missionaries had taken into their homes African boys whom they taught and trained. By the turn of the century many of these boys had grown to be men with considerable training, experience, and leadership ability. Some of them at times felt held down by the perennial white man who stood above them in authority. Missionaries bound by the combined force of their own dedicated conscience and the will of the churches who sent them, do not find it easy to relinquish authority to others who do not have their background, experience, and conviction.

A third factor that led to division in some cases was the conflict of opinion about polygamy. There is a tendency for some missionaries to assume that any time Africans withdraw from the mission to form independent churches, their chief reason is to permit polygamists to be members of the church. This is quite untrue, though it has been one of the factors in some of the divisions that have occurred.

These and other factors all played their part in creating the restlessness that sometimes erupted into divisions, with their resulting ill will, lack of fellowship within the Christian community, and disruption of the Christian witness. They also indicated possibilities of growth and served as a reminder that a vigorous church depends upon developing churches that are soundly New Testament and at that same time an integral, fully indigenous part of the culture in which the churches are planted. Missionaries in Nigeria must find a way to plant churches completely Christian and completely Nigerian. This is no easy task but it does help avoid division.

Divisions in the Eastern Region: Calabar

Historically the first division came not by Africans splitting off but as the result of a difference of opinion between missionaries.

> In the latter part of the 1870's a difference of opinion arose over the administration of the work at Duke Town. A. Ross had been left in charge while Anderson was on furlough.

> The dispute was of such a nature that an investigation was made by the presbytery and a special committee from Scotland. It was thought best that Ross should be recalled, but he refused.
>
> Instead of retiring from Calabar, Ross opened an independent mission very near the Church of Scotland mission and much bitterness followed. The minds of the Africans were confused and the progress of Christianity in Calabar retarded. After the death of Ross the work was carried on by a young man from the Grattan Guinness Institute in London, much to the disfavor of the Church of Scotland.[1]

A later chapter will tell of the entrance of the Qua Iboe Mission into the Calabar area less than ten years later, apparently with the full blessing of the Church of Scotland mission. The first Qua Iboe missionaries came as the result of an appeal from Church of Scotland missionaries to the Grattan Guinness Institute. Guinness himself provided the money for sending the first two volunteers from the Institute. It would be interesting to know whether the independent mission started by Ross later merged with the Qua Iboe mission or returned to the Church of Scotland mission or what became of it.

About this same time (1888) another group of independent churches arose in Calabar and the Cameroons with the withdrawal of the Baptist Missionary Society, which had had a small work in Calabar since 1845. Most of its work was in the Cameroons. When the Cameroons fell under German rule and English was no longer allowed in the schools, the Baptist Missionary Society withdrew at the request of the German government[2] and turned over their work to the Basel mission and the German Baptists. "Many of the churches had declared their independence of any society and were difficult to reach. It soon became evident that these churches did not desire missionary supervision. Beginning with the new century the German Baptists changed their policies and

[1] Knight, Charles Williams, "A History of the Expansion of Evangelical Christianity in Nigeria" (Doctoral dissertation, 1951), pp. 103f.

[2] Maxwell, J. Lowry, *Nigeria, The Land, the People and Christian Progress*, p. 157.

began to open new stations."[3] Since neither German Baptists nor the Basel mission established themselves in Calabar, it left the few small Baptist churches there on their own.

In the early 1930s dissatisfaction arose among adherents of the Qua Ibo Mission in Ibesikpo, a section of Calabar country. A large number withdrew and formed the Ibesikpo United Church. An Ibesikpo boy was studying in America and wrote his townspeople about the Lutheran Church. They thereupon invited the Lutherans to send missionaries to them. In 1935 a committee from the Mission Board of the Evangelical Lutheran Synod Conference of North America visited the area, gave a favorable report, and the following year Henry Nau and wife went to begin work among the Ibesikpo people. They found sixteen churches, each with a school attached.[4] The neighboring missions, Methodist and Church of Scotland, were asked by the Qua Iboe Mission to negotiate an arrangement that would not involve the entrance of a new confessional group into a small area surrounded by long-established missions but matters had already gone too far and the Lutherans began work in 1936.[5] In 1962 the *World Christian Handbook* reported that the Lutheran Church had grown to a communicant membership of 12,132.[6] The mission has a strong medical and institutional program in which most of their 56 missionaries are occupied.

Divisions in the Eastern Region: Lower Niger

After the death of Bishop Crowther in 1891 the Anglican churches in the Lower Niger withdrew from the Church Missionary Society under the leadership of Archdeacon Crowther to form the Niger Delta Pastorate. They continued to recognize the new Bishop but maintained financial independence and self-government. Stock insists that this was not a secession but more of a final step in indigenous development. However, the preceding history shows it evolved in large part

[3] Knight, *op. cit.*, p. 115.
[4] *Ibid.*, p. 205.
[5] Patton, William and Underhill, M. M., *International Review of Missions,* XXVI, p. 65.
[6] Coxill, H. W. and Grubb, K., *World Christian Handbook.*

out of a division of opinion between European missionaries and Africans. A resumé of Stock's account of the story follows:[7]

Continued reports of moral laxity of agents in the Upper River stations for several years prior to 1880 brought the appointment of a committee to investigate and recommend changes in mission administration. The committee included Bishop Crowther and his two African archdeacons and several European missionaries. Rev. J. B. Wood, as secretary of the committee, brought an unfavorable report about the mission. He reported lack of real spirituality and evangelistic zeal among the agents, though moral laxity appeared less flagrant than previous reports had indicated.

Following this report in 1881 the Church Missionary Society committee arranged what was called the Madeira Committee to meet with the Church Missionary Society lay secretary and confer on the affairs of the mission. Mr. Wood would not come. The others, including Bishop Crowther, his archdeacon son, and two other African clergymen met with the European members of the committee. One of the measures proposed was the appointment of an English clergyman as secretary to live on the Niger and be the Bishop's friend and counsellor. Several agents were dismissed.

By this time the actual difficulties within the mission had been embellished with rumors and falsehoods that attracted considerable criticism of the mission from outside, including an attack on the Church Missionary Society in the House of Lords in London.

Under the new organization troubles died down until in 1887 another clergyman, John A. Robinson, was sent to the Niger as secretary. His report on the mission was unfavorable. He was not satisfied with the agents, some of the plans and policies of the mission, or with the results achieved. In 1888 G. W. Brooke visited the river on his way home from the Congo. He and Robinson talked at length and made plans to extend north up the river. Their plans were adopted by the Church Missionary Society committee and involved changes

[7] Stock, Eugene, *The History of the Church Missionary Society*, III, 385-397.

on the Niger. The work on the Upper River, from Lokoja northwards, was in the future to be part of a new mission; and this involved the removal of three or four African agents, who, it was decided, would not fit into the arrangement. One of them was Archdeacon Johnson himself, who was requested to move to Lagos pending further instructions.

The Lower Niger would be a separate mission and three English missionaries were allotted to it. Bishop Crowther would remain the episcopal superintendent of both missions and Archdeacon Crowther retained his position in the Delta. The committee looked with prayerful hope to the more complete combination of European and African in one great work to evangelize the Niger territories. It should be remembered that until this controversy arose the Niger churches had been begun and supervised entirely by Africans.

Under the new organization in the Upper River area an early part of the work was "a work of correction," rooting out and pulling down before building and planting. In the Delta a new committee for the management of the mission was set up, including English missionaries with the Bishop, Archdeacon Crowther, and another able African. Meeting in 1890, this committee was divided Europeans against Nigerians both in matters of policy and personnel for the mission. Although the Europeans succeeded in carrying the dismissal of certain agents, they did not consider this enough. The secretary, acting for the Church Missionary Society, gave separate notice, in its name, suspending still other agents. This brought controversy all over Southern Nigeria and even in England.

A special committee sat in London over this matter and both Mr. Eden, secretary for the Delta Mission, and Brooke went to England for consultation. Through much divided opinion came the report that attempted to register a very kind disapproval of the low moral and spiritual condition of the congregations and the laxity of instruction and discipline from the administration. In an attempt to lessen the blame on the Bishop, the report acknowledged that he had earnestly labored under most serious difficulties in this field.

Neither side of the controversy was satisfied and in June, 1891, John Robinson died of fever, partly attributed to the mental strain over his dissatisfaction with the committee decisions. Less than a year later Brooke died and the new mission was at an end. Robinson and Brooke, both honorable men, dedicated to the salvation of African souls, nevertheless were severe – possibly too severe – in their judgment of their African fellow workers. Their campaign for the correction of the evils on the Niger brought alienation and ill will toward themselves and the Church Missionary Society that would not soon be overcome.

Mr. Eden never returned to Nigeria after the committee meeting in London and resigned in December, 1891, the same month Bishop Crowther died.

> For a time, the Lower Niger mission, as well as the Upper mission, seemed almost to have collapsed. Bonny and its outstations under Archdeacon Crowther had declared their independence; moved thereto undoubtedly in part by resentment at the society's action, yet at the same time honestly believing that in so doing they were only carrying out the society's own policy of Native Church self-support of their Church and clergy.[8]

These years of misunderstanding and conflict of opinion had a very negative effect on the growth of the Church. The report for 1891 showed the Delta mission with 902 communicants. In 1893 there were 397 communicants. And in 1898 only 263 were reported.

In 1895 at the invitation of Bishop Tugwell, Archdeacon Crowther again agreed to be listed among the Church Missionary Society missionaries, although financially independent. This reflected considerable effort on both sides to restore confidence.

By 1930 the Delta Pastorate under Archdeacon Crowther had grown from the first mud and thatch building at Bonny to eleven districts with an average of nearly sixty churches in each, and all self-supporting; this all without resident missionaries and under full direction of Nigerian leadership, an ample validation of Archdeacon Crowther's courageous insistence that Nigerians were capable of directing the expansion of

[8] *Ibid.*, p. 397.

their Church. In Henry Venn's terms the euthanasia of the mission had taken place by a none-too-gentle shove from the younger Church.

"After nearly forty years of separate and independent existence, the Delta Pastorate is now (1930) organically joined to the Church Missionary Society portion of the diocese. Under the new constitution, the two archdeaconries are welded together in one synod that has authority over both."[9] The Niger Diocese grew a hundredfold from 313 communicants in 1900 to 13,852 in 1930. What a monument to the principles of indigenous church growth! Temporary division was far better than continued dissension in this case.

Divisions in Lagos

In Lagos division came among Baptists, Church Missionary Society, and then Methodists. None escaped. The Baptist division came first and was of a temporary nature, but had far-reaching significance on church growth. A growing racial consciousness and a desire for self-determination produced tension in the church. In 1888 a dispute arose over the salary of Rev. Moses Stone, pastor of the First Baptist Church of Lagos. He and all but eight members of the church withdrew, including all the leaders in both the church and school. They formed the "Native Baptist Church," taking the name of "Ebenezer." Duval, one of the later missionaries, wrote,

> This was apparently a heavy blow to our mission, not only in Lagos, but in the whole country. But that which in the eyes of men is a calamity is often used of God for the extension of His Kingdom; and thus it proved in this case. This was the beginning of a movement that spread over the whole country, including the other denominations, who suffered more than we; for our people continued true to the doctrine of the Baptists, and we were eventually reunited in the convention organized some years later.[10]

Twenty years after Ebenezer Baptist Church was formed a secession arose from its membership. "Majola Agbebi with-

[9] Walker, F. Deaville, *The Romance of the Black River*, p. 221.
[10] Duval, *Baptist Missions in Nigeria*, p. 118.

drew as pastor of the Ebenezer church and formed the Araromi Baptist Church in 1908."[11] These two churches, Araromi and Ebenezer, extended arms into many new areas and grew much faster than the mission churches. The mission churches and independent churches were reunited in 1914 with the formation of the Yoruba Baptist Association. Dr. Majola Agbebi was nominated for president by a missionary and was elected.

During the years of separation the independent churches grew mainly by two methods: (1) by sending their leaders into new areas on evangelistic tours, and (2) by providing leadership in places that desired Christianity and asked for help.

One of these extensions was in Ekiti country. Duval tells of a boy captured in Ekiti country during intertribal wars and taken down country. In time he forgot his home, friends, even the name of his town and relatives. Later he became a Christian, attended a mission school and became a house boy for a European who traveled north through Ekiti country. One day on the journey the boy suddenly began to recognize certain landmarks and some of his boyhood memories returned. He thought of two names and kept enquiring until he was restored to his mother and sister. Later he returned to his home town, preaching the gospel to his kinsmen and townspeople without any mission aid or connection. They formed a church that grew to a membership of seven hundred. In 1902, when Dr. Agbebi visited on an evangelistic tour to Ekiti, from whence his father had come, he went to this church. They compared doctrines and the church came under his pastoral care. During the same trip he established other churches in other Ekiti towns and the young man was placed in charge of the group.[12] These churches remained under the supervision of Dr. Agbebi and Araromi church for many years. Note the family connections of both the boy and Dr. Agbebi with these villages where the churches grew. Christianity spreads most easily along lines of kinship and other established intimate relationships. No doubt the ready response in Ekiti

[11] Knight, *op. cit.*, p. 134.
[12] Duval, *op. cit.*, pp. 197-200.

was greatly enhanced by the invitation of kinsmen in whom the people had confidence at a time when they were willing to change. The fact that Dr. Agbebi retained the young man as the leader of these churches encouraged the established plan of conversion through the web of natural relationship and provided stability through continuity of their already accepted natural leader.

In 1902 Rev. Moses Stone responded to invitations from Ijebuland and made a preaching tour there resulting in hundreds of conversions. Ebenezer church paid the salary of Mr. Lewis and Mr. Ologbajo as catechists in Ijebuland from 1902 until 1904, when they resigned.[13] In 1904 Stone "reported after a preaching-teaching mission to Ijebu country, that he had baptized 261 persons, and that all the churches in that area were self-supporting."[14] By that time there were five churches with a communicant membership of 305. This expansion might not have come at this time when the Ijebu people were turning in groups from their former gods if Ebenezer church had not withdrawn from the mission. The division had brought determination on both sides in spite of shortage in personnel to expand and to succeed in establishing strong, self-perpetuating churches. Ebenezer church had the advantage of completely indigenous leadership who understood the African pattern of "group decision" and who had natural channels of relationship with the Ijebu people.

The most rapid expansion of this independent movement took place in the Niger Delta. Church Missionary Society agents had occasionally visited Buguma and founded a school that survived for about six years. Tremendous opposition was aroused by pagan priests and the few strong Christians narrowly escaped martyrdom several times. After the Church Missionary Society withdrew, Rev. William Hughes, a Baptist minister from Wales, came to Buguma, established an industrial school, and began preaching. His compound became the place of refuge for the Christian community. After he went on furlough and saw that he could not return, he

[13] Roberson, C. F. (unpublished notes).

[14] Robinson, Oren C., "The Indigenous Development of Baptist Churches of Nigeria" (Th. M. thesis, 1951), p. 28.

wrote suggesting they contact Dr. Agbebi in Lagos. This they did and, against the advice of his well-meaning friends, he went to restore the work at Buguma.

In 1893 on his first visit he baptized only eight, owing to the prevalence of polygamy. He then encouraged them to keep regular worship and be self-supporting. He taught them to pray in their own tongue, and sing praises to God in native airs, both publicly and in private worship, instead of in English so that the fast-growing membership, many of whom were illiterate, could understand and take part. Soon after, he brought Mr. Teyebi from Lagos, who remained a little over a year to teach them. Before leaving he recommended to Chief Sokari and Dr. Agbebi that W. A. Amakri, a relative of the reigning king, succeed him. Amakri and K. John Bull were taken to Lagos for training and later attended the Baptist Seminary at Shaki. John Bull became pastor at Buguma church and Amakri was ordained and became superintendent of the Baptist work in the Delta district.

During the training of these men, Dr. Agbebi continued to visit and each time baptized several people. He tried to educate the people to extend the Christian Church and implored the members who were traders to propagate the gospel among the heathen. He said, "Trade with the Word of God as you buy and sell your oil and palm kernels." Acting on this advice, Atata Sokari George, a trader and farmer, went to Okaki to sell his yams. There he met and converted two young men, Okiya and Okorio from the Engenni River. Soon they had established a church at their village. The similar witness of other members trading in Abua produced a church there. This process of multiplying churches through trade connections became a common pattern in the delta area and churches were established in several villages in this way.

These churches were called the Delta Mission until Dr. Agbebi's death in 1917. Soon after, according to his wishes, they became a part of the Yoruba Baptist Association, which in turn changed its name to Nigerian Baptist Convention in 1919.

In 1915 Ebenezer church and its branches in Ijebu numbered 345 communicants. Araromi and its Ekiti branches numbered 640. The Delta Mission numbered 2,616. Thus a total of 3,601 communicants were numbered among these independent Baptist churches, most of whom became Christians through the established relationships of their African society.

At this time First Baptist Church of Lagos and its branch in Ikeja, a suburb of Lagos, numbered 448 communicants and the rest of the mission churches in Nigeria had 1,447 communicant members. The inclusion of the Independent Baptist churches accounts for the tremendous rise in the graph (at the beginning of Chapter V) from 1,320 in 1914, when only mission churches were recorded, to 5,650 in 1915, which included the independent Baptist churches.

The more rapid expansion of the independent churches, particularly in the Delta, can be attributed to several factors: (1) The appeal of a purely African controlled church to an increasingly nationalistic-minded people. (2) Less strict supervision and discipline in the Delta Mission due to extreme distance and difficulty of travel. (3) Family, social, business, and other connections of African leaders, which missionaries do not have. (4) African understanding and use of group decision as opposed to the usual missionary approach of individual, isolated conversion.

In 1891 another independent Church was formed in Lagos by seceders from several different Protestant Churches. Their purpose was to establish "a Native African Church, free from foreign control whereby the natives will be able to serve God with a clear conscience."[15] It opened branches in Ilaro and Ijebu in 1892 and in Ebuta Metta in 1893. It developed along the lines of the Anglican Church, having bishops, surpliced choirs, and prayer books. Its present strength (1962) is estimated at 20,000 communicants[16] in churches scattered over much of Southern Nigeria.

In 1901 "Discontented members of the Anglican Church in Lagos formed the Native African Church, commonly known as 'Bethelites.' It followed the Anglican liturgy. The Church allowed polygamy among the members and proved to be a

[15] Talbot, P. Amaury, *The Peoples of Southern Nigeria,* IV, p. 118.

[16] Adejunmobi, T. A. (General Secretary of Christian Council of Nigeria), personal letter to the author, February 21, 1963.

thorn in the flesh to all missionaries and Africans connected with the societies."[17]

"In 1917 a group broke away from the Wesleyan Methodist Erako church in Lagos and formed the United African Methodist Church. Branches were established in the colony and Abeokuta Province."[18] These last two divisions from Anglican and Methodist churches in Lagos have since spread over most of Southern Nigeria but their numerical strength is difficult to estimate with any degree of accuracy. Their break was due primarily to the desire for indigenous leadership and/or the condoning of polygamy. All these divisions illustrate the period of unrest and the need of careful policy review on the part of the missions and Churches concerned in order to produce sound New Testament Churches without alienating the people among whom the Church was being planted.

Divisions and Changes of Affiliation From One Denomination to Another

There have been from time to time small groups or whole churches that have seceded from one denomination and sought affiliation with another. Transfers from one denomination to another still occur. They are sometimes prompted by doctrinal conviction, but more often personal difference or a desire to gain something that they have not been able to get from their former affiliation, such as schools or hospitals. These divisions, of course, bring ill will and disruption of fellowship between denominations within the Christian fellowship. However, they also sometimes spur church growth through competition, renewed evangelistic efforts, and deeper conviction. Purposeful proselytizing from one denomination to another serves only to create confusion and disruption and diverts attention and effort from the primary task of all Christians, to bring unto Christ those who do not know Him. Without any conscious efforts at proselytizing, some changes of affiliation will occur and may be useful in spurring church growth among the unconverted.

In 1916 a division in an interdenominational congregation in

[17] Knight, *op. cit.*, p. 134.
[18] *Ibid.*, p. 134.

Sapele resulted in one group forming the First Baptist Church of Sapele and the other later becoming St. Luke's (Anglican). In 1921 a dispute arose in the Church Missionary Society church in Oginibo. Mr. Makpa and Mr. Obiren withdrew, sought advice from the Baptist church in Sapele, and began a Baptist church in Makpa's house. Mr. Makpa was the son of the chief and was bitterly opposed by his relatives but continued on through persecution. Today the Baptist church is the strongest church in Oginibo and is the mother of twenty-seven churches in other villages in that area.

Similar divisions have occurred in most denominations from time to time. Some have resulted in church growth, as did the above example. Others have produced only ill will, confusion, and stagnation. Division is not God's plan for multiplying churches. Nevertheless, when such divisions occur, both sides face the alternative of seeking vengeance and prolonging the antagonism or facing the challenge of the future with a positive plan for converting the non-Christians about them.

Baptists faced a crisis in 1938 that led to the loss of several churches. Dr. Charles Maddry, executive secretary of the Foreign Mission Board, visited Nigeria. During his visit, several far-reaching plans were made involving policy. Most of the decisions were happily received by all the Nigerians, but one met opposition by some.

Baptist policy had always prohibited the baptism of polygamists, but those who took more than one wife after baptism sometimes escaped discipline. Some also were able to keep their family life hidden until after they were baptized. A new constitution was drawn up by the Nigerian Baptist Convention and each church was required to ratify it in order to be a part of the Convention. It specified that no polygamist could be a member of a Baptist church.

Eventually most of the churches voted approval of the new constitution. Some immediately adopted it but many delayed because it necessitated re-organization and purging of the rolls of all polygamists. In 1940 only 140 of the 211 churches reported in the annual convention meeting a total of 7,338 communicant members. Before the constitution in 1938 there had been 21,214 communicants. The actual report of 7,338 members was noted in the written report to the Foreign Mission Board but the statistical table repeated the membership figure of the previous year, 21,214. Among the churches that finally withdrew from the convention over this were Shaki and Benin City.

In 1942 the pastor of the Baptist Church in Sapele was reported for immorality by members of his church to the Convention. When he was ultimately expelled from the ministry by the Convention, his church and several of its branch churches followed him out of the Convention. The Sapele church and its branch churches together with the Benin church and its branch churches formed an independent denomination called United Baptist Mission. Finally in 1961 the Sapele church returned to the Convention, having reorganized and stricken all polygamists from its rolls.

The failure of the United Baptist Mission was due largely to the lack of provision for training leadership. They were without pastors. Some of their teachers were secured by hiring those disciplined from other Churches. The church services were mainly under the direction of the school teachers, while the control of church affairs rested in the hands of the older and more influential members regardless of either their training or spiritual understanding. The desire to be a part of an organization that had educational opportunities, medical facilities, and possibilities for employment did much to bring dissatisfaction and a seeking for renewed affiliation with the Nigerian Baptist Convention. From 1942 to 1960, while the First Baptist Church saw little growth, a handful of faithful Christians who remained within the Convention formed Bethel Baptist Church and grew to a membership of about six hundred communicants. So today there are two large Baptist churches in Sapele about equal in strength. With proper leadership this could have happened without broken fellowship and bitterness. Greater growth than this could have come if all the energy devoted to this internal strife had been devoted to discipling the multitudes outside, planting churches, and training leadership for the churches.

Some divisions must be expected and need not destroy the

Christian witness. Indeed some divisions result in increased church growth. This gives eloquent testimony to a responsive population with much greater church growth possibilities than have been realized by the Traditional Churches.

While a multiplicity of denominations is not ideal, it is not an insurmountable barrier in Nigeria where innumerable forms, beliefs, and practices are accepted in religion. Christian unity and fellowship are important and are an innate part of the Christian faith. But overemphasis upon this and concentration on maintaining unity can be most costly in terms of failure to convert people outside the Christian faith and to plant churches in responsive populations. Our Christian mission is to make disciples for Jesus, baptize them and teach them to observe all things whatsoever He has commanded. In this task God has promised to be with us. We must not be diverted from this purpose by either vengeful internal strife or by spending all our energies in seeking peace or unity.

The flow of the Christian faith through the natural webs of relationship is clearly seen in many of the purely indigenous Churches described in this chapter. A planned witness for Christ through these channels would bear rich reward for the Traditional Churches as well as the Independent Churches.

Chapter IV. Prophetism and Church Growth

Some Independent African Churches begin by dividing off from Traditional Churches. These are described in chapter III. Other Independent Churches are begun by an individual who, in the role of a prophet, gathers a following and organizes congregations under his supervision. Their shortage of trained leadership and their usual loose organization mean that records of their numerical strength are almost nonexistent, but their significance to church growth is easily seen.

Others who have written on these Independent Churches in West Africa are Geoffrey Parrinder and C.G. Baeta. Robert C. Mitchell and Harold W. Turner are writing now and have kindly permitted the author to see parts of their manuscripts. The purpose of presenting the four Churches described in this chapter and mentioning others is to give a fair and representative picture of the way in which the Independent Churches have developed in Southern Nigeria and the important part they play in the total Christian picture. The inclusion of these Churches in the Nigerian Christian Council might well be explored. Their contribution to the Christian cause can no longer be ignored.

There is a tendency for those in Traditional Churches to brush aside these Independent Churches by saying the people who join them are unstable and backward. This judgment is unfair and inaccurate. Welbourn, dealing with this criticism in his study on East Africa, wrote,

> It is proper to ask, What sort of people join the independent churches? It might be equally proper to ask, What sort of people do not? The forces in African society, centrifugal from the norm of Western government and mission, are immensely strong; and, in many ways, it is surprising to find that any but the most highly acculturated still cling to the norm. But to either question there is no answer in terms of individual psychology . . . , a personal significance which is not available to them in the mission Churches. Some clearly

> seek a legitimization of moral behaviour which is disallowed by the missions. Some are deeply sincere and practice an enthusiasm and evangelical commitment which might put both missionaries and African Christians alike to shame. Few can be regarded either as psychologically abnormal or, in personality, significantly different from the norm of Christian society. The fact is that men of all types are to be found . . . within the Independent Churches.[1]

Referring to these Independent Churches as "spiritual churches," Baeta made the following observation from his study in Ghana.

> People do not join the "spiritual churches" unless they find themselves wanting something or other that the churches are believed to enable them to obtain. Many stay on if their wishes have been realized, or if they are able to continue to hope; many leave again whatever the result of their joining has been. Usually people go for healing after having unsuccessfully tried scientific medicine or African herbal treatment or the fetish priest or all three. . . . A few said they went or would go to them because it was a cheap way of getting healed: "All you need to pay is the collection, and you can make that what you like."[2]

Baeta wrote that these people joined in order to obtain something that they thought the Church was able to provide. The natural question to follow such an explanation is, Why did the Traditional Churches fail to meet the needs? This should be the concern of all genuine Churches and will be dealt with further at the end of this chapter.

In building their ecclesiastical organizations the prophetic leaders, of course, borrowed many elements from the Traditional Churches. On the other hand, they followed the basic pattern of organization of African communities. This included less hard-and-fast application of principles and rules, great dependence upon and adherence to the strong personality of their leaders, group decision by arriving at conclusions through general consensus of opinion, and at the same time considerable freedom for individuals to express them-

[1] Welbourn, F. B., *East African Rebels,* p. 11.
[2] Baeta, C. G., *Prophetism in Ghana,* p. 143.

selves and indulge in personal idiosyncracies. As a balance for all this a very important common characteristic of these prophetic movements is strong teaching to put away fetishes and whole-heartedly embrace Jesus as all-sufficient Lord and God, who is able to provide all needs and to heal all afflictions. As would be expected there has been some syncretism with pagan ideas among some of these movements. Certain objects or forms in some cases take on sacred significance, holding a position somewhat like that of previous fetishes, but possessing their power from Jesus rather than from other gods or spirits or ancestors.

These prophetic movements have been numerous but little effort has been made accurately to record either their beginnings or development. Four of the more important ones will receive attention in this chapter, which illustrates rather than covers the subject in its relation to church growth.

Garrick Sokari Braide

In 1915 a revivalist movement led by a catechist named Garrick Sokari Braide of the Niger Delta Pastorate (Anglican) broke out in the Degema district[3] and spread in less than a year through most of the southern part of Owerri Province.

> Bishop Johnson (an African Bishop) in February, 1916, at a meeting of the Niger Delta Church Board said: "I could almost say it has captured the Pastorate with a few small places excepted." The commission of enquiry appointed to study the situation in the Delta Church reported to the 1918 Synod of Lagos that the districts chiefly affected were Bonny, Obonoma (Abonnema), Bakana, Bile, and Queenstown. "The loss in these districts numerically and financially is considerable. . . ."[4]

Braide was a young Christian worker of promise and was much used in healing the sick by prayer, but belief in his prophetic office soon led to what his Anglican historians called "extravagant excesses." He proclaimed himself to be the second Elijah referred to in Malachi 4:5. "Behold, I will

[3] Maxwell, J. *Nigeria, The Land, the People and Christian Progress*, p. 164.

[4] Mitchell, Robert G., personal letter to the author, April 1, 1963.

send you Elijah the prophet before the coming of the great and dreadful day of the Lord." The people paid him greatest reverence. Even his bath water was thought to be charged with supernatural power and was drunk or mixed with earth and smeared on the body as medicine.

Braide and his helpers are reported to have preached from village to village that "the white man's power was ended;[5] that the native Church was to rule the country under the 'prophet'; that people must repent of their sins, destroy all idols and leave off drinking gin. The European drink traffic was sternly denounced."[6]

In 1916 the "prophet" Braide was convicted and imprisoned on charges of sedition and extortion.[7] This led to a division among his followers that produced at least two new Independent Churches, the Garrick Braide Church and Christ Army Church. By 1921 there were thirty-two Garrick Braide congregations in Owerri Province with 7,280 adherents. The same year Christ Army numbered 21,155 adherents in ninety-one congregations[8] – seventy-four of these in Owerri Province and seventeen in Calabar Province.[9]

The Christ Army Church has continued to spread since 1921 but has splintered into numerous small divisions with no central organization and little cohesion between the branches. Some of these branches show marked syncretism with pagan ideas and practices,[10] while others retain more of the traditional Christian morality and belief.[11]

The antiwhite slogan of Braide's followers was not a rebellion against the Niger Delta Pastorate, which was under the direction of an all-Nigerian staff headed by Archdeacon Crow-

[5] Mitchell doubts that Braide himself actually preached that the "white man's power was ended."

[6] Oldham, J. H., *The International Review of Missions,* VI, 46-47.

[7] Talbot, P. Amaury, *The Peoples of Southern Nigeria,* pp. 118-119.

[8] Maxwell, *op. cit.,* p. 113.

[9] Talbot, *op. cit.,* p. 120.

[10] A description of this syncretism in the Christ Army Church among the Ibibio is given by J. C. Messenger in the article "Reinterpretation of Christian and Indigenous Belief in a Nigerian Naturist Church," *American Anthropologist* (April 1960), Vol. 62, No. 2, 268-78.

[11] Mitchell, Robert C., unpublished preliminary research report. Much of the information that follows is based on this report.

ther. This slogan struck fertile soil because many of these people still harbored feelings of resentment over white domination, which had been a major factor in the withdrawal of the Niger Delta Pastorate from the Church Missionary Society (see Chapter III). Even more important was the political situation at this time. This movement came during the darkest days of World War I for Britain. Every day German victories over the allies were announced. No one could be sure that Britain would survive. In a British colony it should not be surprising then that nationalists should arise to declare "the white man's power is ended." No wonder this declaration appeared seditious to the colonial government at such a time of crisis.

This movement gathered many of its early adherents from already established churches. The conviction and imprisonment of Braide caused many of these to return to their former churches, but certainly not all. Was Braide's movement simply a split from the Anglican Church? Did it grow only by proselytizing Anglicans? The answers to these questions are obvious. Many from the pagan community also joined the movement. This is indicated by the admonition to "destroy your idols" and is supported by the large number of adherents to the two branches of the Braide movement by 1921 when Maxwell reports the Garrick Braide Church with 7,280 and Christ Army with 21,155, making a total of 29,435 adherents.[12] The Church Missionary Society annual statistics report that in 1912 the total adherents of all the Niger Delta Pastorate (Anglican Church) was 7,374. Unfortunately the number of adherents in the Niger Delta Pastorate in 1921 is not known. The lessons to be learned from this movement are: (1) The people were ready for change. They were not satisfied with what they had in their religion. This was a ripe harvest field and yet the traditional churches, though Nigerian controlled, were not reaping its maximum yield. (2) The basic teachings of this movement were both Biblical and moral. "Destroy your idols; repent of your sins; and leave off drinking gin." These people were not looking for a watered-down Christianity with low moral requirements. (3) The key to

[12] Maxwell, *op. cit.*, p. 113.

the readiness of these people to move lies in three factors: (a) The war and the instability that resulted from it brought a new quest for security coupled with a rise of nationalistic feeling. (b) The entire lives of these people had been dependent upon and integrated with their former animistic religion. The physical healing through prayer was a manifestation of the power and closeness of Jesus that the people felt was lacking in their previous experience with Christianity. (c) Braide was a dynamic, positive, optimistic leader who attracted people ready for a change.

Christ Apostolic Church

Though the movement that developed into the Christ Apostolic Church in the 1930s started as a reform movement in the St. Saviour's Church (Anglican) at Ijebu Ode in 1918, it is included in this chapter because its beginnings and early growth came through a series of "prophets" who had visions and dreams and who performed miracles through prayer. The Christ Apostolic Church has grown to be by far the largest of the Independent Churches, having 86,313 adherents (excluding the city of Lagos) by 1958, according to a report from their secretariat to the Western Nigeria Broadcasting Corporation.

Their history began with a series of dreams by Daddy Ali, an elder of St. Saviour's Church. He dreamed that the Church was divided into two parts, a small part who prayed constantly and a large part who remained in darkness and gave little thought to prayer. This resulted in the formation of a prayer group within the church. A vision came to Miss Odulami of this prayer group in which the "use of medicines, eating kola nuts, drinking palm wine, wearing magical girdles, wearing fine clothes, and having Sunday feasts"[13] were sins practiced by members of the Church. These ideas were adopted by the prayer group, who established a very strict moral code and antimedical trend. Also, this group received literature from the Faith Tabernacle of Pennsylvania, U.S.A., that led them to reject infant baptism and around which

[13] Parrinder, Geoffrey, *Religion in an African City*, p. 116.

their theology began to form. After 1920 these prayer bands began to spread to other towns.

By this time spiritual experiences of some of the members and literature from Faith Tabernacle had led them to take a strong stand against every kind of medicine, infant baptism, adultery, drinking, smoking, and jewelry. Bishops Jones and Oluwole each visited them and tried to keep them within the Anglican Church but failed because of their beliefs against infant baptism and curative medicine. In 1922 they formed their own Church named "Precious Stone" (received in a vision) and affiliated with Faith Tabernacle in America. This affiliation was severed in 1925 when it was learned that Pastor A. Clark, the leader of Faith Tabernacle, divorced his wife. This presents a real challenge to critics of African moral ideals.

In 1929 a young Yoruba named Joseph Babalola, a mechanic at Ilofa (about one hundred miles north of Ibadan), began to preach after receiving a series of visions warning him he would die within a year unless he took up the Lord's work. He began to preach in Ilofa but was persecuted. The prayer-band members in Ibadan heard of him and sent for him. They were impressed and sent him on to their headquarters in Lagos, where he was baptized by them. In July, 1930, while the prayer band leaders were having a meeting in Ilesha, Babalola suddenly began to heal, and spontaneously a great healing revival broke out that transformed the prayer movement from a few tiny congregations to a religious movement of great consequence. Huge piles of pagan images were burned after his preaching and large numbers professed Christ as Lord and came into the prayer churches. Both Babalola and another prophet, Daniel Orekoya, were said to have performed miracles. It is notable that even then it was not Babalola's intention to found another Church. He looked upon his role as evangelist-healer. His job was to revive people, preach the gospel, and heal.

Thus large numbers at a time became Christian from the pagan population. This followed the African pattern of group decision described at the beginning of this chapter.

In 1931 the prayer churches were visited by representatives of the British Apostolic Church. Affiliation was agreed upon and missionaries arrived from this body in 1932. They tried to shepherd the flock, helped establish schools and train leaders without interfering in doctrinal beliefs. But troubles arose over the missionaries' use of European medicines and also their failure to consult the churches when appointing new missionaries.[14] The majority of the members and most of the leaders broke away and took the name Christ Apostolic Church.

Notice that this movement, like the Garrick Braide movement, has high moral values and is very Biblical, though uncritically. They require monogamy of both ministers and laymen. They practice only adult baptism by immersion. Alcohol is forbidden. Complete dependence is placed upon prayer and faith for the solution of all problems and the healing of all diseases. This is certainly not a movement toward loose or lax Christian faith and practice. The great attraction to this movement came largely from three sources: (1) the common African belief in the importance and power of visions and dreams, (2) the hope for healing and miracles in meeting the problems of this life, and (3) its African leadership and independence.

This movement began during the terrible world-depression years. Trade had slowed down and outside contacts were diminished at a time when literacy, education, and western civilization were increasing in Nigeria. The graph at the end of Chapter IV (p. 317) shows that these were years (1920-1940) of growth for some of the Traditional Churches as well as for prophetic movements. One wonders, however, if the drop in the graph of the Anglican Church in 1929 was due to the great in-gathering into the prophetic movement of Babalola, beginning in 1929.

Cherubim and Seraphim

A few years before 1920 a man with crippled legs, named Moses Orimolade Tunolase (called by any of these three names by various authors), from Ikarre in Ondo Province, was healed through his own prayer. He then began going from town to town teaching and praying. His following grew

[14] Parrinder, *op. cit.*, p. 117.

rapidly as his story became known. In 1920 he moved to Lagos, where he was unknown, and there made little impression until 1925. In that year a girl in Lagos, named Abiodun Akinsowon, had a series of dreams which convinced her that an angel followed her everywhere she went. This worried her and one day she called him a "devil." She thought that this angered him because soon after she became very sick and lost consciousness. Orimolade was sent for; he prayed over her and she recovered. This brought great attention and popularity to both Orimolade and Abiodun and their prayer meetings in Lagos.

At first Orimolade told his followers to continue in their own churches, but to strive to "worship God in spirit and in truth, depending on God alone and having faith in Jesus Christ." Church authorities, however, opposed some of his activities and he broke away to organize his prayer meetings into full religious services. The organization took the name "The Sacred Cherubim and Seraphim Society" from visions that instructed them to do so.[15]

From 1926 on, this movement grew and spread rapidly over Southern Nigeria under the leadership of Orimolade and Abiodun Akinsowon. In 1929 a quarrel arose and Abiodun broke away to form her own organization. Since Orimolade's death in 1932 there has been continuous division, until now the Secretary of the Nigerian Christian Council estimates there are over 200 separate orders (denominations) of the Cherubim and Seraphim with a combined total of over 2,000 local congregations.[16] (Mitchell suggests considerably lower numbers: a maximum of fifty orders and 1,000 congregations.) Strong efforts were exerted to reunite the various branches in 1948 and again in 1955, but efforts have failed over the selection of the Supreme Father.[17] The Secretary of the Christian Council wrote that the Christian Council favors their getting together.

Because of the lack of unity and central training, and also

[15] MacRow, D. W., "Cherubim and Seraphim," *Nigeria* Magazine, No. 53, 1957, p. 123; Lagos, Nigeria: Exhibition Center, Marina.

[16] Adejunmobi, personal letter.

[17] MacRow, *op. cit.*, p. 131.

because of the importance placed on visions and dreams, the beliefs and practices of the Cherubim and Seraphim vary considerably but some of the distinctive features are:[18] The Revised Version of the Bible is held to be the most important guide to life, and its teachings are supplemented by the wish of God as shown during visions, dreams, or prophecies. (In spite of the high degree of dependence upon the Bible for guidance, the importance placed on visions has brought considerable variations from the main body of Christian thought). They believe in the Trinity and salvation through Christ alone. They depend greatly upon prayer to cure the daily problems of life, and prayer is the greatest aid in the search for salvation. Sins are confessed publicly at special services and use is made of holy water, incense, and candles for cleansing. Using or owning charms is forbidden, though a rod and small cross are both used to perform spiritual acts, such as the driving away of evil spirits and witches. Faith healing is practiced involving the use of holy water. They teach against the use of tobacco and alcohol. Frequent pilgrimages are made to a hill near Ibadan and to the beach near Lagos, places that have attracted attention through visions. These places are considered sacred and conducive to pure worship and prayer, free from distractions. Two sacraments are observed – baptism and holy communion.

Notice in the following features the mixture of ideas from Roman Catholic, Protestant, Muslim, and traditional African culture. All members cross themselves upon entering the place of worship. Shoes are removed before entering and no menstruous woman is allowed to enter. Members in some of the societies turn to the east to sing and pray. There is much drumming, dancing, and lusty singing in the services, sometimes lasting all night. The members are organized in stepping stones of rank and can advance in rank by performing deeds and spiritual activities. All members wear special garb with features delineating their rank. Women occupy important positions in the society.

Several factors can be credited for the beginnings and spread of the Cherubim and Seraphim. (1) In metropolitan

[18] *Ibid.*, pp. 123-133; and Parrinder, *op. cit.*, pp. 120-121.

Lagos and other cities, immigrating strangers from the hinterland have their first encounter with detribalized society in a Western economy and find their problems too great for human wisdom. Many of these take refuge in a form of Christianity that recognizes dreams and visions, as did their animistic religion, rather than in the Traditional Churches that hold vigorously to written creeds and forms. (2) Many of the Nigerian people find the formal Western style of worship foreign to them and are attracted by the free expression and group participation of the Cherubim and Seraphim in drumming, dancing, handclapping, wearing of special garments, recognition of graded ranks, visions and their interpretations, and such features that are familiar in Nigerian society. (3) The down-to-earth emphasis on prayer to meet all problems of *this life* is of far greater concern to many Nigerians, as well as to people all over the world, than just a message of eventual salvation for some future life in eternity. (4) The use of holy water and other symbols for physical and spiritual exercises is a familiar device to people in African society. (5) The Cherubim and Seraphim recognize and make provision for encountering and overpowering evil spirits and witches, which are very real in African society. The usual answer of the Traditional Churches to the problem of spirits and witches is to deny their existence. This is not a satisfactory answer for the multitudes of Nigeria.

The Cherubim and Seraphim are widely spread and well known in Southern Nigeria because of their ostentatious garb, their frequent parades, and their twice-daily very noisy services. Their membership, however, is impossible to determine. They often make the claim that they have won 500,000 converts from Roman Catholicism, Protestantism, Islam, and paganism in Southern Nigeria during the last thirty years.[19] Mitchell, after his research, suggests a much more conservative estimate of 10,000 for all Cherubim and Seraphim in Nigeria.[20] Adding to the confusion on this point, there are no doubt large numbers of temporary or part-time adherents, who briefly affiliate with Cherubim and Seraphim

[19] MacRow, *op. cit.*, p. 119.
[20] Mitchell, personal letter.

to meet a special need and then return to their previous alliance, as will be seen in the study of the following prophetic movement.

The Church of the Lord

Beginning in Ijebu in 1925, an Anglican school teacher and catechist named Josaiah Olulowo Oshitelu had a series of visions that led him to establish the Church of the Lord with himself as the head with the title Primate and Founder. Since 1930 the Church has grown and spread steadily to unknown dimensions. Turner says he has seen written estimates of as high as 400,000 adherents in over three hundred branches but suggests in his research that the parent organization of the Church of the Lord now has about seventy-two branches in Nigeria, most of which have from thirty to sixty members, with a total of about 3,000 adherents. He further estimates that the secessions from this body now total about fifty congregations with about 2,000 adherents. The missionary activities of the Church of the Lord have established about another eighty congregations in Sierra Leone, Liberia, and Ghana with a total of about 4,000 adherents. Turner says, "This agrees at several points with some of the official statements of the Church, and we should fix 10,000 as the uppermost limit for the present strength of the religious movement that stems from Oshitelu. It should be remembered that thousands of others have been active at some time in the Church, or have come under its influence to some degree."[21]

The membership of this Church is highly fluid, with large numbers becoming temporary adherents to meet special needs (e.g., healing of sickness), and then leaving when these needs are met or hope is lost.

Members are welcomed (though not necessarily solicited) from other denominations. A survey made by Turner among 277 members showed seventy-five percent of them came from Traditional Churches, including Roman Catholic, eleven percent from other Independent Churches, and fourteen percent from Islam and pagan religions. Members are allowed to re-

[21] Turner, Harold W., preliminary research toward doctoral thesis.

tain membership in other Christian Churches if they wish, but not in Islam or in pagan religions.[22]

Membership comes from a wide range of social and economic classes with various levels of literacy and education. The Church of the Lord cannot be considered a sect of the lower classes.

Among its distinctive features are the following.[23] The Founder and Primate, Oshitelu, is commonly regarded as a "modern Elijah" and reference is made to John 1:21; Acts 3: 23; 7:37; and Deuteronomy 18:15 as providing Scriptural warrant for his divine commission and unique authority in the Church. The catechism is based on and very much like that of the Anglican Church, the main difference relating to baptism. Only adult believers are baptized by immersion, and rebaptism is required of those coming from other denominations, even Baptists. Polygamy is allowed under some circumstances, but it is not stressed and was not one of the original causes of the founding of the Church of the Lord. Daily prayer is held five times a day. Sprinklings, ablutions, and drinking of holy water are practiced. Special prayer gowns are worn and shoes are removed during services. Menstruous women cannot enter the House of Prayer but may worship in a place assigned. A special "Faith Room" is attached to each House of Prayer for those who desire healing or other help. Supplicants go there to live until their object is attained or they wish to leave. Outward display of emotions form a regular part of supplication – e.g., rolling, rubbing one's face on the ground, sobbing, or crying, whirling around until one falls in dizziness, etc. The Feast of the Tabernacles is observed annually at Ogere, the Church headquarters, with a lengthy ceremony including thirteen days of fasting.

Members are classified according to their degree of association with the Church. Higher degrees of membership, called cross-bearers, are anointed to preach, heal the sick, raise the dead, and work miracles. (Compare Matthew 10:

[22] *Ibid.*

[23] *Ibid.;* Baeta, *op. cit.*, pp. 123-125; and Turner, H. W., "The Catechism of an Independent West African Church," *Occasional Papers* issued by the Department of Mission Studies, No. 9, April, 1961.

7-8, "And as ye go, preach, saying, the kingdom of heaven is at hand. Heal the sick, cleanse the lepers, raise the dead, cast out devils. . . .") Anointment means "separated for the Lord to be overlord over dark powers, Satan, world, witches, wizards, and all spirits of diseases and sickness, to subdue and to cast them out."[24] A small wooden cross, carried by the cross-bearers, is the "key" that carries the power about. This wooden cross is interpreted by many as having special power. Thus syncretism with pagan magic and charms is a grave danger. Membership and leadership is so far very largely made up of the Ijebu tribe of the Yorubas, but missionary activity is gradually changing this.

In response to the author's questionnaire Oshitelu, Primate and Founder of the Church of the Lord, expressed satisfaction at the rate of growth of the Church of the Lord, but did not feel that evangelical Christianity is growing as it should in other denominations in Nigeria. He listed the following things as causes of church growth: (1) Unity and oneness of all Christian Churches; (2) Divine healing and miracles in the churches; (3) Commitment to Christ and rejection of all other gods; (4) Faithfulness to true Christian life and denial of wordly pleasures; (5) Worldwide evangelism.[25] His first point serves to remind the reader that most independent Churches want to see Christianity united, but not at the cost of sacrificing their own convictions or self-government.

It is the author's studied conclusion that the stress placed upon the second point, divine healing and miracles, by the Church of the Lord, is the chief attraction to adherents. Next to that in attracting African members is the typical African form of service indicated by distinctive features listed above and the acceptance of polygamy. The Church of the Lord is born from and fitted to African culture patterns.

Turner found from the personal histories of over 250 members that the central reasons given for joining this Church were as follows:[26]

[24] Turner, *op. cit.*
[25] Oshitelu, J. O., personal letter to the author, February 28, 1962.
[26] Turner, *op. cit.*

Healings, either of convert or a relative or friend	81
Revelations of past history, of dream meanings, of future events	73
General Appeal. "I liked it," or liked some special feature of worship, etc.	43
Troubles removed, which could include sickness, lack of success, etc.	23
Searching for spiritual development, the true way, or real power	18
Conversion, involving change of life, stopping drinking, etc.	15
	253

A handbill put out by the Church advertising a "Spiritual Rally" shows the down-to-earth approach. "Come and hear your Divine Predictions and Revelations. . . . There will be individual testimonies and Prayers, to stamp out the disease in this our present age. What is your Trouble? Your Souls? Salvation? Real Bible Interpretation? And Immediate Healing Power? Are you after Child Bearing? Promotion? Victory over Enemies? etc. Be Present to hear the voice of the Spirit of the Living God."

Numerous other independent Churches have been born in Southern Nigeria out of prophet movements and/or division from other Churches. Parrinder lists fifteen varieties and twenty-five churches in the city of Ibadan alone.[27] Mitchell found that in April, 1962, about 117 Church and Religious Bodies were registered with the Nigerian government. Seven of these were Traditional Churches, eight Ethiopian types, sixty-four Aladura (prayer Churches), fifteen varieties of Cherubim and Seraphim, four varieties of Church of the Lord, fourteen Apostolic type, and twenty-eight others. Each of these registered Churches is a separate denomination and may have many branches. He was told that new Churches arrive at the rate of one or two a week.

Why should this be? Why have the Traditional Churches not been able to contain these prophetic movements? A look at certain common features of most of these movements as

[27] Parrinder, *op. cit.*, pp. 107-132.

illustrated by the cases outlined in this chapter will help answer these questions.

(1) Most of these movements began within already established Churches and only left to form their own Churches when they were suppressed. Both the original divisions and further subdivisions came over central authority and dominance. Such dominance was resented and rejected whether the authority was foreign or African. This presents a puzzling problem with the need for local autonomy and at the same time sufficient guidance toward normal Christian thought and practice. Essential to the solution of this problem is the next point.

(2) Most of these movements are strongly based on a literal, though uncritical, interpretation of the Bible. Even the visions and dreams that spurred prophetic activities were usually based upon Scripture passages. The Bible is our point of contact with these movements. Emphasis on Bible teaching and Bible-centeredness in all Churches is the only bond of Christian unity and is essential to effective evangelism. Broader Bible knowledge leads to better Bible understanding and interpretation. Individual Christians are going to make interpretations of Bible passages and therefore the better they know the Bible, the closer their interpretations are likely to be to the Christian norm. This includes ideas that come through visions and dreams. The only adequate defense against non-Christian syncretism in these movements is thorough Bible study and understanding. A positive contribution that the Traditional Churches might make toword helping the Independent Churches grow in spiritual understanding and Biblical truth would be to offer a thoroughly Bible-based training program for their pastors and teachers. In Ibibioland leaders of some of these churches recently walked miles to go to a short-term Bible school run by a Pentecostal missionary. They take any correspondence course they can get their hands on. They are open for help to the Traditional Churches and, of course, long for recognition.

(3) Some practices show combinations of ideas found in the Bible (especially the Old Testament), Roman Catholic

and Protestant practices, Muslim ideas, and traditional African patterns (i.e., the use of water and oil for anointing, removing of shoes before entering the sanctuary, prohibition of menstruous women from the sanctuary, use of symbols such as rods, crosses, and special garb, recognition of grades in rank and status). Traditional Churches should take care to fit forms of Christian worship and service to the social patterns of the people wherever it does not conflict with the teachings of Scripture. Of course, understanding and careful teaching is necessary to prevent syncretism with other religions; but cultural adaptation is often not syncretism.

(4) An important feature is the complete integration of religion with everyday life and needs. This is especially exemplified in the emphasis on divine healing and miracles and objects of prayer. The traditional thought of Nigerians is that some god or spirit or ancestor is responsible for everything that happens or fails to happen in this life. Nothing should be done, therefore, without appropriate religious ceremony or connection. The author has seen this carried over into African Christian thought. In Traditional Church prayer meetings the most frequent prayer objects are for healing of the sick, safety in travel, success in business or trade, acquiring a job, passing an exam, or winning in a sports event or a court case. Much less frequently prayer is made for purely spiritual matters such as help in winning relatives and friends to faith in Jesus Christ. The people of the prophet movements also pray about and have ceremonies for overpowering evil spirits, witches, and wizards. These "spiritual" things are branded "ignorant superstition" and scoffed at in most Traditional Churches, and so a vital concern of many of the members is suppressed. Failure in this area separates religion from the here-and-now life of the people and brings disillusionment with a Christianity based on and aimed at meeting needs in Western social patterns.

Every church leader who is interested in church growth will do well to ponder these matters in relation to his own Church. Is it Bible-centered and is Bible teaching central in its program? At the same time does the form and pattern of the Church fit the culture? Does the program and teaching of the Church meet the complete needs, fears, and spiritual quests of Nigerians both in the here-and-now and in relation to eternity? It is the author's opinion that failure in these areas is responsible for much of the multiplication of prophet movements and Independent Churches, and is a major factor in the failure to reach the maximum in potential church growth.

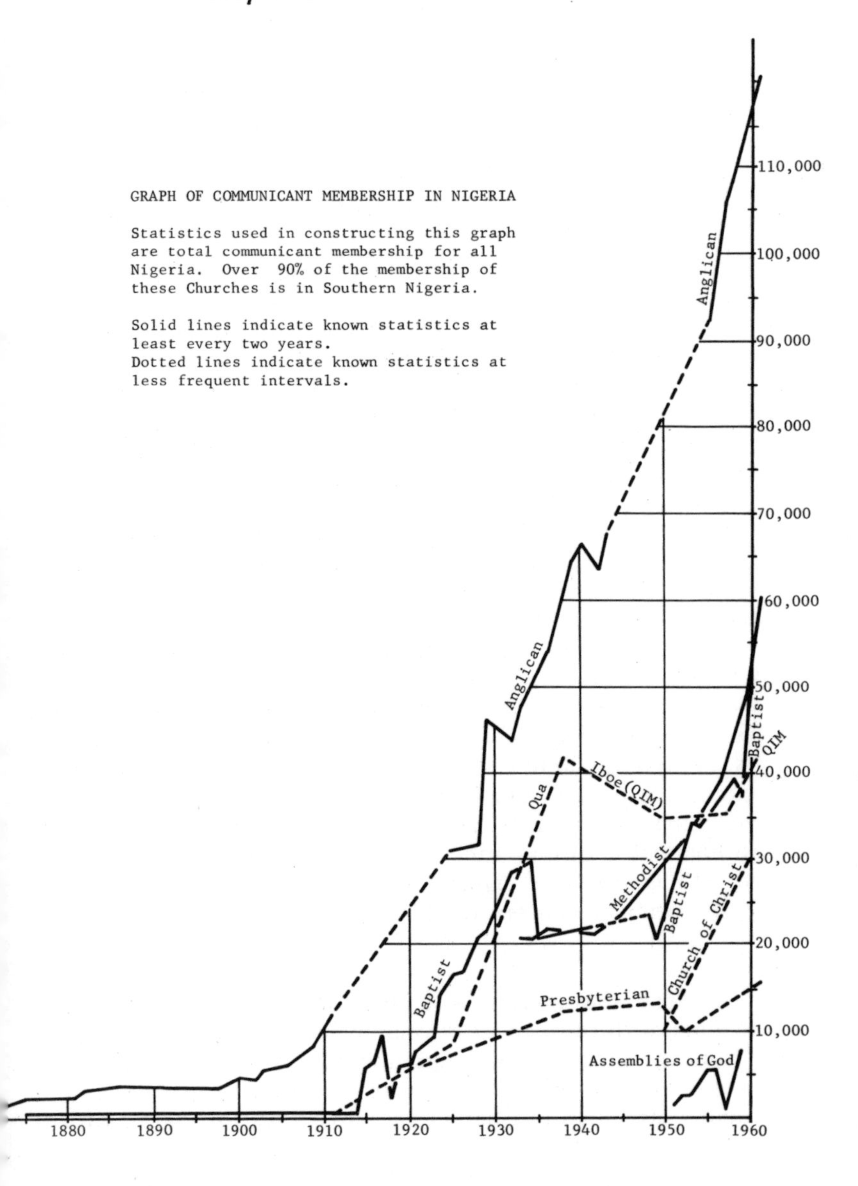
GRAPH OF COMMUNICANT MEMBERSHIP IN NIGERIA
Statistics used in constructing this graph are total communicant membership for all Nigeria. Over 90% of the membership of these Churches is in Southern Nigeria.
Solid lines indicate known statistics at least every two years.
Dotted lines indicate known statistics at less frequent intervals.
Anglican
Anglican
Qua
Iboe (QIM)
Methodist
Baptist
Baptist
Baptist
QIM
Church of Christ
Presbyterian
Assemblies of God
110,000
100,000
90,000
80,000
70,000
60,000
50,000
40,000
30,000
20,000
10,000
1880
1890
1900
1910
1920
1930
1940
1950
1960

Chapter V. The Growth of the Traditional Churches

PROBABLY THE TWO STRONGEST IMPRESSIONS FROM THE FIRST glance at the graph on the preceding page are the lack of church growth during the first fifty or sixty years of "mission work" and the rapid growth during the last twenty years. By 1900 the total communicant membership of all Protestant denominations in Nigeria was slightly over 6,000.

In October, 1962, Harry Boer, missionary principal of the Jos Seminary, wrote, "The Eastern Region consisting of approximately 8,000,000 people officially lists half of them as Christian. In the Western Region with its population of 7,000,000 about 35 percent would designate themselves as Christian."[1] Boer's estimate includes Roman Catholic, Traditional Protestant, Independent, and indeed all who are unwilling to be classified as pagan or Moslem, and it is of total Christian community, not communicants. Boer means there is a Christian community of approximately six and a half million in Southern Nigeria. Table III at the end of this chapter shows that only 561,000 or less than nine percent of these are communicants or full members. However, the story of the development from almost no response in the nineteenth century to nominal Christian adherence of nearly half the population in 1962 is of crucial significance to the Christian mission and is the primary concern of this chapter.

Baptist

Because the author is a Baptist missionary and more familiar with the Baptist development, the story begins there. (Note the graph at the beginning of this chapter.) The lack of growth from 1850 to 1890 must be attributed to the multiple factors described in Chapter II. From 1891 to 1900 the mem-

[1] Boer, Harry R., "The Year of the Elephant," *The Reformed Journal,* Vol. XII, No. 9 (October, 1962).

bership tripled from 111 to 382. It again tripled to 1,081 from 1900 to 1906. This was the period immediately after the split of 1888 in Lagos. Both Ebenezer, the independent church, and the mission churches were stirred to activity. While the independent churches grew in the Delta, Ijebu, Ekiti, and Ibadan, the mission churches grew in Abeokuta, Oyo, Ogbomosho, Shaki, and Iressi.

In addition to the added zeal brought on by the split, another factor entered in. In 1897

> the first Baptist Theological Training School for native workers was established. Missionary C. E. Smith, recognizing the acute need for Nigerians who were able to go out and preach the Gospel in towns and villages which the missionaries could never hope to reach, gathered about him a band of worthy men, gave them a course of Bible study in the vernacular, and sent them out to witness to their fellow men. Many of them did excellent service and a few became pastors of churches. At first the school was a private venture; but, after demonstrating its value, was incorporated into the mission and eventually grew into the Baptist Seminary.[2]

It is amazing that this development in training an indigenous ministry came so late and then had to be proved before being accepted by the mission.

From 1906 to 1909 the membership leveled off and then in 1910 dropped to 610 with a gradual recovery up to 1,320 in 1914. No explanation other than poor record keeping is evident for the drop in 1910. The statistics show a similar drop that year in the number of baptisms, native pastors, schools and scholars. It would appear from this that not all churches got their reports in. More important is the plateau, with membership rising from 1,081 in 1906 to only 1,320 in 1914. This period is described by most authors as a period of institutional expansion. This institutional fever affected the Nigerian people, the government, and the missions.

> Education for the youth of Nigeria was provided entirely by mission societies up to 1899. In the 1890s the government began to take an interest in education and appointed an

[2] Robinson, Oren C., *Indigenous Development of Baptist Churches of Nigeria,* p. 18.

> inspector of schools. The inspector saw the popular demand for education and appealed to the government for a generous support. . . . In 1903 the Education Department was formed and rules and regulations for elementary and secondary education were drawn up. Provision was made for payment of grants-in-aid to all schools working under the system. In 1906 this policy of education was extended over the Colony (Lagos) and Western and Eastern Nigeria. By 1912 there were 59 government primary schools and 91 mission schools in receipt of government grants.[3]

In 1906 Baptists first sent a pastoral student, Nathaniel D. Oyerinde, to America for university training. The author concludes by the institutional developments of this period and the lack of church growth, that the major effort during this time was in getting the institutions going. Emphasis on evangelism and church planting seemed to wane. This did not mean a change in purpose of the missionaries but rather a change in approach. An immediate result of this change was a sharp decrease in growth. At the same time, this change was no doubt a contributing factor to later increases in growth, but one wonders whether much sounder and greater growth would not have taken place, had growth been stressed together with education.

In 1928 Duval expressed an opinion on the importance of mission schools that was and is shared by many. He wrote,

> Twenty years ago our educational work took on added life, and with the coming of new missionaries more interest was given to this branch of the work. In each of the stations and important outstations day schools were established. The graduates of the theological training school were much better prepared than the older class of men, and are expected not only to preach and visit the people, but to establish schools in the towns where they are located. The development of the country and the awakening of the people created a great desire for learning, so that the young men flocked to the night schools, held in the teachers' houses, while the younger boys sought entrance to the day schools. Great sacrifices were made for the privilege of attending. . . . If they were

[3] Knight, Charles Williams, *A History of the Expansion of Evangelical Christianity in Nigeria,* p. 129.

> able to attend a Christian school for a few months, they almost invariably became sincere Christians. The results were so good from a spiritual standpoint that the missionaries began to realize the opportunities of making the boys potential Christian workers. . . . In the Association meeting of 1915 a program was adopted to have a school in each town and village where we had a church, and a high school in each of the main stations.[4]

The school approach has both advantages and disadvantages in church growth, especially in boarding schools and in a society where education is not yet open to the general public. Among the advantages are: (1) It concentrates on the younger members of society who are less bound by traditional ideas than the adults. (2) It creates a community (the school) where Christian social pressures are normal and opposing pressures do not easily intrude. (3) It ensures time and opportunity for Christian growth and understanding after conversion. (4) It offers the combined attractions of intellectual and material advance with new spiritual understanding and beliefs. (5) It gradually produces a higher development in education and potential leadership among Christians than in the general population. Among the disadvantages are: (1) The Christian community might easily be sealed off socially from the rest of the people or lose its opportunity to convert from the masses. (2) The dangerous implication that Christianity is only for the educated is difficult to dispel. (3) It concentrates the efforts and resources of the mission or Church on a few. (This may not be a disadvantage since it does not necessarily limit all efforts to the few and it may ultimately provide the sound base for greater church growth.) (4) Once begun, it is very difficult to reverse this approach. The schools continually grow and expand, demanding increasingly more personnel and resources.

Some schools are essential for training Christian leaders. Beyond that the effectiveness of the school approach depends upon individual circumstances. Since these circumstances vary according to time and place, all must be periodically

[4] Duval, *Baptist Missions in Nigeria*, pp. 173-174.

weighed in order to find the balance that will produce maximum sound church growth.

The graph shows a phenomenal spurt from 1,320 members in 1914 to 9,747 in 1917. (The readers' attention was drawn to this in Chapter III.) During this period the independent Baptist churches joined the mission churches in the Yoruba Baptist Association and the report now included the independent church membership, which had grown larger than that of the mission churches. This reuniting brought joy on both sides and renewed evangelistic efforts were a probable result as well.

The loss of membership, shown on the graph in 1918, is largely a matter of poor records. A new general secretary was elected by the Convention and his multiple responsibilities were far greater than one man could efficiently handle. He was field missionary for Ogbomosho area, the only doctor in Ogbomosho hospital, and general secretary for the Convention as well. Thus Convention reports indicate that only statistics received from local churches each year were recorded. Many churches failed to get in their reports. Added to this was the death in 1917 of Dr. Agbebi, superintendent of the Delta churches. This probably reduced the efficiency of reporting from both Delta and Ekiti districts, which were under his care.

The formation in 1916 of the Sapele Baptist Church was noted in Chapter III. Among the charter members of this new church was a young man named Omatsola, a Warri man and a relative of the Itsekiri king. Omatsola had been educated at Warri and then sent to the Presbyterian school at Calabar. He was a favorite there and refused several promising offers to return to his own Itsekiri people. He became a teacher at Sapele and a leader among the Christians. When the Sapele Baptist Church was formed, he was sent to the Baptist theological seminary in Shaki. Upon his return the church grew phenomenally. From 1918 to 1928

> The work spread among the heathen in all directions, embracing several tribes, so that in some of the meetings five different languages are spoken. The first meeting house was soon found to be much too small, and another had to be erected, which in its turn was replaced, and the members are

> planning the fourth in ten years. The membership of this church in Sapele numbers over 1000.
>
> These people were not satisfied to remain at home, but soon began to visit the towns in the surrounding districts, where churches quickly sprang up. During the ten years there has been on an average of one new church formed every two months with a total membership of over 3,000.[5]

This growth took place through the zeal of a newly organized church under the leadership of a dynamic leader with important family and social connections in the towns and villages surrounding Sapele and Warri. In 1923, only seven years after the Sapele church was formed, four Baptist missionaries made their first visit to the Midwest and found twenty churches had come from this beginning in Sapele. This could not have happened under the isolated individual school approach to conversion. This is what McGavran describes as "people movements,"[6] when Christianity spreads rapidly from individual to individual and from group to group, through family and social ties.

During this same period, spontaneous expansion took place out of the church started in Igede-Ekiti in 1901.[7] Between 1914 and 1925 at least twelve churches were begun in surrounding villages through family or trade contacts.

In 1898 two men from Iressi, some sixty miles northeast of Ogbomosho, became Christian while in Ogbomosho and went home to start a Baptist church. By 1915 this church had only forty members but grew to four hundred by 1928. During this period of rapid growth from 1915 to 1929, fourteen other churches were established in sourrounding villages, each with its own separate membership. Thus a total of possibly 1,000 became Christians through the outreach of this one church in these thirteen years. During its first seventeen years the Iressi church had barely gotten started. Then the fire caught hold in Iressi and sparks flew to other villages through the web of natural relationships, there to ignite similar fires.

[5] *Ibid.*, p. 204.
[6] McGavran, Donald, *Bridges of God,* pp. 11-13.
[7] Roberson, C. F., Unpublished notes.

In 1929 Pastor J. O. Obafemi went to Ekinrin as pastor and in the next few years led this church to establish churches in twenty-four neighboring villages. Thus churches multiplied from village to village.

In terms of social structure what probably happened is this. Inspired and directed by an energetic pastor, thoroughly committed to multiplying churches, the Christians of Ekinrin talked to relatives, market customers, and fellow guild and association members. They aroused interest in neighboring villages, held services for them, and got them started in their own churches. This infectious enthusiasm spread from village to village. People were impressed when they saw lives changed and heard the Christian message from their intimate acquaintances. Christianity was no longer an intrusion from the outside, viewed with suspicion and tolerated by the masses for the few non-conformists who embraced it. Respected and trusted people lived and propagated Christianity in their own society. All this was used by God to multiply churches!

It is probable that the records of 1918 to 1924 are incomplete, so a truer picture of the growth would be to extend the line up gradually from the 1917 membership to join the line on the graph in about 1924. The rapid growth seen on the graph from 1918 to 1934 came as a result of several factors: (1) Christianity was less suspect and persecution less general during this period. (2) Schools multiplied rapidly and were often very effective evangelizing agents, particularly among the students. (3) Some people with important connections and social standing had become Christians and used their influence to spread the gospel. Some of these men were leaders among the multiplying churches. (4) Better-trained Nigerians were coming from the seminary and other schools to provide much-needed capable indigenous leadership, who acted as both local church pastors and often as circuit pastors to other congregations. (5) Laymen were spreading the gospel through relatives, trade, and other social contacts. (6) The combined activitiy of Dr. Green as medical doctor and field missionary tied the treatment of physical suffering at the Ogbomosho hospital to the ultimate purpose of planting churches in local communities. Thus converts in the hospital were led to establish churches in their villages. (7) As churches multiplied and spread geographically more local responsibility and initiative was inevitable, resulting in more natural and indigenous patterns of worship and propagation.

The great loss seen on the graph from 1935 to 1949 is the combined effect of several things. In 1935 again a new man became responsible for keeping statistical records and incomplete returns are obvious between 1935 and 1941. The recorded membership varied little during this period and was identical for the years 1938 and 1939. There are no reports from 1942 to 1947 during the World War.

The visit in 1938 of Dr. Maddry, the subsequent strong stand of the Convention against polygamy, and the effect of this on the graph were discussed in Chapter III. However, several other important policy changes that came out of that visit need to be mentioned here because they affected both the present and future development and growth of Baptists in Nigeria. Plans were made to send outstanding Nigerian pastors to the United States or to England for advanced training. A missionary was made full-time director of the seminary in Nigeria. The Convention was more completely organized with departments to take over responsibilities from the mission. It was decided that the schools should be turned over to the proprietorship of the Convention. By 1947 all schools except the seminary were turned over to the Convention.

More institutions were opened between 1940 and 1950: boys' high schools in Oyo and Port Harcourt, girls' high schools in Lagos and Agbor, teacher-training colleges in Ede and Benin, and hospitals in Eku and Joinkrama.

Rapid growth again took place from 1950 to 1962. It could be that a stronger base, a truer Christianity, and a more effective witness due to the purging of membership rolls in previous years are parts of the reason. As important as these matters are, they probably had less effect upon the present rapid growth than the following factors.

In 1947 the Convention appointed an Evangelism Committee and in 1948 an Evangelism Secretary took office. This gave special emphasis and direction to better evangelism. In 1948 after 98 years of wandering, Baptist headquarters were established in Ibadan. In the years following, offices and departments were stablized and both missionaries and Nigerians gave full time to organization and promotion. More accurate reports, as well as better organization and promotion, have resulted both at headquarters and on the local level.[8]

Both the mission staff and the number of able, well-trained, and experienced Nigerian leaders have grown rapidly. In May, 1950, a special committee was set up to study all matters related to Africanization of posts of leadership in Nigerian Baptist work. The process of transferring responsibilities from mission to Convention has proceeded rapidly in every phase of Baptist work. Nigerian Baptists have demonstrated their missionary fervor by establishing a Home and Foreign Mission Board in 1953. By 1960 Nigerian missionaries served under this board fully supported by Nigerian Baptists in four home-mission fields and in Sierra Leone.

The decade of the 1960s has begun in a period of rapid church growth. It is urgently important if Baptists are to continue to grow beyond 1962 that their attention and efforts be focused upon winning people to Christ and planting churches. While institutions are important and have served as evangelizing agents, the business of operating them must not be allowed to divert the attention of missionaries or Nigerians from the supreme task of making disciples and anchoring them in churches that are evangelistic and missionary. The institutions can be and often have been instrumental in this purpose. This primary evangelistic objective must not be considered the responsibility of only the small percentage of missionaries devoting their major effort to church planting. It must be central in the purpose of every missionary and Nigerian Christian. At the same time the school must not be thought of as the main door to the Church. The era when it might have been thus regarded has ended.

The following table gives revealing statistics at four important points on the graph.

[8] Patterson, I. N., personal letter to the author, February 9, 1963.

TABLE II – BRIEF SUMMARY OF BAPTIST STATISTICS IN NIGERIA

Year	Missionaries	Ordained Nigerians	Unordained Pastors	Churches	Members	Primary School Students
1914	13*	2	34	11	1,320	488
1934	28*	20	165	191	29,646	2,000
1949	119*	33	203	492	20,065	25,000
1961	213*	?	329**	1,265	60,103	86,831

* includes wives ** includes ordained Nigerians

This table implies the following: (1) The development of ordained Nigerians and unordained pastors has been far too small. (2) Compared to most mission fields over a hundred years old, the number of missionaries is large in relation to both the church membership and the number of national clergy. (3) The loss of church membership from 1934 to 1949 while the primary school students grew from 2,000 to 25,000 is tragic and revealing. This would strongly imply that the schools have not been nearly as much of an evangelizing agency as is often claimed by both missionaries and nationals.

Anglican

In 1953 Parrinder wrote,

> The Church of England, through the Church Missionary Society, has by far the greatest sway of Christian bodies in Western Nigeria. It has succeeded to a remarkable extent in forming an indigenous ministry, with over 140 clergy, mostly Africans. In April, 1951, the Bishop of Lagos was elected the first Archbishop of the newly formed Anglican Province of the whole of West Africa. The Lagos diocese was divided into four new dioceses, of which Ibadan was one.[9]

The graph shows that from its beginning in 1842 the Anglican Church has been ahead of all other denominations in communicant membership in Nigeria. At least three important facts contributed to this. Britain had by far the greatest influence of any nation upon Nigeria during the

[9] Parrinder, *Religion in an African City*, pp. 86-87.

nineteenth and twentieth centuries. It is natural that the Church of England should receive psychological and other advantages denied to other denominations. Probably more important is the fact that three of the first Anglican missionaries had extraordinarily good health resulting in long periods of service in Nigeria, while the average missionary in the middle nineteenth century was able to spend less than six years in Nigeria before he died or left for health reasons. Townsend spent forty years, Gollmer spent twenty-one years, and Hinderer spent twenty-eight years in Nigeria. These men and Bishop Crowther gave continuity of policy and stability to the Anglicans not possible to other missions. Of no less importance was the policy stated as early as 1851 to develop a completely indigenous Church. Henry Venn, the general secretary of the Church Missionary Society, urged the missionaries to "organize a native Church, create a Christian literature, and lay plans for days to come. He asked them to aim at self-government and self-support, to put the Bible in the hands of the people, and said how much they were already indebted to Crowther for his translation into Yoruban of a great portion of the Holy Scripture and the liturgy. They were recommended also to start an educational institution at Abeokuta for young men and young women."[10]

Indications that this policy was the dominant aim in the work of the Church Missionary Society can be seen in the following points. (1) A boat named Henry Venn was used on the Niger for the extension and supervision of the Church. (2) Nigerian clergy were used extensively from the beginning. Ajayi points out that this was far more possible for Anglicans and Methodists than for other missions. Anglicans and Methodists had a ready-made African staff, some of whom were well trained, and, indeed, congregations from those coming back from Sierra Leone.[11]

(3) Large portions of the Scripture were translated from the beginning of mission work into Yoruba, Ibo, and other languages. (4) Church liturgy was translated, memorized,

[10] Page, *The Black Bishop,* pp. 107-108.

[11] Ajayi, *Christian Missions and the Making of Nigeria 1841-1891,* p. 413.

and used, enabling a high degree of participation by all in worship. This was especially helpful for the large numbers of nonliterates and semiliterates. The Anglicans did not get sealed off to the small literate school population so easily. (5) Schools were started for the purpose of teaching the people to read the Bible and other Christian literature. By 1854 Church Missionary Society schools had already produced 3,000 literates and imported a printing press to provide them with literature.[12]

(6) The Church was self-supporting. Mission aid was limited to the support and care of European missionaries and necessary grants toward the cost of training institutions, hospitals, and other special agencies.[13] (7) The missionaries sought close friendship and cooperation with chiefs and elders, traditional rulers in the towns and villages. The problem of democracy in the local church did not affect them as much as it did Baptists.

(8) Lay leaders have been used extensively in the churches. Ajayi says of Crowther that

> For all his belief in the value of literacy and academic training, he did not reckon it the most essential outfit of a missionary. He made periodic analyses in 1868, in 1870, and again in 1877 of the qualifications and merits of his (African) mission staff, and on each occasion he came to the conclusion that he depended most on middle-aged men barely literate in English and the vernacular, farmers, carpenters, mechanics, masons, court messengers, stewards on ships and the like by profession, recommended by the Niger Mission Committee in Sierra Leone as men of proven Christian character. One of their chief merits was that they "command more respect with chiefs than young, inexperienced, college-trained men."[14]

(9) The chief function of European missionaries has been to train Nigerians. While this is in keeping with the above-stated policy of indigenous development and has obvious advantages in that direction, it also has weaknesses. The

[12] Walker, *The Romance of the Black River*, p. 82.
[13] *Ibid.*, p. 236, and Hubbard, J. W., *The Sobo of the Niger Delta*, p. 73.
[14] Ajayi, *op. cit.*, p. 513.

greatest of these is the tendency of potential leaders to leave their homes and places in society and cluster around the mission station, reducing their contact with and influence in their own community.

These nine points were most fully followed in the Niger Mission where Bishop Crowther and his completely Nigerian staff were working. If indigenous control does in fact produce greater church growth, it would seem that the Niger Mission under Crowther would have shown the greatest growth during this period. Statistics show that this was true from 1879 to 1888. During this period the Niger Mission multiplied ten times (from 95 to 994) while the Anglicans in Yorubaland merely doubled (from 1,330 to 2,770) in communicants. After 1888, as the troubles in the Niger Mission described in Chapter III grew, the communicants dropped to 263 in 1898 and with a year by year rise and fall did not show steady gain again until after 1910, when they reported only 862 communicants.

Even Crowther did not have the full psychological advantage that might be expected with an African bishop and an all-African staff. He had been considerably Europeanized in his education and training. His thoughts and expressions in a letter of condolence to Mrs. Henry Townsend at the death of her husband could have been that of any English bishop.[15] Because of his friendship with white traders and frequent travel on their ships, he was closely associated with the Europeans in the minds of many of the people among whom he worked.

Nevertheless, the policy of the Church Missionary Society was dominated from the beginning with the idea of creating a Nigerian Church of the Anglican communion. While each of the denominations had identical aims, the Anglicans followed policies that achieved these aims more quickly than most other denominations.

How and where did the Anglican Church grow in Nigeria? National statistics and most histories tend to hide this by

[15] Townsend, George, *Memoir of the Rev. Henry Townsend,* pp. 177-180.

generalities. The 1957 statistics show communicants by diocese as follows:

Niger Delta	**Niger**	**Ondo-Benin**	**Ibadan**	**Lagos**
18,550	48,758	14,226	10,987	12,035

These figures show that tremendous growth had taken place in the Niger diocese. Only a partial description of this can be found in historical records. The headquarters of this diocese is Onitsha, the first station of the Church Missionary Society Niger Mission. By 1930 Walker wrote that in Onitsha, Anglicans had a church of 1,000 Ibos, two smaller Ibo churches and one non-Ibo church, a ninety-bed hospital, a grammar school, a girls' high school, several large elementary schools, and a bookshop.[16] He wrote that sixty miles south of Onitsha in Owerri area, "there are a hundred churches in various stages of development. Twenty-five years ago there was not a single church or African Christian in that area."[17]

Considerably more information is available about the growth of the Anglican Church in Isoko, which was in the beginning also under Onitsha, but was in 1957 a part of the Ondo-Benin diocese. Stock wrote in 1916 of the expansion of the Church into areas out from Onitsha,

> Towns and villages all over the territory on both sides of the river (Niger) have now their little bands of converts, including the Ijaw and Sobo countries, where Mr. Proctor, Mr. Aitkin, and Mr. Rooks have been doing good work. The first confirmation in the Ijaw district was held by Bishop Tugwell in January, 1915. The demand for more teachers is persistent, and the openings are most inviting. There is, in fact, almost a "mass movement," constituting a most urgent call for reinforcements. Mr. Aitkin reported only a year ago that in a few months he had registered 2,000 people who had thrown away their idols.[18]

These movements began within a year or two after Christianity first came to the Urhobo and Isoko country in 1910.

[16] Walker, *op. cit.*, p. 212.
[17] *Ibid.*, p. 216.
[18] Stock, *The History of the Church Missionary Society*, IV, p. 17.

The people had grown tired of certain rules and regulations imposed upon them by their pagan priests. They believed in two worlds, *Akpon* (the present world) and *Erivbi* (the unseen world). Ultimate control of things that happen in *Akpon* is with the Creator, *Oghene,* but more particularly by the *esemo,* departed ancestors who lived in *Erivbi.* There are also a number of beings, called *edjo,* who have only lived in *Erivbi,* except in special occasions when they have taken the human form for their own reasons. Though these *edjo* are fewer than the *Erivbi,* they desired always to make their presence felt in *Akpon.* Through their priests came difficult and suppressing regulations with threats of punishment for the disobedient. A striking example of this was the Aviara clan, the poorest of the Isoko peoples, because the *edjo* forbade them to grow cassava, their staple food. The Christian message to them was, "Do not fear the *edjo;* God the Creator, requires you to worship Him alone, and if you have faith in Him, the *edjo* have no power over you, and you need not fear them." The entire Aviara clan gladly accepted the new Faith, defied the *edjo,* burnt their idols, and grew cassava.

The rate of conversion within other clans depended partly on how firm a grip *edjo* had upon them. At first, severe persecution came to the Christians from the *odio* society, who controlled the worship of the *esemo* and the government of the clan. In the Uzere clan the *odio* tortured and expelled Christians from the clan. In the Okpe clan they plundered the possessions of the Christians. Most Christians stood firm in persecution and eventually won the respect and toleration of the opposition as well as the conversion of large numbers, including some whole villages.

Christianity began with the conversion of a few individuals but these individuals attracted great interest and soon the pattern changed from individual conversion to the decision of groups to burn their idols, leave their taboos, and "become Christian." Hubbard describes this chain reaction in the case of an Urhobo man named Avbaire from an Ughelli village called Iwrogboma. He had heard of Christianity and was interested in it. Visiting in Kuokorhi, he found a man named Oghenerume, who explained to him what he knew. Then they went together to Etefe of the Avburaha clan in

Kwale area to meet a man called Ohro, who was an adherent of the new Faith. They stayed with him for some time learning and then he sent them to Bishop Johnson, a native of Sierra Leone serving the Anglican Church in Nigeria. Bishop Johnson gave them his blessing and told them to return to their home with the message of Christ. On his return to Iwrogboma, Avbaire built a small hut to worship in and worshiped there night and morning. It was not long before he was joined by two men and then a woman from the Ughelli village of Odovhie. In due course the report of the new religion was spread abroad, and Avbaire was joined by people from many clans, particularly Olomu, who asked him to come to their village and free them of the tyranny of *edjo*.

> Thus from Ughelli Christianity reached, through the evangelism of Avbaire and entirely at the people's own request (an area of about 30 miles radius from Ughelli), the Urhobo speaking clans of Ughelli, Olomu, Evbreni, and Ewu, the Urhobo speaking clans on the Forcados river, and the Isoko speaking clans of Emevo, Oue, and Okpe. From them it later spread to Ogo, Agbarha, and Iyede....
>
> In 1912 the clerk of the native court of Uzere, a Jekri by nation, who was a Christian, used to gather the boys and young men of Uzere around him of an evening, teach them Bible stories and simple hymns, and give them instruction in the Christian Faith. As a result a small Christian congregation was formed. From Uzere it spread to the rest of the clan"[19] (including Aviara, mentioned above).

At a period such as this, when people are ripe for change, Christianity can spread rapidly within a clan or other social unit. People see relatives, fellow society members, and others become Christian with happy results and they are made more receptive to the gospel. Christians should be taught to cultivate these opportunities by consistent Christian living and witnessing within their intimate associations. The potential for church growth in this way is especially high in the early stages of a new movement. Though Christians should not limit their evangelistic efforts exclusively to their

[19] Hubbard, *op. cit.*, pp. 276-283.

own family and social groups, they should lay heavy emphasis here. As Christianity spreads in one family or social group, others become interested and more receptive.

In several cases Christianity was not welcomed by the village elders and converts were persecuted. Sometimes Christians were forced to leave their village and go to found a new Christian village. It was during this rapid expansion of Christianity that the Church Missionary Society missionaries realized that a great movement was on foot and began to occupy the area and assist the movement. Walker wrote that an experienced missionary was sent, and the people flocked from every quarter to hear his message. In a few years a hundred towns and villages in the Isoko country had built churches and a score of young men were being trained as evangelists and teachers. The opportunity was so promising that a second missionary was sent. Ill health forced one to retire and the other died of blackwater fever. Two more were sent in 1927 but soon shared the same fate as the first two.

> In his plea for reinforcements the bishop wrote, "During the last ten years (and more especially the last seven), a great mass movement has taken place in the Isoko country. There are now in the comparatively small area (a thirty-mile radius with no large cities) one hundred four churches, many of them very large ones. The churches alone have over 2,600 regular adherents, and the total is about 20,000. At Ozora, at morning and evening prayers, every day in the week, there is an average of nine hundred attending, and more on Sundays. Aviara, the same, and up to 1,500 on Sundays. Uzere has nearly as many; and other churches have very large attendances. Yet the whole missionary strength is one man at home invalided. When a missionary goes round, he is literally besieged morning, noon, and night. In order that he may get his meals, it is not infrequently necessary to get some people to make a sort of cordon round the house to keep the folk off for awhile."[20]

Soon there were large numbers of reversions. When the people found that they could with impunity grow cassava,

[20] Walker, *op. cit.*, pp. 216-218.

and when they were faced with the moral demands of this new faith on their lives, many returned to paganism but did not give up growing cassava. Much of this loss might have been averted had the mission been able to move enough missionaries and Nigerian pastors and catechists here from other areas to create an adequate Christian Urhobo and Isoko leadership soon. "People movements" can be lost through lack of spiritual care. When people move in large numbers toward Christianity, an extremely active and careful follow-up program is essential or one of two things will happen. There will be tremendous loss through reversion or there will result a very watered-down form of semi-Christianity through syncretism with the previous religious beliefs and practices. The great Urhobo and Isoko people movements were not lost but they were badly eroded. In spite of considerable reversions and the failure of the Church Missionary Society properly to staff the area, Anglicans gained a firm foothold, and the graph shows beyond doubt that larger numbers of people came into the Church than left.

While the Church grew rapidly in the Niger area (the Eastern Region and the Midwest, it grew slowly elsewhere in Nigeria. The 1957 communicant membership of 105,308 can be broken down as follows: 33,000 Yoruba, 1,000 Northern Region, and 71,000 Niger. The alarming thing about this is the fact that Anglicans reported 30,237 communicants in Yorubaland in 1940. This means that little growth has taken place since then. The Niger churches reported 32,907 in 1940 and more than doubled in seventeen years by 1957, while the Yoruba churches stood still. Admittedly the population is greater in the Niger mission area, but the percentage of the population that is Christian is lower in Yorubaland than in the Eastern Region. Large numbers await conversion to Christianity throughout Southern Nigeria.

The late Rt. Rev. A. W. Howells, Bishop of Lagos, in his address to the fifteenth Synod of the Lagos Diocese in 1962, expressed alarm at the decline of church growth. While recognizing the great importance of Christian education and literacy, he laid major stress on the need for trained clergymen who would remain as vicars and not yield to the pressure to become teachers and administrators in the rapidly expanding school system in Nigeria. Agreeing with the bishop that this is a very urgent need, but knowing how well-pastored churches both east and west become static, the author would urge that both the clergy and lay leaders of the Church be trained to spread the gospel through the web of kin, clan, trade, and other natural relationships. Thus every Christian should seek to enlist for Jesus Christ all those with whom he has regular contact, whether through kinship, social or business relations, or whatever.

Methodist

The author found it impossible to graph the Methodist growth prior to 1933 when a merging of Wesleyan, Primitive, and United Methodists in England also brought a merging of the Wesleyan and Primitive Methodist missionary societies in Nigeria. Available records for the Primitive Methodist Society before then are very incomplete and Wesleyan statistics often include areas in Dahomey until 1925. However, it is clear that the Wesleyans before the merger as compared to the Primitive Methodist Society had a very poor record of growth. The Wesleyans entered Nigeria at Badagry and Abeokuta in 1842. From the 1840s to the 1880s the Methodist committee in London repeatedly warned Freeman and others not to expand due to the Methodist split in England resulting in little funds and staff. The Primitive Methodist Society began work in the Eastern Region in 1893. Notice their respective communicants (full members) in the following table.

YEAR	WESLEYANS	P. M. S.	Source of Statistics
1899	2,685	88	Knight, p. 123
1918	6,563	3,413	Knight, p. 172
1925	10,004	5,523	Methodist Missionary Society, London
1932	7,646	12,277	Methodist Missionary Society, London

The Wesleyans had a communicant membership of 10,004 in 1925 but declined steadily to 7,046 in 1932. For the next ten years after the merger there was almost no Methodist growth anywhere in Nigeria.

This failure to grow was mainly a result of an over-emphasis on humanitarian service and spreading enlightenment, and an under-emphasis on evangelizing. Education became the doorway to the Church and thus limited the potential and slowed the process. Walker points out that a new secretary of the Wesleyan Missionary Society took office in 1900 with responsibility for the West African field. He was Rev. W. H. Findlay, who had served for eighteen years in South India, where before 1900 there had been much greater development of institutional work. This reflected the feeling of the Committee that the time had come for similar developments in the West African districts. After his first visit to the field, he made the following proposals that were approved by the Committee and carried out in the years following as staff and finances made them possible.

(1) A training institute was urgently needed to supply catechists and teachers. (The implication of this lack of a training school for catechists and teachers after sixty years of mission work is astounding and shows a similar weakness to that of the Baptists during most of this same period). (2) The Lagos high school should be strengthened. (3) Missionary women should be appointed to take charge of girls' boarding schools. (4) Medical missions should be established to deal with physical suffering and strike a blow against fetish priests. (5) Better housing and medical care should be provided for the missionaries.[21]

Walker wrote in 1942 concerning Methodists in the Western Region only,

> During the past 20 years more than 22,000 adult converts have received Christian baptism — always after a period of training and testing. It is required, for example, that the candidate for baptism shall be able to read in Yoruba — unless too old to learn to read. There is no indiscriminate baptism of people who respond to an emotional appeal. Catechumens receive careful and regular instruction in the Christian faith and practice, and there are large numbers who for one reason or another are never baptized. Some find "The Way" too difficult; others make too little progress; and

[21] Walker, F. Deaville, *A Hundred Years in Nigeria,* pp. 113-114.

> there are others who are entangled by polygamy or some other social evil and cannot be baptized – though they may regularly attend the services, contribute to the funds, and otherwise seek to follow Christian teaching.[22]

He states that there were over 22,000 adult baptisms during these twenty years in the Western Region alone and the statistics tell us that at the end of these twenty years there were only 21,541 full members in all of Nigeria. Since the majority of these 21,541 full members were in the Eastern Region, and since there were 11,843 full members already in the Western Region before these 22,000 adult baptisms, there was enormous loss in bringing converts to full membership, even allowing for sizeable error in the figures reported. The fact that "literacy in Yoruba" was required and that "some find 'The Way' too difficult" and "others make too little progress" may indicate that more emphasis was placed on "civilizing" than on "converting."

Perhaps these policies were based on the assumption that Nigeria was going to remain as a British dependency for a very long time, during which most of the educated would become Christian and then gradually Christianity would filter down to the masses and they would rise into a middle-class educated status that would enable them to be Christians. If some such assumption did not lie in the background of thinking, how could these devout Christian leaders have planned for all Nigeria to become churched? Whatever the background, in this new day when the overlordship of a "Christian" power has disappeared and the proletariat rises, the survival of small educated minorities of Christians is assured only if they now spread the faith rapidly to the rest of the people.

Walker concluded his book (1942) with a statement that must have reflected the attitude and policy of the mission.

> For the present, the supreme task is that of thorough training – larger and more efficient provision for training teachers, pastors, evangelists, ministers; the training of boys and girls in our schools, and the more careful training of Christians in our churches. Until, in the not distant future, the

[22] *Ibid.*, p. 133.

> whole Methodist Church in Western Nigeria, strong and devoted to its Redeemer and Lord, shall be mobilized for its supreme task — the evangelization of the yet unreached multitude within its own borders.[23]

Twenty years later the Methodist Church has still to break out of its educational fortress in a campaign to evangelize the "yet unreached multitudes."

One of the brighter pages in Methodist mission history was their early successful church planting in Ijebuland. Repeated attempts had been made by Methodists and others to establish a mission there but the warlike Ijebus had resisted and even threatened to kill any missionaries who passed through their country. In 1891 the British government in Lagos sent an ultimatum to the Ijebu chiefs and a treaty was signed by them to open the roads to safe travel. When the treaty was not honored, troops were sent and the king of Ijebu Ode was captured. Resistance ceased. The Methodist churches in Lagos decided this was the time to enter Ijebuland. A mission party was chosen to investigate and among the party was the Ijebu Prince Ademuyiwa Haastrup, a close relative to the king of Shagamu. They gained audience with the king and were given permission to begin mission work in his city. Other villages under this king were also visited.

Thomas Champness, a former Wesleyan missionary who had tried 30 years before to open the Ijebu tribe to Christianity, had now formed an organization in England called the Joyful News Evangelists with the purpose of sending missionaries to work with the Wesleyans in Nigeria. Three of these missionaries arrived in time to join the men from Lagos in beginning the Ijebu mission. Walker describes the approach made to the Ijebu leaders.

> At least 1,500 people listened while Prince Ademuyiwa — a prince of their own royal house — preached to them in their Yoruba mother tongue . . . they explained the object of their coming that all might hear it. It was most important at the very outset to remove all suspicion that they had any political or military motive. The chief's official speaker came

[23] *Ibid.*, p. 138.

> forward, and kneeling before the Oloja (chief) poured forth a long oration about what the missionaries were expected *not* to do. He spoke of the old established customs of the country, their system of family slavery, their mode of punishing criminals, and their treaties with the Lagos government, and he begged that the missionaries would not interfere with these. Mr. Roe replied that missionaries are not political agents, and do not interfere with the government of the country; if they think they can see better ways of doing things, they talk about it to the king and his councillors. One thing they would not countenance – human sacrifice, and if any such were offered they would publish it to the whole world to the deep disgrace of the Ijebu nation. The Oloja and his chiefs were satisfied; they gave to the mission a very large site for a church and mission house for a catechist, and very soon nearly three hundred men were at work upon it, clearing it and preparing the foundation.[24]

For a few months there was much opposition by the fetish priests but the Shagamu king remained true to his promise of support for the newly founded mission and the opposition died down. "Within three years of its foundation (about 1891), the Ijebu mission had 7 churches, two ministers, eight lay workers, 58 full members, 219 catechumens, 362 scholars, and nearly 2,000 people regularly attending public worship."[25] What a tragedy to note the later decline of this good beginning! In 1925 the Ijebu circuit had 713 full members. They then gradually declined to 533 in 1932. This is the very period of the beginnings of the Church of the Lord with headquarters in Ijebuland (see Chapter IV).

The Methodist church at Ilesha also began through family ties. A man from Ilesha, who had been in Sierra Leone and Lagos and there came in contact with Christianity, became king of Ilesha in 1895. Ademuyiwa (the same man related to the Ijebu king) was closely related to the new Ilesha king through his mother. The new king's daughter was a devoted Christian. The new king agreed to carry on certain pagan customs that he considered necessary as king but refused to live in the palace for it was a veritable temple of the

[24] *Ibid.*, pp. 98-99.
[25] *Ibid.*, p. 102.

heathen gods. He opened his city to missionaries and his daughter became a Sunday school teacher. Methodists began work with Rev. H. Atundaolu, an Ilesha man of the Ijesha clan, who had been captured in his boyhood and taken as a slave to Abeokuta, where he later became a Christian and entered the ministry. Other Ijesha clansmen in Lagos had long encouraged the introduction of Christianity into their home country and had contributed toward it. Thus Christianity flowed to Ilesha (the main town of the Ijesha people) through family connections with Christians living in other cities, and, as in Ijebu, received very helpful support from a friendly king who was influenced by Christian relatives.

Returning to the graph (page 317), the reader will see a significant rise in Methodist communicants since just after the beginning of World War II. By this time a number of well-trained and capable Nigerian clergy had arisen and the mission staff was reduced because of the war. So indigenous control proceeded at a rapid pace. In 1953 Parrinder indicated that Nigerian Methodists had attained a large measure of self-government.[26] This reduced the stigma of white man's religion and opened the way for a freer flow of Christianity through the web of natural relationships.

Perhaps related to the reduction of missionary staff was a dangerous trend pointed out by Parrinder. "Formerly Methodists claimed the highest general standard of education for ministers, but this has sadly declined in recent years. At the time of writing [1953] there is no ministerial Methodist training in Yoruba country (two ordinands have gone to the Eastern Provinces). Catechist training is only now being revived after total neglect for years."[27] It is essential that church leadership, both lay and clergy, be trained, and that their training include a strong emphasis on planting and growing churches. National ministers and catechists need to know how churches multiply in their kind of society and get busy multiplying them.

Calabar Province, a small area of 6,245 square miles in

[26] Parrinder, *op. cit.*, p. 93.
[27] *Ibid.*, p. 94.

southeastern Nigeria, had a 1961 population of 1,540,000. It has been the scene of the multiplication of denominations. Only a few of the more important of these will be discussed here. The first three missions to enter Calabar (Presbyterian, Qua Iboe, and Primitive Methodist) have since worked in close harmony and with comity agreements assigning certain areas to each mission.

Presbyterian

Scottish Presbyterians opened work in Calabar in 1847. They have sought from the beginning to build indigenous churches. In 1954 the Scottish mission dissolved and the European ordained missionaries became ministers of the Presbyterian Church of Eastern Nigeria, no longer ministers of their home Church of Scotland.[28] After a very poor rate of growth from 1933-1957 there has been a twenty-percent increase in the communicant membership of the Presbyterian Church during the last five years, since the change to complete self-control in 1954. The statistics show that in spite of the emphasis on developing an indigenous Church, the growth of this Church has been far too small in an area where other Churches have grown at a much more rapid pace. The author has been unable to gather sufficient information to analyze the causes of this poor growth. Further study on this by the Presbyterian Church with the purpose of greatly increasing sound church growth would be highly rewarding. The statistics for this Church as found in the *Missionary Atlas* and the *World Christian Handbook* are:

Year	1911	1925	1938	1949	1952	1957	1963
Communicants	295	7,694	12,204	13,500	10,908	12,232	15,316

Qua Iboe

In 1887 the Qua Iboe mission entered Calabar in the following manner. Several traders of the Ibunu tribe, a few miles west of Calabar town on the Qua Iboe River, visited Calabar to trade. There they learned of Christianity and when they returned home one of the traders began classes for instruction that he called "God Palavers." He wrote to the Pres-

[28] McFarlan, Donald M., *Calabar,* p. 175.

byterian missionary in Calabar asking for a missionary. The letter was forwarded on to Grattan Guinness of Harley College, London, who read the letter at the college. Samuel A. Bill offered to go in response to the request. Guinness paid his travel with the hope that he could make his own livelihood by trading after arrival in Nigeria. Bill arrived in 1887 and went to the Church of Scotland mission in Calabar for information as to where the Ibunu people lived. He began work along the Qua Iboe river by teaching the alphabet to young people and holding services on Sunday with the help of an English-speaking trader named Williams. He was unable to care for himself financially and had to appeal to friends in Ireland for help. In 1888 Bill was joined by A. Baillie, who before leaving Ireland helped organize a group for the support of the mission under the name Qua Iboe Missionary Association. In 1890 an interdenominational council was formed with headquarters at Belfast and the Qua Iboe Mission was born. The Qua Iboe Mission, like the Presbyterians, has sought from the beginning to build indigenous churches. In 1908 the Qua Iboe council passed a resolution "that all native work should find its support from native sources."[29] Their statistics from the World Christian Handbooks reveal a greater growth than the Presbyterians, but a similar pattern with a drop in the late 1940s and a plateau of no growth from 1933 through 1963. This was the period when the Church of Christ began phenomenal growth in this area. The statistics for Qua Iboe are:

Year	1911	1925	1938	1949	1952	1957	1963
Communicants	245	8,996	41,738	35,000	34,811	35,580	42,692

In Calabar during the twentieth century a large number of "Divers Sects" have sprung up. The Rev. T. A. Adejunmobi, general secretary of the Christian Council of Nigeria, said of them, they are "deeply evangelistic and quasi-zionist. Their creeds, doctrines, and practices are strange conglomerations of those of the established Churches. Leadership in a few instances is comprised of megalomaniacs, and in most

[29] McKeown, Robert L., *Twenty-five Years in Qua Iboe,* p. 90.

of them, of religious fanatics. I feel this movement provides a challenge for leadership training and a specially directed support."[30] Most of these groups have sought aid from and/or affiliation with denominations in other countries and some have been successful. Thus the Lutherans began in the 1930s (described in Chapter III).

Church of Christ

Thus also began the Church of Christ in 1947. Mr. Eugene Peden, one of the first missionaries of this group to work in Nigeria gives the following account of their beginning: After World War II, a Mr. C. A. O. Essien from Calabar Province wrote to the International Correspondence Bureau, a social correspondence club encouraging people of various nations to correspond with each other. From them he acquired information concerning a Bible correspondence course offered by Lawrence Avenue Church of Christ in Nashville, Tennessee. He took the course, and starting a class, he also taught the course to about twelve others. Under Essien's leadership his class began to establish congregations among the Efik and Ibo-speaking people of Calabar and nearby Ibo country. Within the first three years they had 10,000 converts, some from "other religious groups, such as the Church of Scotland, Methodist and the Spiritualist movement, but a great part was converted from pagan worship."[31]

In 1950 two white missionaries from South Africa visited to see what Essien was doing and make plans for the future. In 1952 missionaries were sent from Lawrence Avenue Church of Christ and since then a foreign staff of from six to ten has been kept on the field. In 1950 they reported 158 churches with 10,000 members. In 1955 they reported 200 churches with 20,000 members and in 1962 they reported 475 congregations with 30,000 members. These round numbers suggest that they are estimates rather than accurate statistics, but nevertheless they show phenomenal growth during a time when Presbyterians and Qua Iboes were standing still.

30 Adejunmobi (personal letter).
31 Peden, Eugene, personal letter to the author, January 20, 1963.

Peden attributed this growth to the following:

> (a) We placed the responsibility of preaching on the national preachers. (b) We supported some of the better preachers so they could give full time to evangelism. (c) We conducted many classes for teachers and leaders of the congregations. (d) Each congregation enjoyed self-rule while the American missionaries would instruct, but never took the oversight. We praised them when they made progress. (e) We offered the Bible as the only creed book. The people were interested in studying the Bible and always asked, "What does the Bible say?" (f) Preachers trained for three years in the Bible school were prepared to preach to demand attention.[32]

The Church of Christ emphasis has been on (1) evangelism and church planting, (2) training both laymen and pastors to preach for the purpose of bringing decision, (3) a clearcut system of sharing what the Bible says about baptism, church government, and the like, (4) indigenous control, and (5) converting people to the Church of Christ position from both the pagan population and from other denominations. The first three points give them their growth potential. The last two have brought them many members who were either unacceptable in established Churches, or not content with the teachings or practices of these Churches.

Mennonite

In 1959 the Mennonite missionaries entered Calabar Province under somewhat similar circumstances, but with a very different approach. A group of fifty churches, calling themselves Mennonite churches, invited missionaries from America. Edwin and Irene Weaver were the first to be sent. They found that these churches had splintered from established denominations of the country.[33] Many had split from older denominations because, "they will allow us only one wife, and we need more in order to have enough women to work our farms."[34] Each village wanted its own school, hospital, and

[32] *Ibid.*

[33] Weaver, Edwin and Irene, "The Uyo Story, Part I," *Gospel Herald,* Vol. LV, no. 34 (August 28, 1962), 768-769.

[34] Weaver, Edwin and Irene, "The Uyo Story, Part II," *Gospel Herald,* Vol. LV, no. 35 (September 4, 1962), 781, 887.

mission. Each village wanted the prestige of a white man living there. Some of the "Mennonite" churches were much more pagan than Christian and merely wanted affiliation with a known Christian denomination for prestige and financial help. They "wanted the benefits of a religion without accepting the religion."[35] These same "Mennonite" churches had previously identified themselves with other denominations, which in turn sent them missionaries. But each time when the people failed to conform to the standards of the Church, the missionaries left.

The Mennonite missionaries decided that: (1) It would be very unwise to set low moral standards and accept responsibility for churches or individuals who had left their mother denomination because of requirements for membership. Many of the original fifty churches were therefore never accepted by them. (2) Since it would be unwise to give direct financial aid to individuals and churches, to set up an executive committee of a loose conference of churches and make it responsible for the central funds that came from mission subsidy and local-congregation support. Each congregation is to contribute one pound ($2.80) per month. (3) The missionaries should establish immediate friendship and cooperation with the older denominations in the area, even to the point of helping to staff some of the Presbyterian schools and medical institutions, rather than opening competing institutions.[36] Since the entrance of these missionaries is so recent (1959), no figures are yet available to show growth or lack of it.

Assemblies of God

In 1930 from an unknown source a copy of "Pentecostal Evangel," an Assemblies of God news magazine, found its way into Iboland.[37] It was read and a group of people were stirred by the accounts of the sick being healed and believers baptized in the Holy Spirit. They read their Bibles and prayed for the same experience. God answered their prayers

[35] Weaver, Edwin and Irene, "The Uyo Story, Part III," *Gospel Herald,* Vol. LV, no. 36 (September 11, 1962), 804-805.

[36] Weaver, Irene, "The Uyo Story, Part VI," *Gospel Herald,* Vol. LVI, No. 6 (February 5, 1963), pp. 124-125.

[37] Carmichael, Christine, "Nigeria," p. 4.

and they began to go from place to place preaching to all who would listen. Several small churches were organized, and they sought help from the Assemblies of God in America. In response to this appeal a survey was made of the field and Rev. and Mrs. Everett Phillips arrived to begin work in Nigeria in 1939. The following year they established a Bible school for training national workers. By 1961 there was a missionary staff of 46 working with 377 Nigerian ministers, pastors and lay leaders among 460 churches, and 7,401 communicants.

Now look at the graph at the beginning of this chapter. There was a rather slow start with only 1,319 communicants at the end of the first 12 years. However, when compared to the much longer period that it took the missions to reach this number in the previous century, this was a very fast start. It shows that a new day had dawned in Nigerian missions. Christianity was respectable and even prestigious in much of Southern Nigeria. From 1951 to 1955 the Assemblies enjoyed a 400-percent increase. The sharp dip in the graph from 1955 to 1959 is the result of incomplete reports to board headquarters, from whence these statistics came. For the decade of 1951 to 1961 the graph shows a 600-percent increase in communicants, a healthy rate of growth. However, notice the leveling out on the graph from 1959 to 1961. One wonders whether the time, effort, and financial drive involved in building and opening a high school during these years has been a major cause in producing this plateau in the graph by lessening the emphasis on evangelism and by increasing the financial obligations of the members.

The Sunday school enrollment in 1961 was 33,204 and the total number of believers was 19,415. These figures compared to the communicant membership of 7,401 indicate rather strict rules regulating the admission of members and show a far greater strength than the communicant membership would imply.

Rev. E. Phillips, now the board secretary for Africa, gave the following reasons for rapid growth among these churches: (1) An intensive Bible school program training nationals for the ministry has been carried on since 1940. In 1961 there were four Bible schools with 227 students. (2) The churches have been self-supporting from the beginning. From 1940 to 1942 some financial aid came from the mission. Since that time both churches and schools have been entirely supported by the Nigerians. (3) Nigerian leadership has been used from the beginning in governing both the local churches and the central executive committee. In 1962 there was only one missionary on the executive committee and many local, divisional, and area councils were entirely Nigerian. (4) The twenty-two elementary schools and one high school receive no aid from the mission, except three missionaries to help staff them. (5) A weekly radio broadcast attracts a response of 140 letters a week and enlists people in a Bible correspondence course that had over 10,000 enrolled in 1962. (6) The churches and leaders are deeply spiritual and committed to Christ.[38]

Recognizing the importance of all these factors, special comment should be made on the sixth point. The deep spirituality of these people has two major causes: (1) great emphasis on Bible study, the power of prayer, and evangelism, and (2) the complete integration of the spiritual with every part of daily life. This fits the cultural tradition of the people and is too often neglected by some of the older missions and Churches. Religion is very much involved in the daily activities of life for a Nigerian before he becomes Christian. When he becomes Christian, his new faith must be thoroughly integrated into his complete life and thought. The emphasis placed by the Assemblies of God upon the real power of prayer, the indwelling of the Holy Spirit in the lives of people, and God's concern and involvement in men's everyday activities, makes their message harmonious with the traditional Nigerian thought.

Christian Council of Nigeria

In 1929 the United Missionary Council for education was formed. At their first meeting the council also considered matters of missionary policy. In 1930 the original idea of an education council for Southern Nigeria grew into a much more

[38] Phillips, Everett L., personal letter to the author, October 15, 1962.

comprehensive scheme for a Christian Council for the whole of Nigeria and the name was changed to the Christian Council of Nigeria. The original members of this body were the Methodists, Anglicans, American Baptists, Qua Iboe, and Church of Scotland. Others who have joined since are Salvation Army, Sudan United Mission, Church of Christ in the Sudan. This organization has great influence in Nigeria and has done much to make Christian ideals known and respected in Nigerian society.

Church Union

As early as 1911 a meeting held at Calabar in which representatives of the Church Missionary Society, United Free Church (Presbyterian), Primitive Methodist, and Qua Iboe missions "resolved that the aim of all missionary effort should be the establishment of ONE Church of Christ in Southern Nigeria."[39] Since then the Anglicans, Presbyterians and Methodists have been strong advocates for church union among the Protestant denominations in Nigeria. Baptists and some others have opposed the idea. If it could be effectively demonstrated that church union would aid church growth, there would be a very strong case in its favor. But if it would simply produce a union of static Churches, there would be no gain at all. Lack of the incentive of competition might even retard efforts to enlist the unchurched population. The wide range of church growth among the various Churches in Nigeria indicates many avenues open to exploration to those concerned with increasing sound church growth in the receptive populations of Southern Nigeria.

Hidden within the story of the growth of each of these missions and the resulting Churches can be seen glimpses of some of the causes of growth and/or failure. From the lessons learned in this way, pitfalls to avoid and new paths to tread can be seen as earnest Christians exercise every means at their disposal to bring people to know Jesus as Lord and Master. The joint victory of the evangelical Churches is impressive. They should take courage from each other and press on.

[39] McKeown, *op. cit.*, p. 101.

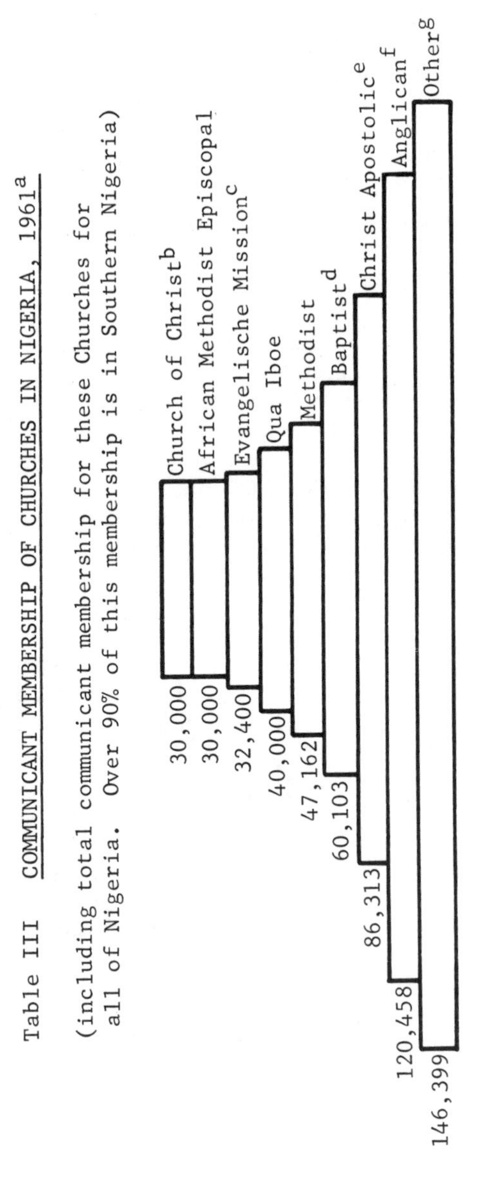

Table III COMMUNICANT MEMBERSHIP OF CHURCHES IN NIGERIA, 1961[a]

(including total communicant membership for these Churches for all of Nigeria. Over 90% of this membership is in Southern Nigeria)

Except where otherwise stated, these statistics were taken from *World Christian Handbook,* Coxill and Grubb, World Dominion Press, London, 1962.

a. Total communicant membership shown in this table – 561,522. Total estimated population of Southern Nigeria – 15,000,000.

b. Statistics from Eugene Peden, Lawrence Avenue Church of Christ, 904 Lawrence Ave., Nashville, Tennessee. This church is sponsor of Church of Christ mission in Nigeria.

c. Evangelische Missions-Gesellschaft in Basel (co-operating with Presbyterian Church of Eastern Nigeria).

d. Statistics from Minutes of the Nigerian Baptist Convention, 1962, with adjustment to delete statistics from Ghana and add statistics for churches not reporting in 1962. For these churches not reporting statistics for the latest previous year were used.

e. Statistics reported by the Christ Apostolic Church secretariat to the Western Nigeria Broadcasting Corporation.

f. Church of the Province of West Africa (Anglican): including Diocese of Lagos, Ibadan, Ondo-Benin, Northern Nigeria, Niger, Niger Delta, and Owerri.

g. Includes statistics for Churches reporting communicant membership from 27 to 19,321. This does not include membership for independent Churches such as Aladura and others because these figures are not available.

Chapter VI. Future Church Growth

THE REAL VALUE OF ANY STUDY OF CHURCH GROWTH IN THE past is its application to the present and future. Based upon the background presented in the first five chapters of this book, what are the possibilities of church growth in Southern Nigeria?

Receptivity

A study of the present receptivity of the people reveals enormous church growth potential. The first paragraph in Chapter V shows that from seven to ten million people in Southern Nigeria are unwilling to be called anything but Christian, although there are less than one million countable communicants among all Evangelical Churches (see Table III). Roman Catholics claim 1,471,925 members and 456,770 catechumens, a total of just under two million adherents in Southern Nigeria.[1] So the Evangelical Churches have a reservoir of from four to seven million nominal Christians, not including Roman Catholics, to bring into full membership. This is a highly receptive population. Its members have already declared themselves to be "Christian" as opposed to Moslem or pagan.

Well over half of these are children. Each new generation needs conversion. Otherwise the Christian movement will revert or degenerate into nominalism. To be "born Christian" and reared by Christian parents is not enough. Every person must have his own vital personal commitment to Jesus Christ as Lord if he is to be truly Christian. This process is illustrated in the following testimony given to the author by a girl from Enugu.

> I was born in a Christian home but when I grew up to about ten years old, I learned from the sermon of Pastor Princewell that my father's and mother's faith would not save me.

[1] *Nigerian Catholic Directory,* 1962.

> I asked my friend with whom I came to church that Sunday to explain to me what the pastor meant. She explained further to me what it meant to be a Christian. The next Sunday in the church we sang the hymn, "Give of Your Best to the Master." I was greatly impressed and after the service I went to the pastor and said, "Please, good pastor, tell me the best I can give to the Master." He answered, "My child, I am not good but Christ is good, and you can surrender your life to Him. That is the best you can give to the Master." The third Sunday an invitation was given by the pastor at the end of the service and I confessed Christ as my personal Saviour.

Many children, born in Christian homes, are brought to decision and personal commitment to Christ through the guidance of parents, friends, pastors, or others in less dramatic circumstances. The fact that in many places the growth of the Church is slower than the population increase is evidence that other children, though born in Christian homes, are never brought to personal commitment and are gradually lost from the Christian family. Too often this occurs because Christian people neglect to reap this most highly receptive harvest.

However, efforts at "perfecting" the nominal Christian population and the children of Christians must not lead to the neglect of evangelism among the present pagan population. It is highly significant that between 1900 and 1960 nearly half of an almost completely pagan population has become nominally Christian. The great prestige that Christianity has gained will continue to open new doors into the pagan reservoir. Receptivity is not uniform at all places at the same time (note Ijebu in Chapter V). Doors must be entered in strength and with purpose when they open. The Churches must be alert to this and constant evangelism on the popular level through relations of kinship, friendship, trade, and social societies will result in an especially intense harvest as individuals and pockets of people become ripe for conversion.

Bishop Samuel Crowther is best known for his effective leadership along the Niger. But his short ministry in Yorubaland among his own people cannot be forgotten. The doors were opened in Abeokuta when ex-slaves, who had become Christians in Sierra Leone, returned home to tell their friends and kinsmen of their new-found faith. It was in this setting in Abeokuta that Crowther won his first convert in Nigeria, his mother.[2]

In 1853 Crowther returned to Ketu, his home town, with Bible in hand to preach to *his people.* He proposed that both the king and the people should receive Christ as their God. The king replied, "Ketu is entirely left open to you; do whatsoever you like in it, and bring whomever you think proper. We will receive them with both hands."[3] The doors were opened wide and Crowther found a ready response among his relatives and clansmen.

In the nineteenth century these open doors were all too few; and when they did open, dedicated Christians with natural bridges of contact were often lacking. The possibilities of church growth today in Nigeria would seem fantastic to the missionaries and national Christians who witnessed faithfully in a generally unresponsive field during the nineteenth century.

In 1962 the author made a survey among 136 Anglican churches and 48 Baptist churches in Benin and Delta Provinces. It revealed multiple bridges of contact with a wide range of the population. In over 90% of these churches the membership was from most sections of the villages and towns. These church members lived with non-Christian relatives and friends. Some sections of the towns were already mostly Christian. Others had a Christian minority living there. These bridges of contact must be used as channels in spreading the gospel. Christian people living in their own society and witnessing among their own people have far greater potential for church increase than large numbers of foreign missionaries or financial aid. How different this is from a mission station where individual converts came for refuge in the nineteenth century!

In most villages today Christians suffer no indignities and are deprived of no advantages enjoyed by other inhabitants.

[2] Page, *The Black Bishop,* p. 92.
[3] *Ibid.,* p. 115.

Christians are respected as never before. When asked if the people of the town respected the churches, 176 out of 226 Baptist members in 48 towns and 483 out of 614 Anglicans in 136 towns, said yes. The Governor of the Eastern Region, His Excellency Sir Francis Ibiam, is a ruling elder in the Presbyterian Church. The King of Ibadan (Olubadan), the largest city in West Africa, is a leader of the Christ Apostolic Church in Nigeria. Many of the traditional rulers, political leaders, and government officials are active Christians in the various denominations. The very respectability and prestige of Christianity demands that now, while the doors are open, Christians act to bring people to a saving knowledge of Jesus Christ.

In the villages where these 48 Baptist and 136 Anglican churches are located, the author gathered information and opinions from 533 people who are not members of these churches. One hundred said they are Christians belonging to other denominations. The information gathered from these 533 people is highly significant as to their receptivity to the gospel: 372 of them come from mostly Christian families; 498 think it is good to have churches in their town; 488 want the churches to grow; 264 are not satisfied with the present growth of the churches; 395 want their whole village or town to be Christian; 242 (56% of the non-Christians) said they would like to be church members.

When asked why they were not members, the 433 non-Christians gave many answers: I am too old. The devil has hold of me. I am the oldest member of my family and responsible for the ancestral shrine. I am all right with my own religion. Everyone cannot be of the same religion; there must be an opposition. I was sick and a native doctor cured me. The church members do not set a good example. The church law is too hard for me to follow. (Surprisingly, only a few mentioned polygamy, though this was, no doubt, a cause for several others not being members.) The church contribution is too much. No one has talked to me about this.

Most of these answers were honestly given and deserve careful consideration by the Churches. These 433 non-Christians represent multitudes throughout Southern Nigeria who have a high respect for Christianity, who want churches to grow, and many of whom desire to become Christians themselves. How could a population be more receptive?.

How Nigerians Become Christians

In such a highly receptive population how can the potentially responsive be reached and enlisted? An anthropological and sociological study of the people concerned sheds much light at this point. Some of the principles helping us decide on an effective course of action are:

(1) Southern Nigerians have very close personal attachments between blood and marriage kin. People from the same village or section of town and members of the same society, association, or guild know each other intimately and have a high consciousness of kind. Markets have important social as well as economic functions. They often form a network of inter-village as well as intra-village relationships that can be valuable avenues of disseminating the gospel. These attachments and relationships between Christian and non-Christian are the most effective bridges of contact available to Christian evangelism. They are down-to-earth, natural, purely indigenous relationships within society.

Illustrating the flow of Christianity along these natural avenues of contact is the spread of the Church through kinship connections in Ekiti (Chapter V) and in Sapele (Chapter V); through trade connections from Buguma (Chapter III) and by Crowther along the Niger (Chapter II).

(2) Keith Hamilton concluded from his study *Church Growth in the High Andes* that "Churches made up of the people of one homogeneous unit grow better than those made up of several. Church growth is more rapid and healthier when it occurs in some one homogeneous unit."[4] He defined a homogeneous unit as a society whose members are bound together by a sense of kind or a tribal consciousness.

This statement will meet with instant indignation by some Christians because it seems to ignore the Christian ideal of oneness in Christ of all nations and tribes and peoples. However, recognition that the close personal ties of family, clan, and tribe are the most fertile avenues for spreading the gos-

[4] Hamilton, Keith E., *Church Growth in the High Andes*, p. 116.

pel does not imply bigotry or attitudes of superiority toward others. Indeed the church doors must be open to all who would enter. At the same time the advantages of high receptivity within homogeneous units must not be ignored. When churches can be formed of people who already have close personal ties, then in becoming Christians, they are not socially dislocated. Non-Christian friends and relatives recognize the church as a part of their society and not a threat to their solidarity. Their language and forms of expression can be employed. The people "feel at home" in this church.

This principle is illustrated by church growth patterns in Port Harcourt in Eastern Nigeria. The city was created with the establishment of a seaport and government center. People of many of the tribes of Nigeria migrated there to work but did not consider Port Harcourt their home.

The one Baptist church there includes members from many tribes. Students from the Baptist high school form over half the congregation when school is in session. Because of these two factors the services are conducted in English. And thus they attract only the better-educated detribalized population. This church has had very little growth.

Methodists and Anglicans each have two congregations in Port Harcourt. Each of these congregations is dominated by people from one of the several tribes and services are usually in the language of that tribe, though others are welcome to attend and may become members. These churches have grown, each within a homogeneous unit. Can they therefore be said to be less Christian than the Baptist church, which has no feature that would appeal more to one tribe than to another?

(3) A strong system of seniority reinforces both authority and responsibility. Much attention is given to meeting the approval of those who are senior. Chiefs and even family heads traditionally have religious as well as temporal authority and responsibility. This means that the conversion of, or at least the respect and friendship of, the older generation is essential to major church growth. True, the conversion of the chief and elders will not automatically bring a whole village to Christ. Nor does inability to convert them doom

evangelism to total failure. But winning their respect and friendship is an inestimable aid in persuading those under them to follow Jesus Christ as Lord.

Note in Chapter II how schools and medical institutions won the friendship of chiefs and elders and became effective instruments of evangelism and training. See also the important place in spreading Christianity played by King Pepple in Bonny (Chapter II), Prince Ademuyiwa in Ijebu (Chapter V), and the king and his daughter in Ilesha (Chapter V).

(4) Decisions affecting the group are usually arrived at through discussion among senior members of the group until general agreement is found. Then the decisions are announced by the head men and the whole group is expected to abide by them. People acting separately and apart from the group may or may not be subjected to disciplinary action, but are certainly not looked upon with favor. They have threatened the solidarity and security of the group. Thus if through group decision individuals or subgroups are permitted to leave their former gods and follow Jesus, then Christianity becomes an accepted and natural part of the society. Its spread is far more likely than if it comes in as a foreign element challenging the cohesion of the group. This process of group decision is the natural and accepted way in the societies of Southern Nigeria. They do permit individual differences but within the knowledge and understanding of the group. Individual conversions do occur, but usually Christianity spreads most naturally and rapidly along lines of established relationships and it is common to see relatives or friends converted in rapid sequence, or sometimes simultaneously in groups.

Again Hamilton's findings in the High Andes are applicable here. He wrote,

> We shall get group conversion, if: (a) we set our sights on winning to Christ many individuals in every close-knit family and village unit through a deliberate approach to the entire group; (b) we recognize that we are dealing with individuals who decide everything from the most insignificant detail of their lives to the most important through group discussion; and, (c) we train Christians to present in their own way and to their own folk the "possibility of several persons together

> accepting Christ." Christians should tell about individuals becoming Christians in groups small or large, remaining at their customary place of abode, doing their ordinary work, and maintaining community with their own people."[5]

This is what happened in the Garrick Braide and the Babalola movements (described in Chapter IV), when large numbers moved and hugh piles of fetishes were burned. This is also what happened in the chain reaction of conversions in Isoko (Chapter V). Note also that individual conversions occurred more easily among the freed slaves in Sierre Leone because they were separated from kinsmen and village pressures (Chapter II).

(5) Religion is integrated into every part of life. Christian ceremonies and rules of behavior are therefore incorporated into all social and economic organization and activity. When traditional religions are replaced by Christianity, the Church must replace the old religion in all its functions or expect syncretism or dual alignment of its members. They will become fully Christian only if the Christianity given to them meets their full spiritual need (i.e., the spiritual need of every aspect of their lives). The deficiency of a formal, western-oriented Christianity not integrated with the everyday life of the people is a major cause of nativistic movements.

In the author's survey among 136 Anglican and 48 Baptist churches in Benin and Delta Provinces, 526 of the 614 Anglican members and 162 of the 226 Baptist members who responded said their families are mostly Christian. This further illustrates web and group movements. An analysis of conversion experiences sheds further light on how Nigerians become Christian.

Table IV shows patterns of conversion compiled from questionaries filled out by students in Baptist teacher training colleges in Nigeria. Notice the very high rates of "influence to conversion" played by parents and by school. The emphasis placed by Baptists upon a definite conversion experience even for those reared in a Christian home is seen

[5] *Ibid.*, p. 120.

in the large number of conversions at the age span of eleven to twenty.

A similar questionnaire was given to twenty-five Christian students at the University College of Ibadan from varied denominational affiliations. The results were alarming. All but one said both of their parents were Christian. Nineteen said they were Christian from birth or youth, and only six recalled a definite time of conscious commitment to Christ. They listed the following influences that led them to be Christian: Parents – 19, School – 6, Teacher – 2, and Friend – 1. This survey indicates almost no church growth beyond biological growth. Children of Christians become Christians. Few others do. In a highly receptive Southern Nigeria population, still more than half non-Christian, such stagnation is tragically unnecessary.

Influence of Christian Schools and Medical Institutions on Church Growth

The strong emphasis on the institutional approach to missions begun in the nineteenth century and strengthened in the early twentieth century is still present today. The reasons given are: (1) to gain respect, confidence of the people, and thus entry into their hearts; (2) to bring people into a Christian environment where they can be converted; (3) to bring progress to the people (primarily a humanitarian motive); (4) to train indigenous leadership; and (5) to keep "our people" from being proselytized by others who will give them institutions.

All of these reasons have factual basis. Evidences of the influence of Christian institutions on church growth are many. J. B. Gaultney, a medical missionary, said to the author, "When I enter a village and tell the chiefs and people I am from Eku Baptist hospital, there is an immediate response of welcome." It is common for villages to send word to church leaders and say, "If you will give us a school or dispensary, the entire village will become Christian."

Although the results are seldom as good as the promises, institutions do open doors. Christian institutions are also largely responsible for the fact that Christian influence in

Nigeria far exceeds what might be expected by the numerical strength of the churches. The long history of education through church schools has resulted in a predominance of Christian-educated leaders in Southern Nigeria today. In an analysis of baptisms in 1960, district by district, J. E. Mills, Secretary of Evangelism for the Nigerian Baptist Convention, said, churches "around some of our institutions are helped in winning people by the ministry of the institutions."[6] Note that this was true of only some of the institutions. Others seemed to have no positive effect upon church growth.

In 1961 the author visited Ovwodokpokpo, about thirty-five miles east of Warri, having heard that a Baptist church had sprung up there spontaneously. An old man was leading a congregation of about thirty in worship services. He had been very sick two years before and after spending all his money for treatment from the native doctor, was still no better. Someone suggested that he go to Eku Baptist hospital some thirty miles away. When he got there the doctor admitted him, treated him, and told him about Jesus. The nurses who ministered to his needs also took time to tell him about Jesus. A man they called chaplain came to preach each day in the ward and then also went around to each bed and talked to the people about Jesus. The old man said, "After some days of this I began to realize that these people were trying to help me because of Jesus, who was their God. They were different from other people because of Jesus. So I took Jesus to be my God and was filled with such peace and satisfaction that I determined to go back to my people, when released from the hospital, and tell them what I had come to know." A church resulted.

This hospital has an intensive regular evangelistic program with a careful follow-up program: (a) The gospel is preached daily to every patient with the objective of bringing him to a definite decision for Christ. (b) Evangelism is the planned responsibility of every member of the staff. (c) Religious records are kept on each patient and all decisions are recorded. (d) Information on each decision is sent to the church nearest the patient's home when he is discharged from

[6] Mills, J. E., "Open Letter to Nigerian Baptists," July 28, 1961.

the hospital. (e) One or two days a week the chaplain makes field trips to visit former patients in their villages to see whether they have followed through on their decision and are active in a church. (f) Most of the senior staff members of the hospital (including the doctors) have regular itinerant responsibilities in the churches of the areas around the hospital.

This program has been carefully worked out to bring the influence of the hospital to bear in the greatest possible degree upon planting and multiplying churches.

The author offers two considered conclusions regarding Christian institutions in Southern Nigeria: (1) An institution does not automatically bring conversions. Often institutions expand more rapidly than personnel and finances to operate them increase. This diverts efforts from evangelism and church planting to merely keeping the institutions themselves functioning. This has happened all too often in Nigeria. If evangelism and enlistment of persons into local churches is an aim of the institution, careful planning must be done to bring students and patients to decide concerning Christ. Then careful nurturing and training of the new converts must be done, baptizing them and enlisting them in ardent evangelism to win others to Christ and His Church. The example and influence of the teachers and medical workers will be purposely used for this process or unwittingly used against it. Christian teachers and medical workers, both missionary and national, should have definite responsibilities for and active participation in the planting and expansion of churches. Where all this is done, institutions will have positive usefulness in church growth. (2) The government is increasingly taking into its own hands both education and medicine and thus reducing the opportunities and influence of the Churches through these social services. As this process continues the Churches need to find new ways to minister spiritually to the patients and students. Additional provision will also need to be made for the training of laymen for all levels of church leadership. A thorough religious education program within each local church will be increasingly essential.

Problems That Need Solutions

In 1961 Tai Solarin, an influential Nigerian educator and writer, wrote in the Lagos *Daily Times*, the newspaper with the widest circulation in West Africa, that Christianity has no future in Nigeria. He quoted from a speech that he had made in 1954, branding the Protestant Churches begun by foreign missionaries as "imposed Christian Churches" and saying that by 1984 their numerical strength would be one-half what it was in 1954. He said the Roman Catholic Church would be reduced by one-third. And he concluded, "All faiths indigenously African, that is native, together with all shades of Africanized Churches . . . will have doubled, if not trebled their present numbers, for their tenets will be so much more in keeping with African nationhood."[7]

Solarin was very conservative in his estimate of growth for the "indigenously African" Churches, and entirely wrong in his prediction for other Churches. Statistics show that Anglicans, Baptists, Methodists, Roman Catholics, and others have made very substantial numerical gains thus far since 1954. Indeed Anglicans have grown some 25% and Baptists and Methodists have increased more than that (see graph at the beginning of Chapter V). Evidently Mr. Solarin in 1961 quoted his predictions of 1954 without bothering to investigate what results the intervening years had already brought.

This limited growth should not be an occasion for sitting back and rejoicing. In 1962 the author gathered opinions from many of the leaders of Protestant denominations in Nigeria (both missionaries and Nigerians) through questionnaires and personal conversation and found almost unanimous concern for the slow rate of growth. These opinions weighed with the author's personal experience suggest the following problems that need solutions:

(1) There is almost universal failure to keep accurate record of progress and make adjustments in policy, emphases, and budget distribution needed to secure maximum church growth. Records and statistics are often incomplete and

[7] Solarin, Tai, "Future of Christianity in West Africa," Lagos, Nigeria *Daily Times* (September 16, 1961).

poorly kept and thus are misleading. Records are also ignored, forgotten, or explained away when people are not satisfied with their results or implications. Constant awareness of how much church growth is occurring in each section of the land, why the churches are growing and why they are not, where receptive populations are located, and a willingness to face up to failures and needed changes, is essential if Church leaders want to realize the best possible results from their dedication, their prayers, and their expenditure in personnel and resources for the purpose of expanding Christ's kingdom.

(2) Christians often lack spiritual depth and fail to live up to their professed beliefs and purposes. This is not peculiar to Nigeria. It is equally true in other nations and was a problem even to the Apostle Paul. "The good that I would I do not: but the evil which I would not, that I do" (Romans 7:19). However, let not the universality of this problem ease the conscience of Christians guilty of spiritual laxness. "Shallow Christianity," which does not change life and character, does not bring a satisfying relationship with God; nor does it convince others.

(3) Evangelism, the actual winning of people to Jesus Christ, and the actual planting of churches, is neglected far too much. Church leaders, missionaries, pastors, and laymen involve themselves in multitudinous activities that are good but are not bringing people to personal commitment to Christ. Dr. Cal Guy, a noted American missions professor, dealt with this problem in his important chapter, "Eliminating the Underbrush," in *Church Growth and Christian Mission*. He pointed out that many missionaries by example have – no doubt unintentionally – taught national pastors and leaders to spend vast amounts of time and effort on material matters, while neglecting the spiritual.

> A week spent in hearing missionaries plan their next year's work is illuminating. Budgets, salary scales, repairs, rents, and scholarships take hours. While the bulk of their planning ought to concern the spiritual thrust, most of it deals with matters material and mechanical. Part of this is an outgrowth

of the subsidy system, part a product of the American environment transferred overseas, and part failure to understand the essential function of planning sessions.[8]

Matters both important and trivial constantly arise to divert Christian people from their primary function of bringing others to know Him who offers salvation to all. Only definite purpose and determination to win people to Christ and enlist them in active Christian service under the leadership of the Holy Spirit will guard against such diversion.

(4) The shadow of foreignness still hangs over Christianity. Dr. E. B. Idowu, professor of religion at the University College, Ibadan, said to the author,

> The real difficulty of the Church in Nigeria is it has not really become indigenous. It is patterned after the European Church and often controlled by the parent foreign mission. The fault lies both with missionaries who try to guide and control and with the nationals, who try to mimic or copy the foreign "masters." People do not really know what Christianity is because of misemphasis. They do not know that to be Christian is "to be in Christ." We have used foreign terminology, standards, and patterns, and there is no bridge between the old and the new life. We need Christian literature, visual aids, and other materials produced in Nigeria by Nigerians and with a Nigerian setting. If you are going to help Nigeria you must take chances. Indigenization must come.

Dr. Eugene Nida, anthropologist, author, and vicepresident in charge of translations for the American Bible Society, distinguishes between indigenous and indigenized Churches.[9] Indigenized Churches, he says, were begun by foreign leadership with foreign patterns and later handed over to nationals but retained most of their foreign patterns. They are still not really native to the culture and cannot therefore be called indigenous. A truly indigenous Church is born out of the culture of the people and is a natural, integral part of the culture.

An indigenous Church (Nida's definition) need not be any

[8] Guy, Hodges, McGavran, and Nida, *Church Growth and Christian Mission.*

[9] *Ibid.*

less Christian than one whose worship forms, architecture, organization, or other patterns were copied from Europe or America. Indeed a Church is more Christian if its patterns are understood by the people and thus readily brings them to personal commitment to Jesus Christ as Lord.

Patterns and features should not be condemned merely because they are used in other cultures. Nor should they be superimposed on a culture where they do not fit naturally just because they are the tested and proven way somewhere else. Sharing ideas by two groups across cultural lines is beneficial only if the right of adaptation or complete rejection is retained by each. Thus a truly Nigerian Church may have many features like those of Churches in other places but these features will belong to the people rather than bear the mark of foreignness. This problem merits careful attention by Nigerian Churches that have past or present relationships of dependence upon missions from other lands.

One of the primary principles of indigenization is: self-support must accompany self-government. A Church cannot be considered fully indigenous, even though it is self-governing, if it is dependent upon an outside body to carry on its program. This is a reasonable principle but it has built-in dangers. When even indirect control is exerted over a Church through foreign subsidies, foreign patterns will be imposed upon it. A missionary may understand another culture quite thoroughly but seldom does he escape completely the ideals, thought patterns, sense of values, and experiences he has acquired from his own cultural background. These he considers good. These he thinks the younger Church ought to do. This is often called cultural overhang. Nationals trained abroad also sometimes imbibe foreign standards of what is good and impose these on the younger Churches.

While the knowledge and experience of a missionary are among the important factors that qualify him to go as an ambassador for Christ to a foreign land, he must be conscious of his own cultural overhang and the danger of unwittingly presenting Christ and His Church in Western garb. They thus appear foreign to those he would win. The long years of foreign aid, in personnel and money, along with the acculturation process through mission schools and other factors, have produced Churches in Nigeria patterned closely after those in England and America. These Churches have for the most part become a part of the Nigerian culture but too many still retain a foreign flavor. Only Nigerian Christians can change this, and they deserve missionary understanding and cooperation. Motives for change should come from a desire to bring salvation through Jesus Christ to the rest of the people of Nigeria in a way that they can understand and accept. Mere nationalism is not a good motive for change to indigenous ways. Christian principles, as found in the Bible, should not be violated, for the Bible must be the basis of judgment on ideals and actions, rather than what is learned from another culture.

(5) The practice of polygamy has been a difficult problem from the very beginning of Christian missions in Nigeria. It has received frequent review with the hope of finding a solution consistent with Christian principles and understandable to the people in African society. The most recent study was made in a consultation on African independent church movements arranged by the Department of Missionary Studies of the World Council of Churches in September, 1962. The conference found the subject of polygamy "the most difficult, the most interesting, and the most important" of their study. Their final statement on the subject was:

> The negative attitude hitherto adopted by the older churches towards members of polygamous homes has been no small barrier to converts to Christianity. In respect to this issue, a loveless, censorious and legalistic approach has developed which does not reflect the spirit of our Lord Jesus. The church is called to be a minister of Christ's redeeming power and grace, not His punitive instrument. In the judgment of many of us, the polygamous status of a new convert from a non-Christian background should be no barrier to his acceptance into church membership. However, Christians within the fold must be taught to appreciate and practice standards of home life based on the mind of Christ, which, among other things, include monogamy.[10]

[10] Hayward, Victor E., "African Independent Church Movements," *The International Review of Missions,* Vol. LII, No. 206, 168.

Note the middle-of-the-road position advocated. "Standards of home life based on the mind of Christ" must be learned and practiced by Christians. Among them is monogamy. On the other hand, "the polygamous status of a new convert from a non-Christian background should be no barrier to his acceptance into church membership." Note that this last sentence is the opinion of "many of us," not the consensus of the consultation.

This procedure has not been that followed by most of the Traditional Churches in Nigeria, which have steadily refused to accept polygamists as full members of the Church. They require that a person separate himself from his polygamous relationships before he can be baptized. Some Churches will baptize the wives, maintaining that they are not responsible for the husband's action in taking other wives. Other Churches will baptize neither husband nor wives, saying that a wife can either dissuade her husband from taking other wives or she can leave him when he does. This is economically feasible since most Nigerian women are financially independent of their husbands. They are traders or have their own farms or other means of livelihood.

One weakness of this traditional position is that it has received so much attention that Christianity appears legalistic and foreign. The basis of Christianity, which is spiritual rebirth and a personal relationship with God through Jesus Christ, is lost sight of. Whatever the position on polygamy, it is imperative that consistent emphasis be placed on spiritual rebirth followed by spiritual development through Bible study and dependence upon the Holy Spirit both individually and collectively.

Another weakness of the traditional position on polygamy is more subtle. Combined with the school approach, it confines evangelistic drive largely to youth. Polygamy for them is no problem – yet. They are won to Christ through the schools, grow up, marry, and continue as good Christians. A few are lost by lapsing to polygamy. It is presumed that the old polygamous adults in the population will die off and their places will be taken by more and more youth who have become Christian in the schools. Since direct evangelization of adults is hampered by the polygamous men who cannot be baptized, the "youth approach" seems normal and reasonable.

Thus large sections of society are left untouched and a double standard of life develops. "The old polygamists" may die off, but polygamy does not. A strong alternative to Christianity remains alive and flourishes ready to opt for secularistic materialism, Islam, Communism, or some other allegiance.

To meet this weakness the Churches in Nigeria should make a determined effort to win adults. Churches that cannot accept polygamists, should make redoubled efforts to win every non-polygamous adult. The barrier put up by polygamy must not prevent large regular accessions of adults to the Church. Reliance on the school as the main way into the Church must be renounced. The school door will, of course, continue to be used, but the door of adult conversions, especially multi-individual conversions, must be forced open and kept open.

(6) Developing a training program to produce adequate leadership for every level of responsibility in the Churches is essential. At least five levels of training are needed. First is basic training for every member. This is being done by most Churches in catechism or inquirers' classes and Sunday school Many of the smaller congregations do not have these classes because there is no leader for them.

This suggests the second level of training that is urgently needed and is for the most part neglected, training local unpaid leaders for small churches. Multitudes of smaller churches in Southern Nigeria are unable to support a seminary-trained pastor. This problem is being met in the following ways: (a) Aid for the pastor's salary from a central fund of the denomination or from the mission. (b) Local preseminary training for young men who serve as pastors on a bare subsistence salary during this training. (c) Teachers or leaders from stronger churches sent to help neighboring smaller churches without salary. (d) Local unpaid leaders, who may be church founders, senior persons in the church, or educated persons, chosen because they can read and are interested in, or at least willing to be, church leaders.

These local unpaid leaders frequently become church leaders regardless of their spiritual maturity, and carry on their responsibilities without benefit of any training. Locally they often become the voice and the primary authority of the church with no other qualification than that they, for one reason or another, have become the "church leaders."

Many of these church leaders have performed an admirable and worthy service and have been used of God in leading others to know and worship Jesus Christ. They know their people and the ways of their people. They are an integral part of the society with all the advantages of kin and social interrelationships. They are often natural leaders, who are respected and understood by the people. Bishop Crowther found such men his most valuable assistants. The only thing many of them lack is training for their task. If they were given basic training locally, which did not separate them from their people in their natural relationships, no better leaders could be found. What better investment could be made than a problem of lay leadership training that increased the effectiveness of these local leaders in smaller churches? Such a program would necessitate little financial outlay but would require itinerant directors or teachers who understand and appreciate the value and potential usefulness of these local leaders. They should be given basic Bible teaching, training in church leadership, preparation for teaching inquirers, and methods of evangelism (including an understanding of how churches grow in their society).

The third level needed is training for pastors or catechists serving in churches that can pay a relatively small salary. In several areas Baptists have local pastors' schools to provide this level of training. Most of these schools conduct classes four days a week for six months each year and the course is arranged for two years of this plan. These students serve as pastors in small churches during their training. Their salaries are small and they have provided leadership in places where it is sorely needed. Those who are able to pass the entrance exam usually go on to seminary for the next level of training, while new students in the pastors' schools take up the work in the churches they have left.

The fourth level is at least three or four years of training for pastors to serve in larger village churches and smaller town and city churches. There has been considerable training of men on this level in the past twenty years.

The fifth level is for top leadership in administrative posts, department heads, pastors in large city churches, and other places of responsibility that demand a very high level of education. Levels four and five are essential to every indigenous Church, but no more so than the first three levels.

An important emphasis in the training of all levels of Christian leadership is an understanding of how people in that society become Christian. Studies of church growth should be made and attention focused upon this as the primary task before every Christian.

Factors That Will Produce Church Growth

The factors most often mentioned as causing church growth by the Nigerian Church leaders polled by the author were:

(1) Christians must be humble but courageous and militantly evangelistic.

(2) Spiritual depth and willingness to follow the leadership of the Holy Spirit are imperative.

(3) Intensive and widespread Bible teaching must be done among all the population, including those not yet literate.

(4) The Churches in Nigeria must be thoroughly Christian and at the same time thoroughly Nigerian.

In support of and supplementary to these factors the author suggests the following:

(1) The church must become an accepted, respected, integral part of the community life. This is already the case in some places. The people must feel that it is their church and they, as Christians of that community, are responsible to uphold the Christian faith and work for the conversion of the whole community. Aids to this end are: (a) democratic church government and as much local autonomy as possible; (b) development and training of local leadership for both pastoral and lay responsibilities; (c) orders of service and programs of activities conforming as much as possible to the natural patterns and customs of the community social life; (d) services conducted in the language and dialect of the

people – with separate services in multi-language areas if possible; (e) music developed from within, not relying indefinitely on foreign tunes in a foreign tongue, or even translations, which do not fit the tonal pattern of Nigerian languages. With the tonal languages of Southern Nigeria, the words must match the beat of the music or the meaning is changed; (f) active participation of all (including illiterates) in worship services and activities of the church. A simple liturgy to be memorized and used regularly in services is useful at this point; and (g) self-support. If foreign aid is felt to be advantageous at first, it should be clearly understood and used only as a temporary aid, not an indefinite crutch and symbol of foreign domination.

(2) A regular program of evangelism should be carried on continuously. (a) Lay members should be taught their responsibility to witness and how to witness to their relatives and friends about the saving power of Jesus. (b) Visitation, evangelistic meetings, open-air services, and other activities supplementary to the regular worship services should be used, supported by regular prayer for the salvation of those to whom they witness. (c) Definite emphasis should be put on the bringing of family and ethnic groups to recognize and accept Jesus Christ as Lord. As individuals are won, immediate efforts should be made to win their families and close associates as rapidly as possible so new converts will not be wrenched from their former group relationships.

Multi-individual decisions should be actively sought. It is normal for the residents of the multitudinous villages and hamlets of Southern Nigeria to make important decisions together, at the same time, after talking matters over, and keeping the same leaders as they had before. These multi-individual and mutually interdependent decisions fit society in Southern Nigeria. They are often loosely called "group conversion." The advantages and methods of "group conversion" should be taught and programs of evangelism aimed at winning persons in their natural groups rather than winning individuals and isolating them from their family and social circles. (d) More emphasis should be given to evangelism in worship services – aimed at bringing people to personal commitment to Jesus. (e) Pastors and catechists should be trained for and encouraged to work for community acceptance, and carry on intensive and consistent efforts to bring people to Christ individually and in groups.

(3) Ethnic groups must be cultivated and watched for ripeness to change. Unconverted pockets of population in cities and in the country should be charted, entered, and won for Christ. Sufficient mobility in personnel and funds should be maintained to enable adequate staffing of areas according to changes in the rates of response. Where a "people movement" takes place, it is essential that a well-trained staff be sent in for one purpose – to train local leaders from that population. As soon as this is accomplished they could be moved elsewhere. This will preserve the advantages of the continual spread of the gospel along normal channels within the homogeneous unit. It will also develop leadership from among those converted in the movement, who understand the avenues of its spread and who are fired by their involvement in it. They have far greater potential usefulness than outsiders brought in "cold," who do not understand the situation.

Enormous sound church growth is possible now in the tremendously receptive populations of Southern Nigeria, but it will not come without careful planning and great effort directed purposefully to that end. Such potential calls for regular careful evaluation of opportunities, and willingness to adjust resources and procedures on every level in order to attain maximum sound church growth. The traditional way, the convenient way, the way that is adapted to personal desires and ambitions must not thwart a positive planned program of winning the multitudes to Jesus Christ in a population that is ripe unto harvest. In this day of rapid change in the minds and hearts of Nigerian people, what will be the response of Christian leaders who bear the responsibility of this harvest? The doors of opportunity that open wide today will not wait long to be entered by some religion or ideology, and once entered, the doors will again close. The Christian imperative is clearly to enter the doors with Christ's message of salvation, bearing that message through the sociological channels through which it can pass most easily and understandably. Will Christians heed this clarion call in the day of opportunity?

BIBLIOGRAPHY

Chapter I

Ajisafe, A. K. *Laws and Customs of the Benin People.* Lagos: Kash and Klare Bookshop, 1945.

———. *Laws and Customs of the Yoruba.* London: Routledge, Lagos, CMS Bookshop, 1924.

Bascom, W. R. "The Sanctions of Ifa Divination," *J. Roy. Anthrop. Inst.* Vol. LXXI (1941), 43-54.

———. "Ifa Divination," *Man,* Vol. XLII, No. 21 (1942), 41-43.

———. "The Principle of Seniority in the Social Structure of the Yoruba," *Amer. Anthrop,* Vol. XLIV (1942), 37-47.

———. "The Relationship of Yoruba Folklore to Divining," *J. Amer. Folklore,* Vol. LVI, No. 220 (1943), 127-131.

———. "The Sociological Role of the Yoruba Cult Group," *Amer. Anthrop.,* Vol. XLVI, i, Part 2, Memoir 63 (1944).

———. "West Africa and the Complex of Primitive Cultures," *Amer. Anthrop.,* Vol. L (1948), 18-23.

Basden, G. T. *Among the Ibos of Nigeria.* London: Seeley Service, 1921.

———. *Niger Ibos.* London: Seeley Service, 1938.

Bindloss, H. *In the Niger Country.* Edinburgh, 1898.

Bradbury, R. E. *The Benin Kingdom and the Edo-Speaking Peoples of South-Western Nigeria.* London: International African Institute, 1957.

Buchanan, K. M. and Pugh, J. C. *Land and People in Nigeria.* London: University of London Press, 1961.

Burns, A. C. *History of Nigeria.* London: Allen & Unwin, 1942.

Coleman, James S. *Nigeria Background to Nationalism.* Los Angeles: University of California Press, 1960.

Dennett, R. E. *Nigerian Studies, The Religious and Political System of the Yoruba.* London: Macmillan, 1910.

Ellis, A. B. *The Yoruba-Speaking Peoples of West Africa.* London: Chapman & Hall, 1894.

Egharevba, J. U. *Benin Laws and Customs.* Lagos: Service Press, 1947.

———. *A Short History of Benin.* Ibadan: University Press for CMS Bookshop, Lagos, 1953.

Fadipe, N. A. "The Sociology of the Yoruba" (Doctoral dissertation, University of London, 1939).

Forde, Daryll. *The Yoruba-Speaking Peoples of South-Western Nigeria.* London: International African Institute, 1962.

Forde, Daryll, and Jones, G. I. *The Ibo and Ibibio-Speaking Peoples of South-Eastern Nigeria.* London: International African Institute, 1962.

Goldie, J. E. *Sir George Goldie and the Making of Nigeria.* Oxford: Blackwells, 1960.

Green, M. M. *Land Tenure in an Ibo Village.* London: Percy Lund, Humphries, 1941.

Howell, E. Milford. "Tribal Laws and Social Customs That Afflict Mission Work in Southern Nigeria" (Th.M., thesis, Southwestern Baptist Theological Seminary, 1952).

Idowu, E. Bolaji. *Olodumare, God in Yoruba Belief.* London: Longmans, 1962.

Johnson, S. *The History of the Yorubas.* Lagos: CMS Bookshops, 1937.

Leonard, A. G. *The Lower Niger and Its Tribes.* London: Macmillan, 1906.

Lloyd, P. C. *Yoruba Land Law.* London: Oxford University Press, 1962.

Lucas, J. Olumide. *The Religion of the Yorubas.* Lagos: CMS Bookshops, 1948.

Meek, C. K. *Ibo Law.* London: Kegan Paul, 1934.

———. *Land, Law and Custom in the Colonies.* London: Oxford University Press, 1946.

Okojie, C. G. *Ishan Native Laws and Customs.* Yaba: John Okwesa & Co., 1960.

Omoneukanrin, C. O. *Itsekiri Law and Custom.* Lagos, 1942.

Parrinder, E. Geoffrey. *African Traditional Religion.* London: Hutchinson House, 1954.

———. *Religion in an African City.* London: Oxford University Press, 1953.

———. *West African Religion.* London: Epworth Press, 1961.

Pinnock, James. *Benin, The Surrounding Country, Inhabitants, Customs, Trade.* Liverpool, 1897.

Roth, H. Ling. *Great Benin: Its Customs, Art and Horrors.* Halifax, 1903.

Talbot, P. Amaury. *Life in Southern Nigeria. The Magic, Beliefs, and Customs of the Ibibio Tribe.* London: 1923.

———. *The Peoples of Southern Nigeria.* 4 Vols. London: Oxford University Press, 1926.

———. *Tribes of the Niger Delta.* London: Sheldon Press, 1932.

Thomas, N. W. *Anthropological Report on the Edo-Speaking Peoples.* 2 Vols. London, 1910.

———. *Anthropological Report on the Ibo-Speaking Peoples of Nigeria.* London: Harrison, 1914.

Welch, J. W. "The Isoko Tribe," *Africa,* Vol. VII (1934),160-73.

West, Ralph L. "A Study of Indigeneity Among Nigerian Baptists" (Doctoral dissertation, New Orleans Baptist Theological Seminary, 1953).

Westermann, D., and Bryan, M. A. *Languages of West Africa.* London: Oxford University Press for International African Institute, 1952.

Chapter II

Ajayi, J. D. Ade. "Christian Missions and the Making of Nigeria 1841-1891" (Doctoral dissertation, University of London, 1958).

Bowen, T. J. *Central Africa: Adventures and Missionary Labors in Several Countries in the Interior of Africa from 1849 to 1856.* Charleston: Southern Baptist Publication Society, 1857.

Duval, Louis M. *Baptist Missions in Nigeria,* Richmond, Va.: Education Department, Foreign Mission Board, S.B.C., 1928.

Goerner, H. C. *Exploring Africa.* Nashville: Broadman Press, 1950.

Green, C. Sylvester. *New Nigeria, Southern Baptists at Work in Africa.* Richmond, Va.: Foreign Mission Board, S.B.C., 1936.

Howell, E. Milford. "Nigerian Baptist Leaders and Their Contribution" (Doctoral dissertation, Southwestern Baptist Theological Seminary, 1956).

Hunter, J. H. *A Flame of Fire.* Aylesbury and Slough: Hazell Watson and Viney, 1961.

Livingstone, W. P. *Mary Slessor of Calabar.* New York: George H. Doran Co., n.d.

Maddry, Charles E. *Day Dawns in Yoruba Land.* Nashville: Broadman Press, 1939.

McFarlan, Donald M. *Calabar – The Church of Scotland Mission.* London: Thomas Nelson & Sons, 1957.

Miller, Basil. *Mary Slessor, Heroine of Calabar.* Grand Rapids: Zondervan Publishing House, 1946.

Nigeria Catholic Directory. Yaba, Nigeria (National Office, 7 Simisola Road, Suru-lere, P.M.B. 1043), 1962.

Page, Jesse. *The Black Bishop.* London: Simpkin, Marshall, Hamilton, Kent and Co., n.d.

Pinnock, S. G. *The Romance of Missions in Nigeria.* Richmond, Va.: Education Department, Foreign Mission Board, S.B.C., 1917.

Southon, A. E. *Gold Coast Methodism.* London: Cargate Press, 1934.

Westermann, Diedrich. *Africa and Christianity.* London: Oxford Press. 1937.

Chapter III

Coxill, H. W., and Grubb, K. *World Christian Handbook.* London: World Dominion Press, 1962.

Knight, Charles Williams. "A History of the Expansion of Evangelical Christianity in Nigeria" (Doctoral dissertation, Southern Baptist Theological Seminary, 1951).

Maxwell, J. Lowry. *Nigeria, The Land, the People and Christian Progress.* London: World Dominion Press, n.d.

Patton, William, and Underhill, M. M. *International Review of Missions.* Vol. XXVI. London: Edinburgh House, 1937.

Robison, Oren C. "The Indigenous Development of Baptist Churches of Nigeria" (Th. M. thesis, Southern Baptist Theological Seminary, 1951).

Stock, Eugene. *The History of the Church Missionary Society*. Vol. III. London: CMS, 1899.

Talbot, P. Amaury. *The Peoples of Southern Nigeria*. Vol. IV. London: Oxford University Press, 1926.

Walker, F. Deaville. *The Romance of the Black River*. London: CMS, 1930.

Chapter IV

Baeta, C. G. *Prophetism in Ghana*. London: SCM Press, 1962.

MacRow, D. W. "Cherubim and Seraphim," *Nigeria* Magazine, No. 53, 1957.

Messenger, J. C. "Reinterpretation of Christian and Indigenous Belief in a Nigerian Naturist Church," *American Anthropologist*, Vol. 62, No. 2 (April 1960).

Oldham, J. H. *The International Review of Missions*. Vol. VI. New York: Missionary Educational Movement, 1917.

Parrinder, Geoffrey. *Religion in an African City*. London: Oxford University Press, 1953.

Welbourn, F. B. *East African Rebels*. London: SCM Press, 1961.

Chapter V

Boer, Harry R. "The Year of the Elephant," *Reformed Journal*, Vol. XII, No. 9 (October 1962).

Carmichael, Christine. "Nigeria." Springfield, Mo.: Foreign Mission Department of Assemblies of God, n.d.

Hubbard, J. W. *The Sobo of the Niger Delta*. Zaria, Nigeria: Gakiya Corp., 1948.

McFarlan, Donald M. *Calabar*. London: Thomas Nelson & Sons, 1957.

McGavran, Donald. *Bridges of God*. London: World Dominion Press, 1955.

McKeown, Robert L. *Twenty-five Years in Qua Iboe*. London: Morgan and Scott, 1912.

Townsend, George. *Memoir of the Rev. Henry Townsend*. London: Marshall Brothers, 1887.

Walker, F. Deaville. *A Hundred Years in Nigeria*. London: Colgate Press, 1942.

Weaver, Edwin and Irene. "The Uyo Story," *Gospel Herald*, Vol. LV, Nos. 34, 35, 36 (August 28, September 4, and September 11, 1962).

Weaver, Irene. "The Uyo Story, Part VI," *Gospel Herald*, Vol. LVI, No. 6 (February 5, 1963).

Chapter VI

Guy, Hodges, McGavran, and Nida, *Church Growth and Christian Mission*. Harper & Row, 1965.

Hamilton, Keith E. *Church Growth in the High Andes*. Lucknow, U.P., India: Lucknow Publishing House, 1962.

Hayward, Victor E. "African Independent Church Movements," *The International Review of Missions*. Vol. LII, No. 206. London: Edinburgh House (April 1963).

Mills, J. E. "Open Letter to Nigerian Baptists." Ibadan, Nigeria: Baptist Building (July 28, 1961).

Solarin, Tai. "Future of Christianity in West Africa," Lagos, Nigeria *Daily Times* (September 16, 1961).

Index